This book is for
Tom, Michelle, and Caitlin McCraw

THE
FOUNDERS
AND
FINANCE

THE
FOUNDERS
AND
FINANCE

How Hamilton, Gallatin, and Other Immigrants
Forged a New Economy

THOMAS K. McCRAW

THE BELKNAP PRESS OF HARVARD UNIVERSITY PRESS

Cambridge, Massachusetts, and London, England

2012

Library of Congress Cataloging-in-Publication Data

McCraw, Thomas K.
The founders and finance : how Hamilton, Gallatin, and other immigrants forged
a new economy / Thomas K. McCraw.
p.   cm.
Includes bibliographical references and index.
ISBN 978-0-674-06692-2 (alk. paper)
1. Hamilton, Alexander, 1757–1804.   2. Gallatin, Albert, 1761–
1849.   3. United States. Dept. of the Treasury—History.   4. Finance,
Public—United States—History.   5. Monetary policy—United States—
History.   6. United States—Economic policy.   7. United
States—History—Revolution, 1775–1783.   8. United States—
History—1783–1865.   9. United States—Politics and
government—1783–1865.   I. Title.
HJ261.M37   2012
330.973'04—dc23   2012014006

Contents

Part II
ALBERT GALLATIN
1761–1849

Part III
THE LEGACIES

To extinguish a Debt which exists and to avoid contracting more are ideas almost always favored by public feeling and opinion; but to pay Taxes for the one or the other purpose, which are the only means of avoiding the evil, is always more or less unpopular.

—Alexander Hamilton,
Report [to the House of Representatives] on a Plan
for the Further Support of Public Credit,
January 16, 1795

Introduction

The United States government started out on a shoestring and almost immediately went bankrupt. To fight its War of Independence from Britain, it borrowed from banks in Holland and wheedled large sums from France, Britain's great rival. The Continental Congress continually asked the new state governments for funds but never received more than a fraction of what it needed. Desperate for cash, Congress made extravagant use of the printing presses, churning out stacks of paper money. The quick depreciation of this currency gave rise to the phrase "not worth a Continental."

The War of Independence not only impoverished the country, but also left it burdened with the highest public debt it has ever experienced, measured against the income of its government. Unpaid interest on the debt grew larger year by year, during the deep depression that persisted throughout the 1780s. There seemed to be no way out—the more so because "these United Colonies," as the Declaration of Independence called them, were now "Free and Independent States." From Massachusetts, New York, and Pennsylvania in the North to Virginia, the Carolinas, and Georgia in the South, the thirteen states differed in many of their basic economic interests and some of their core ideas. Not until the late 1860s, after the Civil War, did people speak of the nation in the singular: "the United States *is*" rather than "the United States *are*."

During the first forty years after 1776, the new country could have broken apart because of its financial problems, which were related to sectional disputes and even more to foreign affairs. It happened to be blessed, however, with a handful of people who understood finance and also grasped the economic potential of the American *national* future. A disproportionate number of them were recent arrivals from almost a dozen different places overseas. This book shows how they put the United States on a sound institutional footing to manage its finances, and how some of their ideas grew out of their experience as immigrants. It highlights what they did more than what they wrote and said.[1]

The achievements of one of them, Alexander Hamilton—who came from St. Croix in the Danish West Indies—are well known. But a great deal of fresh research on Hamilton and a more thorough look at how he went about his work underscore the influence of his overseas origins. In addition, a closer analysis of the parts other immigrants played in the financial affairs of the early Republic reveals a much larger role than they have usually been accorded. It also illuminates the strengths and weaknesses of the major founders who had been born in North America—and why they depended on financial policies designed by recent arrivals.[2]

Did other aspects of governing rely on immigrants to the same extent that finance did? No. During the first fifty years under the Constitution, only six of the sixty persons appointed to presidential cabinets had been born abroad. Five of those six became secretaries of the treasury.[3]

When George Washington was inaugurated as president in 1789, one of the first tasks he faced under the new Constitution was to establish a national executive administration. Because of the immense debt left over from the War of Independence, financial affairs would be among the most critical concerns. The candidates Washington considered for secretary of the treasury were Robert Morris, who had come from the English port of Liverpool, and Alexander Hamilton, who had emigrated from the Caribbean.

Twelve years later, when Thomas Jefferson took office in 1801 as the first Republican president (no relation to the present-day party of that name), he, too, appointed a foreign-born secretary: Albert Gallatin, who had come from Geneva; and he reappointed him in 1805. Jefferson's successor, James Madison, also appointed Gallatin—in 1809 and again in 1813. Later, when Gallatin left office to negotiate the end of the war with Britain that had begun in 1812, Madison appointed, in sequence, two more immigrants: George W. Campbell (from Scotland) and Alexander James Dallas (from Jamaica).

Thus, four of the first six secretaries of the treasury were born overseas. They served for twenty-one of the first twenty-seven years under the Constitution—78 percent of that period. Was this a remarkable circumstance? Compared to later patterns of appointment, exceedingly so. Of the next sixty-seven secretaries, serving into the twenty-first century, only two were born abroad, and their combined service lasted less than two years out of almost two hundred.[4]

Why would immigrants occupy such a sensitive office 78 percent of the time from 1789 through 1816, versus 1 percent of the time since? Did the foreign-born constitute a greater proportion of the U.S. population during the early years? No. The rate of immigration had been sluggish before the Revolutionary War, and a very high percentage of the population was native-born. The U.S. Census did not begin to record foreign births until 1850. But other data suggest that in 1775 the number of persons born abroad, including those from Africa, was no more than about 8 percent of the population, and likely less. Immigration then dropped during the fighting of 1775–1783, and during most years of the Napoleonic Wars and the War of 1812.

In 1816 the proportion of foreign-born was probably no more than about 4 percent, among the lowest in U.S. history.[5]

—❧—

When the Revolutionary War began in 1775, many of the colonies had experienced at least 125 years of settlement. Almost all of the major founders came from families long resident in North America. John Adams's first American ancestor arrived in 1620 aboard the *Mayflower;* Benjamin Franklin's, in 1635; James Madison's, in 1653; George Washington's, in 1659; and Thomas Jefferson's, in 1672. By contrast, Alexander Hamilton came in 1772 and Albert Gallatin in 1780.[6]

Much of this book is about Hamilton and Gallatin, whom most experts regard as the two greatest secretaries of the treasury. But they were only two of about ten newcomers who shaped the early financial contours of the country. The names of some other members of this group may be recognizable, if only vaguely: Robert Morris, Haym Solomon, John Jacob Astor, Stephen Girard. But even Gallatin, who served as secretary longer than anyone else ever has, is unfamiliar to most people.[7]

Did it make a difference that the most important architects of the American economy were immigrants? This is like asking whether it made a difference that four of the first five presidents, who served for thirty-two of the first thirty-six years under the Constitution, were slaveholding Virginia planters. Certainly they were iconic figures: George Washington, Thomas Jefferson, James Madison, and James Monroe. Yet they, like most people everywhere, tended to look at the world through the lens of their native milieu—in their case, the landed class of colonial Virginia. As adults, each these four presidents came to own very large plantations. Their holdings in Virginia totaled about 23,000 acres—the equivalent of almost thirty-six square miles.[8]

As Emerson wrote in 1860, "If a man owns land, the land owns him." The extent to which land (as opposed to liquid capital) dominated Virginia's culture is reflected in the number of banks chartered during the nation's first decades. In 1781, when Virginia was the largest and most populous state, not a single bank existed anywhere in the country. By 1837, there were 627. Of these, Massachusetts had 123 banks, New York 98, Pennsylvania 49, but Virginia only 6. Each bank increased the money supply in the state where it was chartered—promoting commerce, manufacturing, and faster economic growth.[9]

Robert Morris played the major role in securing a charter for the nation's first bank, which opened in Philadelphia in 1782. Alexander Hamilton drafted the charter for its second, founded in New York in 1784. They and other financial innovators from overseas took a more commercial and cosmopolitan perspective than the landowners in Virginia and most other states, especially in the South. The stories told here suggest that their being immigrants broadened their insights and shaped their behavior. They did not fit the image of immigrants popularized in the famous poem written by Emma Lazarus in 1883 and etched on the Statue of Liberty. They were not tired, or wretched refuse, or members of huddled masses. Nearly all of them came alone and full of vigor. The economic foundations they laid were a vital part of the promise that drew the millions of immigrants who followed them.[10]

Even in the eighteenth century, abundant land attracted more newcomers than any other endowment of North America. But it did not attract most of the protagonists of this book. Rather, these agents of financial change arrived with a mentality about cash and credit different from that of most people born in the thirteen colonies, and from that of other immigrants as well. The innovators analyzed here were nonfarming, urban people comfortable with the tools of public finance—with money, taxation, government spending, and other means of making the United States first solvent and then prosperous. As the nation's chief financial officers, they moved money across oceans and across national, state, county, and city borders. Dealing both domestically and with European bankers and governments, they thrust their country into a new economic relationship with the Atlantic world.

In this sense, their wanderlust and readiness for bold action never died. Compared to other founders such as the four Virginia presidents, they remained personally rootless. They saw capital as rootless, too—movable, portable, migratory in the same sense that they themselves were. Theirs was an agrarian age, and most people throughout the world were farmers tied to the land—as slaves, serfs, renters, or owners. But the immigrants in this book were not. They had no plantations to inherit or other businesses built up by their parents and grandparents. Their ties to any state or community ran less deep than those of native-born settlers. They had no North American genealogy, no ancestral farms or manors. But neither did they intend to return to the homelands they had left.

Being rootless themselves, they were better able to appreciate the intrinsic rootlessness of money—and how its mobility could serve the public good. As a character in one of William Faulkner's novels expresses it, "We were foreigners, strangers, that thought differently from the people whose country we had come into without being asked or wanted." Yet this same character of Faulkner's recognizes an obligation not to demean local customs but instead "to respect anybody's love for the land where he and his people were born and to understand that a man would have to act as the land where he was born had trained him to act." The immigrant financiers were engaged in a constant task of reconciling what they knew about money and credit with what the executives who appointed them believed.[11]

Morris, Hamilton, and Gallatin had experiences and habits of thought different from those of the native-born planters Washington, Jefferson, and Madison. Even as teenagers, Morris and Hamilton had worked long hours in merchant houses. Gallatin had been the best student in his mathematics classes at elite academies in Geneva. All three had grown up in cities rather than on farms or plantations. They dealt more with movable capital than with immovable land, and they trusted their own ability to manage both public and private finance. For the first two generations of U.S. history, these three immigrants and others like them influenced national financial policies more powerfully than did citizens born in the thirteen colonies. And over the next two hundred years, their ideas formed much of the framework for American economic development.

Today, the U.S. Treasury Building in Washington, D.C., stands right next to the White House. Its five acres of space occupy three city blocks. On the opposite sides of its 466-foot length are two pillared façades, each overlooking a spacious plaza. A large bronze statue of Alexander Hamilton dominates one plaza. On the other side is a similar statue of Albert Gallatin. There are no other statues. Nor do monuments to only foreign-born statesmen adorn the British, French, German, Brazilian, Chinese, Indian, or Japanese equivalents of the U.S. Treasury. That idea seems ludicrous on its face.

Hamilton and Gallatin were political enemies with partly competitive visions of the nation's future and of the best ways to fulfill it. During the two centuries since they left office, many of their differing ideas have survived, vying for dominance. Hamilton exemplifies energetic government and vigorous federal programs for economic growth. Gallatin symbolizes low taxes and less intrusion by government. Their views still underlie debates over the proper roles of the public and private sectors, the appropriate level of taxation, and the character of the national debt.

Of course, the United States has changed drastically since their time—having fought a Civil War, ended slavery, spread the Republic across the North American continent and beyond, multiplied its population more than a hundred times over, and become the world's largest economy. But the contest over their ideas has endured. The frequent compromises and recurrent fusions of Hamilton's and Gallatin's ideas have sometimes produced bizarre and even harmful results. In the long run, however, they have yielded outcomes of immeasurable benefit to the country. This book shows how those ideas evolved and were first put into practice.

PART I

Alexander Hamilton
1757–1804

FIGURE 1. Statue of Alexander Hamilton overlooking the south plaza of the Department of the Treasury, Washington, D.C. Sculpted by James Earle Fraser, dedicated in 1923.

CHAPTER I

St. Croix and Trauma

Of the six major "founders" of the United States, Alexander Hamilton was the only immigrant. He was also much the youngest of the six: fifty-one years younger than Benjamin Franklin, twenty-five younger than George Washington, twenty-two younger than John Adams, fourteen younger than Thomas Jefferson, six younger than James Madison. Hamilton alone died violently, in his famous duel with Aaron Burr. He also had the shortest life—only forty-seven years. Washington lived to be sixty-seven, Adams into his nineties, the other three into their middle eighties.

All were true revolutionaries. As Benjamin Franklin remarked in 1776, "We must all hang together or assuredly we shall all hang separately." Yet as soon as the United States achieved independence, the revolutionaries began to quarrel with one another over the shape the new nation should take. In consequence, the 1790s, the first decade under the Constitution, was probably the most contentious period in American history except for the 1850s and 1860s, which brought the Civil War. And despite the romantic picture later generations painted of the founders, nobody escaped condemnation. Even George

Washington almost quit public life because of the partisan in-fighting. The founders attacked one another without mercy, often through newspaper articles and pamphlets they wrote under pseudonyms.

Alexander Hamilton, the visionary immigrant who shaped the nation's future economy, absorbed more abuse than anyone else (and inflicted a good deal himself). The tasks assigned him and the audacity with which he pursued them guaranteed that this would happen. "Never," he wrote in 1800, "was there a more ungenerous persecution of any man than of myself. Not only the worst constructions are put upon my conduct as a public man but it seems my birth is the subject of the most humiliating criticism."[1]

Hamilton came from a complicated background that was certain to incite rumor and gossip. To this day, no one knows with complete assurance when or where he was born, or even who his father was. The year was likely 1757, as he himself believed, but may have been 1755, as one official record indicates. Not that it makes much difference. By all accounts he was a boy wonder. His birthplace was probably the small West Indian island of Nevis, near St. Kitts and St. Croix. At that time, Nevis contained about 1,000 whites and, to work the island's sugar plantations, 8,000 enslaved blacks.[2]

Hamilton was the most romantic and dashing of the founders. He likely inherited his good looks—"a face never to be forgotten," as one of his sisters-in-law called it—from his mother, Rachel Faucett, a beautiful woman of British and French Huguenot descent. She was a native of Nevis and a minor heiress. At sixteen she was married to Johann Lavien, a flashy but cruel Dane nearly twice her age. Together with her mother, who had arranged the marriage, Rachel then moved to Lavien's home in St. Croix—the largest of the Danish Virgin Islands, lying about seventy-five miles southeast of Puerto Rico.[3]

A few years later, after bearing a son, the headstrong Rachel

abandoned her husband, child, and mother. She began living on
nearby St. Kitts with James Hamilton, the ne'er-do-well fourth
child of an aristocratic Scottish family. Rachel and James did
not marry, but Rachel gave birth to two sons, whom she named
James and Alexander Hamilton.

In 1765, when James was about ten and Alexander ("Elicks")
eight, the family moved back to St. Croix. Not long afterward,
the elder James Hamilton abruptly left the island, deserting his
family and never seeing them again. Meanwhile, Johann Lavien
had divorced Rachel on grounds of adultery. For that offense
she spent two months imprisoned in a dank fortress, a harsh
punishment even for that time and place. The divorce decree
read that she had abandoned her husband and child and had
"given herself up to whoring with everyone." This was too cruel
a judgment, but Rachel likely did have other lovers besides
James Hamilton.[4]

After her release from prison, she opened a small store in
St. Croix's capital city of Christiansted, a port heavily involved
in the sugar trade. She and her sons lived over the store, as was
customary in eighteenth-century towns. For a while the little
family got along fairly well. Elicks clerked in his mother's shop
and began to learn rudimentary lessons about business.

At that time the Caribbean sugar islands, despite their beauty,
were among the unhealthiest places on earth. Their fetid conditions and sweltering climate gave rise to persistent yellow fever,
malaria, and typhoid fever. Lifespans were notoriously short—
for planters, slaves, and everyone else, including the large number of British sailors stationed in the West Indies.

Not long after their move to St. Croix, Elicks and his mother
fell ill, probably with yellow fever. They lay in bed together in
their small quarters, becoming sicker by the hour. After a few
days, Rachel died as Elicks slept. He woke up to find her lifeless
body. She was thirty-nine years old; Elicks, nine. A male cousin
then adopted him and his brother, but soon afterward the
cousin committed suicide. Within the same year, an aunt, uncle,
and grandmother also died. Meanwhile, a court in St. Croix
awarded Rachel's property to the son she had borne to Johann

Lavien. That son, now in his twenties, had moved to another island but returned to claim his inheritance—leaving Rachel's two Hamilton sons destitute.

Such an extraordinary run of bad luck might have been almost laughable had it not been so tragic. The deep wounds the Hamilton boys suffered never healed. Nobody fully "gets over" experiences such as theirs. The adult Alexander Hamilton's extreme sensitivity to insult, his frequent lack of discretion, his impulsiveness, and his pleasure in outsmarting his enemies had roots in the devastating psychological shocks of his youth.

After their mother's death, James and Elicks were split up—still another blow to both of them. James was apprenticed to a carpenter and for the rest of his life had little contact with his brother. Elicks was taken in by the family of his young friend Ned Stevens. This gesture by the Stevens family, together with the uncanny physical resemblance of Ned and Elicks, led some people to speculate that he and Ned were not mere friends. They may have been half-brothers as well. Ned's father had known Rachel for many years.[5]

Hamilton's boyhood could hardly have been more different from those of the other founders—especially Washington, Jefferson, and Madison on their large Virginia plantations. Yet even at this stage, it was clear that Elicks had supreme intellectual gifts. By the age of nine, he had begun to show the boldness and self-reliance that would characterize his later years—an unblinking assessment of his circumstances and a resolve to master them. Denied the security and affection of a close family circle, indeed of much real childhood at all, he developed by his early teens a habit of focused, unremitting work. None of the other founders had greater powers of concentration or so little taste for leisure. And none except Franklin started working so early.

At the time Rachel died, St. Croix had a population of about 24,000, more than 90 percent of whom were enslaved. Hamilton's close contact with so many human chattels almost surely shaped his ardent lifelong opposition to slavery. Sugar plantations dominated the island's eighty-three square miles. (By comparison, Manhattan has twenty-three.) The culture of St. Croix, like that of the rest of the Caribbean, was stratified: a few wealthy planters at the top, enslaved masses at the bottom, and in between a motley group of traders, fortune seekers, and itinerant seamen. The small city of Christiansted, where Elicks lived, contained 3,500 people, only about 850 of whom were white. Most of the whites were of English and Scottish descent, plus a few officials from Denmark, which had acquired the island from France in 1733. Elicks grew up speaking English but became fluent in French as well, most likely from his mother's teaching.[6]

After her death and his move into the Stevens household, he found a job in the local merchant house of Beekman and Cruger, New York–based traders. He worked under Nicholas Cruger, who was ten years his senior. The firm did a lively import-export commerce centered on the sugar economy, and Hamilton learned valuable lessons about business: bookkeeping, inventory control, short-term finance, scheduling, and the pricing of merchandise. He became an expert on the fluctuating exchange rates of the many different national coinages and currencies in circulation. He grew familiar with the bills of credit issued by numerous merchants.[7]

In all, his duties in the Cruger enterprise thrust him into adulthood. During one of Nicholas Cruger's frequent absences, the fourteen-year-old Hamilton wrote detailed instructions to ship captains in the firm's employ. One message warned a captain against the consequences of delay (the following documents are in their original spelling, as are all other quotations in this book):

St. Croix Nov. 16, 1771
Here with I give you all your dispatches & desire youll proceed immediately to Curracoa. You are to deliver your Cargo there to Teleman Cruger Esqr. agreable to your Bill

[of] Lading, whose directions you must follow in every respect concerning the disposal of your Vessell after your arrival . . . Remember you are to make three trips this Season
& unless you are very diligent, you will be too late as our
Crops will be early in.

Then, three months later, upbraiding the same captain on his
failures:

St. Croix Febru 1, 1772
Reflect continually on the unfortunate Voyage you have just
made and endeavour to make up for the considerable loss
therefrom accruing to your Owners.[8]

A letter Hamilton wrote at the age of twelve to his friend
Ned Stevens captures his fervent drive and self-awareness.
Among his thousands of surviving letters, this is one of the most
revealing:

Ned, my Ambition is prevalent that I contemn the grov'ling
and condition of a Clerk or the like, to which my Fortune &c. condemns me and would willingly risk my life tho'
not my Character to exalt my Station. Im confident, Ned
that my Youth excludes me from any hopes of immediate
Preferment nor do I desire it, but I mean to prepare the way
for futurity. Im no Philosopher you see and may be jusly
said to Build Castles in the Air. My Folly makes me ashamd
and beg youll Conceal it, yet Neddy we have seen such
Schemes successfull when the Projector is Constant I shall
Conclude saying I wish there was a War.

Glory in war was practically the only route to distinction available to a boy of his situation at that time and place. He would
soon get his war, and would make the most of it.[9]

In 1772, a powerful hurricane struck St. Croix, and the fifteen-year-old Hamilton's account of it, published in the *Royal*

Danish American Gazette, brought him some local notice: "It seemed as if a total dissolution of nature was taking place. The roaring of the sea and wind, fiery meteors flying about in the air, the prodigious glare of almost perpetual lightning, the crash of the falling houses, and the ear-piercing shrieks of the distressed, were sufficient to strike astonishment into Angels . . . But see, the Lord relents. He hears our prayer. The Lightning ceases. The winds are appeased. The warring elements are reconciled and all things promise peace."[10]

In addition to his gift for writing, the young Hamilton had a deep conceptual intelligence and first-rate analytical powers. Despite his almost complete lack of formal schooling, he also had a quick and cold-blooded facility with numbers. His job with the Crugers brought him into contact with people from ports throughout the Americas, as well as western Europe. The rest of his early knowledge about the outside world came from his mother's excellent collection of books.

It was his work, however—and his being put in charge of the Cruger operation during his superior's absences—that taught him the core principles not only of retail and wholesale management, but also of finance. These principles included the nature of credit and the importance of compound interest, ideas not well understood in that era even by many businesspeople. This knowledge and experience, acquired so early, played a big part in Hamilton's future triumphs as U.S. secretary of the treasury.

CHAPTER 2

New York and Promise

In the eighteenth century, it was common practice in the West Indies to help talented white boys go abroad for further education. Hamilton had no family financial support other than that of his cousin Ann Lytton Venton, whom he later called "the person in the world to whom as a friend I am under the greatest Obligations." But he made the journey to North America with the additional help of several St. Croix sponsors who had been impressed by his account of the great hurricane. Among them was Hugh Knox, a radical Presbyterian minister with connections in New York and New Jersey.[1]

Bearing letters of introduction to prominent families in those two colonies, Hamilton sailed away from St. Croix in October 1772. He was fifteen and a half years old and looked even younger because of his small size. Hugh Knox's wealthy friend William Livingston welcomed the young immigrant at his mansion in Elizabethtown, New Jersey. Hamilton studied for almost a year at a nearby Presbyterian school run by a recent graduate of the College of New Jersey (now Princeton). He then tried to get into the same college himself but was denied admission. In the fall of 1773, he enrolled as one of seventeen first-year students admitted to King's College (now Columbia University), which at that time was located in lower Manhattan. He was not a regular member of the class but attended as a private student of anatomy, Latin, and mathematics.

He also read the classics—Plutarch's *Lives* in particular—as well as more recent works by Hobbes, Locke, Montesquieu, Blackstone, and Hume, all of whom influenced his future writing. His friends at King's College remembered him as studious and given to composing doggerel verses. (Hamilton had a sense of humor, but he seldom allowed it to surface, then or at any other time.) They also recorded a habit of his that stayed with him for the rest of his life: pacing back and forth in his rooms for hours, talking to himself—composing oral arguments as he worked out problems of logic and presentation. In all, he was a striking, zealous, and altogether memorable young man.[2]

Hamilton was fortunate in settling in New York rather than, say, Boston or Savannah. Since the period of the initial Dutch settlement—1613 to 1664, when the English took the area and New Amsterdam became New York—it had established itself as the most cosmopolitan city in the thirteen colonies. As a busy port full of sailors, New York had been open to immigrants from many nations. When Hamilton came, the city was a roiling mix of 25,000 people clustered in lower Manhattan. So, during this time of his life, he experienced almost no nativist prejudice.

He also arrived in North America at the best possible moment for someone aspiring to distinguish himself. The Boston Tea Party occurred during his first academic year at King's College (1773–1774), and a similar event soon took place in New York City, where crowds dumped imported tea into the harbor. Britain's Parliament, in a monumental mistake, responded by passing the punitive Coercive Acts (called in America the Intolerable Acts), and real resistance started to coalesce throughout the colonies. In 1774, the First Continental Congress convened

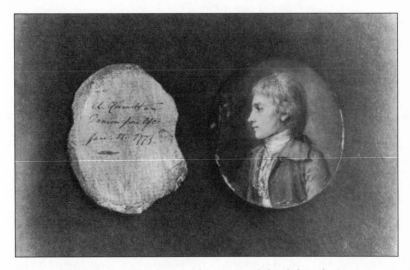

FIGURE 2. Alexander Hamilton on his sixteenth birthday, three months after arriving in North America. Until his mid-thirties, he always looked younger than he was. The notation on the left, which is on the reverse of the drawing, reads: A. Hamilton, Drawn from life, Jan. 11, 1773.

and imposed a complete ban on British imports. At that time, such a reprisal against the mother country was not far from armed rebellion. It brought the colonies to the brink of revolt.

—⁂—

The War of Independence, which began the next year, was about many different issues: the ideology of "republicanism" (literally, representative government in which the electorate and not a monarch is sovereign); Britain's withdrawal of self-governing mechanisms that the colonists had long enjoyed; the corruption of American-based British customs collectors and other officials; and, perhaps most important, the nature of empire itself— the social and cultural estrangements that over the next two centuries prompted all other colonies to break from their European parents. As John Adams remarked, "The Revolution was effected before the war commenced. The Revolution was in the hearts and minds of the people." It evolved from 1760 to 1775 and preceded the firing of the first shot. "Thirteen clocks were made to strike together," wrote Adams, "a perfection of mechanism which no artist had ever before effected."[3]

To the extent that identifiable events brought on the Revolution, an unusual number of them had to do with money—what the Roman statesman Cicero had called the "sinews of war." By the mid-eighteenth century, the British government was devoting about 80 percent of its revenues to war or to interest on its debts from prior wars. Parliament, reasonably enough, believed that the colonists should pay more for their own defense, especially after the expensive French and Indian War (1754–1763) in North America. That conflict had turned into a world war on land and sea in which about a million people died and Britain's national debt almost doubled. By the war's end, the British Empire had gained vast tracts in India, Canada, and elsewhere, and was overextended. From London's point of view, the cost of imperial control should now be spread so as to ease the crushing burden on taxpayers in the home islands. But a succession of British politicians—George Grenville, Charles Townshend, Lord North—misread sentiment in North America and made a series of disastrous decisions about taxing the colonists.[4]

Britain had thirty colonies in the New World, but only thirteen seriously resisted the new revenue measures. Neither the Canadian colonies, nor the Caribbean, nor the mid-Atlantic island of Bermuda showed much spirit of defiance. By contrast, people in the thirteen "continental colonies" opposed every new policy that would cost them money. And there were many such measures, beginning in the early 1760s.

The most offensive was the Stamp Act of 1765—the first direct tax (as opposed to tariffs on imported goods) levied by the British after more than 150 years of North American settlement. Had it remained in effect, it would have hit the colonial economy hard because it applied to so many kinds of transactions. It taxed a wide range of documents: newspapers, pamphlets, land grants, attorney's licenses, other legal certificates, and even playing cards. Many of these items now had to be printed on stamped paper imported from Britain.[5]

Intense uproar in most of the thirteen colonies followed passage of the Stamp Act. Parliament repealed it in 1766, after protests not only from the colonists but also from English merchants who exported goods to America. But a series of similar measures followed: the Townshend Acts of 1767, which taxed paper, glass, paint, lead, and other items; the Tea Act of 1773, which brought on the Boston Tea Party. Still, few people on either side of the Atlantic imagined a formal break with the mother country, let alone a long and bloody war. Well into the 1770s, a majority of the colonists still hoped for a peaceful settlement.

One of the most striking aspects of the eventual separation was how long it took—how protracted the interval was between the initial stirrings of independence and the establishment of the American government under the Constitution. Issues between the mother country and some of the thirteen colonies had begun to deteriorate as early as the 1750s. They became more serious in the 1760s, and flared into violent revolution in 1775. But not until 1789 did George Washington take the oath of office as president of the United States.

Thus, when we speak of the Revolution and the basic decisions about how the new country was to be governed, we are talking about a process that consumed almost four decades. Washington and thousands of other colonial soldiers had fought alongside British redcoats in the French and Indian War of 1754–1763. That conflict began before Alexander Hamilton was even born. By the mid-1770s, as John Adams later estimated, American public opinion was about equally divided into three camps: pro-British, pro-independence, and undecided. The preferred medium of persuasion was the pamphlet, of which Thomas Paine's *Common Sense* (1776) became the most famous.

In December 1774, Hamilton, who was now almost eighteen and living in lower Manhattan, joined in the flurry of pamphlets. He published a spirited essay of about forty pages titled *A Full Vindication of the Measures of the Congress,* signing it "A friend to America." To the natural-rights arguments of many pro-independence pamphleteers, he added an economic dimension: Britain needed the colonists more than they needed Britain. "The colonies contain above three millions of people [the actual figure was about 2.4 million]. Commerce flourishes with the most rapid progress throughout them. This commerce Great Britain has hitherto regulated to her own advantage. Can we think the annihilation of so exuberant a source of wealth, a matter of trifling import." Concluding on a note of defiant confidence, he pronounced the colonial economy self-sufficient: "We can live without trade of any kind." This assertion was at best debatable, but the essay was an impressive debut for someone so young.[6]

Two months later, in February 1775, Hamilton followed with a longer and more mature piece called *The Farmer Refuted,* which he published under the sobriquet "A sincere friend of America." He wrote this new pamphlet in response to a well-argued attack on the Continental Congress by "A. W. Farmer"— who was Samuel Seabury, later the first American Episcopal bishop. Hamilton's response to Seabury would have done credit to a learned writer with theoretical training and practical experience in high politics. When he wanted to, Hamilton could be as stirring a stylist as any of the other founders. In contrast to Jefferson, he seldom chose this route, preferring instead to present sequential arguments unadorned with high-flown language.

The Farmer Refuted, however, is an exception. Full of vivid metaphors, it shows Hamilton at his thrilling rhetorical best. Parts of the pamphlet are as eloquent as anything he ever wrote, and some passages bear reading more than once:

> The sacred rights of mankind are not to be rummaged for, among old parchments, or dusty records. They are written,

as with a sun beam, in the whole *volume* of human nature, by the hand of the divinity itself; and can never be erased or obscured.[7]

Coming from a mostly unschooled young immigrant, *The Farmer Refuted* was nothing short of a *tour de force*—the first of many Hamilton would produce over the next three decades. And the war he had wished for was now only two months away.

CHAPTER 3

War and Heroism

After years of simmering, the War of Independence exploded in April 1775 on the fields of Lexington and Concord in Massachusetts. In New York City, Hamilton began drilling daily with other volunteers in the yard of St. George's Church. Later in the year, during the evacuation of cannon from the Battery at the southern tip of Manhattan, he came under British fire for the first time. In January 1776, New York's Provincial Congress ordered that an artillery company be organized for the defense of the city. Soon Hamilton, now nineteen years old, received his appointment as a captain. He made such a strong impression on his fellow officers that two generals asked him to be their aide-de-camp. He declined, because he wanted distinction in the field rather than staff work behind the lines. In January 1777, however, after Hamilton's exemplary combat service as an artillery captain in the battles of Trenton and Princeton, George Washington requested his services. Hamilton could not refuse an invitation from the commander of the Continental Army.[1]

Of the thirty-two junior officers who served as Washington's aides during the war—usually four or five at a time—Hamilton was far and away the most talented. Another aide was Aaron Burr, whom Washington disliked and who lasted less than a month. Hamilton stayed more than four years with Washington and would have been welcome for much longer. Among the general's aides, he was one of the very few who did not come from a well-established colonial family. (Another was his close friend James McHenry, an immigrant from Ireland.) He lived during those years in Washington's own "family," as the head-quarters unit called itself. Members of the family bunked in tents or in commandeered houses—eating together, working side by side, seeing one another constantly. It was the closest community in which Hamilton had ever lived, and he loved it.[2]

As head of the national army, Washington carried on an immense correspondence. Scores of messages poured out of his headquarters every day. Hamilton, a quick and articulate drafts-man, wrote hundreds of these messages and orders, often with the barest minimum of instructions. He developed a knack for anticipating Washington's wishes, adapting his own prose to the spare and businesslike style favored by the general.[3]

As time went by, he grew about as close to Washington as it was possible to become. He sensed something of the father he never had, and the childless Washington likely had reciprocal feelings. On the other hand, given the upheavals of Hamilton's childhood, he wanted to avoid relying too much on anyone besides himself. He enjoyed the attention of Washington and other high-placed sponsors but remained stubbornly independent. As he wrote his close friend John Laurens of South Carolina, a wealthy young planter who had been another of Washington's aides, "You know the opinion I entertain of mankind, and how much it is my desire to preserve myself free from particular attachments."[4]

His chip-on-the-shoulder attitude contributed to occasional quarrels with Washington. The general, despite his dignified bearing, had a violent temper, far worse than Hamilton's. Their infrequent arguments were always over some imagined slight by one against the other. But even if Washington had been exceptionally warm-hearted, which he was not, he could hardly allow himself to be seen playing favorites with any of his aides. Circumspection therefore prevailed on both sides, even as the Washington-Hamilton relationship remained close.

The two men complemented each other perfectly. Washington's no-nonsense demeanor, his maturity of judgment, and his imposing physical presence—well over six feet and 200 pounds—commanded universal respect. The juvenile-looking Hamilton, by contrast, was about 5'7" and 125 pounds. Another of Washington's aides called him "the little lion," and the nickname stuck. Overshadowed by Washington (and later by Thomas Jefferson, who stood about 6'2"), Hamilton was slender for that time but not particularly short. James Madison was about five-four; Napoleon, five-three.

Hamilton brought to the Continental Army the kind of resourceful, incandescent brilliance that Washington needed and knew just how to use. Unlike most officers, even most generals, Hamilton always thought strategically. The mere task of keeping the Continental Army together—an assemblage from thirteen independent states, each of which also had its own militia—could easily have failed. The army chronically ran short of money and supplies. It was plagued by desertions and dependent on financial help from France, Britain's historic enemy. Because Washington lacked the funds to assemble a larger force, he lost more big battles than he won. He avoided full-scale engagements with the British, who fielded a much larger and more professional group of soldiers. He kept his army intact by making quick strikes and elusive maneuvers.

Even as an eighteen-year-old, Hamilton had anticipated this unorthodox way of fighting. In *The Farmer Refuted,* published in February 1775, he had described the most effective course to follow if war came: "The circumstances of our country put it in our power to evade a pitched battle. It will be better policy, to harass and exhaust the [British] soldiery, by frequent skirmishes and incursions, than to take the open field with them, by which means they would have the full benefit of their superior regularity and skill." He seemed to be a born military strategist, just as he would later become a consummate economic strategist.[5]

———

Among Washington's aides, it was always Hamilton who received (or sought out) the hardest assignments. He drafted plans to institute new military regulations, to reform the inspector general's office, and—most remarkably—to reorganize the entire army. All of this would have been heady stuff for anyone, let alone a penniless, illegitimate, West Indian immigrant barely out of his teens. Yet Hamilton blossomed. Despite his emotional insecurities, he had total confidence in his own abilities and seemed able to do anything. In an age unfamiliar with complex management, he proved a superlative administrator, with a sure sense of managerial hierarchies.

He dealt routinely with public officials at the highest levels. As Washington's representative, he never hesitated to upbraid senior army officers—including such men as General Horatio Gates, the acclaimed victor at the Battle of Saratoga—in the same tone he had used with Caribbean ship captains. Because he had no resources or family of his own, however, he remained well aware of his own vulnerability. This was one reason why he often asked Washington for a field command of his own—a position in which he might achieve national renown through some conspicuous act of heroism. As the years passed, Hamilton came to resent the general's refusal to let him go. In any war, this is a familiar story: the brilliant staff officer whose close assistance is vital to his chief but who instead wants to fight independently in the field. Seldom has it been a more dramatic story than in the prolonged tension between Hamilton and Washington.[6]

Among his many other duties, Hamilton was the ranking French speaker on Washington's staff, and he managed the stream of officers from France who showed up expecting to be placed at the head of American troops. He did become close friends with the Marquis de Lafayette, who was two years younger than Hamilton and regarded him as a foreigner like himself, helping a new country to win independence. And Hamilton kept a constant eye on the behavior of Congress in Philadelphia. Like Washington and most others in the army, he became frustrated to the point of incredulity at what was happening in Philadelphia. The national government seemed almost irrelevant to the fighting in the field—disorganized to the point of impotence.[7]

Most of all, Hamilton *wrote*—hundreds, ultimately thousands of pages: orders, letters, reorganization plans, essays on strategy, ideas for financing the war, the occasional political tract. Seated at his camp desk day after day, the weeks turning into years, he recorded in his smooth, plain script a huge body of work. His surviving papers, almost by themselves, constitute a military history of the Revolutionary War. During his first four years of service, he never took a furlough. The army had become his household, Washington's "family" his own. He had no other home.[8]

The one missing ingredient remained the very thing that had led him to join the army in the first place: glory in battle. He wanted more than a desk job, even if that desk stood at the epicenter of the Revolution. Thus continued the protracted struggle with his chief, who dreaded losing his unmatched talents. As he wrote Washington, he had many times "explained to you candidly my feelings with respect to military reputation, and how much it was my object to act a conspicuous part in some enterprise that might perhaps raise my character as a soldier above mediocrity." To understand how strongly Hamilton felt about this is to grasp the essence of his character. He had a passionate drive to achieve what in his time was called "Fame" and what today we would call immortality.[9]

He finally decided that he had to leave Washington's family, regardless of the general's wishes. Though he had just turned twenty-four, he was a lieutenant colonel and a seasoned veteran. Before he joined Washington's staff, he had fought in the battles of Monmouth, Trenton, and Princeton. Two of his horses had been shot from under him. But he had never had a significant field command of his own.

In early 1781, after years of sparring, Washington relented and agreed to release him within a few months. By that time, as Hamilton wrote his friend James McHenry, another Washington aide, "The Great man and I have come to an open rupture. Proposals of accom[m]odation have been made on his part but rejected. I pledge my honor to you that he will find me inflexible. He shall for once at least repent his ill-humour." But this was just one more quarrel among many and did not last long. Its importance lay in its timing. At last Hamilton would get his chance to head a large group of soldiers in combat.[10]

After Hamilton left Washington's headquarters, his moment of true glory came in the fall of 1781, during the decisive Battle of Yorktown in Virginia. There he was put in command of three light infantry battalions—but only after still another tiff with Washington, who wanted to place a French officer in charge because it was a joint operation. Hamilton's orders were to seize a fortified British position, a redoubt that blocked a full advance by the Continental Army. It was the kind of opportunity he had been dreaming of for years.[11]

Washington decided on a daring night-time assault on the redoubt, so as to gain the advantage of surprise over the British. In another bold stroke, he instructed Hamilton to have his men unload their pistols and muskets and attack only with swords and bayonets. Hamilton's troops silently crept up on the British, then surged into the trenches and began screaming like madmen. After ten or fifteen minutes of vicious hand-to-hand fighting, the Americans overwhelmed the startled enemy soldiers and captured the redoubt. Hamilton, sword in hand and the first person to leap into the fray, could not have written a better script or carried it off with more élan. It was the perfect culmination of his time in the army, and it made him a legitimate national hero.[12]

His fondness of things martial ran deep. Even in civilian clothes, he was vain about his appearance and seemed always ready for inspection. Though not quite a dandy, he dressed impeccably and carried his slender frame as straight as a ship's mast. John Adams, who once called him "the bastard Brat of a Scots pedlar," also spoke of him as "the Bloody Buoy" [*sic*], an allusion to his love for battle and perpetually youthful appearance. With his reddish-blond hair, bright blue eyes, and fair complexion, Hamilton continued to look like an adolescent until his thirties.[13]

Yorktown effectively ended the Revolutionary War, even though the British still blockaded the coast and held New York City, Charleston, Savannah, and other key positions. Two more years of skirmishes, sea battles, and diplomacy passed before the signing of the 1783 peace treaty. Hamilton, satisfied with his measure of glory, left the army soon after the Yorktown campaign, having served for more than five years. One of his last acts was to renounce, as he wrote Washington, "all claim to the compensations attached to my military station during the war or after it"—a reference to the entitlement of half-pay that Congress awarded officers of the Continental Army. This gesture typified Hamilton's sometimes impulsive temperament. Perhaps he did it because he wanted to put the army behind him symbolically. The war was not yet over, and he may have felt a bit remorseful about leaving, as his letter to Washington hints. But he certainly could have used the money.[14]

FIGURE 3. General George Washington at Princeton, 1779, by Charles Willson Peale. Washington was forty-seven years old at the time, and his commanding presence could hardly be more apparent. The U.S. one-dollar bill should display the face of this Washington, rather than that of the diminished old man with severe dental problems.

FIGURE 4. Lieutenant Colonel Hamilton, age twenty-four, in a trench at the 1781 siege of Yorktown, where he became a war hero. Painted by Alonzo Chappel in 1857.

CHAPTER 4

Love and Social Status

Hamilton had arrived in North America in 1772 as a rootless fifteen-year-old. By 1780, despite his achievements, he remained acutely aware of his tenuous position in the new nation. He had worked closely with George Washington at the highest levels of the army, but once the war ended he would have no standing in American society, no logical destination. "I am a stranger in this country," he wrote. "I have no property here, no connexions." Nothing in his life was settled, as it was for all the other founders. He would have to reinvent himself again—choose a profession, find a place to live.[1]

During the latter years of the war, he had also begun to think about getting married. In April 1779, when he was twenty-two years old, he sent a half-facetious letter about marriage to John Laurens, who had left Washington's headquarters to fight the British in his native South Carolina. Laurens distinguished himself by proposing that slaves who enlisted in the Continental Army be given their freedom. White South Carolinians spurned his suggestion.

"As we are upon the subject of wife," Hamilton wrote his

friend, "I empower and command you to get me one in Carolina." He then listed the requisite qualifications. "She must be young, handsome (I lay most stress upon a good shape) sensible (a little learning will do), well bred." Concerning her political views, "I am indifferent what side she may be of; I think I have arguments that will easily convert her to mine. As to religion a moderate stock will satisfy me. She must believe in god and hate a saint. But as to fortune, the larger stock of that the better."[2]

Finding an attractive mate during wartime was not as difficult in this particular conflict as one might think. The circumstances of the Revolution—intermittent fighting, adjournment of active hostilities during most winters—made it possible for army officers to participate in at least some social activities. During these interludes, Hamilton took a conspicuous part and always cut a romantic figure. At parties, balls, and other gatherings held near the headquarters of the Continental Army, he stood out. So did Washington, who was a charming host and an excellent dancer.

Hamilton, with his good looks and courtly manners, attracted a lot of attention from women. Abigail Adams once wrote her husband, "When I have seen that cock sparrow, I have read his heart in his wicked eyes. The very devil is in them. They are lasciviousness itself." In 2011, a professor published an article in an academic journal titled "The Erotic Charisma of Alexander Hamilton." More than any other founder, he had real glamour.[3]

During the war, he carried on numerous flirtations—one with the socially prominent Kitty Livingston of New York, another with the beautiful Cornelia Lott of New Jersey. Despite his vanity, Hamilton did not regard himself as a truly handsome man, because of an indentation between his nose and forehead. That imagined flaw, which is barely visible in his portrait on today's ten-dollar bill, violated the classical Greek and Roman ideal of an uninterrupted straight line.

Probably because of his mother's ill fortune, Hamilton had

complicated feelings about women that he never fully resolved. He had strong sexual impulses but was not over-aggressive or promiscuous in the manner of some of his contemporaries, notably Aaron Burr and Gouverneur Morris. Often he went out of his way to help women who seemed to be in distress. Some, such as the clever young Peggy Shippen Arnold, exploited his well-known gallantry for their own purposes. Wife of the traitor Benedict Arnold and fully knowledgeable about her husband's intrigues, Peggy Arnold regaled Hamilton with false tales of her own betrayal that reduced him to jelly.

The woman who would become his wife first crossed his path not in Carolina, where he had asked John Laurens to look, but in upstate New York. He met Elizabeth Schuyler in 1777 at the Albany home of her father, Major General Philip Schuyler, a veteran of the French and Indian War and one of the highest-ranking officers in the Continental Army. At that time, Hamilton was twenty and Elizabeth nineteen. Their encounter was brief and came to nothing, as Hamilton rushed to complete his business with General Schuyler.

Three years later, however, in February 1780, Elizabeth Schuyler arrived in Morristown, New Jersey, for a visit with some of her relatives. By sheer coincidence, they happened to live near the house George Washington was using for his winter quarters. Soon, as a matter of course, Hamilton met Elizabeth again. This time it was love at second sight, and Hamilton lost his head altogether. In response to one of Elizabeth's notes to him, he wrote, "I cannot tell you what exstasy I felt in casting my eye over the sweet effusions of tenderness it contains." Before long he was wandering around as if in a daze. Tench Tilghman, his roommate and another of Washington's aides, pronounced his friend "a gone man." Hamilton began to spend every available minute with Elizabeth (he usually called her Eliza, and sometimes Betsey). Within a month he had decided that he must marry her. Eliza, fortunately, was just as smitten as he was.[4]

"I venture to tell you in confidence," Hamilton wrote another Schuyler daughter, Margarita, "that by some odd contrivance or other, your sister has found out the secret of interesting me in everything that concerns her . . . She has good nature affability and vivacity unembellished with that charming frivolousness which is justly deemed one of the principal accomplishments of a *belle.*" In his diary, Tench Tilghman described Eliza as "a brunette with the most good-natured, lively dark eyes that I ever saw, which threw a beam of good temper and benevolence over her whole countenance." A portrait of Eliza confirms this description, highlighting the unusual combination of piercing eyes—so dark as to appear dominated by black pupils and devoid of irises—with a forthright and interested expression, as if something amusing may be about to happen.[5]

She was the second of five Schuyler daughters. There were also three sons. The Schuylers—land-rich, Dutch-descended patroons long resident in New York—were one of the most prominent families not only in their state but in all of North America. General Schuyler's mother had been the wealthy Cornelia Van Cortlandt. His wife was the former Catherine Van Rensselaer, heiress to huge acreages of New York farmland. Philip Schuyler was a skilled but controversial soldier and landowner, beloved by many of his associates but resented by others because of his blunt, businesslike manner.

Though rooted in aristocratic New York society, General Schuyler showed an unpretentious attitude toward Hamilton. The younger man had worried for years about his own place on the American social scale. He well knew that despite his dazzling success as Washington's aide, he was engaged in a precarious high-wire act. The war could not continue forever, and then where would he go? Unlike all the other founders, he had no family in the United States, no lifelong friends, no home except Washington's headquarters. He would never feel secure in the way that his future rivals Jefferson and Madison did. After

Eliza's arrival in Morristown, he had every reason to doubt that the Schuylers would consider him a suitable match for their daughter.

Philip Schuyler, however, was a close friend of George Washington, who had no question whatever of Hamilton's extraordinary talents and integrity. Then, too, the United States prided itself on being a new kind of country where merit was supposed to supersede ancestry. So, after thinking the matter over, Schuyler decided in Hamilton's favor. The young man's lowly origins would not prevent his acceptance by so prestigious a family.

On April 8, 1780—scarcely two months after Eliza came to Morristown—the general informed Hamilton by letter that he and Mrs. Schuyler would give their blessing to the marriage. Hamilton was not only exhilarated by this news, but also a little incredulous at the warmth of his welcome. The wedding was scheduled for December 1780, eight months later. It would take place at the Schuyler mansion in Albany. No relative of Hamilton would be able to attend; his sole guest would be his immigrant friend and fellow Washington aide James McHenry.[6]

During the summer of 1780, Hamilton wrote John Laurens: "Next fall completes my doom. I give up my liberty to Miss Schuyler." By this time, he could appraise a little more clinically the woman he was about to marry. "Though not a genius she has good sense enough to be agreeable, and though not a beauty, she has fine black eyes—is rather handsome and has every other requisite of the exterior to make a lover happy. And believe me, I am a lover in earnest."[7]

Hamilton's obsession with personal independence required that he never take a penny from Eliza or her family. And despite his earlier remarks to Laurens about finding a wife with a large fortune, he never did. Unlike most people who excel in finance, he had little interest in becoming rich. Nor did he want to mislead Eliza about his prospects. As he wrote her shortly before the marriage, "Do you soberly relish the pleasure of being a poor mans wife? Have you learned to think of a home spun preferable to a brocade and the rumbling of a waggon wheel to the musical rattling of a coach and six? Will you be able to see with perfect composure your old acquaintances flaunting it in gay life, tripping it along in elegance and splendor, while you hold an humble station and have no other enjoyments than the sober comforts of a good wife?" Hamilton was not joking. He concluded his letter with a direct warning: "Your future rank in life is a perfect lottery." But Eliza was the perfect match. The love on both sides was passionate and genuine, transcending any difference in backgrounds.[8]

The Schuyler connection instantly endowed Hamilton with social standing he could have attained in no other way. Only eight years earlier, he had arrived in North America as a penniless, illegitimate, teenaged orphan. Since then he had become the most influential aide to the most powerful man in the United States. And now he was a member of one of the country's most celebrated families and on the verge of becoming an authentic war hero at Yorktown. Two years after the marriage, Philip Schuyler wrote Eliza that she could not have chosen a better husband. Hamilton "affords happiness too exquisite for expression. I daily experience the pleasure of hearing encomiums on his virtue and abilities from those who are capable of distinguishing between real and pretended merit. He is considered, as he certainly is, the ornament of his country." To say that Hamilton had "married up" does not begin to express the spectacular social ascent his alliance with the Schuyler family brought about. He was still an outsider, but not nearly so much as before.[9]

Some people thought that his dash and mercurial temperament formed a better fit with Eliza's older sister, the glamorous Angelica Schuyler. However, for reasons almost nobody understood, Angelica had earlier eloped with the dull and stolid John Church, an English merchant with lucrative U.S. commercial connections. Church made a fortune during the war, and afterward he and Angelica spent part of their time in England. For the rest of her life, Angelica played the coquette with dozens of attentive men, including her brother-in-law. She and Hamilton

FIGURE 5. Elizabeth Schuyler Hamilton at age twenty-nine, seven years after her marriage. Painted in 1787 by Ralph Earl, a well-known artist who had been imprisoned for debt. Alexander Hamilton arranged for this portrait, other clients followed, and Ralph Earl was soon able to pay his debts and win his release.

wrote numerous flirtatious letters to one another, full of double entendres. But there is no convincing evidence that they had a sexual relationship.

Meanwhile, Eliza, his true love, helped her husband in a thousand ways: indulging his obsessive penchant for work, organizing their households in a long series of rented accommodations, even taking his dictation for some of *The Federalist Papers* in 1787 and 1788. She bore eight children and spoke not a word in public when Hamilton became involved in a sensational extramarital liaison during the 1790s. She endured the deaths of both her husband and her oldest son in senseless duels, and acted with courage and dignity throughout her life. Of the entire Revolutionary generation, Eliza survived longest. As late as the 1850s, when she was in her mid-nineties, she was still attending dinner parties in Washington, looking after the reputation of "my Hamilton" fifty years after his death. Marrying her was one of the wisest things Hamilton ever did.[10]

After the Battle of Yorktown and his resignation from the army in 1781, he and Eliza moved to her hometown of Albany. Hamilton had decided to become a lawyer, and he began one of his typical crash programs of study. In New York, the privilege to practice was restricted to men who had passed the bar examination, a step that normally came after a three-year apprenticeship with an established lawyer. Not wishing to wait so long, Hamilton took advantage of a legislative waiver for military veterans (and an additional one enacted specifically for him) and passed the examination within a few months after he began his study.[11]

In preparation for the exam, he worked with Robert Troup, who had been his roommate at King's College. Because he was trying to skip the required apprenticeship, it was necessary for Hamilton somehow to master the complex procedures of New York courts. In organizing the notes he made during his intense concentration, he produced the first manual of civil procedure ever written in the United States. His "Practical Proceedings in the Supreme Court of the State of New York" ran to seventy printed pages, and for decades afterward was used by hundreds of law students. He was admitted to the bar in 1782.[12]

In that same year, Hamilton's constituents elected him to the New York legislature, and soon thereafter as one of the state's delegates to the Confederation Congress. (Its name changed from Continental Congress after the ratification of the Articles of Confederation in 1781.) In August 1782, he wrote John Laurens about what should come next, the war being almost over: "Peace made, My Dear friend, a new scene opens. The object then will be to make our independence a blessing. To do this we must secure our *union* on solid foundations; an herculean task . . . Quit your sword my friend, put on the *toga,* come to Congress. We know each others sentiments, our views are the same: we have fought side by side to make America free, let us hand in hand struggle to make her happy."[13]

In South Carolina, however, the war had not quite ended. Twelve days after Hamilton wrote this letter, Laurens was killed in a skirmish with the British. Losing his closest friend was yet another blow in what seemed an endless series of personal traumas. But Hamilton had already demonstrated the resilience that would characterize his entire life.

Not long after Laurens's death, he wrote Lafayette that "I have been employed for the last ten months in rocking the cradle [of his and Eliza's new son] and studying the art of fleecing my neighbours. I am now a Grave Counsellor at law, and shall soon be a grand member of Congress." He had moved his family from Albany to New York City and begun his legal career, setting up a law office in his house at 57 Wall Street. With so much history already behind him, he was still just twenty-six. For the next five years, he pursued a lively legal practice while also taking an energetic hand in New York politics and the affairs of Congress at Philadelphia.[14]

Many of Hamilton's colleagues at the bar believed him to be

the best trial lawyer of his generation. "I need not tell you," Robert Troup later wrote, "how far he surpassed us all in abilities." In his early practice he represented several affluent "Tories" (former Loyalists to the British Crown) whose property had been confiscated by the New York state government. Some of his clients had collaborated with the British army, which occupied New York City for nearly the entire war. They were good clients, ready to pay generous fees. But besides needing their business, Hamilton wanted to create a hospitable environment so that they would not move their wealth from the United States to Canada. This idea of husbanding all possible financial resources was based on his vision of the nation's economic future. It presaged some of his policies as secretary of the treasury ten years later.[15]

In 1783, after he began to attend sessions of Congress as one of New York's five delegates, Hamilton wrote a letter to George Washington describing the divisions within the legislature. "There are two classes of men Sir in Congress of very Different views—one attached to state, the other to Continental politics. The last have been strenuous advocates for funding the public debt upon solid securities [new federal bonds], the former have given every opposition in their power." Delegates who elevated the broad national interest over narrow loyalty to their states, he told Washington, were "the men who think continentally."[16]

Nobody thought more continentally than Hamilton himself. As he wrote in a pamphlet published in 1782, "There is something noble and magnificent in the perspective of a great Federal Republic, closely linked in the pursuit of a common interest, tranquil and prosperous at home, respectable abroad; but there is something proportionately diminutive and contemptible in the prospect of a number of petty states." He had seen this kind of pettiness up close during his youth in the Caribbean. There, imperial and local rivalries prevented cooperation that would have benefited all of the island colonies.[17]

Now he saw it on the continent as well—far more clearly

than his contemporaries, most of whom felt stronger loyalties to their states than to the new nation. Hamilton had ties to New York, but they did not run very deep. Here his immigrant origins served him well, giving him a more national orientation—a more single-minded devotion to the Union than that of perhaps any other founder.

CHAPTER 5

The Roots of His Thinking

By the time Hamilton reached his middle twenties, his basic ideas had crystallized. There is not much in *The Federalist Papers* of 1787–1788 or in his great *Reports* to Congress as secretary of the treasury during the 1790s that his writings of a decade earlier did not foreshadow. Because these ideas so powerfully influenced the future of the United States, they are worth a close look. They ripened during the years 1779–1782, and concerned four interrelated subjects: finance, foreign relations, the optimal nature of the American union, and the strategy that would best promote national security and prosperity, as opposed to states' rights.

During the 1770s and 1780s, the situation confronting Hamilton and all other would-be designers of American policy was unprecedented: a new country was emerging from a colonial past. Never before had there been a successful revolution by any colony against its European parent—not in the British Empire, the Spanish, the French, the Dutch, or the Portuguese, all of which included huge tracts of land scattered across the globe. There was no template, no obvious series of steps to take. The

Declaration of Independence was an eloquent manifesto but not a plan for governing a nation.[1]

Even under the Articles of Confederation, which were ratified by the states in 1781, the civilian part of the national government still consisted almost solely of Congress. No true executive branch existed, no federal court system, no clear power to tax, no authority or mechanism for regulating trade. Congress borrowed money from abroad, printed its own currency, and received substantial financial and military help from France. But aside from this, both Congress and the army depended almost entirely on the states for funds and other trappings of government. The Articles of Confederation represented a step forward, but only a baby step. Hamilton chafed under this system, both before and after the Articles were ratified.

Overhanging all postwar affairs were two daunting issues: finance and foreign relations. During the war, there had been a good deal of trading with the enemy—so much that it became routine. The British army in North America, the largest expeditionary force in history up to that time, had to be fed and maintained. It could hardly be supplied from the faraway British Isles or the trickle of supplies coming out of Canada. Many Americans therefore conducted a regular, large-scale business with the British. Once the war ended, so did this trade with the enemy—to the detriment of the national economy. Some Americans who had engaged in commerce with all kinds of customers found their trading patterns disrupted, if not cut off altogether, especially on the seas.

What the ex-colonists hoped for was open markets for U.S. exports to Europe, the West Indies, and South America. In April 1776, the Continental Congress had ended traditional mercantilist restrictions by opening American ports to the ships and cargoes of all countries. This was a radical step for that time, rooted in revolutionary idealism and military need. The Americans hoped other countries would reciprocate, but the plan did not work. The European imperial powers would not give up their own closed systems.[2]

Even after the war, Britain continued to insist that many American cargoes be landed first in England. They would then be taxed and "re-exported"—often in British merchant ships— to other destinations, including British colonies. American commerce was therefore restricted and sometimes shut out from some of its best markets, particularly in the Caribbean. Throughout the 1770s and 1780s, and well into the 1790s and 1800s, the crucial issue of foreign trade festered. The problem taxed the minds of Hamilton and the other founders and affected the livelihood of every commercial center in the new nation. It caused a series of annual balance-of-payments crises that seemed to worsen every year.[3]

American merchants had hoped to buy imports with funds they accrued abroad from purchasers of American exports. The failure of these hopes meant an adverse trade balance, causing in turn a chronic outflow of gold and silver ("specie" or "hard money"). During much of the 1780s, it meant general economic depression.

With hard money in such short supply, both Congress and seven of the thirteen states let the printing presses roll. They issued large amounts of paper currency that depreciated very fast. Some state currencies quickly lost 75 to 80 percent of their value. (The Constitution of 1789 put a stop to state issues, ending a practice that had begun much earlier, when the states were colonies.) Economically, the 1780s was likely the worst decade in American history except for the 1930s. And since the country was not yet a nation in anything but name, persistent economic crisis raised the specter of political disintegration. Nobody recognized this possibility better than Hamilton.[4]

The war had been extremely expensive, costing about $160 million in 1780 dollars—a huge sum for that time. It was more than the total budget of the national government over the *twenty years* from 1790 to 1810—years in which most federal spending went toward paying interest and principal on the war debt. Economic disruptions were severe, especially in New York, New Jersey, Georgia, and South Carolina, the four states where much of the fighting took place. By 1779, Washington's Continental Army had been forced to pay for civilian crops and farm animals using currency or vouchers issued by Congress that soon lost their value.

Paying with worthless notes amounted to outright confiscation, and it was hard even for strong supporters of the Revolution to endure the seizure of their property. Unrest in both the army and the countryside began to reach a dangerous level. As Hamilton wrote from Washington's headquarters in 1780, the army had reached the verge of breakdown. "It is now a mob, rather than an army, without clothing, without pay, without provision, without morals, without discipline. We begin to hate our country for its neglect of us; the country begins to hate us for our oppression of them."[5]

Even after the war ended in 1783, America's external economy was still tied to the British Empire almost as tightly as it had been before the Revolution. And while the country's imports rose by more than 69 percent during the twenty years from 1770 to 1790, its exports grew by only 2.7 percent, one twenty-sixth as much. This was a path to disaster. For the period 1787–1792, more than 90 percent of all imported manufactures came from Britain. As against this incoming flood, only 43 percent of America's small quantities of exports went to Britain and its empire; 25 percent went to the French Empire, 10 percent to the Dutch Empire, 8 percent to the Spanish Empire, and 6 percent to the Portuguese Empire (mainly Brazil). At none of these destinations were American traders as welcome as they wished to be. Nowhere did American merchants sell as much as they could have in the absence of imperial restrictions. Nor, back home, could the thirteen states come to agreement among themselves as to what to do about it.[6]

Heavy dependence for public funds on import tariffs (customs duties or "imposts") made foreign policy inseparable from economic policy. Until the new government under the Constitution entered office in 1789, customs duties belonged not to the national government but to whatever state included the port where the incoming goods happened to enter. This was one of the many elements that had made the financing of the Revolution so chaotic.

Then, too, both before and after 1789, such heavy reliance on imposts deepened sectional discord. Many Southerners disliked having to pay tariffs on imported British goods. They believed that the North, where manufacturing was more highly developed, could supply its local consumers with a larger amount of domestically made products than the South was able to do. This meant, in turn, that the South was having to buy proportionately more British goods, and, accordingly, having to contribute more than its share of duties on manufactured imports. And yet, tariffs on British imports furnished the bulk of all federal income. A reduction or stoppage of this income would imperil the new nation's independence. The intertwined issues of finance and foreign relations therefore tended to divide the country along sectional lines of North versus South.[7]

Because we know how this story turned out—that the Union survived and prospered—it is hard to imagine how perilous the situation of the 1780s and 1790s actually was. But what happened later, during the Civil War of the 1860s, makes the hazards of the earlier situation of sectional conflict more vivid. It becomes easier to imagine the harsh realities of the 1780s and 1790s. Without wise management and a lot of good luck, these conditions could have split the fledgling United States into two or more countries whose independence would have remained unpredictable.[8]

Certainly a disastrous fate for the new nation preyed on the imagination of Alexander Hamilton. He knew from his turbulent boyhood that things could fall apart on short notice. During the war, he had seen from his special vantage point at Washington's headquarters that everything that could go wrong often did. Soldiers were not paid, supplies failed to arrive, and there was nothing to wear. Troops deserted and went home in disgust. Congress issued paper money that became worthless. The national government seemed helpless. "Our countrymen," he wrote John Laurens in 1780, "have all the folly of the ass and all the passiveness of sheep." For a person who loved order in addition to liberty, the spectacle was unbearable. At one point late in the war, Hamilton feared that the outcome might be a British loss without an American *national* victory.[9]

Sometimes Hamilton wondered why the heavily taxed British continued to fight. As he wrote Eliza Schuyler four months before their wedding, "The affairs of England are in so bad a plight that if no fortunate events attend her [in] this campaign, it would seem impossible for her to proceed in the war. But she is an obstinate old dame, and seems determined to ruin her whole family, rather than to let Miss America go on flirting it with her new lovers [France], with whom, as giddy young girls often do, she eloped in contempt of her mothers authority."[10]

On the other hand, the outcome of the war and future of the American union were still far from certain. Just a month later, Hamilton wrote another letter to Eliza suggesting that if the American confederation should disintegrate, then they might settle after their marriage in the State of New York, which was relatively self-sufficient. And if that didn't work, then neutral Geneva might be a suitable haven. Hamilton was always thinking ahead. The experiences of his youth had bred into his personality an insecurity that taught him to take nothing for granted.[11]

By 1780 the U.S. economy was in real trouble. To buy one silver dollar (actually a Spanish peso that was called a dollar) required about a hundred paper Continental dollars. There was no agreement on what to do about the fiscal crisis, nor any governmental structure for resolving other problems. The big questions were how to organize for final victory in the war and how to plan for economic recovery afterward, given the extreme weakness of the national government.[12]

Hamilton's analysis of this situation is evident in a series of letters and articles he wrote from 1780 through 1782. In these documents—whose aggregate length is equivalent to a medium-sized book—he presented both a diagnosis of the situation and a prescription for its reform. His approach is best summarized in a long letter of September 3, 1780, to James Duane, an influential New York delegate to the Continental Congress who had asked for his views.

Hamilton's letter to Duane, written three days before his conjectures to Eliza about perhaps moving to Geneva, is uncannily prescient. The outcome of the war was in doubt, the Articles of Confederation had not yet been adopted, the Constitutional Convention lay seven years in the future, and his service as secretary of the treasury a decade away. When he wrote the letter, he was twenty-three years old and still Washington's aide-de-camp. But he had long since begun to think continentally.

"The fundamental defect is a want of power in Congress," he told Duane. "The idea of uncontrolable sovereignty in each state, over its internal police [policies], will defeat the other powers given to Congress, and make our union feeble and precarious." Congress, therefore, should either demand the power to operate an effective government, or, if that failed, call a "convention of all the states" to write what amounted to a new constitution. In either case, the national legislature "should have complete sovereignty in all that relates to war, peace, trade, finance, and to the management of foreign affairs." In order to exercise its authority, "Congress should instantly appoint the following great officers of state—A secretary for foreign affairs—A President of war—A President of Marine—A Financier—A President of trade."[13]

Here, in 1780, Hamilton was calling for a new government for the United States, and it is the first known proposal for a constitutional convention to come from any of the founders. Although even the Constitution of 1787 said nothing about cabinet departments of government, many of Hamilton's ideas materialized in 1789, when Congress began to create departments. What he had called "presidents" became cabinet "secretaries" in the kind of full-fledged executive branch he favored.

In his 1780 letter to Duane, Hamilton went on to argue that it was especially important to do something about finance. Despite his youthful business background, Hamilton was not yet an expert on this subject, but he had begun to read widely about finance in 1777, at the age of twenty. He wrote copious notes to himself that drew on the works of European authorities, and, later, also on his own experience at Washington's headquarters in trying to pay for the war. He saw very early that without an effective financial system, the drive for a truly independent new country would fail, sooner or later.

As he conceived it, there were four urgent needs, all interrelated: an immediate loan from abroad to help finance the war, a new foundation for both public and private credit, a system of paper money, and a national bank. As he continued in his letter to Duane, "It has been to me astonishing how any man could have doubted at any period of our affairs of the necessity of a foreign loan." There simply was not enough money left in the United States for the continuation of the war.[14]

Then, too, a system of public finance (that is, government bonds that could be bought and sold by private investors) "never was long supported in any country on a national scale, where it was not founded on the joint basis of public and private credit." Both the government itself and private investors must be part of the system. "The only certain manner to obtain a permanent paper credit is to engage the monied interest immediately in it by making them contribute the whole or part of the stock and giving them the whole or part of the profits." Here Hamilton had in mind the Bank of England, which had been established in 1694. At that time, England's economy had been mired in the kind of crisis now besetting the United States. In 1780, by contrast, Hamilton could write that "the Bank of England unites public authority and faith with private credit; and hence we see what a vast fabric of paper credit is raised on a visionary basis. Had it not been for this, England would never have found sufficient funds to carry on her wars; but with the help of this she has done, and is doing wonders." Even as Hamilton wrote, the Bank of England was still a private, profit-making institution.[15]

"It is true," he concluded in his letter to Duane, that "the individuals in America are not very rich, but this would not prevent their instituting a bank; it would only prevent its being done with such ample funds as in other countries. Have they not sufficient confidence in the government and in the issue of the cause? Let the Government endeavour to inspire that confidence, by adopting the measures I have recommended or others equivalent to them." There is little in Hamilton's programs as secretary of the treasury during the 1790s that is not foreshadowed in this letter of 1780—however "hastily written," as he described it.[16]

Less than two years after his letter to Duane, Hamilton—now out of the army and practicing law in New York—wrote for a newspaper a series of six essays titled "The Continentalist." They total nearly 10,000 words, or about thirty pages of an average-sized book. Together, the essays flesh out the prescriptions set forth in his earlier letters. Hamilton was still in his mid-twenties, but his style of analysis and persuasion had now matured.[17]

One of the biggest economic problems the United States faced, he wrote, was an adverse trade balance. The large excess of imports over exports caused a steady outflow of gold and silver and a consequent shortage of money within the country. Hamilton believed that something had to be done about this problem.[18]

In the situation of an unfavorable balance of trade, Hamilton argued, anyone who knew the history of Europe must reject the idea of a hands-off policy by the American government. He cited the record of the most successful economies of Europe in order to show how the American people's apparent preference for laissez-faire was hurting their own economy. "Trade may be said to have taken its rise in England under the auspices of [Queen] Elizabeth; and its rapid progress there is in a great measure to be ascribed to the fostering care of government in that and succeeding reigns." The same was true of France, and again it was easy to identify when and by whom the change had been carried out. "France was much later [than England] in commercial improvements, nor would her trade have been at this time in so prosperous a condition had it not been for the abilities and indefatigable endeavours of the great COLBERT [Louis XIV's innovative finance minister]." Of all European countries, one of the best examples supporting Hamilton's argument was Holland. "The Dutch, who may justly be allowed a pre-eminence in the knowledge of trade, have ever made it an essential object of state."[19]

Americans, because of their determined drive for independence, had been too ready to ignore these economic lessons of history. They liked to find fault with almost all Old World practices, whether bad or good. "It is too much characteristic of our natural temper to be ingenious in figuring out and magnifying the minutest disadvantages, and to reject measures of evident utility." Americans' penchant for accentuating the negatives in European experience was understandable but dangerous. "Unless we can overcome this narrow disposition and learn to estimate measures, by their general tendency, we shall never be a great or a happy people, if we remain a people at all."[20]

In "The Continentalist," Hamilton was writing in conscious opposition to the laissez-faire prescriptions contained in Adam

Smith's *Wealth of Nations,* published in 1776, the same year that the American Declaration of Independence was signed. Smith's argument was appropriate for Britain, which by then was an advanced nation with too many regulations—but not for a developing country such as the United States, which had too few. The federal government was going to have to take a stronger role, especially in finance. Otherwise, Hamilton believed, the United States could not survive as a nation. He was arguing not for high protectionist tariffs, but only for some means to increase exports, limit imports, and exert better control over monetary and fiscal policy. As matters stood, the government was doing none of these things well, if at all.

CHAPTER 6

Robert Morris, Hamilton, and Finance

In Hamilton's long letter of September 1780 to James Duane, he had recommended that Congress appoint executive officers to be in charge of trade, foreign policy, and other departments, including finance. For this last office, which he regarded as the most important, he recommended only one candidate: Robert Morris of Philadelphia. Morris, Hamilton wrote, "could by his own personal influence give great weight to the measures he should adopt."[1]

When Hamilton sent his letter in 1780, the legislature had no clear authority to appoint executive officers. But in 1781, when the Articles of Confederation were at last ratified, Congress did move toward additional executive control. The country was in an emergency, the war's outcome remained uncertain, and financial problems pressed harder than ever. Among the new executive offices was superintendent of finance, and some legislators favored Hamilton himself for the job. He was still just twenty-four, however—too young and inexperienced. Congress therefore appointed Robert Morris, Hamilton's own choice and that of other well-informed advisers. Morris proved to be something of a short-term savior. He was forty-seven years old at the time, a prominent merchant with a compelling personal history.[2]

Born in Liverpool to unmarried parents, Morris had no recollection at all of his mother. She abandoned him as an infant, leaving him to be raised by her own mother. When he was a small boy, his father, also named Robert Morris, was sent to Maryland by his employers, who dealt in tobacco grown by planters in the Chesapeake colonies. British law required that all tobacco exported from America go directly to British ports, thus giving the mother country a trade monopoly.

Tobacco imported into Britain carried a tariff of 200 percent of its wholesale value, and for more than a century it had provided lucrative revenues to the British Crown. Then, as today, customers were willing to pay high prices for tobacco, liquor, and other semi-psychoactive items. Robert Morris Sr. operated as a factor (middleman) in Oxford, Maryland, then a lively tobacco port. He bought crops from colonial planters and arranged for their shipment to England. Gradually he became prosperous, though he never achieved real wealth. In 1747, when Robert Jr. was thirteen years old, his father sent instructions that he come to Maryland. Morris Jr. left the Liverpool household of his grandmother—reluctantly, as he is supposed to have told friends; there are no reliable surviving records.

Besides being an immigrant, Morris Jr. had other things in common with Alexander Hamilton: an agile mind, a quick facility with numbers, and a turbulent childhood. His father neglected him during the year after their reunion, and then sent him to live with Morris Sr.'s friends in Philadelphia. A year after that, the father was killed in a freak accident at the age of thirty-nine, the same age Hamilton's mother had been at her death.[3]

Then came a fateful and fortunate step for the young man's

future, almost analogous to Hamilton's appointment as aide to George Washington. His father's friend apprenticed the fifteen-year-old Morris to the firm of Charles Willing, mayor of Philadelphia and one of its leading merchants. Philadelphia at that time was the largest and liveliest city in the thirteen colonies. Five years after Morris joined his firm, Charles Willing died. By that time Morris, now twenty years old, had demonstrated a canny sense of business and a remarkable maturity. After completing his seven-year apprenticeship, he soon became the partner of Willing's son, Thomas, a capable businessman only three years older than Morris himself. In 1757, the two young men, who were close friends, established the merchant and shipping house of Willing Morris & Co. Over the next twenty years, it became one of the city's most innovative and profitable firms.[4]

Willing Morris & Co. dealt not only in shipping, but also in marine insurance and in handling other merchants' bills of credit. Its dozens of ships traveled to ports in Britain, Europe, and especially the Caribbean, carrying items such as flour and timber outward from the colonies, and manufactured goods and sugar inward. Sometimes they ventured as far as India and China. In addition to cargoes of goods, they brought many indentured servants across the Atlantic to America, and on a few occasions they participated in the slave trade. From time to time Morris himself owned one or two slaves, who worked in his household.

In 1763, six years after the formation of the business partnership, Thomas Willing was elected mayor of Philadelphia, and Morris began to take a larger role in managing the firm. Morris had earlier fathered a daughter with a woman he did not marry and had made provision for the daughter's upbringing. He also gave employment in his firm to a half-brother his own father had sired out of wedlock soon after Morris Jr. arrived in America.[5]

In 1769, now thirty-five, he married Mary White, the twenty-year-old daughter of a distinguished Maryland family. Mary was the sister of William White, who later became Chaplain of the Continental Congress, Episcopal Bishop of Pennsylvania, and Presiding Bishop of the Episcopal Church, USA. Again like Hamilton, Morris managed to leave his messy family affairs behind and improve his social status by marrying up. Eventually he and Mary had seven children.

⁘

When the War of Independence began in 1775, Hamilton had been in North America for only three years, since 1772. Morris, by contrast, had emigrated in 1747 and had lived in the colonies for twenty-eight years. He had watched as the long series of events leading up to the war gradually unfolded. By the time of the Stamp Act of 1765, he was well on his way to wealth. But he supported the resistance to that measure and to nearly every other similar step taken by the British.

Most other prosperous merchants and planters hedged their bets more carefully, and Morris himself occasionally wavered. Like the majority of North American colonists, he continued for more than a decade after the Stamp Act to hope for a peaceful settlement. During that period, he steadily grew wealthier. He did not attain the affluence of many southern planters, some of whom owned immense acreages and well over 500 slaves. But he made himself one of the richest businessmen in the colonies.

He looked the part: tall, well-dressed, his once-slender frame expanding over the years to the ample girth expected of well-to-do merchants at that time. He acted his role well, building a lavish Philadelphia mansion and hosting elegant parties. But Morris never lost the common touch. His genial personality made him as much at home with longshoremen on the Philadelphia docks as in the drawing rooms of colonial elites. He got along well with Benjamin Franklin and worked with him on public affairs of both Pennsylvania and the city of Philadelphia—and later, when Franklin was minister to France, on financing the War of Independence.[6]

Despite his consistent opposition to punitive measures by the British, Morris seldom struck a radical posture against the mother country. He was not given to the kind of unbridled oratory used by men like Samuel Adams and Patrick Henry to excite turmoil. Even after the war started in 1775, Morris still held out hope for a negotiated settlement short of total separation from Britain. So did most other Americans, especially in Pennsylvania and New York. Once the British army threatened the safety of Philadelphia, however, Morris began to move decisively. In the tangled politics of Pennsylvania he remained a political moderate but cast his lot with those opposing the British. He sent dozens of his company's ships to Europe to procure gunpowder, which was in short supply in the colonies. He often used his firm's credit, and sometimes his own personal funds, to complete these purchases.

Throughout this early period of the war, Morris tried to maintain his middle-of-the-road position, while becoming more involved in politics. In 1775 he was elected to the Committee on Public Safety for the defense of Philadelphia; also in 1775, to the Pennsylvania House of Delegates; and in 1776, to the Continental Congress. There he became a leader in committees concerned with money, commerce, and naval operations. During the early years of the war, Morris chaired the Secret Committee on Commerce. If the Revolution were to fail, members wanted their business and other private connections to be endangered as little as possible. Hence, the membership of several committees remained hidden.

During the summer of 1776, in Congress's initial ballot on the Declaration of Independence, the Pennsylvania delegation voted no by a margin of four to three. Morris, one of the four, believed even after a year of fighting that a less radical settlement might still be worked out. On the second ballot, however, he and another delegate abstained, making the Pennsylvania vote three to two in favor so that the Declaration would be unanimous among the states. Morris then signed the document, his name appearing just to the right of the huge, flourishing signature of John Hancock.

Of all the founders, only Morris and Roger Sherman of Connecticut signed all three defining documents of the new United States: the Declaration of Independence (1776), the Articles of Confederation (1778), and the Constitution (1787). With his endorsement of the Declaration, Morris committed himself for good. His firm owned scores of merchant ships—and as the war heated up, it acquired scores more. Morris converted many of them to heavily armed privateers and sent them out to prey on British merchant vessels. He saw nothing wrong with this, but others eventually would, since he sometimes profited personally.

In 1777, when the British army seemed once more on the verge of capturing Philadelphia, Congress moved its headquarters to Baltimore. But Morris stayed behind. For three months he managed the government almost single-handedly, until the danger subsided and the other delegates returned. During that period and many others during the eight years of fighting, his role in financing the war remained so vital that his power in the national government was second only to that of George Washington. He and Washington became close friends, and when the general came to Philadelphia he usually stayed at Morris's house.

The new Confederation Congress of 1781 provided for a financial executive, as Hamilton and others had suggested. When Morris was elected superintendent, Hamilton wrote him a detailed letter about what should be done. Since 1777, Hamilton had been learning more about finance, devouring dozens of books on the subject. In preparation for this letter to Morris, he asked a friend to send him five more books, all by English and Scottish writers: David Hume's *Political Discourses* (1752), Malachy Postlethwayt's *Universal Dictionary of Trade and Commerce* (1751), Wyndham Beawes's *Les Mercatoria Rediviva; Or, The Merchant's Directory* (1751), and two books by Richard Price: *Observations on the Nature of Civil Liberty* (1776) and *Additional Observations on the Nature and Value of Civil Liberty* (1777). These were standard treatises of the period, and Hamilton's use of them reflects his obsessive drive to educate himself about finance and public policy.[7]

"I was among the first who were convinced," he wrote Morris in 1781, "that an administration by single men [as opposed to committees] was essential to the proper management of the affairs of this country. I am persuaded now it is the only resource we have to extricate ourselves." He went on to say that he had recommended Morris to James Duane for the post of financial executive and had learned with "the greatest satisfaction" that Morris had been nominated. "In the frankness of truth I believe, Sir, you are the Man best capable of performing this great work." Nothing was more important to the success of the Revolution. "'Tis by introducing order into our finances—by restoring public credit—not by gaining battles, that we are finally to gain our object."[8]

As in his letter to Duane, Hamilton then set forth his views on what should be done. He confessed to Morris that "I pretend not to be an able financier," having lacked the "leisure or materials to make accurate calculations." Nevertheless, his reading had convinced him that much could be learned from the experience of advanced European nations: "1st by examining what proportion the revenues of other countries have borne to their stock of wealth," and "2dly by comparing the result of this rule with the product of taxes in those states which have been the most in earnest in taxation"—Britain, France, and Holland.[9]

Hamilton took up the difficult question of estimating the resources of a country and calculating what percentage could be allocated to government without harming the country's economy. These issues were (and still are today) impossible to answer with precision. But Hamilton—following some of the authorities he had just read—wrote Morris that a country's "circulating cash" was a reasonable proxy for its wealth, and that in wartime about one-fourth of that wealth might be allocated to government.[10]

No single European country offered a useful model. In France, "the rich have gained so entire an ascendant that there is a constant sacrifice of the ease and happiness of the people to their avarice and luxury." The situation in England and Holland was not quite so bad, but still similar. So the relevant European systems would have to be modified before any emulation by the United States. Americans, though in desperate need of public revenues to fight the war, would never accept the high tax levels characteristic of France, Britain, and Holland.[11]

Hamilton then took up one of his main points: "the institution of a National Bank. This I regard, in some shape or other as an expedient essential to our safety and success." There had never been a bank in colonial America and there were still none in the United States. In many countries, banks were viewed with justifiable suspicion. They often seemed to lend beyond their means and in economic downturns to run out of cash, leaving depositors destitute. "But all that has been said against them," Hamilton wrote Morris, "only tends to prove that like all other good things they are subject to abuse and when abused become pernicious. The precious metals by similar arguments may be proved to be injurious; it is certain that the mines of South America have had great influence in banishing industry from Spain and sinking it in real wealth and importance." Here Hamilton—still just twenty-four years old—exhibited a sophisticated understanding of money and its relationship to a nation's "real" economy of goods and services.[12]

Regardless of public prejudice, he was convinced that the United States had to have a banking system in order to promote the nation's credit, both public and private. Public credit "gives power to the state for the protection of its rights and interests."

Private credit "facilitates and extends the operations of commerce among individuals. Industry is increased, commodities are multiplied, agriculture and manufactures flourish, and herein consist the true wealth and prosperity of a state."[13]

Banks, the chief instruments of credit, "have proved to be the happiest engines, that ever were invented for advancing trade." Britain in particular had ingeniously used banks in financing its many wars. "'Tis by this alone she now menaces our independence." In short, the path to developing the sinews of war led to banks and the credit they furnished both for governments and for the private sector. Hamilton explained to Morris his own ideas for an American national bank, "which I rather offer as an outline than as a finished plan." He listed twenty "Articles" for the proposed bank: a capital of £3 million to be raised by the sale of 30,000 shares of £100 each to private investors, "this stock to be exempted from all public taxes and impositions whatsoever." Then came details about the bank's relationship to the national government (a loose one: it was to be a private, profit-making institution); about its management; and about its role in creating additional currency, thereby increasing the nation's money supply and stimulating its economy.[14]

In the rest of his letter, Hamilton suggested methods for financing and ultimately repaying the huge national debt from the Revolution. Here he was looking far into the future: "According to my plan at the end of thirty five years, these states will have paid off the whole debt contracted on account of the war; and in the meantime will have a clear [annual] revenue of four millions of Dollars for defraying the expenses of their civil and military establishments."[15]

Then came one of the most widely quoted statements Hamilton ever made—one used by both his supporters and detractors over the next two centuries and beyond: "A national debt if it is not excessive will be to us a national blessing; it will be a powerfull cement of our union." The key word in this quotation is "national." Hamilton's concern in 1781, when he wrote his letter to Morris, was the same as it had been since 1777: that the

Revolution might succeed in securing the colonies' independence from Britain, but not in producing a permanent union of the states—that is, a genuine nation.[16]

Morris sent a cordial reply to Hamilton's letter. "I have read it with that attention which it justly deserves and finding many points of it to Coincide with my own Opinions on the Subject, it naturally Strengthened that Confidence which every man ought to possess to a certain degree in his own judgement. You will very Soon See the Plan of a Bank published and Subscriptions opened for its establishment, having already met with the approbation of Congress." This proved to be too optimistic a prediction. Even in his letter to Hamilton, Morris acknowledged that the capital of the bank would fall "far Short of your Idea and indeed far Short of what it ought to be."[17]

The superintendent went on to say: "My office is new and I am Young in the execution of it. Communications from Men of Genius & abilities will always be acceptable and yours will ever Command [my] attention." In all, this initial exchange of letters between Hamilton and Morris began a close personal relationship. In the years ahead, both men worked to put the chaotic finances of the new nation on a sounder footing. The task, as Morris wrote George Washington in 1781, was "more than Herculean Labour." The nation's finances were in a complete mess.[18]

After five years of war, Congress had issued $241.5 million in paper money, whose value had gradually dropped to about two cents on the dollar. Almost no gold or silver remained in circulation. Congress had begun borrowing money through domestic loans in 1776, and the army soon began to issue its own certificates of indebtedness (IOUs) for food, munitions, and other supplies. Meanwhile, by 1780 the states had printed bills of credit in excess of $200 million and were in no position to help the national government borrow money. Beginning in

1777, Congress had started to receive large loans—some from Holland, but most through the efforts of Benjamin Franklin in France—which by 1783 totaled almost $8 million. Unlike all the other sums, the foreign loans were actually worth their face value. Also in 1777, Congress had begun to ask the states for money (it had no legal authority to require payment). By 1780, these requests totaled $95 million, of which about $55 million had been paid—but in paper money of uncertain worth. By the time Robert Morris became superintendent of finance in 1781, the United States had long been bankrupt. Morris understood this situation all too well. He accepted his new job on the condition that his efforts would be directed forward, to financing the ongoing war, not backward to paying existing debts.[19]

He had a small staff to help him, the most important member being his skillful assistant, Gouverneur Morris (no relation), a wealthy and aristocratic New Yorker. Twenty-nine years old in 1781, Gouverneur Morris was a colorful character given to having affairs with any willing women he could find. At age twenty-eight, he lost his left leg and had it replaced with a wooden device. Ostensibly the amputation had been necessary because of a road accident, but many people believed its actual cause was a leap from the bedroom window of a married woman whose husband had suddenly appeared out of nowhere. Gouverneur Morris stayed with Robert Morris throughout his tenure as superintendent of finance, and he performed his duties with distinction.[20]

Also assisting Robert Morris in raising money for the war was Haym (or Hyam) Solomon, still another important immigrant financier. Born in 1740 to Portuguese Jews who had been driven from their native land, Solomon grew up mostly in Poland. In 1772 he left Europe for New York, where he worked as a commission agent and broker. He also became a leader of the anti-British Sons of Liberty. In 1776 and again in 1778, he was captured and imprisoned by the British. Sentenced to death as a spy, he escaped occupied New York and fled to Philadelphia, where he brokered loans, bills of exchange, and other financial

FIGURE 6. Gouverneur Morris (left) and Robert Morris, by Charles Willson Peale, 1783. Robert Morris was superintendent of finance at the time, and Gouverneur—who seldom met a skirt he didn't chase—was his assistant. Both were delegates to the Constitutional Convention of 1787, where Gouverneur Morris played a major role, probably second only to that of James Madison.

instruments. Few reliable records of Solomon's activities survive, but he is believed to have arranged a loan of $400,000 in 1779 to help pay troops of the Continental Army and soldiers from France who assisted in the war. Solomon's language skills facilitated the movement of French and Dutch loans to the government, and as the official Broker to the Office of Finance he worked with Superintendent Morris on a variety of tasks: arranging the sale of government bonds, handling bills of exchange, and obtaining promissory notes to help pay for the war. He also lent money to several members of Congress, including James Madison. The total amount Solomon raised for the Revolutionary cause has been estimated at $658,000, a large sum for that time, which likely included a substantial contribution of his own funds.[21]

In Robert Morris's first year as superintendent, he recommended the creation of a bank, of which there were still none in the entire country. Congress complied, and the federally chartered Bank of North America opened its doors in Philadelphia on January 7, 1782. Hamilton, both in his letter to Morris and also in one of his six "Continentalist" essays, had urged that Congress not only charter such a bank but also give it sufficient powers to operate as a central bank, with broad discretion over national finance.

The Bank of North America never attained this kind of power. It remained a modest enterprise, under the leadership of Thomas Willing, Morris's former business partner, who was elected its president. But at least the bank made a plausible start, and it provided significant help in financing the war. Over the next few years, Morris and Hamilton often corresponded, exchanging suggestions on how to meet the nation's financial crisis. Both the bank and numerous other aspects of Morris's attempts at financial reform anticipated those of Hamilton almost a decade later. Each man was an ardent nationalist, like many other immigrants. Each wanted to increase the fiscal power of the central government because the states were so tight-fisted and Congress lacked any direct authority to raise funds.[22]

Like most patriot-entrepreneurs during the Revolution, Morris saw no reason to separate his personal business from that of the government, especially during the early years of the war. He made excellent use of his wide network of private commercial connections in Europe and the Caribbean to procure arms, gunpowder, and other munitions necessary to fight the war. He managed to negotiate bargains that nobody else in the government could have executed. In hundreds of individual transactions, Morris sometimes profited personally, but often he did not. Because of the extreme uncertainties of oceanic trade during wartime, the profit or loss on individual voyages often took months or even years to be determined. Scores of British vessels surrendered to Morris's privateers, but his firm lost about the same number of its own ships.[23]

One of the most striking examples of Morris's resourcefulness came in 1781, on the eve of the Battle of Yorktown. Washington's Continental Army had run out of money at the very moment when it might be able to strike a conclusive blow. In response to Washington's urgent request—it was a genuine emergency—Morris almost miraculously procured the necessary funds. He then disbursed them in small increments, so as not to give soldiers large sums that might encourage them to desert and return home to their families. He personally signed 6,000 bills of currency, in the process risking some of his own credit. The army, now able to pay for essential supplies, then made its strenuous march from New York and Pennsylvania to Virginia for the siege of Yorktown, which turned out to be the decisive engagement of the war.[24]

Morris continued to operate his private shipping and mercantile affairs along with those of the government, though much less so after his appointment in 1781 as superintendent of finance. This commingling of public and private affairs was common in the eighteenth century, but in the context of a revolution it made Morris a controversial figure. He endured criticism from many quarters, much of it vicious and personal. He became the most conspicuous early example of the conflict-of-interest problems that have plagued federal service from that time down to the present, especially in finance. Morris had many merits, and did his job well. But he was no saint, any more than the other founders were; and his extravagant lifestyle made him an easy target for more feverish revolutionaries. James Madison supported him, however, and an official investigation by Congress, made at Morris's own insistence, exonerated him of wrongdoing. Ironically, had he been less open and generous, he would have been less vulnerable to this kind of attack.

If Morris had valued his personal fortune more than American independence, as many of his critics charged, he could easily have cashed out in 1775, returned to his native England, and lived a life of monied ease. Many wealthy "Loyalists" did decamp for Canada or England. Morris, by contrast, risked his life, threw himself into the effort of financing the war—the most arduous nonmilitary assignment of the entire Revolution—and discharged it with energy, patience, and distinction.

In the mass of surviving records from his years as superintendent, 1781–1784, the impossibility of total success becomes clear. The major barrier turned out to be the failure of Congress to gain control over import duties. The government came tantalizingly close to achieving this aim, which would have solved many of its financial problems at one stroke. But under the Articles of Confederation a single state could block such a move, and Rhode Island chose to do so. Had that not occurred, the subsequent history of the 1780s, and even of the United States in the long term, could have turned out differently. If Congress had possessed this taxing power, then the Constitutional Convention of 1787 conceivably might never have taken place at all.

Without that authority, Congress and its chosen executive officer, Robert Morris, stood no chance of success. In the fall of 1781, for example, Congress asked the states for a total of $8 million to be paid during 1782. By early 1783, only $420,000 had been remitted, or a little more than 5 percent. Morris's diary during his time as superintendent, and the collected letters to and from his office, fill nine volumes of about 500 pages each. Most of these documents pertain to the thousands of individual transactions necessary to raise money for the war. But they are also full of Morris's own revealing remarks about the difficulty of his task, and of how much worse it became year by year. By 1783 Morris had almost given up altogether, as the makeup of Congress itself had changed and there was no likelihood at all of gaining control over import duties. The evolving situation becomes vivid in the tone of his comments, read in sequence:

December 19, 1781, letter to the governors of North Carolina, South Carolina, and Georgia: "I have no System of Finance except that which results from the plain self-evident dictates of Moral Honesty . . . I expect that your State will immediately pass Laws to collect by the days named, the Sums called for from them for the year 1782."[25]

February 2, 1782, diary entry: "The greatest part of my time since in office has been consumed in hearing the Tales of Woe . . . which I cannot prevent in any other way than by declining personal interviews."[26]

August 29, 1782, letter to George Washington about the refusal of the states to contribute enough money to support the army: "I pray that Heavan [*sic*] may direct your mind to some mode by which we may be yet saved. I have done all that I could and given repeated Warnings [in messages to state governors and legislatures] but it is like preaching to the dead."[27]

October 21, 1782, letter to the governors of all thirteen states: "How long is a Nation who will do nothing for itself to rely on the Aid of others [i.e., gifts from France and loans from Dutch banks]? How long will one Part of a Community bear the Burdens of the whole? [A few states contributed sums approaching their fair share; most did not come close.] How long will an Army undergo Want in the Midst of Plenty? How long will they endure Misery without Complaint, Injustice without Reproach, and Wrongs without Redress?"[28]

March 14, 1783, letter to General Nathanael Greene on Morris's decision to resign from office: "I had no alternative. I saw clearly that while it was asserted on all Hands our Debts ought to be paid, no efficient Measures would be adopted for the Purpose."

After much persuasion by Congress and the army, Morris withdrew his resignation shortly afterward and agreed to stay.[29] He did resign in November 1784, frustrated by his ceaseless attempts to raise money. In his final "Statement of Accounts," issued in March 1785 and printed in 500 copies he sent to Congress, Morris reflected on the larger meaning of the nation's fiscal irresponsibility:

> No treason has operated, or can operate, so great an injury to America, as must follow from a loss of reputation. The payment of debts may indeed be expensive, but it is infinitely more expensive to withhold payment. The former is an expense of money, when money may be commanded to defray it; but the latter involves the destruction of that source from which money can be derived when all other sources fail. That source, abundant, nay almost inexhaustible, is public credit [i.e., the nation's ability to borrow] . . .
>
> The inhabitant of a little hamlet, may feel pride in the sense of separate independence. But if there be not one government which can draw forth and direct the combined forces of united America, our independence is but a name, our freedom a shadow, our dignity a dream.[30]

Coming from such an affable and mild-mannered person as Morris, this language paints a picture of stark national irresponsibility toward financial affairs. Morris held the office of superintendent for almost four years, from early 1781 to late 1784. Through foreign loans, sales of domestic securities, and the investment of several million dollars of his own fortune, he managed somehow to maintain the country's financial and military situation—constantly juggling accounts and trying in every conceivable way to keep the government afloat. Complete success proved impossible, but by wide consensus at the time, no other person could have come closer to it than Morris.

As Alexander Hamilton and many others well understood, Morris's inability to achieve his goals did not derive from the strategy he pursued. Instead, the failure originated from a structural flaw in the Articles of Confederation: the absence of any provision for the national government to raise money through import duties and other taxes. Many years later, Chief Justice John Marshall wrote, in what became a famous Supreme Court decision, that "the power to tax is the power to destroy." But the reverse is true as well. Lack of the power to tax—in this case, no direct way to gather the sinews of war—almost cost the United States its fight for independence from Britain.

CHAPTER 7

The Constitution

The failure of Morris's program gave even more force to Hamilton's sense of urgency. It prompted him to push hard to get rid of the Articles of Confederation and create a new constitution. Under the Articles, each state had one vote, regardless of its population. Unanimous consent was required to amend the Articles, and the approval of nine of the thirteen states was necessary to pass any legislation at all. After Morris resigned as superintendent of finance, Congress chose to replace him with a three-person committee, which proved ineffective. The stalemate over financial policy continued.

As Hamilton often pointed out, a coordinated economic strategy for the new nation remained impossible under the Articles of Confederation. The thirteen states were just too disparate in their populations (tiny Rhode Island with about 60,000 people, mighty Virginia with ten times as many) and in their core economies (shipping and some manufacturing in Pennsylvania, New York, and New England; slave-based agriculture in the South). Even individual states were at odds within themselves.

New York, in population only the fifth largest of the thirteen states at that time, was split into two main factions: the emerging Manhattan metropolis, with its teeming ethnic mix of 30,000 people; and the rural estates of the Hudson Valley, where families such as Hamilton's in-laws, the Schuylers, presided in semi-feudal fashion. Political divisions within the state remained strong, and Hamilton's alliance with the Schuylers put him at odds with the powerful anti-Federalist political machine headed by George Clinton, who served as governor of New York from 1777 to 1795. The Clintonians, who favored the power of the states over that of a strong central government, consistently opposed the Federalists Philip Schuyler and Hamilton, and in state politics they won more often than they lost. Eventually they allied themselves with the Jeffersonians. So Hamilton never had the solid state base in New York that Jefferson and Madison, despite some politically tangled circumstances in Virginia, had in that state.[1]

Sometimes the relationship between the national government and individual states bordered on the ridiculous. Rhode Island, for example, blocked not only the effort to shift control over import duties to Congress, but some other crucial national funding bills as well—even as it printed reams of state currency backed by no assets at all. The country's financial system remained essentially a mess. Once the war ended in 1783, Hamilton sent a letter of congratulations to John Jay, who had helped to negotiate the peace treaty. Hamilton added, however, that the real work of nation building had hardly begun: "Our prospects are not flattering . . . The road to popularity in each state is to inspire jealousies of the power of Congress, though nothing can be more apparent than that they have no power."[2]

He worried especially about economic affairs. So did several other founders. By contrast, some prominent Virginians—

not including James Madison—regarded the basic issue of the 1780s as one of locating new markets for their tobacco after the Revolution ended the British monopoly. Then, too, many powerful Virginians, such as Arthur Lee and Henry Lee, saw little or no role for the federal government in addressing economic matters, which they regarded as the purview of individual states. Thomas Jefferson knew about most national economic problems, but he spent the latter half of the 1780s in Paris as U.S. minister to France. So, despite a stream of letters from Madison, he had no immediate vision of how much worse the economic situation was becoming.

———

Hamilton did see it, with visceral clarity. For him, the glass was usually half-empty, but he always had a plan for how it should be filled. He was in his most natural element as a shaper of what today would be called macroeconomic policy—national issues pertaining to money, taxes, public expenditure, and employment. He never liked the role of delegate, although he served as one on four occasions: the Confederation Congress in 1782–1783, the Annapolis Convention of 1786, the Constitutional Convention of 1787, and the New York Ratifying Convention of 1788. Despite his formidable gifts as a public speaker, he was uncomfortable in all four settings. His mind always darted ahead, too fast for the usual pace of deliberation. His disposition ran more to action than discussion.

He had been especially frustrated by the endless dialogues in the Confederation Congress on the subject of public finance, which by now he understood better than anyone except Robert Morris. During his year of service in Congress, Hamilton had firmly clarified his views about finance, and particularly about why imposts should be taken away from the states and given to the national government. James Madison's notes of the proceedings portray Hamilton as having "disliked every plan that made but partial provision for the public debts; as an inconsistent & dishonourable departure from the declaration made [earlier] by Congs. on that subject"—namely, that comprehensive arrangements must be made for funding the debt.[3]

Hamilton was forever pushing for a thorough engagement with all of the new nation's problems. Early in his tenure as a delegate to the Confederation Congress, he drew up a long resolution calling for a new convention with "full powers to revise" the Articles of Confederation. This was a radical proposal, and his twelve-point outline called for many provisions that were later incorporated into the Constitution of 1787. But in the Congress of 1783 he lacked the necessary support and did not submit his resolution. In 1786, as the American economy continued to worsen, New York itself blocked another attempt by Congress to get control of the imposts. The port of New York took in more customs duties than any other in the country, and both the city and the state were loath to give up control of these funds.[4]

Hamilton, disgusted with this situation, became one of the moving spirits behind the Annapolis Convention of 1786. Initiated by James Madison and others, the meeting at Annapolis was a key way-station on the road to the Constitutional Convention of 1787 in Philadelphia. Only nine of the thirteen states appointed "commissioners" to Annapolis, and four delegations either never left their home states or failed to arrive on time—strong clues to the general lack of interest in a tighter national union. But the gathering of five delegations did result in a strong call for a more substantive meeting of all the states. Hamilton's fellow commissioners, by now familiar with his compelling prose style, chose him to draft the 1,200-word Address of the Annapolis Convention. The "national circumstances," he wrote, were so serious as "to render the Situation of the United States delicate and critical, calling for an exertion of the united virtue and wisdom of all the members of the Confederacy." The Annapolis commissioners called for a convention of all thirteen states, to begin in May 1787.[5]

———⊷⊷———

To the surprise of many politicians, that momentous convention attracted delegates from every state except recalcitrant Rhode Island. It assembled in Philadelphia on May 14, 1787, and deliberated in secret for four months. In all, fifty-five delegates attended, eight of whom were immigrants, including Hamilton and Robert Morris. Hamilton was thirty years old by this time, but he still showed the *wunderkind*'s exasperation with drawn-out proceedings. He soon grew impatient—and when he did speak, he tended to express himself too strongly. If Madison's account of his comments is correct, Hamilton occasionally crossed the line that separates candor from indiscretion. Had the meetings not been closed to the press and the public, some of his remarks might have cut short his political career. The same was true of other strong nationalists who said what they thought—notably Gouverneur Morris, who drafted important parts of the Constitution and spoke 173 times, more than any other delegate. Closing the proceedings therefore turned out to be crucial to the Convention's success.[6]

The issue of slavery, for example, inevitably disturbed the delegates. Many owned slaves themselves, and all knew that sectional discord between the northern and southern states might prevent broad agreement on a new form of government— even though many northern states themselves contained a few slaves. But if there was to be a Constitution at all, then there would have to be some serious compromises. In the end, the two most important were the agreement counting each slave as three-fifths of a person and an arrangement not to abolish the transatlantic slave trade for at least twenty years.

The three-fifths clause—in the eyes of later generations a hideous provision, the most notorious passage in the entire

4,400-word text of the Constitution—had little to do with anyone's calculation that a slave was exactly 60 percent of a human being. Rather, it derived from a miserable bargain about how to allocate political power in the House of Representatives and the Electoral College. (Senators at this time were elected not by popular vote, but by state legislatures. Every state's numbers in the Electoral College were—and still are—the sum of its congressmen and its two senators.) Because each state's population determined the number of its congressmen, southern states would have had a tremendous advantage if every slave had been counted as one person. The northern states would never have accepted this, so some adjustment would be necessary.[7]

The idea of a three-fifths compromise had originated four years earlier, in a proposal by James Madison during a debate in the Confederation Congress of 1783. The issue at that time was not about voting, but about taxes: how to count slaves as property in a proportional system of tax levies on the thirteen states. The delegates knew that some kind of alteration in counting slaves would be essential to any successful legislation. Most southerners wished to minimize the fraction (and thereby their own taxes) while most northerners wanted to maximize it. After each side had settled on a negotiating figure—one-half proposed by some Virginians and three-fourths by New Englanders—Congress in effect split the difference and adopted Madison's three-fifths proposal.[8]

The three-fifths idea carried over into the debates at the Constitutional Convention four years later. There it was sponsored by Roger Sherman, a prominent delegate from Connecticut, and James Wilson of Pennsylvania, an immigrant lawyer from Scotland. In 1783, when the discussion had been mainly about property and taxes, some northern representatives had wanted to count each slave as one full person in the population, for tax purposes, while some southern representatives had suggested that none at all be counted. At the Constitutional Convention of 1787, when the primary issue had shifted from taxable property to political power, these positions were precisely reversed. In each case, the resulting bargain was the three-fifths compromise.[9]

It was both a northern and a southern idea, the result of negotiations to preserve the Union. Hamilton, an opponent of slavery who had joined the New York Manumission Society at its second meeting in 1785, lamented that without the clause, "no union could possibly have been formed." So the curse of slavery became an integral part of the nation's foundational document. The delegates' embarrassment is reflected in the final draft of the Constitution, which avoids any mention at all of the words "slave" or "slavery." Instead, it employs euphemisms such as "other persons" and "a person held to service or labor." Rather than speak openly of the "slave trade," the Constitution uses the expression "importation of Persons."[10]

As the convention of 1787 dragged into its second month, Hamilton grew exasperated with the inability of most delegates to look beyond the narrow interests of their own states and think continentally. In addition, they seemed to have become paralyzed when trying to choose between the "New Jersey Plan" (for a weak central government) and the "Virginia Plan" (for a strong one)—the latter outlined primarily by James Madison.

On a hot day in mid-June, Hamilton rose to speak on these touchy subjects and held forth for about six hours. And although the proceedings were supposed to be closed, his words leaked out and caused problems throughout the rest of his political career. According to Madison's notes, Hamilton said that "in his private opinion he had no scruple in declaring, supported as he was by the opinions of so many of the wise & good, that the British Govt. was the best in the world: and that he doubted much whether any thing short of it would do in America." While this statement may have been defensible (what major country had a better system?), hatred for Britain still ran high in several states. Not only was Britain a monarchy, but it also had the kind of rigid class structure that many Americans were trying to overthrow.[11]

Hamilton also suggested that senators should "hold their places for life or at least during good behavior," and the president for life. Equally damaging, he observed that society was divided into two classes, the few and the many. "The voice of the people has been said to be the voice of God; and however generally this maxim has been quoted and believed, it is not true in fact. The people are turbulent and changing; they seldom judge or determine right. Give therefore to the first class a distinct, permanent share in government [mainly in the Senate]. They will check the unsteadiness of the second, and as they cannot receive any advantage by a change, they therefore will ever maintain good government."[12]

If Madison's report is accurate, then Hamilton seems to have become caught up in his own rhetoric, as often happens when powerful orators engage in heated debate. But it has never been certain that he completely believed or would have publicly stood by everything he said in the secret proceedings. The same was true of many other speakers as they explored different alternatives. John Dickinson of Pennsylvania, for example, suggested that state legislatures be given the power to impeach the president. Benjamin Franklin proposed that the new government have a one-house legislature and no president at all, but a council of three executives.[13]

Then, too, there are major differences between some of Hamilton's remarks and what he wrote a few months later in *The Federalist Papers*. The most likely explanation for the indiscretions in his long speech is that it was an ingenious tactical maneuver. By proposing such an extremely strong government, he was trying to break what he saw as a logjam, an impasse among the delegates. His proposals would get rid of the New Jersey Plan altogether and put the Virginia Plan in a different light: as a middle way, when in fact it was far stronger than that.[14]

Shortly after his speech, Hamilton left Philadelphia feeling gloomy, convinced that the delegates would never consent to a strong national government. Rhode Island had not even bothered to send a delegate. And the other two New York delegates at the convention, the Clintonians Robert Yates and John Lansing Jr., had departed permanently after six weeks' attendance, believing that the convention was exceeding its mandate merely to revise the Articles of Confederation. So the state no longer had a quorum, and Hamilton thus had no vote on the many issues in the proceedings. During his absence, however, the encouraging words he heard from ordinary citizens made him more optimistic. He then wrote to Washington, who was still presiding over the Convention and anxious for Hamilton to come back: "I am more and more convinced that this is the critical opportunity for establishing the prosperity of this country on a solid foundation . . . [T]here has been an astonishing revolution for the better in the minds of the people. The prevailing apprehension among thinking men is that the Convention, for fear of shocking the popular opinion, will not go far enough."[15]

Hamilton returned to Philadelphia and participated in the remaining debates. He served on the Committee of Style and Arrangement, along with Madison and four others—including Gouverneur Morris, who chaired the committee and wrote the famous Preamble that begins "We the People . . ." When their final draft of the Constitution was ready (it followed the Virginia Plan more than any other), Hamilton proposed that all delegates sign it even though many, not least he himself, still had strong reservations. For what lay ahead, he believed that the appearance of unanimity by all delegates was vital.

A substantial minority, however, did not sign, and here the difference between immigrant and native-born delegates was significant. Of the fifty-five delegates who had assembled in Philadelphia, thirty-nine signed the Constitution. Seven of the eight immigrant delegates signed and one did not. By contrast, of the forty-seven native-born delegates, thirty-two signed and fifteen did not—including two of the three from New York and four of the seven from Virginia. Thus, seven to one among the immigrants were willing to sign, as compared to thirty-two to fifteen (or just over two to one) among the forty-seven who were native-born. This difference suggests that Hamilton, Morris, and other immigrant delegates took a more national perspective than their native-born counterparts. Many of the latter were suspicious of a strong national government and oriented more toward their individual states.[16]

With the battle in Philadelphia now over, the battle for ratification of the Constitution by the states could now begin, and its outcome was far from certain. For this effort, Hamilton labored mightily over *The Federalist Papers,* which to this day is considered the finest American contribution to political theory and administration ever written. Hamilton and his nationalist allies James Madison and John Jay composed, under tremendous time pressure, eighty-five newspaper articles that systematically analyzed and defended every part of the Constitution. Hamilton conceived the project, recruited his collaborators, and wrote fifty-one of the essays himself—exactly 60 percent. Many show him at the height of his rhetorical powers. Madison wrote twenty-nine essays, just as powerful and persuasive as Hamilton's. John Jay fell ill and contributed only five. All three writers published over the signature "Publius," as it was the custom of the time to remain anonymous and use classical names. On the whole, Hamilton's essays go into detailed analyses of the institutional design of the new government and how it would operate. This is a more prosaic and less elegant subject than Madison's assignment of laying out the constitutional theory, and in some ways a more difficult one to write about. The extraordinary combination of the two is what made *The Federalist Papers* so powerful and compelling, both at the time of their composition and for later generations, including our own. Never in American political history has there been a better team of two writers working on one big project than Hamilton and Madison.[17]

The immediate purpose of *The Federalist Papers* was to shape public opinion in New York, where a flood of anti-Constitution propaganda had issued forth and ratification seemed unlikely. Madison estimated the odds against success in New York at about two to one. Meanwhile, newspapers in many other states also published *The Federalist Papers,* as their own ratifying conventions gathered. So the influence of the essays went far beyond New York alone. Many other writers besides Publius also flooded the press with articles favoring the Constitution. Of the ninety-two existing newspapers in the United States at that time, about eighty published primarily pro-Constitution arguments. This percentage did not necessarily reflect the views of the editors, who were hungry for copy of any kind. Nor did it mirror public opinion as it stood. Rather, it indicated the energy and determination of nationalists like Hamilton and Madison to change that opinion.[18]

At the New York Ratifying Convention, Hamilton addressed his fellow delegates long and often. Again his theme, hammered relentlessly, was that the new nation must be bound into a tight union or centrifugal forces would pull it apart. Hamilton fought with all his strength and vitality for the Constitution and against its opponents. They were a formidable group, including Governor George Clinton and his many allies, such as Robert Yates and John Lansing, who had been New York's other two delegates to the Philadelphia convention. During the debates, Hamilton not only wrote fifty-one of *The Federalist Papers* and spoke at length in favor of ratification; he also published acidulous newspaper attacks on the Clintonite opposition, using classical pseudonyms. Like the great courtroom litigator he had already become, he left no stone unturned in pressing his case.

In the end, and to the surprise of most people, New York ratified the Constitution—by the narrow margin of 30 to 27. Within a short time afterward, the required nine states had affirmed the document, and it took effect in 1789. Hamilton's long quest for a workable national government now stood on the brink of achievement. Over the next five years he would come fully into his own, as the major player in the epic drama about to unfold.

His task would be very difficult. As the historian Carl Becker once remarked, the Revolution was not only about independence, or "home rule." It was also about the new system of government, or "who should rule at home," an equally divisive issue. Hamilton's passion about who should rule at home matched his hunger for home rule. For him, it would have to be the national government first and the states second.

Many popular currents continued to run in the opposite direction, however, and Hamilton well understood why. "We love our families, more than our neighbours," he had said at the New York Ratifying Convention. "We love our neighbours, more than our countrymen in general. The human affections, like the solar heat, lose their intensity, as they depart from the center . . . On these principles, the attachment of the individual will be first and forever secured by the state governments." In consequence, the centripetal *national* pull of the new Constitution had to be strengthened as a countervailing force. If it were not, the Union would split apart. Hamilton intended to do everything in his power to prevent that outcome.[19]

Once the new government was organized in 1789, President Washington offered the post of treasury secretary to Robert Morris. But Morris, now fifty-five years old, wanted to attend to his many business ventures. Nor did he wish to take on the daunting task that would face the new secretary—a task with which he was all too familiar. He therefore declined the offer, recommended the thirty-two-year-old Hamilton for the post, and then agreed to serve as a senator from Pennsylvania. Washington, who knew better than anyone else the remarkable reach of Hamilton's abilities, took this advice and appointed his former aide-de-camp.[20]

It proved to be a narrow escape for the country. Robert Morris had begun a downhill slide, investing in canal companies, steam engines, and—disastrously—in large tracts of land. In 1791, he purchased immense areas in upstate New York. He also invested in the District of Columbia and bought, on credit, six million acres in the South, an area larger than five of today's fifty states. He seemed unable to control his passion to make more money. By the late 1790s, his fortune had evaporated and his debts approached $3 million—a huge sum for that time. In an ignominious climax, Morris was arrested in 1798 and jailed for debt. He spent three-and-a-half years in prison, then five more in obscurity until his death in 1806. Like many successful financiers, Morris had come to believe in his own infallibility. An immigrant entrepreneur who overreached himself, he paid a grievous price.[21]

Meanwhile, secretary of the treasury Alexander Hamilton proceeded to turn in the most impressive economic performance in the history of American statecraft—against heavy odds and at great psychological cost to himself.

CHAPTER 8

New Government, Old Debt

By the time Hamilton took office in 1789, the War of Independence had been over for six years. The Constitution had been written and ratified, after almost two years of arduous bargaining among the states. The framework of a new federal government was being set up. What should that government now do? Not much, many Americans believed. In their eyes, the national crisis was over and the state governments would suffice for most public needs. Everyone should go home and savor the fruits of the Revolution and the Constitution. The time had come to enjoy the peace, raise crops, engage in routine commerce, and live a tranquil life with families and friends—without interference from either Britain or a too-powerful United States government.

Hamilton, Madison, and other well-informed leaders saw things differently. From their perspective, what had happened before 1789 was only the beginning—essential first steps, but far from bringing a viable nation into being. The Constitution was a marvelous outline, but it contained no detailed organizational structure for the government. It said nothing at all, for example, about cabinet departments. Congress would have to decide how many there would be, if any, and how they should relate to one another. The existing staff of public employees remained woefully insufficient.

These details of setting up the new government could be worked out, but even more daunting issues loomed. The United States owed huge foreign and domestic debts from the Revolution and had no coherent plan for paying them. Nor were military threats a thing of the past. Britain, France, and Spain still laid claim to vast territories adjacent to the United States. The British occupied a string of forts west of the Appalachian Mountains, and maintained alliances with Indian tribes hostile to American settlement. Spain owned Florida and controlled the vital port of New Orleans.

Even if the peace of 1783 lasted, many of the best foreign markets for American goods—the West Indies and to some extent South America—remained wholly or partly closed to them. The imperial systems of Britain, France, Spain, Holland, and Portugal were still intact. Without some adjustment, the domestic demand for U.S. agricultural products would be insufficient to support its farmers, who constituted the vast majority of the labor force.

As Hamilton saw it, unless the United States paid its debts, managed its foreign policy wisely, and made the most of its economic opportunities, then the gains of the Revolution could be lost. The Union itself might disintegrate. The arguments during the four-month Constitutional Convention—harsh, caustic debates that were repeated again and again in all the state ratifying conventions—showed deep fissures among the American people. Disputes ranged across a wide array of issues: the overall role of government, the appropriate division between state and national authority, and the divergence of political and economic interests in a union of dissimilar sections. There was no escaping the degree to which New England, the Middle Atlantic region, the Chesapeake areas, and the Deep South differed from one another. Equally troublesome were lingering contrasts among individual states. Some were large, some small; some agricultural, some commercial; some slave, some free.

———∞———

The government official whose vision most resembled Hamilton's was the new president, George Washington. After a long trip north from Mount Vernon, interrupted by raucous local celebrations along the way, Washington took his oath of office on April 30, 1789. On that occasion, his mood consisted of about equal parts confidence and misgivings. The swearing-in occurred at Federal Hall on Wall Street in New York, at that time the nation's capital city.

One of the first orders of business was to provide the new government with desperately needed funds. The most reliable source would be import duties. The Tariff Act, quickly passed by Congress and signed by Washington, gave the national government an independent source of income. At last, fourteen years after the start of the War of Independence, import duties would belong not to individual coastal states, but to the federal government. And for the next 124 years, until the Sixteenth Amendment legalized a federal income tax in 1913, revenues from tariffs composed by far the national government's principal source of funds.[1]

Advised by Hamilton and others, Congress set most duties at 5 to 10 percent of the value of incoming goods. The legislators imposed an additional 10 percent duty on merchandise carried by foreign ships. This measure gave American vessels a significant advantage in what was called the "carrying trade." During the 1790s, the average level of import duties was gradually raised to about 20 percent.[2]

In the new government, Hamilton saw himself—accurately, as it turned out—as the most important federal official except for the president. As he conceived his role, the U.S. secretary of the treasury would be rather more of an executive officer than the traditional European-style finance minister. In effect, Hamilton would serve as prime minister under President Washington. Over the next few years, he sometimes wrote privately of "my administration" and "my commercial system."[3]

The original three cabinet members were Hamilton, secretary of state Thomas Jefferson, and secretary of war Henry Knox, a former Boston bookseller and the Continental Army general in charge of artillery during the Revolution. The office of attorney general, occupied by Edmund Randolph of Virginia, was a part-time position not yet considered of cabinet status.

By the time Hamilton began his work at the Treasury Department in September 1789, he had studied finance for more than a decade. His learning ran deep. In addition to his voracious earlier reading, he had absorbed a cornucopia of insights from the writings of the world's leading contemporary financial experts: the French finance minister Jacques Necker, the Irish philosopher George Berkeley, the French mercantilist Jean-François Melon, the Dutch scholar Isaac de Pinto, and the British-American writer Samuel Gale. In addition, Hamilton ordered his staff at the Treasury and customs collectors in port cities to provide him with detailed statistical reports. Theory could take him only so far, and he needed as much hard data as it was possible to get.[4]

Hamilton had a clear idea of what he wanted to do, and in what sequence. His first priority would have to be the national and state debts, because without success on those fronts he could accomplish little else. As part of implementing his plan, he would need a national bank—an institution far larger than the Bank of North America that Robert Morris had persuaded Congress to authorize in 1782. Finally, Hamilton was determined to diversify the American economy beyond its traditional focus on agriculture.

He had enough people in the Treasury to help him accomplish these goals, but only barely. His immediate staff numbered thirty-nine, including his assistant and five clerks. The Treasury's auditor, who worked directly under him, had twelve clerks of his own. Outside the national capital, Hamilton had charge of customs revenue collectors at port cities—very important officials—and also of the 297 inspectors and others who worked for the collectors. He oversaw fifteen additional general supervisors and twenty inspectors, thirteen keepers of federal lighthouses, and assorted others. To guard against smuggling, Hamilton organized the Revenue Cutter Service, which later became the United States Coast Guard. The total number of federal employees working under him reached 570, and they made up the great majority of the U.S. civil government.[5]

Jefferson at the State Department oversaw a tiny office with four or five clerks, plus a small corps of ministers assigned abroad, in foreign capitals. He returned from France in September 1789 and did not take up his official duties until March 1790, by which time Hamilton had been at work for six crucial months. He was quick to notice Hamilton's far larger staff and was much rankled by his greater influence. Jefferson barely knew Hamilton, and regarded the younger man (Jefferson was forty-seven; Hamilton, thirty-three) as an upstart from a remote Caribbean island. Knox at the War Department had only four civilian employees and one active army regiment, but he remained on good terms with Hamilton. The federal establishment as a whole grew about four-fold from 1790 to 1800, but even then it remained minuscule compared to the civil services of European powers.[6]

Working alongside his staff, Hamilton did an inordinate amount of the Treasury's daily business himself. In contrast to Robert Morris, he toiled in modest surroundings, as he had done at

Washington's field headquarters. A French visitor to the Treasury found the secretary sitting "in a long gray linen jacket" at an unadorned pine table covered with a green cloth. Files lay neatly on crude shelves. The entire furnishings of the office, the visitor estimated, had cost perhaps ten dollars.[7]

As secretary, Hamilton cared a great deal about "energy" in administration. In his outline of the long speech he gave at the Constitutional Convention, he had written, "It is said a republican government does not admit a vigorous execution," then had argued that this need not be true. He made the same point in *The Federalist Papers,* which are full of references to "energy" and effective organization.[8]

Having risen against great odds by means of his own talents, Hamilton was a meritocrat who believed that nothing of significance could be left to chance. He never ceased to emphasize the importance of energetic government and constant monitoring. At the New York Ratifying Convention, he had said, "There are two objects in forming systems of government—Safety for the people, and energy in the administration. When these objects are united, the certain tendency of the system will be to the public welfare."[9]

His thinking contrasted with that of some other founders, especially Jefferson. Whereas Hamilton extolled activism, Jefferson remained preoccupied with the virtues of agrarian living and the need for quiet reflection as prerequisite to correct decision making. In 1787, when Madison sent him a copy of the new Constitution, Jefferson replied from Paris, "I am not a friend to a very energetic government. It is always oppressive." He went on to say that "I think our governments will remain virtuous for many centuries; as long as [the people] are chiefly agricultural; and this will be as long as there shall be vacant lands in any part of America. When they get piled upon one another in large cities, as in Europe, they will become corrupt as in Europe." Two such differing views of the nation's future represented seeds of dissension between Hamilton and Jefferson that were certain to sprout once the new government began doing business.[10]

In the case of Hamilton, the question naturally arises: energetic administration toward what end? Here his answer was the good of the nation as a whole, not of any particular state or section. His thought centered on national economic aggregates—in agriculture, industrial production, and finance. In addition, he understood better than any other founder—indeed, better than any other American of his generation who left enough records to judge—how everything in the national economy was related to everything else. A first-class student of both economics and administration, he saw that in the construction of grand strategy, every move must be coordinated so as to make the whole of public policy exceed the sum of its parts. And this is what he proceeded to do as secretary.[11]

The first step had to be the establishment of the nation's credit—its ability to borrow from abroad and from its own citizens. In both Britain and America at this time, indebtedness was often construed as a moral issue, and the verdict was usually negative. Many critics associated consumer credit with irresponsible behavior and usurious pawnbroking, and commercial credit with wild projects leading to ruin. Government ("public") credit seemed worst of all: forcing a nation to impose high taxes, facilitating unpopular wars fought with borrowed money, enriching financiers who had inside information, and promoting corruption in the legislature.[12]

In 1789, when Hamilton entered office, at least fifty different coinages and currencies from different countries, U.S. states, and even private companies remained in circulation—Spanish dollars, British pounds, Dutch guilders, and numerous others. Counterfeiting had also been flourishing, and the entire situation bewildered average citizens. It had become very hard to determine what certain coins and paper notes were actually worth.[13]

The vast public debt owed by the American government comprised a motley concoction of state and federal paper obligations. To thousands of American holders of the many different instruments of federal debt—bonds, currency, IOUs, and other instruments issued by Congress and the army—Hamilton calculated that the government owed about $29 million in principal and $11.4 million in unpaid interest. The amount due French and Dutch creditors was $12 million, including $1.8 million of unpaid interest. The debts owed by the thirteen states, some of which had issued large sums of promissory notes and currency with little or no gold or silver backing, were impossible to determine with much accuracy. Hamilton estimated the figure at about $25 million, and the total state and federal debt at a "par" value of about $79 million (that is, the *face* value of all instruments, as opposed to what they would bring on the open market). This represented a slight overestimate, primarily because of the uncertainty of state debts, and the actual figure was about $74 million.[14]

But the mere act of adding up these numbers obscured the complexity of the problem: the extreme diversity in the sources of the debt, the different interest rates and maturities attached to various instruments, and the disparate groups of American and foreign creditors who held securities in all categories. Nor did the total figure say anything at all about the actual market value of the debt, which was much less than its par value of $74 million. The domestic holders of many types of federal and state securities would have gladly sold them for ten to twenty cents on the dollar.

Almost nothing except the foreign debt was worth anywhere near its par value. And even if the numbers could somehow be made precise, they alone could not express the economic and political stakes at issue. The stark fact was that the United States had long been in a state of bankruptcy. Hamilton believed that if the country could not somehow make itself creditworthy, then it could not survive as a union.

—⊷—

Because of Hamilton's experiences as a youth in St. Croix, followed by his years at Washington's headquarters during the Revolution, the issue of national security in a world of warring empires always lay near the front of his mind. Hamilton reasoned that the preservation of liberty required not only an energetic government, but also a strong military. The Constitution, after all, mandated that the federal government "provide for the common defense."[15]

Hamilton knew that it would take a fair amount of money to build and maintain a sufficient shield against threats from Europe. The ability to raise that money hinged on America's creditworthiness. All future attempts to borrow depended, in turn, on the country's ability to deal with its huge existing debt. As Hamilton saw it, continued liberty demanded an immediate and effective engagement of that debt.[16]

Simple arithmetic, however, seemed to make the debt problem intractable. Hamilton believed that in the short-to-medium term the federal government would take in about $2.8 million per year, a tiny sum in the face of a $74 million debt. The resulting relationship of debt to income would be 26.4 to 1, a huge ratio, by far the highest in American history even down to the present time.

In 1789, few people agreed even on how to calculate the total debt. Arguments over the various debts had been going on for at least a decade, and the debates over funding them had become more acrimonious with each passing year. "Funding" did not mean paying the debts immediately, which would have been impossible. Instead, it meant what today would be called refinancing. It meant setting up a program for making regular interest payments and, eventually, beginning to reduce the

$74 million principal. Nationalists wanted to consolidate the federal and state debts and fund them both. Individual states differed on whether the federal government should take over all state debts or whether each state should fund its own debt. The foreign debt, the most pressing issue, could perhaps be refinanced through another big loan from abroad.

The Constitution of 1787 represented a major victory for the nationalists, but actual implementation of a nationalist fiscal policy was something else entirely. Hamilton and other nationalists had argued that the federal government's claim on tariff and tax revenues must take priority over those of the states. Following this logic, the secretary opposed plans for individual states to pay off their debts. Many had begun to do so, imposing heavy state taxes, and Hamilton wanted them to stop. He and his allies reasoned that the power to tax was indispensable to national sovereignty—a way to glue the Union more tightly together.

Before he took office in 1789, Hamilton knew that there might have to be some sort of downward adjustment in the total amount owed. But by how much, and in what way? No one knew what level of interest should apply if the debt were refinanced. Nobody could predict what Congress would do about the divisive issue of "assumption" by the federal government of the states' debts. It remained unclear whether any of the principal on any of the debts would ever be paid, and, if so, when. The entire financial situation was about as chaotic as it could be.

CHAPTER 9

The Fight over the Debt

To bring order out of this chaos, Hamilton proposed bold, almost breathtaking action. When Congress created the Treasury Department in 1789, it required that the secretary report to both the president and the House of Representatives. This provision gave the treasury secretary the opportunity to initiate legislation, a power even Washington believed he himself did not possess as president. In Hamilton's long *Report Relative to a Provision for the Support of Public Credit,* submitted in January 1790, he presented the most forceful and persuasive case he could make, and ended by suggesting a complex package of legislation. He began his argument by pointing out that the debt was "the price of liberty." The new nation could not have secured its freedom without the money lent to the national and state governments by foreign bankers and American citizens. He then recommended that Congress pass laws to meet four related problems.[1]

First, Hamilton asked for immediate authority to repay at face value the entire principal on the debt owed to foreign creditors, plus the unpaid interest. He would do this by means of new foreign loans taken out for this specific purpose—that is, a complete refinancing of the $12 million owed to European creditors. This part of his plan went forward without much opposition, and new loans from Europe were soon negotiated, to Hamilton's great relief.[2]

Second, to manage the domestic part of the national debt, he proposed that the Treasury issue new federal bonds to replace the total principal of all old securities, again at their entire face (or par) value. The new bonds would carry no dates of maturity. Nor could their holders receive from the Treasury more than a specified dollar amount each year.

Hamilton reasoned that the no-maturity provision would buy time for the national economy to grow. To increase the incentives for purchasers, he suggested a provision that would prohibit the Treasury from buying back its bonds even if interest rates declined. (In modern jargon, this provision is known as "call protection.") And the ceiling on annual payments to bondholders would insulate the Treasury against excessive demands, should it run short of funds.

Third, Hamilton suggested that the federal government assume all of the war debts of the states, and fund these debts at par in the same way he had outlined for the federal debt.

Fourth, in his boldest step, Hamilton proposed—though subtly—that the average interest rate on the new bonds be about 4 percent, rather than the 6 percent rate that was supposed to be paid on most existing securities. This cut represented an immense reduction of the total amount of money the government would have to pay for the next two decades. (Almost one-third, since nearly every dollar the Treasury intended to disburse was for interest on the debt, and not principal.) In order to guarantee that interest payments would be issued when they came due, his plan provided that the government set aside part of its substantial receipts from import duties. This measure would eliminate the need for regular appropriations and thereby avoid bitter annual controversies in Congress. Hamilton also took the unusual step of specifying that interest on the debt would be paid in gold and silver. This was an unexpected guarantee that went far toward reassuring potential investors. Altogether, the elements of his plan contained many departures from the way most governments conducted their financial affairs.

Hamilton partially cloaked these changes in a flurry of technical terms that only sophisticated investors would fully understand. And although they could not cash in their bonds by selling them back to the government, they could sell them to other investors. Because the market value of the new securities would be so much greater than that of the old ones, liquidity would increase for investors and for the nation as a whole. Trading among holders of the new federal bonds led to the creation of the first efficient securities market in the United States, the forerunner of the New York Stock Exchange.[3]

Even in long retrospect, when it is clear how well Hamilton's program worked out, it is equally clear that the little lion was taking an extremely big gamble. Both he and the investors who bought the bonds were betting that the American economy, once on a sound footing, would prosper sufficiently to increase the government's income and confirm the soundness of the new securities. Without rapid growth, the Treasury would not receive enough money to pay the interest on the debt, let alone conduct the normal affairs of government.

Hamilton believed that if Congress would enact his plan, then future economic growth would be far more robust than most people expected. When he became secretary, economic conditions seemed to be improving a bit. But there was no guarantee that in the short run the federal government would take in the $2.8 million per year he was counting on, and at first, receipts were much lower. The extraordinary audacity of his plan is evident in the actual federal revenues for his time in office—some of which have only recently been discovered, more than 200 years after the fact:[4]

Year	Receipts	Debt-to-receipts ratio
1789	$0.162 million*	457 to 1
1790	$1.6 million	46 to 1
1791	$2.6 million	29 to 1
1792	$3.7 million	21 to 1
1793	$4.7 million	17 to 1
1794	$5.4 million	15 to 1

*Collected for only part of the year

By the year 1800, in large part because of Hamilton's policies for economic growth, annual federal revenues had reached $10.8 million. At that time the debt-to-income ratio had shrunk to about 8.6 to 1. Throughout this period, and for years thereafter, payment of interest on the debt consumed the great bulk of federal revenues (87 percent for 1792, for example). But looking forward from the time of Hamilton's 1790 *Report*, rather than in retrospect as in the tabulation above, nobody could have known that economic growth would accelerate so rapidly as to ease the debt burden to such an extent. In 1790, the political atmosphere surrounding financial policy remained very tense, and Hamilton's legislative proposals thrust him into the biggest fight of his life.[5]

———

In 1790, when he sent his *Report* to Congress, few people questioned that something had to be done about public credit. But his specific program ignited an immediate firestorm of controversy. There were deep divisions in Congress and throughout the country over whether to fund the debt at par, and even stronger disagreements over whether the federal government should assume the debts of the states.

On the issue of funding the debt at par, a chorus of critics correctly pointed out that the market value of most outstanding instruments was nowhere near their face value. Thus, funding at par seemed to put the Treasury in the position of making a huge and pointless gift to "speculators." So there was much talk in favor of what Hamilton's opponents called "discrimination."

A discrimination plan would distinguish between original holders of Continental securities, on the one hand, and those who had purchased them since, on the other. The former were portrayed as deserving contributors to the war effort, the latter as wealthy predators who had bought certificates from the original holders at a price far below their face value. Under a policy of discrimination, the Treasury would partially reimburse the original holders and pay a remaining fraction of face value to the final purchasers.

As an abstract proposition, discrimination seemed reasonable and just, but Hamilton immediately saw that it would plunge the Treasury into an administrative nightmare. Most securities had been bought and resold again and again by a series of intermediate holders. Adjudicating their claims with any degree of fairness would require hundreds of investigators and judges. And the process itself would be long, drawn out, and contested by those who were dissatisfied with the results.

Even without the administrative problem of discrimination, the act of failing to pay existing holders the face value of their securities would be, as Hamilton wrote, "a breach of contract." And the sanctity of contracts was a foundational principle of the rule of law. Even as a practical matter, reneging on payment of the debt at par would imperil future attempts to sell federal bonds, both at home and abroad. Paying less than face value to any debt holder would amount to a partial default by the United States government. It would set a disastrous precedent at the very moment when the Treasury was planning to seek essential new domestic loans. It would therefore undercut the nation's creditworthiness and ultimately its safety.[6]

In addition, Hamilton wanted to tie what he called "the monied interest" (wealthy Americans) as tightly as possible to the federal government, rather than to individual states. Only in that way could the new union prosper as a *nation,* and paying the face value of the debt to all holders would go far toward binding the monied interest to the federal government. A firmer union had long been the chief goal of the nationalists, who had fought for almost a decade against the constraints of the Articles of Confederation. In writing the Constitution and working so hard for its ratification, they had finally won their fight.

In the midst of the campaign to get his program through Congress, Hamilton was astounded when the leader of the opposition turned out to be James Madison—his longtime fellow nationalist, the principal architect of the Constitution, and his close collaborator on *The Federalist Papers*. Madison had also helped to shepherd the Tariff Act of 1789 through Congress, and in earlier years had favored funding the debt at par. But he had begun to pay more attention to the wishes of his Virginia constituents, most of whom opposed it. He was also personally repelled by the thought of rewarding "speculators."

Madison, who was at this time the most powerful and respected member of Congress, now argued against funding the debt at par and instead for discrimination through what he called a "composition" (compromise). Under this idea, both the original and final holders of government securities would be fairly compensated, and intermediate holders ignored. In an eloquent statement, Madison acknowledged the unorthodoxy of his proposal but not its complexity. Nor did he show any awareness of the administrative quandaries that would follow when different classes of creditors began to clamor for maximum payments to themselves. As Descartes had written more than a century before, "A man is incapable of comprehending any argument that interferes with his own revenue." And that psychological problem now beset Hamilton on all sides.[7]

The secretary stood his ground. Despite his youth, Hamilton was a veteran soldier and administrator, as well as a trained lawyer who had argued many cases before hostile juries. Madison, for all his wisdom and talents, lacked these particular experiences. The split between Madison and Hamilton also reflected traditional divisions between agrarian and urban interests. In the United States, as in most other countries, there was a mutual lack of respect between large-scale landholders on the one hand and financial "speculators" on the other. In one of his "Continentalist" essays of 1782, Hamilton had written of "the collision and rivalship, which almost always subsist between the landed and trading interests." Sometimes the feeling approached open and reciprocal contempt. It frequently erupted in exchanges of insults and, at worst, the occasional duel.[8]

In the context of financing the War of Independence and its aftermath, however, any definition of the word "speculator" was problematic. In 1790s America, most people who were called "speculators"—apart from land speculators, a large and varied cohort that included Washington, Franklin, and other founders—were actually town and city merchants of moderate wealth who lived by their wits, rather than on incomes from inherited lands. Although Madison was a talented political theorist, he derived his income from a slave-staffed Virginia plantation that he stood to inherit. Madison's close friend Jefferson had already inherited his landed fortune (along with debts from his wife's father), and saw most issues the way Madison did. Despite their intellectual brilliance, both men lacked anything approaching Hamilton's knowledge of business and finance.[9]

So did almost everyone else. Opposition to Hamilton's plan was not confined to southern planters. The American people as a whole remained skeptical toward nearly every issue related to debt and credit. And there were indeed well-financed people touring the countryside and buying up old securities on the likelihood that Congress would fund the debt. As a result, negative responses to Hamilton's proposals poured in from everywhere.

A typical complaint came from the pen of William Manning, a self-taught Massachusetts farmer and veteran of the Battle of Bunker Hill. Admitting that he had "Nither Larning nor abilitys," Manning wrote that any policies "that touch a Mans Interest or his Eydeayes thereof" were certain to be controversial. "The Grate Question is how Shall Restitution be Made & Justis Done in this Case when Nither Congress nor the States have Either Mony nor Credit to Do it with." This was an accurate portrayal of Hamilton's problem. But in Manning's view, the secretary's plan, with its "Measures so Glareingly unjust," favored the rich over the poor. "Their is nothing which Excites Jelocye betwen these few and Many More than the alterations of Money affares." Although Madison and others wrote smoother protests, none of Hamilton's opponents put the matter more forthrightly than William Manning.[10]

Yet Hamilton's plan seemed the only route to a prompt and sound establishment of the nation's credit. He had presented a deft argument and in parts a very technical one. Thomas Jefferson, who did not join the government until two months after Hamilton submitted his *Report,* could not fathom all the details of the plan and believed—incorrectly—that Hamilton himself did not fully understand it. As a Maryland congressman complained in 1790, the secretary's proposals were so complicated as to "be above the comprehension of persons in general." Here, for example, is a representative passage in which Hamilton describes one of the seven options Congress might offer holders of each $100 in federal bonds: "To have sixty-six dollars and two thirds of a dollar funded immediately at an annuity or yearly interest of six per cent. irredeemable by any payment exceeding four dollars and two thirds of a dollar per annum, on account both of principal and interest; and to have, at the end of ten years, twenty-six dollars and eighty-eight cents, funded at the like interest and rate of redemption."[11]

Although it is not evident on a first reading, this option would result in an actual interest rate not of 6 percent for the $100 in question, but of 4 percent (6 percent of $66.67 equals 4 percent of $100). Also, the purchaser could not sell the bond back to the government and could not receive more than $4.67 annually for principal and interest combined. Then, too, the plan seems to imply a maturity of ten years, when in fact Hamilton's language does not specify any date for full payment of the principal. In his example, at the end of ten years the original principal of $100 would have been reduced by only $6.45 ($100 minus $93.55, which is the sum of the other two figures mentioned: $66.67 plus $26.88). Under this plan, about thirty-four years would be necessary to pay off the $100 in full.[12]

Hamilton was not trying to deceive prospective buyers of securities. Most investors were knowledgeable domestic merchants or overseas financiers. They would grasp the specifics of his plan after a few minutes' calculation with pencil and paper. These investors, Hamilton believed, would quickly see that receiving 4 percent of something was far preferable to getting 6 percent of nothing.[13]

Investors who held old government instruments now paying nothing were anxious to exchange them for sound securities paying regular interest in gold or silver. Hamilton was offering them this opportunity. But he was not openly repudiating part of the total debt by emphasizing a one-third reduction in the interest rate.[14]

For Hamilton himself, it was clear that there were not just two "classes" of people who took different positions toward funding the debt, but several others as well. The farmer William Manning and most critics saw only the first two: those who wanted discrimination and those who wanted funding at par. But Hamilton's plan had to deal with at least five categories of claimants because there were so many different types of debt with so many different maturities and rates of interest. "It is easy to perceive," he recalled later, "that such a heterogeneous mass of opinions not merely speculative but actuated by different interests and passions could not fail to produce much embarrassment to the person who was to devise the plan." This was another expression of the extreme pressure he felt himself under.[15]

There was, of course, no ideal solution. But Hamilton believed that decisions had to be made, whatever the pros and cons perceived by affected players. Thus, he could not be persuaded by arguments from Madison and others that profit making by speculators, in itself, was a sufficient reason to avoid funding the debt at par. The task of an executive officer was not to achieve perfection, but to devise and then carry through the best alternative among a list of flawed options.

This was a lesson he had begun to learn in his youth, when he was managing Nicholas Cruger's shipping business in St. Croix (he regarded that experience as the most useful economic training of his life). Later, his four years as George Washington's aide-de-camp had strongly confirmed the lesson about decision making. Most important for the debt crisis of 1790, he had witnessed Robert Morris's four-year effort during 1781–1784 to persuade Congress to deal with the deficit problem—an effort that had ended in frustration and failure. Hence Hamilton's sense of extreme urgency in pushing forward his plan.[16]

In the end, he prevailed with surprising ease on the question of funding the national debt at par. The House of Representatives, more persuaded by his logic and tenacity than the country at large had been, defeated Madison's proposal for discrimination by a vote of 36 to 13. Hamilton savored his victory, but not for long. This was only the first part of the fight. The far more difficult political issue was his insistence that all state debts be assumed by the federal government. And on that question Madison had the votes to defeat him.

The issue of state debts was full of built-in unfairness and could hardly have been more troublesome. Some states, including Virginia, Maryland, Georgia, and North Carolina, had already made substantial progress in paying down their debts. Others still owed huge sums: Massachusetts and South Carolina about $5 million each, the two states aggregating 40 percent of the total estimate of $25 million. Several other states owed less than $1 million, and Delaware only $50,000. There were few correlations between the population of a state, the size of its debt, and its ability to pay.[17]

As a committed nationalist and an immigrant without hereditary ties to any state, Hamilton cared little about these differences. But his debt-assumption proposal outraged many members of Congress who cared a great deal. And here again Hamilton felt that Madison was double-crossing him. The first House ballot on federal assumption of the state debts failed by a vote of 32 to 29. Despite Madison's majority—and the prospect that the gap would grow larger, since some congressmen from North Carolina who opposed assumption had not yet arrived in the capital—Hamilton would not budge. The assumption of state debts was the keystone of his grand plan to force the American confederation into a tighter union. The responsibility to fund all public debts carried the power of first call on tax levies, and Hamilton was not going to let that power remain in the hands of state governments. Without debt assumption, as he later wrote, the federal government would be "under all the entanglements and imbecilities of a complicated clashing & disordered system of Finance."[18]

Week after week, however, Madison and his majority in Congress stood just as rigid and uncompromising as Hamilton. The secretary searched for any means of winning a few more votes, but without success. Madison blocked assumption motions four times in Congress; and on the funding plan as a whole, the legislature debated for almost the entire congressional session—from February to August 1790. Hamilton had every reason to fear that the crucial debt-assumption part of his plan was going to fail.

Finally, in one of the most pivotal episodes in early U.S. history, an ingenious bargain broke the logjam. The terms of the bargain were concluded during a dinner suggested by Hamilton and held in New York City at Thomas Jefferson's rented house on Maiden Lane, two blocks north of Wall Street. At that dinner, Madison, Jefferson, and Hamilton agreed that Philadelphia should replace New York as the nation's capital for a period of ten years—an idea calculated to win one or two Pennsylvania votes for Hamilton's plan. Thereafter, a new town, built in a federal district along the Potomac River on the border between Maryland and Virginia, would become the permanent capital.

Hamilton would have preferred that the capital remain in New York. But having no hereditary native state himself, he was not as concerned about its location as the more section-conscious Virginians were. In return for the secretary's support of the move south, Madison agreed to provide enough votes to swing the House in favor of Hamilton's bill. The bargain was consummated, and the House vote taken. Madison did not change his own negative ballot, but he apparently persuaded two congressmen from Virginia and two from Maryland—all four of whose districts lay near the Potomac River—to change theirs. A few other votes shifted as well, and what had been a 32-to-29 margin against the assumption bill in April 1790 was reversed in July: 32 to 29 in favor. Ten years later, a hot, muddy, and ramshackle town on the Potomac became the national capital—fulfilling a long and, it had been thought, utterly impractical dream of George Washington himself, who had chosen the area.[19]

The act of Congress on funding and assumption became law on August 4, 1790, and a very complicated measure it proved to be. Institutional foreign creditors would be paid in full through the returns from a new loan to be negotiated with Dutch banks. Other holders of the national debt, after exchanging their old securities for new ones, would be paid, in effect, 4 percent interest on two-thirds of the new securities, starting in 1792. The remaining one-third of new securities would earn 6 percent, but those payments would not begin until 1800.[20]

In 1792, state creditors would start receiving 6 percent interest on four-ninths of their securities and 3 percent on one-third. For the remaining two-ninths of securities, they would be paid 6 percent interest, but not until 1800. There would be a "sinking fund" for the eventual payment of the principal of the consolidated debt, but the details remained a little obscure.[21]

Because it would take so long to pay the principal, the general reduction of the de facto interest rate from 6 to 4 percent amounted to an unacknowledged cut of about one-third in the amount of money the government would have to allot toward the debt over at least the next decade. This was the simple goal that Hamilton had in mind all along. But he had been compelled to devise a long series of intricate measures in order to reach it.

After a year of tireless work, he finally had his entire funding plan written into law. "Had a single session [of Congress] passed," he recalled, ". . . without some adequate provision for the debt the most injurious consequences were to have been expected." To get his plan enacted, he had used all his ingenuity, all his powers of persuasion, all the help he could obtain from any source, and every compromise that would not damage his grand design.[22]

If he had failed in the First Congress, at the launching of the new government—which he correctly judged as the most propitious moment—he believed that nobody could ever succeed. The stakes could hardly have been greater or his triumph more dramatic. But the level of personal stress had been high, and it was far from over. For Hamilton, it would never be over. It would ebb and flow, but it would never end.

CHAPTER 10

The Bank of the United States

The move to Philadelphia late in 1790 facilitated better organization of federal offices and more efficient communication among them. The tight physical constraints of lower Manhattan had forced the government into cramped quarters. The First Congress had met at Federal Hall on crowded Wall Street, which is barely half a mile long. Philadelphia, by contrast, was much more spacious. It had been the largest and most populous city in the thirteen colonies and remained so for three decades after independence. The city had hosted the Constitutional Convention of 1787 and remained the capital of Pennsylvania until 1798.

Unlike New York, Philadelphia contained many government buildings, including the Pennsylvania State House and convenient spaces for the Treasury, State, and War departments. The headquarters of the three were almost adjacent to one another. The federal House and Senate met in Congress Hall, a large new building first intended to serve as the Philadelphia county courthouse. On Chestnut Street, Congress Hall stood next to the State House, where both the Declaration of Independence and the Constitution had been signed. (The restored

State House, now one of the nation's great landmarks, was re-named the Hall of Independence in 1824 and Independence Hall in 1852.) For the residence of President Washington, the federal government rented the ornate mansion of Robert Morris in downtown Philadelphia. When Washington left office in 1797, his successor, John Adams, moved into the same quarters.

At the turn of the nineteenth century, the most imposing building in Philadelphia was none of these structures. That distinction went instead to the Bank of the United States, built during the 1790s to house one of the key institutions of Hamilton's grand financial plan. This part of his program became public in his *Report on a National Bank*—sent to Congress in December 1790, four months after the passage of legislation to fund the national and state debts. Like those proposals, the bank bill ran into immediate opposition. Most of the congressmen and senators who would vote on the bill had only a vague idea of how banks are supposed to work. Some had no idea at all.[1]

In 1790, when Hamilton submitted his *Report,* there were only three banks in the United States: the Bank of North America, located in Philadelphia and set up in 1782 at the behest of Robert Morris, and two others established in 1784—the Bank of Massachusetts, located in Boston, and the Bank of New York, which Hamilton himself had helped organize and whose charter he had written. So there had been some progress, but the nation's institutional credit system was still in its infancy.[2]

In preparing for the legislative battle, Hamilton conducted extensive research on banks located in other countries. A friend touring Britain wrote him that England contained about fifty banks that issued their own currency, and Scotland had thirty more. "Many people here are of opinion," Hamilton's friend added, "That the Prosperity & flourishing State of Britain, Is owing far more to the Establishment of *Bank's* then to the Na-tionall Debt. Certain it is that Scotland alone owes allmost all its Improvement in Agriculture, Commerce & Manufactures to the Institution of Banks."³

Hamilton began his *Report* with an elementary and much-needed lesson in finance. "It is a well established fact, that Banks in good credit can circulate a far greater sum [in paper cur-rency] than the actual quantum of their capital in Gold & Sil-ver." Because it was very unlikely that all depositors would withdraw their money at the same time, banks could issue cur-rency in much greater amounts than their reserves of gold, sil-ver, and federal bonds. (Today these are called "reserve require-ments," and the structure itself is known as a "fractional reserve system.") As Hamilton put it, "The extent of the possible excess seems indeterminate; though it has been conjecturally stated at the proportions of two and three to one."⁴

Thus, Hamilton wrote, "the money of one individual, while he is waiting for an opportunity to employ it, by being either deposited in the Bank for safe keeping, or invested in its Stock, is in a condition to administer to the wants of others, without being put out of his own reach . . . [This] keeps the money itself in a state of incessant activity." In effect, Hamilton's plan pro-vided for reserve requirements not of two or three to one, but of five to one, which proved not to be excessive. He went on to say that a Bank of the United States would facilitate the collec-tion of taxes and permit the government to make payments and secure loans more easily.⁵

Like a trial lawyer addressing a jury, Hamilton then flattered his audience, the House of Representatives, by adding that "it would be to intrude too much on the patience of the house to prolong the details of the advantages of Banks." Instead, he listed "their disadvantages, real or supposed," and proceeded to demolish every conceivable argument against his proposal. One vital detail, he emphasized, was that the Bank of the United States be mostly a private, profit-making institution. The gov-ernment would supply $2 million of the bank's original $10 mil-lion capital, but the remaining four-fifths must come from private investors. At this time, the total capital of the country's existing banks hardly exceeded $2 million.[6]

The twenty-five-member board of directors would be private individuals, not public appointees. The Bank of the United States could have branches in several cities throughout the country, in addition to its home in Philadelphia. These branches would enable the government to spend money far away from the places it had been collected, without having to move the assets physically—a tremendous advantage. The bank's charter, by act of Congress, would run for twenty years, expiring in 1811, when it could be renewed or terminated. The bank would be a limited-liability corporation, although Article 7.9 of its charter stated that directors would be personally liable if the bank could not redeem notes it issued in excess of $10 million.

Hamilton saw the requirement that the Bank of the United States be a profit-making institution as a way to control the government's temptation to issue notes not backed by gold and silver. That tendency to print money had run amok during the Revolution. In Hamilton's new plan, the Bank of the United States, not the Treasury Department, would issue paper currency. "The stamping of paper," he argued, "is an operation so much easier than the laying of taxes, that a government, in the practice of paper emissions, would rarely fail in any such emergency to indulge itself too far." Therefore, it was necessary that the new bank "be under a *private* not a *public* Direction, under the guidance of *individual interest,* not of *public policy* . . . What nation was ever blessed with a constant succession of upright and wise Administrators?" And to prevent other types of abuse by politicians, Hamilton's *Report* specified that the Bank of the United States could lend no more than a total of $50,000 to the national government or to any state "unless previously authorized by law."[7]

In these provisions, Hamilton was trying to kill four birds with one stone. A large and powerful group of Americans opposed the existence of all banks because they remained suspicious of all paper money. Having been fleeced when they accepted paper currency issued by the Continental Congress and the states, a majority of citizens had full confidence only in gold and silver.

A second group opposed a national bank not for economic but for political reasons. They regarded Hamilton's proposal as still another scheme for centralizing power in the federal government at the expense of the states. (In both the twentieth and twenty-first centuries, the existence of the Federal Reserve System has offended people who think this way. Ever since the establishment of the Fed in 1913, members of Congress and others have periodically proposed that it be abolished.)

A third faction fought the creation of a national bank because it would compete with state-chartered banks they themselves wanted to establish. In many cities, merchants wished to set up their own banks and start doing business. They saw Hamilton's plan as a bid for semi-monopolistic financial powers that would interfere with their own plans. They anticipated—quite accurately—that a federally chartered bank would have stronger backing in gold and silver reserves than most state-chartered banks would. It might also come to exercise de facto regulatory powers over state institutions by refusing to accept their banknotes at face value.

Still another group, the most sophisticated of the four, saw the unmistakable need for a national bank. But they had little faith in the ability of a purely public institution to resist the temptation to issue unlimited banknotes backed by no reserves. This fourth group included the "monied interest" whom Hamilton was determined to seduce into depositing their funds in the Bank of the United States and investing in its securities. This is why he emphasized in his *Report* that the bank would remain under private and not public control, and forbidden to issue currency without gold or silver backing. In his overall plan for national economic development, he believed that the financial resources of the monied interest would be essential. So, too, would the political support that would follow their investment.

He was relying on the principle laid down in the biblical Book of Matthew: "For where thy treasure is, there will thy heart be also."

—⁕—

Hamilton knew just how to relate the new bank to the funding and assumption acts Congress had just passed. His *Report* specified that the bank's capital be $10 million, of which the Treasury, at the discretion of the president of the United States, could buy and retain $2 million of its own shares. The remaining $8 million in bank shares would be purchased by both domestic and foreign investors. They were to pay one-fourth of the purchase price ($2 million) in gold or silver, and the remaining three-fourths ($6 million) in the new federal bonds authorized by the funding acts.

Hamilton's aim was to augment the nation's money supply by "monetizing" the federal and state debts. That is, he would deposit in the Bank of the United States not only gold and silver, but also federal bonds: interest-earning securities whose value would be established in the open market. Thus, bank reserves in the form of gold, silver, and government bonds would form the basis for a new paper currency. This currency, issued not by the Treasury but by the bank, would vastly increase the country's supply of money and therefore stimulate its economy. Soon afterward, Hamilton sent in his important *Report on a Mint,* which confirmed the dollar as the national currency and provided for the government's coinage of gold and silver.[8]

The House passed Hamilton's bank bill by the one-sided vote of 39 to 20. After the Senate also passed the bill and sent it to Washington for his signature, the president asked secretary of state Jefferson and attorney general Edmund Randolph for their opinions. Jefferson, in addition to regarding Hamilton as an immigrant upstart, detested all banks, and opposed this one in particular on the additional grounds of unconstitutionality. Both he and Randolph returned a negative verdict. They argued that the Constitution said nothing about incorporating banks or any other kinds of business. In effect, they were recommending that Washington veto the bank bill. Jefferson's message was strongly phrased, and although he hedged a bit on the matter of a veto, there could be little question that this is what he wanted. Randolph and Jefferson were Virginians, and most politicians from their state opposed Hamilton's bank bill. Washington, also a Virginian but more of a nationalist than the other two, was genuinely undecided. As a contingency, he asked James Madison to draft a veto message.[9]

The president then put the question to Hamilton, giving him the written objections from Randolph and Jefferson. After a week of feverish composition, the secretary produced a long and sophisticated response. He began by noting that the essence of both Jefferson's and Randolph's objections lay in their narrow interpretation of federal powers under the Constitution: "The objections of the Secretary of State and Attorney General are founded on a general denial of the authority of the United States to erect corporations." From this beginning Hamilton constructed a step-by-step rebuttal of both the premises and specific arguments employed by Randolph and particularly by Jefferson.[10]

"A strange fallacy seems to have crept into the matter of thinking & reasoning upon the subject," Hamilton wrote. "An incorporation seems to have been regarded as some great, independent, substantive thing—as a political end of peculiar magnitude & moment; whereas it is truly to be considered as a *quality, capacity,* or *mean* to an end." In other words, incorporation of the Bank of the United States was a type of measure clearly contemplated by the Constitution in its "necessary and proper" clause about what the federal government could or could not do.[11]

If Jefferson's reading of the Constitution were correct, Hamilton went on to say, it would be "as if the word *absolutely* or *indispensibly* had been prefixed" to the necessary and proper clause. "Such a construction would beget endless uncertainty and embarrassment. The cases must be palpable & extreme in which it could be pronounced with certainty that a measure was absolutely necessary, or one without which the exercise of a given power would be nugatory. There are few measures of any government, which would stand so severe a test."[12]

Furthermore, although Jefferson's letter to Washington had referred to the adequacy of existing state banks, Hamilton pointed out that his reasoning would prohibit not only the national government but also the states from incorporating a bank. "It is to be remembered, that there is no *express* power in any State constitution to erect corporations." This was a telling detail that Hamilton knew from his research in drafting the charter of the Bank of New York in 1784, whereas Jefferson likely did not.[13]

But Hamilton was just beginning his evisceration. "There are two points in the suggestions of the Secretary of State which have been noted that are peculiarly incorrect. One is, that the proposed incorporation is against the laws of monopoly, because it stipulates an exclusive right of banking under the national authority. The other is that it gives power to the institution [i.e., the Bank of the United States] to make laws paramount to those of the states."[14]

On both points, Hamilton repeated, Jefferson was mistaken. The bank bill "neither prohibits any State from erecting as many banks as they please, nor any number of Individuals from associating to carry on the business." So the charge of monopoly had no basis whatever. "And with regard to the second point"—that the bill would give the bank power over state laws—"there is still less foundation." The bylaws of a bank govern only its own organization. "They are expressly not to be contrary to law; and law must here mean the law of a State as well as of the United States."[15]

Hamilton then posed a hypothetical situation: "A nation is threatened with a war. Large sums are wanted, on a sudden, to make the requisite preparations. Taxes are laid for the purpose, but it requires time to obtain the benefit of them. Anticipation is indispensible. If there be a bank, the supply can, at once be had; if there be none loans from Individuals must be sought. The progress of these is often too slow for the exigency." What Hamilton described here actually occurred twenty-one years later, in 1812, in the war between the United States and Britain. The country had no national bank at that time, and narrowly escaped financial and military catastrophe.[16]

Hamilton ended his long letter to Washington with an expression bordering on open contempt. Not only did the objections Jefferson and Randolph had raised to the bank go against what an expert would conclude about the Constitution; they also contravened "impressions that any mere spectator would entertain concerning it." Jefferson's objections in particular had stung Hamilton. And, as always when he felt personally attacked, he gave better than he received. His response made Jefferson look like a naïf, a petulant child who knew little about constitutional law and nothing about finance.[17]

Whatever its motivation, this reply of Hamilton's amounted to yet another *tour de force*—one of the most compelling documents he ever wrote. It ran to about 16,000 words, the equivalent of fifty pages in an average-sized book today. Its relentless logic quickly won President Washington's approval, and he signed the bill. Twenty-eight years later, Hamilton's paper formed the basis for chief justice John Marshall's opinion in *McCulloch v. Maryland* (1819). That case established broad implied powers for the federal government under the Constitution. Even today, it remains one of the most important decisions in the Supreme Court's history—a fact that would have pleased Hamilton for many reasons. Among the founders, he had always been among the most ardent proponents of judicial review, and Jefferson among the least ardent.[18]

After Hamilton's bank bill became law, he caused the Treasury to issue $2 million in federal bonds for the purchase of 5,000 shares of bank stock at the standard price of $400 per share. He thereby provided the $2 million public capital specified in his plan. The Bank of the United States then lent $2 million to the federal government, at an annual interest rate of 6 percent. This kind of adroit gambit was not specified in Hamilton's original *Report*. Indeed, it seemed to have been forbidden by the proviso that the bank could not lend any government more than $50,000. The maneuver was an example not only of Hamilton's audacity, but also of the lengths to which he was forced to go because of the financial straits of the federal government. He had anticipated such a possibility when he included the phrase "unless previously authorized by law" in his original *Report*. Congress authorized the $2 million loan, in Section 11 of the bank's charter.

When it came time to choose a president for the new institution, the bank's directors elected the distinguished Philadelphian Thomas Willing. Again, this former partner of Robert Morris and mayor of the city filled an important financial role, as he had done earlier when he headed the Bank of North America. Willing served with distinction and remained president of the Bank of the United States from 1791 until poor health forced him to resign in 1807.[19]

So, in the end, Hamilton got his bank, just as he had won his fight over funding and assumption. He seemed to be conquering every obstacle. The American economy was beginning to boom, the new federal bonds were selling above their face value, state taxes were declining because of the federal assumption of state debts, and Hamilton was running circles around the native-born opposition.[20]

But he was paying a heavy price for his victories. The extreme pressure from continuous opposition by figures as formidable as Jefferson and Madison would have strained anyone. The scornful tone in parts of his response to Jefferson's protests over the bank signaled that Hamilton might be starting to crack under the pressure. However tough he could be, he was only human, and he had his weaknesses.

FIGURE 7. The Bank of the United States, in Philadelphia. Its grand façade symbolizes Hamilton's vision for the nation's financial system. The building was completed in 1797 and still stands today, on Third Street. It has red-brick sides that do not show up well in this engraving.

One of these was for women, as had become evident earlier, during his time in the army. In the summer of 1791, shortly after his bank victory, he became involved in a passionate affair with a beautiful twenty-three-year-old swindler named Maria Reynolds, whom he allowed to seduce him. She and her husband had devised a clever scheme to blackmail Hamilton into giving them inside information about Treasury business from which they could profit. They took advantage of Eliza Hamilton's absence from Philadelphia during much of the summer (along with the Hamiltons' children, she spent several months in Albany visiting her parents). Maria Reynolds pressed the affair with the isolated Hamilton, and he did little to resist. Ultimately, he paid blackmail money to the Reynoldses but never disclosed any facts about the Treasury that would have aided their more ambitious scheme. The affair ended early in 1792, about ten months after it began.[21]

Inevitably, since the community of government in Philadelphia was so small, some members of Congress became aware of what was happening. A committee of three confronted Hamilton, who managed to persuade them that his sins were entirely of the flesh and did not compromise the duties of his office. The congressmen remained quiet, and Hamilton was lucky to escape exposure. Not until five years later, in 1797, did the full details of the Reynolds affair become public, in spectacular revelations described later in this book (see Chapter 13).

Meanwhile, Hamilton's financial system, including the Bank of the United States, was being firmly woven into the fabric of American finance. By 1800, in addition to the flagship institution in Philadelphia, there were four branches of the bank (in Boston, New York, Baltimore, and Charleston), and four more were about to be created (in Norfolk, Savannah, Washington, and New Orleans). Individual states had authorized nearly thirty other banks, whose charters largely followed Hamilton's model for the Bank of the United States. Its provision for limited liability was one of the keys to the success not only of the Bank of the United States but also of the many state banks that followed in its train. Limited liability meant that shareholders did not have to risk their entire personal fortunes, as they did in most English banks, which were organized as partnerships. The American financial system was now on its way to becoming the best in the world, and Hamilton's triumph could hardly have been more sweeping.[22]

CHAPTER 11

Diversifying the Economy

Hamilton was determined to make the American economy broad and diverse. It should have vibrant manufacturing, financial, and trading sectors, as well as agricultural. In late 1791, he issued the third of his major treatises as secretary of the treasury: the *Report on the Subject of Manufactures*. Now almost thirty-five years old, he was the most powerful person in the country with the exception of Washington. In preparing his *Report*, he read still more economic treatises and deluged his subordinates with questions and requests for statistics. He worked on the document periodically for eleven months, writing at least five drafts. He sent it to Congress in December 1791, a year after his proposal for the Bank of the United States.

The *Report on the Subject of Manufactures* presented a panoramic analysis of the American economy and Hamilton's vision of its future. He explored the relationship between agriculture and industry, the proper role of manufacturing, the contours of the American business system, and the best methods to promote economic growth. As in his first two reports, Hamilton addressed some extremely contentious subjects—in this case, even more multifaceted than public credit and the bank.

Compared to the two earlier reports, the *Report on the Subject of Manufactures* is less a legislative program than a philosophical discussion of the problems and opportunities facing a developing country. As with the other documents, Hamilton's immigrant origins helped him to see with unusual clarity both the country as it was and what it might become. His frame of reference, as always, was the nation as a whole. Despite his growing ties to New York, his *Report* contained no special pleading for any state or section.

Rather, the document radiated with suggestions for the application of energetic government to promote manufacturing nationwide. It was what today would be called a "macroeconomic" plan. "Macroeconomics," a word not invented until the twentieth century, is about aggregates, and Hamilton—remarkably—wrote of "the *aggregate* prosperity of manufactures, and the *aggregate* prosperity of Agriculture," adding that the two "are intimately connected." Toward the end of the document, he reiterated that "in the affairs of a Country, to increase the total mass of industry and opulence, is ultimately beneficial to every part of it."[1]

Hamilton began the *Report* with a discussion of the existing popular consensus on the superiority of agriculture to other economic pursuits. This notion boiled down to the proposition that it is more "natural" for people to toil in fields than in shops or factories—the closer to nature, the better. In the 1780s Jefferson had written, in his book *Notes on the State of Virginia*, that "those who labour in the earth are the chosen people of God, if ever he had a chosen people . . . While we have land to labour, then, let us never wish to see our citizens occupied at a workbench . . . The mobs of great cities add just so much to the support of pure government, as sores do to the strength of the human body."[2]

Anticipating the protests of Jefferson and Madison (who did indeed greet his *Report* with hostility), Hamilton praised agriculture but declared that commerce and manufacturing were no less natural, virtuous, or necessary. He framed part of his argument in the context of a world given to the kind of almost constant warfare that had characterized the eighteenth century. Such a world, he pointed out, posed continual dangers to an agrarian country unable either to buy the items necessary for its self-defense or to manufacture its own. Every nation needed "the means of *Subsistence habitation clothing* and *defence* . . . The extreme embarrassments of the United States during the late War, from an incapacity of supplying themselves [with needed food, clothing, and munitions], are still matter of keen recollection."[3]

In a more general sense, he wrote, "The substitution of foreign for domestic manufactures is a transfer to foreign nations of the advantages accruing from the employment of Machinery." This, in itself, was a powerful reason to mechanize parts of the American economy. The country suffered from a chronic shortage of workers and would benefit mightily from the use of labor-saving machinery.[4]

Thinking broadly about human nature, Hamilton argued that adding industry to agriculture would satisfy Americans' inherent drive to employ their talents to the fullest. "The results of human exertion may be immensely increased by diversifying its objects. When all the different kinds of industry obtain in a community, each individual can find his proper element, and can call into activity the whole vigour of his nature." Allowing people to do what they did best would benefit the entire community. "The spirit of enterprise," as he called it, "must be less in a nation of mere cultivators, than in a nation of cultivators and merchants; less in a nation of cultivators and merchants, than in a nation of cultivators, artificers and merchants."[5]

Hamilton then pointed out that the United States in 1791

had far more land than people to inhabit it. In this "very peculiar situation," the attraction of cheap land would likely cause too many settlers to move to the countryside. There, they would produce more crops than they could sell either at home or in overseas markets, where U.S. products were often shut out by imperial restrictions. "The United States are to a certain extent in the situation of a country precluded from foreign Commerce." Imports would continue to come in, but exports would remain limited. The need for a more diversified economy was therefore self-evident.[6]

Workers who remained in commercial and manufacturing centers, rather than moving to cheap lands as farmers, would not only produce finished goods; along with their families, they would also augment the domestic market for food. As immigration continued, the whole process would become a virtuous economic circle. If this did not occur, Hamilton warned, "the prospect of a successful competition with the manufactures of Europe must be regarded as little less than desperate . . . If Europe will not take from us the products of our soil, upon terms consistent with our interest, the natural remedy is to contract [i.e., reduce] as fast as possible our wants of her."[7]

But to contract America's wants from Europe meant manufacturing them at home, in North America. Hamilton then stated, in the most prescient sentence in his entire *Report,* that skilled immigrants "would probably flock from Europe to the United States to pursue their own trades or professions, if they were once made sensible of the advantages they would enjoy." He had already taken steps to induce what he called "artificers" (master craftsmen) to emigrate from the Old World to the New.[8]

This was often a dangerous business for both the artificers and anyone trying to persuade them to leave. At that time, Britain—the clear leader in the emerging industrial revolution—had strict laws against the emigration of trained craftsmen or even the export of machinery. As Hamilton's ally Thomas Digges wrote him from Belfast, any "person attempting to inviegle away an artist is subject not only to very rough treatment, but a fine of 500£ & 12 months imprisonment." Nevertheless, Digges, a native of Maryland, reported that he himself had "been the means of sending [to America] 18 or 20 very valuable artists [i.e., artisans] & machine makers in the course of last year."[9]

One of several Americans engaged in recruiting foreign craftsmen, Digges had also ordered from a Dublin bookseller 100 copies of Hamilton's *Report on the Subject of Manufactures,* "in order to distribute it with ease, & for disseminating its information among many Manufactoring Societys here as well as in England, (where I will take 3 or 400 Copys in a few days) and by so getting it read, induce artists to move." Like Hamilton, Digges and others wanted to bring the emerging industrial revolution to the United States: "The beauty & benefits of *machinery* is such, & has so much reduced the [cost of] manufacture of various articles, by the reduction of manual labour, as to make it incredible to those who have not seen and contemplated machinery."[10]

Foreign artisans had already begun to move to the United States, bringing with them the early fruits of the machine-based industrial revolution. The most conspicuous example was Samuel Slater, who immigrated in 1789, the same year Hamilton became secretary of the treasury. In England, Slater had apprenticed in a water-powered cotton mill designed on principles pioneered by Richard Arkwright, the greatest inventor-entrepreneur of Britain's mushrooming textile industry. During the years of his apprenticeship, Slater had committed to memory the details of Arkwright's machinery and factory design. With the blueprints imprinted on his brain, Slater disguised himself as a farm boy and slipped out of England on a ship bound for the United States.[11]

He arrived in New York and soon moved to Providence, Rhode Island. There he entered into partnership with members of the Brown family, who functioned as early venture capitalists.

The Browns—for whom today's Brown University is named—had grown wealthy through Atlantic commerce. They wished to funnel part of their fortune into domestic manufacture, exactly the kind of sequence Hamilton had in mind. They had built a cotton mill, but lacked the expertise to put together the complex machinery and make it work.[12]

Samuel Slater supplied this expertise. His first mill, erected at nearby Pawtucket Falls, produced machine-spun cotton thread, which became the foundation of the industrial revolution in America. Cotton cloth was far cheaper than silks or woolens, and, unlike them, could be repeatedly washed. Within two decades, cotton came to dominate the huge markets for clothing, bed linens, curtains, and sailcloth. Men could now afford five or six shirts made of cotton, rather than one or two made of wool; women, a half-dozen dresses, rather than the usual two. Cheap cotton cloth also made underwear available to masses of people for the first time in human history. (Few people could afford silk or linen, and wool was far too scratchy.) In the *Report on the Subject of Manufactures,* Hamilton mentioned the "celebrated cotton mill" near Providence as an example of how manufactures might develop in the United States.[13]

⸺⸙⸺

He went on to point out that the rapidly recovering national economy made the time ripe for promoting manufactures in a way that would have been impossible during the depressed 1780s. "Industry in general seems to have been reanimated. There are symptoms indicating an extension of our Commerce. Our navigation [shipping] has certainly of late had a considerable spring, and there appears to be in many parts of the Union a command of capital, which till lately . . . was unknown." Here Hamilton was not only stating the facts, but implicitly praising the success of his own programs: funding the national debt at par, assuming the state debts, and setting up the Bank of the United States. "Since the Revolution, the States, in which manufactures have most increased, have recovered fastest from the

injuries of the late War, and abound most in pecuniary resources." Still, because market forces alone would not accomplish the object of promoting manufactures on a national basis,
it "may therefore require the incitement and patronage of government."[14]

But how? Toward this end, Hamilton put forward a host of
proposals. He argued that the usual European method—a high
tariff designed to protect domestic manufacturers against cheap
imports—must be used with special restraint by the United
States. The country's fiscal program depended on relatively low
tariffs on British imports as a reliable source of revenue. High
protective tariffs would help manufacturers, but would also
raise consumer prices and reduce the federal government's income.

About 90 percent of that income derived from tariffs, of
which three-quarters came from British imports. Hamilton
therefore proposed, and the House of Representatives passed
(by a vote of 37 to 20), tariff increases that would help domestic manufacturers in a few industries without being so prohibi-
tively high as to exclude imports altogether. These increases
covered only fourteen items, such as nails and spikes (from one
cent to two cents per pound), sailcloth (from 5 percent of its
wholesale price to 10 percent), firearms and weapons (5 percent to 15 percent), printed books (5 percent to 10 percent),
and iron (7.5 percent to 10 percent).[15]

Hamilton called for no changes in existing tariffs on several
common items such as lead manufactures, and he asked for de-
creases in tariffs on raw materials needed by domestic American producers. The tariff on sulfur for gunpowder would drop
from 5 percent to zero, as would tariffs on copper, silk, and sci-
entific books.[16]

His most controversial proposal applied to "bounties"—that
is, direct subsidies paid by the federal government to producers
of such items as wool, window glass, and cotton cloth. He cited
the common practice of many industrialized countries in granting bounties, and went on to enumerate their special advan-

tages. They were "more positive and direct" than any other method, and would produce quicker results. They would avoid "the inconvenience of a temporary augmentation of price," which was one of the disadvantages of tariffs. And bounties did not, like protective tariffs, have "a tendency to produce scarcity."[17]

Here, however, Congress drew the line, even though bounties had proved useful in promoting industry in other countries. Because bounties would inevitably be paid to some manufacturers but not others, the method could be portrayed as unfair. And the administration of such a system would open the door to corruption after Hamilton left office. He himself remained enthusiastic about the use of bounties—but in the context of the American polity, the method was not in the cards, whatever its economic merits. Jefferson, Madison, and their allies opposed nearly everything in the *Report,* and the section on bounties gave them useful ammunition.

So did Hamilton's work in promoting the Society for the Establishment of Useful Manufactures (formed earlier in 1791). This was a mostly tax-exempt public-private corporation aimed at developing an industrial park in northern New Jersey, near the fifty-foot falls of the Passaic River. In his *Report,* Hamilton listed seventeen manufactured products for which there would be "an encouraging assurance of success in future attempts." These products included paper, pottery, carpets, and wire. But the Society failed at first because the requisite investment capital, supply of artisans, and management expertise did not yet exist in the United States. The basic idea, however, ultimately succeeded. By 1820, the city of Paterson had become one of the leading industrial centers in the country, its mills powered by the Passaic River falls.[18]

———

Apart from tariff adjustments, Congress mostly ignored Hamilton's *Report on the Subject of Manufactures*—not because it was incorrect in its analysis, but for three other reasons. First, during 1790 and 1791 the House and Senate had debated at extraordinary length Hamilton's proposals for funding the debt at par, assuming the states' debts, and establishing the Bank of the United States. The country's political system could absorb only so much, and Hamilton's third major *Report* went too far, at least in the immediate practical sense. Then, too, the *Report* ran into what by now had become a reflexively negative response from Hamilton's enemies to anything that he proposed. Both Madison and Jefferson denounced the document. And some of the secretary's suggestions, however fertile and imaginative, were ahead of their time. As the experience in Passaic with the Society for the Promotion of Useful Manufactures showed, the nation did not yet possess the necessary resources to implement parts of his plan.

On the other hand, as a philosophical meditation on the position of the United States in the world and the future of the national economy, the *Report on the Subject of Manufactures* was the most thoughtful and far-seeing of all Hamilton's writings. As the economist Joseph Schumpeter wrote 150 years later, it represented "'applied economics' at its best"—a thoroughgoing plan for the development of a nation. Schumpeter went on to say that Hamilton "was one of those rare practitioners of economic policy who think it worth while to acquire more analytical economics than that smattering that does such good service in addressing audiences of a certain type."[19]

Like Schumpeter, who became an academic pioneer in the study of entrepreneurship, Hamilton attached great importance to the innovating role of an entrepreneurial elite. The Jeffersonians, by contrast, put conspicuous faith in yeoman farmers and urban mechanics, and in doing so reaped major political dividends. Hamilton believed that real economic breakthroughs required the leadership of visionaries like himself, whether in the public or the private sector. He did not, as his enemies charged, favor the rich so much as he respected talented entrepreneurs and managers, whom he regarded as scarce assets.

This is why he wanted to encourage the immigration of people like Samuel Slater, and to put them in touch with investors like the Brown family of Providence.[20]

———⊶⊷———

Hamilton remained in office until early 1795, implementing the legislation he had sponsored from 1790 to 1793—and in most cases had written himself. He oversaw the conversion of an economy that had long been in depression to one of booming prosperity, and he knew that he himself had been the major contributor to the change. As the historian Richard Sylla has pointed out, when Hamilton became secretary of the treasury in 1789, the United States had no plan for funding its huge debts. It had no stable currency, no sound credit system, no central bank, no reliable securities markets, and almost no corporations. By 1795, Hamilton's policies had corrected all of these deficiencies. The United States enjoyed the highest credit rating in European financial markets of any country in the world. Hamilton endured enormous personal abuse during these years, but he also had the satisfaction of seeing most of "my commercial system" put into place.[21]

In addition to causing the establishment of the Bank of the United States and devising a system to fund the debt, Hamilton had created a hospitable setting for large privately financed enterprises. During the entire colonial period, only eight for-profit corporations had been chartered in what became the United States. During the 1790s, 311 such corporations were chartered, almost all by individual states for public purposes: turnpikes, bridges, canals, banks, waterworks, and fire and marine insurance companies. A total of 3,884 entrepreneurs participated in these ventures, pooling their capital for expensive projects. Most could not have done so without the corporate form, which offered limited liability to stockholders, the opportunity to buy and sell shares, and—barring bankruptcy and liquidation—institutional permanence. Proprietorships and partnerships usually ended when individual businesspeople died. Corporations endured. Their abuses would have to be regulated by governments, but they held tremendous advantages over other forms of business organization.[22]

What Hamilton's policies had achieved, in combination with events, was the promotion of long-term business confidence, setting the stage for the release of immense economic energy. His programs had helped to shape the distinctive American balance between political stability on the one hand and capacity for economic growth on the other. They had made it plausible for entrepreneurs to think big thoughts and entertain risky new ventures. They had made it easier for energetic individuals, whatever their social or national origins, to rise in American society, just as Hamilton himself, a poor boy from abroad, had done. In his time, such a rise was restricted mostly to white men. Over the very long term, white women and people of color would have much better opportunities as well.[23]

It had all been a great adventure, a monumental achievement of planning and execution. The 1790s turned out to be a remarkably prosperous decade, far more so than the 1770s or 1780s. The economy expanded rapidly and the capabilities of the federal government grew, in both cases aided by emerging networks of communications. The number of post offices increased from 75 to 903, the mileage of post roads from 1,875 to 21,000, the number of newspapers from under 100 to 250.[24]

Hamilton alone cannot be credited with these changes, of course. But he excelled as an administrator, as well as an economic visionary and planner. Beginning in 1789, he imposed a new discipline on the financial staff he had inherited from the Confederation period and on the customs services formerly run by the individual states. He caused a quantum leap in the efficiency of these officials, and far beyond that of the prewar British colonial administrators. Hamilton and his successors needed (and, because of his reforms, received) reliable schedules for the receipt and disbursement of funds, solid data on a variety of other economic matters, and accurate reports on changing conditions—all delivered by a corps of dependable subordinates. This was a singular accomplishment, without which the funding and assumption plans, the Bank of the United States, and the entire fiscal system could not have worked well.[25]

Had Hamilton been less brilliant, less intrepid, or less persistent in pursuing these goals, we would likely never have heard of him. Certainly he would not be ranked among the major founders, alongside Franklin, Washington, Adams, Jefferson, and Madison. He possessed supreme talents and honed them with constant study and dedication. He seemed able to outwork any of his contemporaries and to elicit the best efforts from the Treasury's civil servants. The political scientist Leonard D. White, an eminent scholar not given to overstatement, wrote in 1948 that Hamilton was "the greatest administrative genius of his generation in America, and one of the great administrators of all time."[26]

In pursuit of his goals, which could hardly have been more ambitious, Hamilton had exerted almost superhuman effort for more than twenty years. He had filled many roles: as a teenaged pamphleteer justifying strong action against Britain; as a captain of artillery and as Washington's aide-de-camp during the War of Independence; as a moving spirit behind the Constitutional Convention of 1787; and as the principal author of *The Federalist Papers*, whose purpose was to get the Constitution ratified. Once he became secretary of the treasury, he had devised a comprehensive and audacious economic program for the new nation and had persuaded Congress to enact it. Almost from the moment of his arrival from St. Croix, he had composed reams of letters, pamphlets, essays, speeches, and reports—of compelling persuasive power. Theodore Roosevelt judged that Hamilton was "the most brilliant American statesman who ever lived, possessing the loftiest and keenest intellect of his time."[27]

FIGURE 8.
Alexander
Hamilton in
1792, then
thirty-five and
at the height of
his powers
as secretary of
the treasury.
Portrait by John
Trumbull.

FIGURE 9.
Portrait bust of
Alexander Hamilton
by Giuseppe Ceracchi,
c. 1793—a likeness
especially treasured
by Eliza Hamilton
and other family
members.

FIGURE 10. Alexander Hamilton in his later thirties, painted by John Trumbull in 1804 from his own earlier portraits and sketches. This is one of the best-known of all Hamilton images, showing what one of his sisters-in-law called "a face never to be forgotten."

Four of Hamilton's compositions would remain classics forever. His three great *Reports*—on public credit, the Bank of the United States, and manufactures—have been republished many times in the years since he wrote them. Their total length is the equivalent of a 220-page book. Along with contributions to the classic *Federalist Papers*, a landmark 500-page book still widely sold today, Hamilton's *Reports* attest to the power of his thought and its continuing relevance to contemporary issues.

In 1789, only seventeen years after his arrival in North America, he received the chance to design the outlines of a national economy. This was not a job for the faint-hearted under the best of circumstances—and one all but unknown in modern history for so young a person, let alone an illegitimate immigrant to a new country. And in undertaking the task, Hamilton soon found himself involved in something approaching mortal combat against two of the most talented, powerful, and highly pedigreed men in the country: James Madison, the principal author of the Constitution; and Thomas Jefferson, the draftsman of the Declaration of Independence. Among the many consequences of his ceaseless conflicts with these two other eminent founders was the evolution of the nation's first political party system.

CHAPTER 12

Tensions and Political Parties

The Constitution said nothing about organized political parties. Yet the subject was hardly absent from the minds of the delegates to the Philadelphia Convention of 1787 or to the state ratification conventions that followed. An enormous amount of discussion and argument centered on "factions" and "parties." Few delegates to any of the conventions wished to replicate the recent English tradition of Tories versus Whigs, with alternating majorities in Parliament and attendant systems of patronage. Most delegates favored a representative republic that could somehow remain immune to these institutions, which, like the monarchy, would lead to corruption.

On the other hand, many delegates—and hundreds of other influential politicians throughout the country—did question whether a *large* republic would work well. Citing Montesquieu and other writers, they argued that only small and homogeneous republics could survive over the long term. They feared that the kind of republic contemplated by the Constitution would split apart. The country was just too big and diverse: South versus North, big states versus small, slave states versus free, farmers versus merchants, poor people versus rich. The better solution, some argued, would be a loose confederation of about three units: New England, the Middle Atlantic states, and the agrarian and slaveholding South. Most political power would remain with the individual states.

The size of a viable republic was one of the most difficult questions that supporters of the Constitution had to address. In *Federalist* No. 9, published in 1787, Hamilton raised it directly, citing "the tempestuous waves of sedition and party rage" that had plagued "the petty [city-state] republics of Greece and Italy." Titling his piece "The Utility of the Union as a Safeguard against Domestic Faction and Insurrection," he began to point the way toward a possible resolution of the issue.[1]

In an immediate follow-up with the same title "continued," James Madison wrote in *Federalist* No. 10 a rich and eloquent essay that made No. 10 the most widely quoted of all eighty-five *Federalist Papers*. In essence, Madison argued that the division of authority between state and federal governments, together with the choice of trustworthy congressmen and senators, would make a big republic more practicable than a small one—"the great and aggregate interests being referred to the national, the local and particular to the State legislatures."[2]

In the large republic envisioned for the United States, Madison wrote, the diversity of elements in the national government would cancel out narrow partisan interests. None could gain a majority in the national legislature without compromising with other "parties"—a word Madison construed as what he called "factions" and what today would be called "interest groups." The achievement of a voting majority for any bill in both the House and Senate would become difficult, thereby protecting the interests of all groups. Only policies with broad national appeal would be enacted.

Madison's *Federalist* No. 10 has often been analyzed by political scientists, historians, lawyers, and judges. Interpretations of its meaning, like that of the Constitution itself, have diverged according to the use a given writer has wished to make of the argument. But most analysts have agreed that the thrust of both Hamilton's *Federalist* No. 9 and Madison's No. 10 opposed the rise of political parties. As Justice John Paul Stevens wrote in a Supreme Court decision of the year 2000 that cited *Federalist* No. 10, "Parties ranked high on the list of evils that the Constitution was designed to check."[3]

That dream, of course, did not come true. Within five years after Hamilton and Madison wrote their essays, a full-fledged American party system was emerging. Among the many causes, three stood out, beginning with the split over Hamilton's financial system. The closely related issue of foreign policy deepened the fissure. The Jeffersonians habitually called their opponents "Anglomen" for their alleged preference for England over France, while Hamilton and his allies countered by labeling the Jeffersonians "Francophiles." The third element in the rise of organized parties was the inflammatory tone of newspapers, which could turn simmering differences into public infernos, like oil poured onto a roaring fire.

In 1790, Madison's opposition in Congress to Hamilton's funding and assumption bills had caught the secretary of the treasury completely by surprise. Madison's new stance seemed to come out of nowhere, and it jolted Hamilton as much as anything that happened during his years as secretary. It foreshadowed an almost irreparable rift between Washington and Hamilton on the one hand and Madison and Jefferson on the other. It also presaged the origins of the first party system: the Republican Party of Madison and Jefferson; the Federalist Party of Washington, John Adams, and Hamilton.

In 1792, Hamilton described his feelings about what he saw as Madison's betrayal in a long letter to Edward Carrington, a Virginia friend whom he had known in the army. (Carrington was also a collector of customs at this time, which made him technically a subordinate of Hamilton.) The letter was one of the most candid and heartfelt that Hamilton ever wrote, and it was not made public until long after his death:

> When I accepted the Office, I now hold, it was under a full persuasion, that from similarity of thinking, conspiring with personal goodwill, I should have the firm support of Mr. Madison, in the *general course* of my administration. Aware of the intrinsic difficulties of the situation and of the powers of Mr. Madison, I do not believe I should have accepted [the appointment as secretary] under a different supposition.
>
> I have mentioned the similarity of thinking between that Gentleman and myself. This was relative not merely to the general principles of National Policy and Government but to the leading points which were likely to constitute questions in the administration of the finances. I mean (1) the expediency of *funding* the debt (2) the inexpediency of *discrimination* between original and present holders (3) The expediency of *assuming* the state Debts.[4]

Madison had clearly expressed his support for funding and assumption at par in comments he made at the Confederation Congress during 1783, when Robert Morris was superintendent of finance. If internal debts were not assumed by the federal government, Madison had averred, "What then would become of the confederation? What would be the authority of Congress? What the tie by which the States could be held together?" Now, with no warning to Hamilton, Madison was reversing himself on the biggest and longest-standing financial questions faced by the American government.[5]

"Add to this," Hamilton continued in his letter to Carrington, "that a variety of conversations had taken place between him and myself respecting the public debt down to the commencement of the New Government in none of which had he glanced at the idea of a change of opinion. I wrote him a letter after my appointment [as secretary, in 1789] in the recess of Congress to obtain his sentiments on the subject of the Finances. In his answer there is not a lisp of his new system."[6]

Hamilton believed that Madison had then double-crossed him a second time on "the question of an assumption of the state Debts by the U States." That issue "was in discussion when the convention that framed the present Government was sitting at Philadelphia; and in a long conversation, which I had with Mr. Madison in an afternoon's walk I well remember that we were perfectly agreed in the expediency and propriety of such a measure."[7]

Mystified and hurt by Madison's reversals, Hamilton surmised that they derived from two sources: the views of Madison's Virginia constituents and those of his close friend Thomas Jefferson, the secretary of state. Jefferson, Hamilton wrote, "with very little reserve manifests his dislike of the funding system generally; calling in question the expediency of funding a debt at all." A stronger reason was that, in both Madison and Jefferson's eyes, Hamilton's financial program bore too much resemblance to that of Britain—a nation both men detested. But Hamilton did not yet understand the depth of their convictions.[8]

Several months after the battle over assumption of state debts, Jefferson's adamant objections to the Bank of the United States once more stung Hamilton. In Jefferson's letter to President Washington about the bank bill, Hamilton told Carrington, Jefferson had "not only delivered an opinion in writing against its constitutionality & expediency; but he did it *in a stile and manner* which I felt as partaking of asperity and ill humour towards me."[9]

In the fight over the Bank of the United States, as with the funding and assumption bills, Hamilton wrote, "I prevailed." Yet his repeated victories only enraged the Virginians all the more. "This current of success on one side & defeat on the other have rendered the Opposition furious, & have produced a disposition to subvert their Competitors even at the expence of the Government." Henry Knox, the secretary of war, was being attacked as well—"a man who generally thinks with me & who has a portion of the Presidents good Will & confidence."[10]

Hamilton had concluded, he wrote Carrington—underlining the passage for emphasis—"*That Mr. Madison cooperating with Mr. Jefferson is at the head of a faction decidedly hostile to me and my administration, and actuated by views in my judgment subversive of the principles of good government and dangerous to the union, peace and happiness of the Country.*" He went on to say, in words perhaps more prophetic than even he realized, that "'Tis evident beyond a question, from every movement, that Mr. Jefferson aims with ardent desire at the Presidential Chair." The words in this long letter, Hamilton acknowledged, were "strong expressions." But, however candid and indiscreet, they were mailed privately to his old friend Carrington, who had no real political power.[11]

On May 23, 1792, three days before Hamilton wrote to Carrington, Thomas Jefferson had sent a blistering letter to President Washington about Hamilton and what Jefferson believed to be undue influence in Congress by monied interests. He referred again and again to "the corrupt squadron of paper dealers" who were debauched by Hamilton's funding, assumption, and bank schemes and who threatened the existence of republican government. If unchecked, the financial system "will be the instrument for producing in future a king, lord and commons, or whatever else those who direct it may chuse." Never one to understate his case, Jefferson informed Washington that it would all end in "the most corrupt government on earth, if the means of their corruption be not prevented."[12]

Jefferson went on to say that "whenever Northern and Southern prejudices have come into conflict, the latter have been sacrificed and the former soothed"—a remarkable statement in light of the slavery question. The public debt also remained controversial. Jefferson, who for most of his life was heavily in debt to a variety of American and English creditors, no doubt believed, as he said, "that the owers of the debt are in the Southern and the holders of it in the Northern division." But he had framed the question incorrectly, betraying his poor understanding of finance. The owers of the public debt were the American people as a whole, not those of one section more than another. Then, too, as recent research has confirmed, holders of the debt included wealthy investors in Virginia, South Carolina, and other southern states, who had purchased substantial quantities of federal bonds.[13]

Washington paraphrased Jefferson's letter and sent it to Hamilton over his own signature, keeping intact the expression "corrupt squadron" and many other passages without identifying their original author. Hamilton, as was his habit, counterattacked with a long and scathing response. He defended his financial system and vigorously denied what Jefferson had called his "Monarchical" aims.[14]

At this point, the only thing Hamilton and Jefferson seemed to agree on was that Washington must remain president for a second term. Washington himself, heartsick over the bitter feuding between his two closest cabinet advisers, wrote them both in late August 1792, pleading for more harmony. He was not successful. On September 9, 1792, both Hamilton and Jefferson replied to Washington, each denouncing the other in vehement language:

> *Hamilton:* "I *know* that I have been an object of uniform opposition from Mr. Jefferson, from the first moment of his coming to the City of New York to enter upon his present office. I *know,* from the most authentic sources, that I have been the frequent subject of the most unkind whispers and insinuating them from the same quarter. I have long seen a formed party in the Legislature, under his auspices, bent upon my subversion."

> *Jefferson:* "When I embarked in the government, it was with a determination to intermeddle not at all with the legislature, and as little as possible with my co-departments. The

first and only instance of variance from the former part of my resolution, I was duped into by the Secretary of the treasury, and made a tool for forwarding his schemes not then sufficiently understood by me [i.e., the bargain of 1790 that traded assumption of state debts for moving the capital to Washington, D.C.]; and of all the errors of my political life, this has occasioned me the deepest regret . . . If it has been supposed that I have ever intrigued among the members of the legislature to defeat the plans of the Secretary of the Treasury, it is contrary to all truth."

Hamilton: "As long as I saw no danger to the Government, from the machinations which were going on, I resolved to be a silent sufferer of the injuries that were done me . . . But when I no longer doubted . . . I considered it as a duty, to endeavour to resist the torrent, and as an essential mean to this end, to draw aside the veil from the principal Actors."

Jefferson: "When I came into this office, it was with a resolution to retire from it as soon as I could with decency . . . I will not suffer my retirement to be clouded by the slanders of a man whose history, from the moment at which history can stoop to notice him, is a tissue of machinations against the liberty of the country which has not only received and given him bread, but heaped it's [*sic*] honors on his head."

This allusion to Hamilton's immigrant origins was rare for Jefferson, though not for many of his allies.[15]

It is worth remembering that whereas Jefferson and Madison came from wealthy, distinguished, and long-established Virginia families, Hamilton had arrived in North America as an unaccompanied immigrant—a destitute, illegitimate fifteen-year-old. He knew not a soul and had only tenuous connections through letters of recommendation. In an era that valued honor above all other virtues, he had been forced to create his own out of whole cloth. And however heroic his service in the War of Independence had been, however high he married up into the Schuyler family, and to whatever heights he rose in the councils of the nation, he was always fighting against his own questionable past.

The psychological effects of his unusual predicament could hardly have been clearer. In December 1792, three months after Jefferson's letter to Washington, Hamilton wrote his friend John Jay: "Tis not the load of proper official business that alone engrosses me; though this would be enough to occupy any man. Tis not the extra attentions I am obliged to pay to the course of legislative manoeuvres that alone add to my burthen and perplexity. Tis the malicious intrigues to stab me in the dark, against which I am too often obliged to guard myself, that distract and harass me to a point, which rendering my situation scarcely tolerable interferes with objects to which friendship and inclination would prompt me."[16]

Jefferson's most drastic act came just a month after Hamilton wrote these words. In January 1793 he secretly composed ten resolutions condemning Hamilton and gave them to his fellow Virginian, Representative William Branch Giles, for introduction into the House. (Jefferson's authorship was not discovered until 1895, a century later.) The tenth resolution read: "That the Secretary of the Treasury has been guilty of maladministration in the duties of his office, and should, in the opinion of Congress, be removed from his office by the President of the United States." Giles, though something of a hothead, deleted this tenth item and softened some of the others. When he introduced them in the House, all nine were defeated by a large margin.[17]

So the wish to avoid a party system had perished, perhaps inevitably, over strong differences in views about the country's future. The impending war between Britain and France, together with provocative newspaper coverage of Republican and

Federalist politics, cemented the party system into American government.

———◆———

In 1793, Britain and France began a war that would last twenty-two years, until the final defeat of Napoleon at Waterloo in 1815. During much of this war, France and especially Britain purchased large quantities of American goods. Most of those cargoes were carried in thousands of American merchant ships—neutrals in the "carrying trade" and therefore, in principle, not subject to attack by either side. Periodically, however, even in the war's early phases, one belligerent or the other would attack American commercial ships and seize their contents. Britain, with the more powerful navy of the two, took great pains to prevent American cargoes from reaching France or its allies.

In 1792, Hamilton had foreseen a mortal danger to the United States in the emerging hostilities. Both Madison and Jefferson were enamored of France and favored commercial sanctions against Britain, which they despised. The phenomenon of Anglophobia ran deep in most parts of the United States, and remained a strong element in arguments over the nation's foreign policy for at least two generations after 1776. Many Americans believed that Britain was intent on recolonizing the United States. "This disposition," Hamilton wrote, "goes to a length particularly in Mr. Jefferson of which, till lately, I had no adequate Idea. Various circumstances prove to me that if these Gentlemen were left to pursue their own course there would be in less than six months *an open War between the U States & Great Britain.*"[18]

Such a war would devastate America's financial system. The Treasury relied almost completely on tariffs, and Britain was by far the biggest exporter to the United States. The stark fact was that the government was essentially running on levies charged against British imports. Hamilton, taking up his pen once more, wrote a series of ten newspaper articles over the signatures "Pacificus" and "Americanus," arguing against helping France in its war against Britain. That kind of policy would hurt the Americans far more than the British: "Nine tenths of our present revenues are derived from commercial duties," and "a substitute cannot be found in other sources of taxation, without imposing heavy burthens on the People." As secretary of the treasury, Hamilton dealt with this issue every day, whereas Madison and Jefferson did not. But no one questioned that something had to be done about Britain's depredations against American shipping.[19]

Facing the possibility of war, President Washington sent Chief Justice John Jay to London in 1794. Jay's assignment was to negotiate a settlement of commercial issues and other disputes still pending more than a decade after the Revolution. The treaty Jay worked out, which had partly been designed by Hamilton, came before Congress in 1795 and promptly turned into the nation's biggest political dispute of the decade. The country split along both sectional and emerging party lines. The North, most businesspeople, and nearly all Federalists favored the treaty. The South, many farmers, and almost all Jeffersonians bitterly opposed it as unduly favorable toward the British.

Jefferson, having quarreled with Washington and lost every important battle to Hamilton, had left office in December 1793, before the Jay Treaty's negotiation. He had retired to Monticello, where he began to direct the building of a national political party. A very astute politician, he wrote hundreds of letters and entertained frequent visitors. The controversy over the Jay Treaty moved him to vigorous action.

—⚬⚬⚬—

Hamilton, having seen his fiscal system through to completion, left the cabinet himself at the end of January 1795, after five-

and-a-half years' service. In response to Hamilton's letter of resignation, Washington wrote what was, for him, a very warm
tribute:

> After so long an experience of your public services, I am
> naturally led, at this moment of your departure from of-
> fice—which it has always been my wish to prevent—to re-
> view them.
>
> In every relation, which you have borne to me, I have
> found that my confidence in your talents, exertions and in-
> tegrity, has been well placed. I the more freely render this
> testimony of my approbation, because I speak from oppor-
> tunities of information wch cannot deceive me, and which
> furnish satisfactory proof of your title to public regard.
>
> My most earnest wishes for your happiness will attend
> you in your retirement, and you may assure yourself of the
> sincere esteem, regard and friendship of
>
> Dear Sir Your affectionate
>
> Go: Washington[20]

At that time, the Jay Treaty had been negotiated but had not
yet come before the Senate for ratification or the House for the
funds necessary to implement it. The Federalists controlled the
Senate at this time, but the Republicans had gained a majority
in the House. They had mounted a coordinated and effective
attack against the Jay Treaty, and they expected to win. Jefferson wrote Madison from Monticello that the treaty was "the
boldest act they [the Federalists] ever ventured on to undermine
the constitution."[21]

Hamilton, meanwhile, was writing in notes to himself that
the Republicans could not seem to grasp the indissoluble connection between foreign policy and finance—between the nation's safety and the sinews of war. "Reason and experience
teach that the great mass of expence in every country proceeds
from War. Our experience has already belied the reveries of
those Dreamers or Impostors who were wont to weaken the

argument arising from this source by promising to this country perpetual peace. How narrowly have we thus far escaped a war with a great European power?" War with Britain would not only expose the United States to mortal danger, but it would also cut off its major source of revenue: tariffs on imported British goods.[22]

In response to intense Republican efforts to kill the treaty, Hamilton put his prolific pen to work yet again in the public press. Writing this time as a private citizen, he turned out another *tour de force*. During the summer of 1795, he composed twenty-eight newspaper essays in defense of the treaty, publishing them under the pseudonym "Camillus"; then four separate articles signed "Philo Camillus." He enlisted the help of the capable senator Rufus King of New York, who wrote ten additional essays, which Hamilton edited.[23]

As a rhetorical achievement, the Camillus essays approach Hamilton's performance in *The Federalist Papers*. They range widely as they explore the world situation, in addition to defending the specific provisions of the Jay Treaty. Their effectiveness is apparent from Jefferson's reaction in a letter to Madison: "Hamilton is really a colossus to the anti-republican party—without numbers, he is an host within himself. They have got themselves into a defile, where they might be finished; but too much security on the Republican part, will give time to his talents and indefatigableness to extricate them. We have had only midling performances to oppose to him—in truth, when he comes forward there is nobody but yourself who can meet him . . . [F]or god's sake take up your pen."[24]

Jefferson might have done this himself, but—ever the careful politician—he always shied away from public involvement in press controversies. Nor did Madison take up his pen in the way Jefferson had urged, and the Jay Treaty went forward. In June 1795, with Washington's strong support, the Senate ratified the treaty by a vote of 20 to 10, the two-thirds minimum that was required. This action only intensified the national uproar against the treaty. One Pennsylvania senator's home was attacked, a Kentucky senator was burned in effigy, and others voting for ratification were mercilessly vilified in print. The controversy was not about to die down.[25]

The unusual depth of sectional discord became evident during the House debate on appropriations to implement the treaty. Not much money was at stake, but a negative vote could have killed the treaty. In the initial ballot, Congressmen from the North voted 35 to 5 for the appropriations; those from the South, 41 to 3 against. Not until April 1796, ten months after the Senate's ratification, did the House finally vote to fund the treaty, by the bare margin of 51 to 48.[26]

Throughout the entire controversy, Madison and Jefferson maintained their opposition. Madison's ill-advised demand that Washington produce the official documents guiding the treaty's negotiation caused a rupture between Madison and the president—much as Jefferson's squabbles with Washington and invective against Hamilton had opened a rift between Jefferson and the president in late 1793. Prior to those episodes, Washington had been close to both men. But one of the president's greatest strengths was his sureness of judgment. In the case of a potential armed conflict, he knew better than anyone else where to draw the line. His personal intervention saved the Jay Treaty. It likely prevented a renewed war with Britain, for which the United States was wholly unprepared.[27]

In that crucial goal, the treaty succeeded. It also gave American ships freer access to Britain's Caribbean colonies and provided for the evacuation of British forts in the Northwest Territory—the present-day Midwest. It did not, however, resolve numerous other American grievances: Britain's intrigues with Indian tribes to impede westward American expansion, and—most important—Britain's forcible "impressment" of American seamen into the Royal Navy. Britain also had a list of its own unresolved grievances: the refusal of U.S. state courts to enforce payment of prewar debts to British creditors; the confiscation of property belonging to returning Loyalists in the United States; and the unsettled boundaries between British Canada and the American Northwest Territory. All of these issues, on both sides, remained mostly unresolved for more than a decade, the period prescribed in the Jay Treaty. Most of them would be decided only by the War of 1812 between Britain and the United States.[28]

Despite some of the treaty's unfavorable terms, the U.S. government could not afford to cut off its main source of income, which was duties on British imports. So although the treaty mostly favored the British, it not only averted a possible war and relieved the pressure on American commerce—it also bought precious time for the Americans to develop their economy. Washington and Hamilton had won yet again, and the Republicans could hardly have been more disappointed.

Much recent literature on this period has characterized Hamilton's approach as aspiring to the kind of "fiscal-military state" that had become a European pattern during the seventeenth and eighteenth centuries: very high taxes, large standing armies and navies, and, for some countries, aggressive expansionism. To the extent that Hamilton had a military cast of mind and was preoccupied with protecting the United States from foreign threats, this is not an implausible description. But measured by the actual levels of taxation in the United States and of American military forces relative to the population, compared to those of Britain and European powers, the characterization fails. Hamilton well knew from his long experience in the army and the Treasury that the American people would never support British or European levels of taxation or of large standing armies and navies.[29]

The protracted fight over the Jay Treaty solidified the emerging two-party system in American politics. At the same time, it increased the intensity of partisan political journalism in the United States. Newspapers allied with one group denounced policies of the other, with degrees of acrimony that grew much stronger as the 1790s progressed. The number of newspapers increased from fewer than 100 in 1790 to about 250 in 1800, aided by the Postal Service Act of 1792. That act made transmission of "exchange" copies between newspapers free, and many papers reprinted articles from others. The same 1792 legislation made mailings to subscribers extremely cheap. A spurt of growth in the number of papers toward the close of the decade gave a powerful impetus to the Republican Party, since more of the new editors were Republicans than Federalists.[30]

During the 1790s, most papers were four pages long and appeared once or twice a week. They were devoid of illustrations and filled with advertisements and random reports from the United States and Europe. In addition, most papers ran anonymous opinion pieces signed with classical names similar to "Publius" of The Federalist Papers and "Camillus" in the fight over the Jay Treaty. The papers did not typically earn substantial profits, and were more often owned by working-class printers than by "gentlemen." During the 1790s and early 1800s, many printers gradually turned into professional editors and—in a major new development—became powerful political figures themselves.[31]

One of the most important journalists was John Fenno, a Bostonian whose Gazette of the United States began publication in New York during April 1789, with financial backing from Massachusetts investors. Unlike most other newspapermen of the time, Fenno was not a printer but an entrepreneur, and his Gazette supported the nationalist program of Hamilton and Washington. Fenno published his paper twice a week and moved the Gazette from New York to Philadelphia when the government itself moved. In addition to the editor's own essays, the paper carried articles by John Adams, and also many pieces by Hamilton under various classical pseudonyms. Hamilton steered Senate and Treasury printing jobs to Fenno, and occasionally lent him money.[32]

As policy disputes heated up, so did the tone of essays in the Gazette of the United States. Jefferson, who seemed to see monarchical tendencies everywhere, became concerned at what he regarded as the drift of Fenno's paper. Irate at the existence of what struck him as a press organ of the government, he decided to retaliate. He hired the well-known poet and journalist Philip Freneau as a translator for the State Department, paying him a modest salary. Freneau had been James Madison's college roommate.

After taking up his government post in Philadelphia, Freneau spent almost no time translating—Jefferson himself was fluent in French, the only foreign language known by the new hire. Freneau's real function lay in setting up the *National Gazette,* which began publication in October 1791 and soon established itself as an effective rival of Fenno's *Gazette of the United States.* Like Fenno's paper, Freneau's had an influence far beyond the national capital, in cities where other Republican-oriented newspapers republished its articles.[33]

In pseudonymous pieces he wrote for Fenno's paper, Hamilton exposed Freneau's patronage appointment to the State Department. He went on to point out that Freneau's real function was to undermine the administration, of which Jefferson was himself a member. In his accusations, Hamilton—who had steered federal contracts to John Fenno but had never hired him as a government employee—had his opponents dead to rights. Jefferson and Freneau parried the thrusts ineffectively—their responses to Hamilton's disclosures were clumsy and untruthful—and they paid the price of intense embarrassment.[34]

These alliances between cabinet members and newspapermen did credit to nobody. Although both papers seemed to become more strident with each successive issue, a slight edge in vituperation went to Freneau's *National Gazette.* James Madison sometimes wrote signed or pseudonymous articles for the paper, and it was Freneau who gave the name "Republican" to the Madison-Jefferson party. In addition to its ceaseless attacks on Hamilton and his programs, the *National Gazette* often criticized George Washington as well. When Washington asked Jefferson to fire Freneau from the State Department, Jefferson refused, replying that the editor "has saved our Constitution." This was another step in the alienation of Washington from both Jefferson and Madison.[35]

The scurrilousness of both *Gazettes*—and even more so of other papers published later in the 1790s—outdid almost anything in the mainstream American press of the twenty-first century. Their tone bore a greater resemblance to that of today's partisan blogs and radio talk shows—unbridled, undocumented, and often anonymous. The main difference lay in the quality of the prose. As stylists, Hamilton, Adams, Madison, and other contributors—including Fenno and Freneau—were far superior to all but a handful of today's journalists and bloggers. But they were often just as brazen.[36]

Fenno's *Gazette of the United States* continued publication after its editor's death in 1798—its name having changed in 1797 to *Gazette of the United States and Philadelphia Advertiser*. John Ward Fenno, the founder's son, edited the paper for two more years, then sold it in 1800 to Philadelphia investors. The paper's political influence thereafter declined, along with the power of the Federalist Party. But during the 1790s it had been a mighty organ, especially during the battles of 1791–1793. So had Philip Freneau's *National Gazette* until its demise in 1793, two years after its establishment. Both papers had subsisted on a shoestring, and Freneau's shoestring proved shorter than Fenno's.

The disappearance of Freneau's *National Gazette* signaled no diminution in pro-Republican journalism. Even before asking Freneau to start a paper in 1791, Jefferson had unsuccessfully approached the twenty-one-year-old Benjamin Franklin Bache, a precocious journalist and the grandson of his namesake. The fiery Bache had declined Jefferson's request to start a paper opposing Fenno's *Gazette of the United States,* having founded his own journal, the *General Advertiser,* in 1790. After several changes in name, it became the *Philadelphia Aurora.* Bache was soon attacking Hamilton's financial program and the Washington-Adams administration with even more fervor than Philip Freneau. As a Philadelphia insider, he was able to lace his articles with personal references, especially to John Adams but sometimes to Washington as well. He kept it up for most of the 1790s, and the *Aurora* established itself as the most important newspaper of that decade. Bache became a major political player to an extent that neither Fenno nor Freneau had ever reached.[37]

After the ratification of the Jay Treaty in 1795, the *Aurora* turned into an almost purely political paper devoted to the Republican cause. In 1796 Bache broke the story that Washington would not stand for reelection to a third term. He also confirmed the long-suspected rumor that Jefferson, who had spent the mid-1790s building a powerful political machine, would be a candidate for the presidency.[38]

Meanwhile, Bache was beginning to run out of money and his attacks on the Federalists were growing ever less prudent. He sealed his fate when he wrote on the day of Washington's departure from office in 1797: "If ever there was period for rejoicing, this is the moment . . . [T]hat the name of WASHINGTON from this day ceases to give a currency to political iniquity; and to legalize corruption, . . . this day ought to be a JUBILEE in the United States." After unrestrained assaults on the Adams administration and the passage of the Sedition Act of 1798, Bache was arrested and jailed. Out on bail, he contracted yellow fever during the epidemic of that year in Philadelphia, and died at the age of twenty-nine before standing trial.[39]

But his short career—a curious mixture of courage, originality, and indiscretion—was a watershed in the evolution of political journalism in the United States. It was also a portent of what lay just ahead for Alexander Hamilton: a public disclosure and uproar over the adulterous affair he had carried on with Maria Reynolds several years earlier, in 1791–1792.

CHAPTER 13

The Decline

The whistle-blower in the Reynolds affair was James Callender, a mercurial immigrant journalist given to inflammatory rhetoric. In his native Scotland, having published in 1792 a scathing pamphlet on corruption and war called "The Political Progress of Britain," he escaped prosecution by going first to Ireland, then to the United States. There he settled at age thirty-four in Philadelphia, the nation's capital. Callender was soon writing anonymous articles for Benjamin Franklin Bache's *Aurora* and other newspapers. His denunciations of Federalist policies and his satires of Federalist leaders took a particularly vicious tone. He enjoyed naming names, and he spared nobody: Washington, Adams, Hamilton, and every other prominent Federalist.[1]

In June and July 1797, Callender brought out two pamphlets titled "The History of the United States for the Year 1796" and "Sketches of the History of America." In both, he detailed Hamilton's adulterous affair of 1791–1792 with Maria Reynolds, a married woman. He charged that Hamilton had corrupted his position at the Treasury to enrich himself, Mrs. Reynolds, and her husband, all three of whom Callender portrayed as conspirators.

He had learned both stories—the true one about Hamilton's sexual affair and the false one about Hamilton's abusing his office—through a circuitous series of tales involving about a dozen tellers. It has never become certain how Callender acquired the documents to support his account of the affair. But the key informant seems to have been James Monroe, a protégé of Jefferson and later the fifth president of the United States. Along with two other congressmen, Monroe had questioned Hamilton privately about the episode in 1792.[2]

When Callender published his pamphlets in 1797, Hamilton felt compelled to reply. Many of his friends advised him to remain silent, but that had never been his way. His lifelong practice had been to defend himself in writing, compulsively and often at excessive length. But in this case it proved to be the most foolish decision he ever made. He brought out a ninety-five-page pamphlet titled

OBSERVATIONS
of
CERTAIN DOCUMENTS
Contained in no. V and VI of
"THE HISTORY OF THE UNITED STATES
for the Year 1796"
in which the
CHARGE OF SPECULATION
against
ALEXANDER HAMILTON
LATE SECRETARY OF THE TREASURY
IS FULLY REFUTED
WRITTEN BY HIMSELF
PHILADELPHIA
1797.

Hamilton devoted the first thirty-seven pages to the story of his affair with Maria Reynolds and the attempt by her and her husband to obtain inside Treasury information, money, or both.

Then he appended fifty-eight pages of supporting letters and other documents. The entire pamphlet resembled one of Hamilton's legal briefs—on behalf of a client who happened to be himself.[3]

In defense of his honor in managing the nation's finances, he noted the vicious attacks by the opposition press on every leading Federalist, including Washington: "The most direct falsehoods are invented and propagated, with undaunted effrontery and unrelenting perseverance." He hinted that the source of the general press assault was Jefferson and the Republicans.[4]

Then he denied any interest in becoming wealthy: "No man ever carried into public life a more unblemished pecuniary reputation, than that with which I undertook the office of Secretary of the Treasury; a character marked by an indifference to the acquisition of property rather than an avidity for it." After further remarks, including a confession of adultery for which "I can never cease to condemn myself," he proceeded to a detailed account of his assignations with Maria Reynolds.[5]

When their affair began in 1791, he was thirty-four years old and under a good deal of pressure at the Treasury—composing his *Report on the Subject of Manufactures,* in addition to his many other duties. Reynolds was a beautiful twenty-three-year-old and for Hamilton an irresistible temptress.

> Some time in the summer of the year 1791 a woman called at my house in the city of Philadelphia and asked to speak with me in private. I attended her into a room apart from the family. With a seeming air of affliction she informed me that . . . her husband, who for a long time had treated her very cruelly, had lately left her, to live with another woman, and in so destitute a condition, that though desirous of returning to her friends she had not the means—that knowing I was a citizen of New-York, she had taken the liberty to apply to my humanity for assistance.[6]

Maria Reynolds identified herself to Hamilton as having been born into a good New York family, which was true enough. But her tale of abandonment by her husband, James Reynolds, was not true. The two of them, along with others, were in fact engaged in an elaborate scheme to swindle the U.S. Treasury. The plan would begin with a seduction of Hamilton, whose gallantry toward women was well known. To Mrs. Reynolds's lament at their first meeting, Hamilton replied

> that I was disposed to afford her assistance to convey her to her friends, but this at the moment not being convenient to me (which was the fact) I must request the place of her residence, to which I should bring or send a small supply of money. She told me the street and the number of the house where she lodged. In the evening I put a bank-bill in my pocket and went to the house. I inquired for Mrs Reynolds and was shewn up stairs, at the head of which she met me and conducted me into a bed room. I took the bill out of my pocket and gave it to her. Some conversation ensued from which it was quickly apparent that other than pecuniary consolation would be acceptable.[7]

The initial success of the seduction was followed by "frequent meetings with her, most of them at my own house; Mrs. Hamilton with her children being absent on a visit to her father." Here Hamilton glossed over the embarrassing fact that Eliza was pregnant with their fifth child and that he had encouraged her to visit General Schuyler in New York. Meanwhile, Maria Reynolds "mentioned to me that her husband had solicited a reconciliation, and affected to consult me about it . . . She told me besides that her husband had been engaged in speculation, and she believed could give information respecting the conduct of some persons in the department which would be useful."[8]

Persuaded in this way, Hamilton met James Reynolds, who "confessed that he had obtained a list of claims from a person in my department which he had made use of in his speculations. I invited him, by the expectation of my friendship and good offices, to disclose the person." Reynolds named former assistant secretary of the treasury William Duer, a known speculator who had left the government before it moved from New York to Philadelphia. None of this was news to Hamilton, and he now began to have suspicions about what the Reynoldses were up to.[9]

By this time, however, he seemed to be in the grip of a full-fledged sexual obsession:

> The intercourse with Mrs. Reynolds, in the mean time, continued; and, though various reflections, (in which a further knowledge of Reynolds' character and the suspicion of some concert between the husband and wife bore a part) induced me to wish a cessation of it; yet her conduct, made it extremely difficult to disentangle myself . . . My sensibility, perhaps my vanity, admitted the possibility of a real fondness . . . Mrs. Reynolds, on the other hand, employed every effort to keep up my attention and visits.[10]

When it became evident to the Reynoldses that they were not going to extract any inside information or Treasury funds from Hamilton, they settled on simple blackmail. As the price of their silence, Hamilton paid them about $1,100, in several installments, out of his own pocket. His annual salary at the time was $3,500.[11]

The affair had lasted for about ten months by the time Hamilton finally forced himself to break it off. Because so many of his meetings with Maria Reynolds occurred at his own home near the government offices in Philadelphia, a discovery was all but inevitable. He had been almost unbelievably reckless in imagining that his enemies would not find out what had been going on.

They did. When James Monroe and the two other congressmen visited him at his home to inquire about the matter, Hamilton confessed to the adulterous relationship. But he produced enough letters between himself and the Reynoldses to convince his visitors that his only vice had been sexual. He had paid blackmail but had compensated the would-be swindlers in no other way. All three legislators professed themselves satisfied that the secretary's sins did not compromise the Treasury or involve public funds, and were therefore no business of the government.

Hamilton had been extraordinarily fortunate that no public disclosure occurred during his time in office. But information of this sort always has a life of its own. It never dies away. Moreover, Hamilton had made a bad mistake in giving to the three congressmen a large sheaf of incriminating letters between him and the Reynoldses. Before returning them to the secretary, the congressmen passed them along to John Beckley, the clerk of the House and an ardent Jeffersonian. Beckley made copies of every letter. As party politics intensified during the 1790s, these copies of the Reynolds correspondence became a ticking time bomb.

When James Callender set off the bomb in 1797—and even more so when Hamilton replied at such length in a published pamphlet—both his friends and his political opponents were incredulous at the degree of his foolhardiness. The Federalist newspaperman Noah Webster asked how Hamilton could "degrade himself in the estimation of all good men, and scandalize a family to clear himself of charges which no man believed." Some sort of pathology seems to have been at work, perhaps related to Rachel Faucett's behavior and disgrace thirty years earlier in St. Croix.[12]

Hamilton explained in his pamphlet that he had included in it all copies of the Reynolds correspondence "in order that no cloud whatever might be left on the affair." In other words, in order to protect his public reputation as a trustworthy steward of the nation's finances, he was willing to sacrifice his personal reputation as a faithful husband. By his own extreme standards of honor as a public man, the tradeoff made perfect sense.[13]

But what of his family? The noblest behavior throughout the entire matter was that of Eliza Hamilton. The Republican paper *Aurora* vilified her as well as her husband. "Art thou a wife?" it asked, sparing no malignity. "See him, whom thou hast chosen for the partner in this life, in the lap of a harlot!" A public word from Eliza might have ended Hamilton's career. But she remained silent and steadfast. Though undoubtedly hurt, she seems to have regarded the exposé as only the latest of an endless series of political assaults on her husband.[14]

James Callender could hardly believe that the bomb he had detonated had produced such damage, and so much of it self-inflicted by Hamilton. After reading the ninety-five-page "Reynolds Pamphlet," he wrote Jefferson: "If you have not seen it, no anticipation can equal the infamy of this piece. It is worth all that fifty of the best pens in America could have said agt. him, and the most pitiful part of the whole is his notice of you." James Madison, after receiving a copy of the pamphlet from Monroe, wrote to Jefferson: "The publication under all its characters is a curious specimen of the ingenious folly of its author. Next to the error of publishing at all, is that of forgetting that simplicity & candor are the only dress which prudence would put on innocence."[15]

John Adams, who had never liked Hamilton and who, as president, was having to contend with him as a rival leader of the Federalist Party, commented that he had shown himself to have "as debauched morals as old Franklin, who is his Model more than any man I know." The younger man's boundless ambition could be traced to a "superabundance of secretions" that he "could not find whores enough to draw off." Later, Adams referred to Hamilton's "fornications, his adulteries, his incests"—the latter presumably with Angelica Church, his attractive sister-in-law. Hamilton did indeed have a weakness for women. But despite herculean attempts by his contemporaries and similar efforts on the part of historians for more than 200 years, no reliable evidence has ever been found that he strayed from his marital vows except with Maria Reynolds.[16]

Even so, the Reynolds affair damaged his reputation permanently and removed any chance that he might become president. (Though born abroad, he was eligible because the Constitution opened the office to men who had been citizens at the time of its adoption, in 1789.) The Reynolds matter remained the most notorious scandal of its kind in American politics for 200 years—until the Clinton-Lewinsky affair of the 1990s, and the revelation in 1998–2000 that DNA and other evidence proved with virtual certainty Thomas Jefferson's paternity of the children of his slave Sally Hemings.[17]

The charges of Jefferson's relationship with Hemings were first published in 1802 by the editor of the *Richmond Recorder*, a Federalist newspaper. That editor was none other than James Callender, who had developed a grievance against Jefferson and had changed political sides. By that time president of the United States, Jefferson had the good sense to ignore the charges, and they soon faded from contemporary importance.

Hamilton held no public office when the Reynolds controversy broke in 1797, but he still wielded a great deal of power in the Federalist Party. He had already drafted most of Washington's 1796 Farewell Address to the nation, the most memorable public statement of Washington's career, and had remained very active in the government. Oliver Wolcott, his successor at the Treasury, consulted him almost constantly and followed his advice to the letter. Secretary of war James McHenry, the only fellow officer who had been able to attend Hamilton's wedding to Eliza twenty-five years earlier, was still a close friend and confidant who often sought his counsel. Secretary of state Timothy Pickering, another friend, held even more adamant views about policies toward France and England than Hamilton did. All three were holdovers from the Washington administration, and each was far closer to Hamilton than to the president, John Adams. With no tradition to guide him, Adams had retained Washington's entire cabinet.[18]

From 1798 to 1800, the dominant issue in national politics

was the "Quasi-War" between the United States and France. This conflict was still another by-product of the Jay Treaty. The French, who were falling more and more under the control of Napoleon, resented that treaty's apparent favoritism toward Britain. The two great powers were deep into the all-out conflict that would mark European history from 1793 until 1815. In this long and bloody contest, Napoleon gradually attained supremacy in Europe, while at sea the much enlarged British navy thwarted both the French navy and its frequent ally the Spanish navy.

During the 1790s, as part of their fight against Britain, French warships and privateers began to seize scores and ultimately hundreds of American merchant ships. In response, the Adams administration—prodded by Hamilton and his allies—built up both the army and the navy, and augmented military expenditures in anticipation of a possible war with France. The Hamilton faction emphasized strengthening the army in particular, the Adams faction the navy. This division of opinion, oddly enough, became one of the most contentious issues of Adams's presidency and weakened the Federalist Party still further. Adams finally overhauled his cabinet in 1800, but by then it was too late. In the election of that year, he lost the presidency.

Hamilton, meanwhile, was called back to military duty in 1798, during the Quasi-War with France. George Washington, by now sixty-six years old and in poor health, accepted command of the army on the condition that Hamilton be made a major general, second in rank only to Washington. Hamilton then spent twenty-one months of hard work reorganizing the army. The conflict with France occurred entirely at sea, but Hamilton enjoyed being addressed as "General" for the remaining years of his life. In mid-1800, Adams cooled the dispute by starting negotiations with the French.[19]

Late in 1800, Hamilton wrote a long and scathing essay about Adams's shortcomings as president. He had reason to believe that it would be published, and it was. The essay appeared too late to have much effect on the election of that year, and its apparent purpose—wholly unrealistic—was to persuade Federalist presidential electors to cast their votes for Charles Cotesworth Pinckney, the South Carolinian who was on the ballot as Adams's running mate. The essay did not amount to quite the debacle the Reynolds pamphlet had been, but again it showed Hamilton's discretion and judgment at its worst. He simply could not restrain himself from speaking out when he should have remained silent.[20]

In 1801, he founded the *New York Evening Post*, which today lays valid claim to being the nation's oldest continuously published daily newspaper. But the most significant event of that year for Hamilton concerned his family. His oldest son, Philip—named for General Schuyler—fought a duel to defend an alleged insult against his father. Captain Charles Eacker, a twenty-seven-year-old lawyer and army veteran, had made a speech praising President Jefferson and criticizing Hamilton. Shortly afterward, during a play at a theater, Philip Hamilton and a friend burst into Eacker's box and insulted him in the presence of his female companion and another couple.

In response, Eacker first took the field of honor against Philip Hamilton's friend, a confrontation in which neither man was injured despite having fired two shots apiece. Then Philip and Eacker fought a duel as well. Their encounter took place across the Hudson River from Manhattan in Weehawken, New Jersey, at a spot often used by duelists. The practice was illegal in both New York and New Jersey, but the prohibition was more rigorously enforced in New York.

Once on the dueling grounds, both men hesitated for a moment after the signal to fire. Eacker then shot Philip, who died the next morning. He was only nineteen, unusually talented, and as handsome as his father had been at the same age. His parents were devastated. Hamilton felt responsible, not only because his son had died defending Hamilton's honor but also because he had advised Philip either not to fire at all or to throw away his shot. Not long afterward, Eliza gave birth to their eighth child, a son whom they also named Philip. The family called him "Little Phil."[21]

—⊶⊶⊷—

Philip's death was perhaps the most painful blow that ever struck Alexander Hamilton, and he did not recover emotionally. Over the three remaining years of his life, from the age of forty-four to forty-seven, he changed far more than most middle-aged people ever do. A portrait of him at this time shows a different person from the vigorous, self-confident, and often vain figure of earlier paintings. Instead, he wears a grave and sad expression, that of someone who, though of strong character, has borne too much adversity.

After Philip's death, Hamilton spent most of his time practicing law and trying to put the family's finances on a stronger footing. He still wrote for the public press, but without his old verve and persuasiveness. His essay in response to Thomas Jefferson's first Annual Message as president, for example, had little of the compelling force of his earlier efforts. He seemed to sense that his time had passed, and he began to return to the religious roots of his childhood. On Sunday mornings he read Scripture to his family at their new country house in upper Manhattan—a small estate he had named the Grange, after a house in Scotland his ancestors had occupied.

Hamilton enjoyed his rural retreat at the Grange, but for him things were never going to be the same. Three months after Philip's death, and with Jefferson, Madison, and Albert Gallatin in control of the national government, he wrote Gouverneur Morris, "Mine is an odd destiny. Perhaps no man in the U States has sacrificed or done more for the present Constitution than myself . . . Yet I have the murmur of its friends no less than the curses of its foes for my rewards. What can I do better than withdraw from the scene?"[22]

Hamilton had remained very active in public affairs after leaving the Treasury in 1795. But without the restraining hand of Washington, he had gradually grown less discreet, more erratic, and much more self-destructive. When Washington suddenly died in 1799, Hamilton wrote a friend, "Perhaps no man in this community has equal cause with myself to deplore the loss. I have been much indebted to the kindness of the General, and he was an Aegis very essential to me." Nothing Hamilton did during the years from 1796 to 1804 could match his achievements in the Revolutionary War, as the main author of *The Federalist Papers,* and his magnificent performance as secretary of the treasury. Yet he already knew with certainty that he had achieved Fame—that he would be a historic figure of the first magnitude.[23]

So did other founders, who were also living out years of diminished distinction knowing that they had earned a place in the American pantheon. All had completed their most important work by 1804, the year Hamilton died. John Adams survived until 1826, but he had made his greatest contributions during the 1770s and 1780s, and had become politically irrelevant on the day he left the presidency in 1801. Jefferson also survived until 1826. He died on July 4, the fiftieth anniversary of the Declaration of Independence and the same day as the death of Adams, with whom he had been exchanging a long and warm series of letters. But the greatest of Jefferson's many contributions had been the Declaration of 1776, the democratizing thrust of the Republican Party during the 1790s and early 1800s, and the Louisiana Purchase of 1803, secured during his first presidential term. James Madison lived until 1836, and he, like Jefferson, served two terms as president. But Madison's signature historical moment had come in 1787, as principal author of the Constitution.

One often-overlooked consequence of the unusual longevity of Adams, Jefferson, and Madison was their continued denigration of Hamilton after his death. They outlived him by a collective seventy-six years, although the three of them were older than Hamilton by a total of forty-two years. After 1804, Jefferson and Madison did not have a great deal to say in public

FIGURE 11. An idealized and undated image of the Grange, Alexander Hamilton's country retreat in upper Manhattan and the only house he ever owned. Completed in 1802, two years before his death, it remained in the family until the 1830s. In 1848, Eliza Hamilton moved from New York to Washington, D.C., where she died in 1854 at the age of ninety-seven. She survived "my Hamilton" by fifty years, fiercely defending his reputation to the very end.

FIGURE 12 *(opposite, above).* Philip Hamilton not long before his death in November 1801, at the age of nineteen. He was killed in a duel that began over an insult to his father's honor.

FIGURE 13 *(opposite, below).* Philip Hamilton's death crushed his father, altering even his appearance. The Albany artist Ezra Ames captured the change in a somber portrait of Alexander Hamilton, done in 1802 and copied by Ames himself in this version dated c. 1810.

about Hamilton, but what they did say and write hurt his reputation.

Even while Hamilton was still alive, John Adams spoke of him as "a foreigner." In 1813, nine years after Hamilton's death, Adams wrote that he "was not really an American." This comment embodied New England provincialism at its worst. Hamilton's life could hardly have been a more quintessentially American saga: that of a destitute immigrant boy without connections, able to triumph because of his extraordinary talents, fortitude, capacity for sustained and arduous work—and the fabulous possibilities offered by his adopted country.[24]

CHAPTER 14

The Duel

As a way to settle affairs of honor, dueling was not rare during Hamilton's time, but neither was it very common. Most duels did not end fatally, even though the distance between the combatants was usually ten or twenty paces. Duels occurred most often between military officers. Hamilton's exaggerated sense of honor and his long service in the army seemed to predispose him to involvement in more duels than most men—occasionally as a principal, sometimes as a second, others as a peacemaker. But the only time he actually took the field of honor as a principal occurred in his duel with Aaron Burr in 1804.[1]

Besides that, the closest Hamilton came to dueling was in 1797, during the uproar over the Maria Reynolds scandal. Furious at James Monroe for refusing to confirm his account of his dealings with Maria and James Reynolds, Hamilton challenged Monroe to a duel. After months of angry charges back and forth, the feud ran out of steam. Ironically enough, the key figure in averting violence was Aaron Burr, whom Monroe had asked to be his second.[2]

By 1804, Hamilton and Burr had known each other for almost thirty years, since their service as officers during the War of Independence. Later they came into frequent contact as law-yers practicing in New York City, but they never developed a congenial relationship. Both were ambitious, energetic, and politically influential. Burr came from a distinguished colonial family. His maternal grandfather was Jonathan Edwards, the most prominent American theologian of his time, and Burr's father had served as president of what became Princeton University.

In the New York governor's race of 1789, both Hamilton and Burr had opposed the reelection of George Clinton, the head of a powerful political machine. Clinton had been governor for twelve years, and he won yet again. In order to strengthen his faction, Clinton then offered Burr the appointive office of state attorney general, and Burr accepted. Thereafter, Hamilton and Burr drifted in opposite political directions. In the senatorial election of 1791, held in the New York legislature, Burr de-feated the incumbent Philip Schuyler, Hamilton's father-in-law. As the two-party system evolved, Burr cemented his alliance with Clinton and also with the Jeffersonians. The Virginia Re-publicans had little fondness for Burr, but New York was a piv-otal state for their party.

As early as 1792, Hamilton had written in a letter that Burr was "unprincipled, both as a public and private man." As time passed, the two seemed to develop a mutual dislike that came to a head during the presidential election of 1800. Burr was on the ballot essentially as Thomas Jefferson's running mate. When a foul-up by Republican electors caused a tie in the Electoral College between Jefferson and Burr, Hamilton did everything he could to secure the election of Jefferson. He disliked both candidates, but much preferred Jefferson to the unscrupulous Burr. After Jefferson won, the Republican Party's distrust of the wily new vice president increased. Early in the presidential elec-tion year of 1804, he was dropped from the ticket in favor of George Clinton, the veteran New Yorker. Burr then ran for gov-ernor of New York but lost—partly because of Hamilton's opposition but mostly because the Clinton machine gave him in-sufficient support.[3]

Still the sitting vice president of the United States but now more hypersensitive to criticism than ever, Burr was in no mood to accept further setbacks. When Hamilton continued to dis-parage him, Burr decided on a challenge. Hamilton could easily have avoided the duel—the extent of his public comments fell short of the open personal insults contemplated by the *code duello*—but he chose not to. In his view, a refusal would have stained his honor, and his son's tragic death less than three years earlier likely affected his decision as well. If Philip had given his life defending his father's honor, was not the father compelled to take the same risk?

When Hamilton went to his fatal "interview" with Burr early on the morning of July 11, 1804, he was full of conflicting emo-tions. He explained his attitude toward Burr and the duel in private notes he had composed during the thirteen days before-hand. With his lawyer's habit of writing down his thoughts in systematic fashion, he went over the arguments, pro and con:

> I am certainly desirous of avoiding this interview, for the most cogent reasons.
>
> 1. My religious and moral principles are strongly op-posed to the practice of Duelling, and it would even give me pain to be obliged to shed the blood of a fellow creature in a private combat forbidden by the laws.
>
> 2. My wife and Children are extremely dear to me, and my life is of the utmost importance to them, in various views.
>
> 3. I feel a sense of obligation towards my creditors; who in case of accident to me, by the forced sale of my property, may be in some degree sufferers. I did not think my self at

liberty, as a man of probity, lightly to expose them to this hazard.

4. I am conscious of no *ill-will* to Col Burr, distinct from political opposition, which, as I trust, has proceeded from pure and upright motives.

Lastly, I shall hazard much, and can possibly gain nothing by the issue of the interview.

But it was, as I conceive, impossible for me to avoid it. There were *intrinsick* difficulties in the thing, and *artificial* embarrassments, from the manner of proceeding on the part of Col Burr.

Intrinsick—because it is not to be denied, that my animadversions on the political principles character and views of Col Burr have been extremely severe, and on different occasions, I, in common with many others, have made very unfavorable criticisms on particular instances of the private conduct of this Gentleman . . .

The disavowal required of me by Col Burr, in a general and indefinite form, was out of my power . . .

As well because it is possible that I may have injured Col Burr, however convinced myself that my opinions and declarations have been well founded, as from my general principles and temper in relation to similar affairs—I have resolved, if our interview is conducted in the usual manner, and it pleases God to give me the opportunity, to *reserve* and *throw away* my first fire, and I *have thoughts* even of *reserving* my second fire—and thus giving a double opportunity to Col Burr to pause and reflect.[4]

Hamilton had no wish to kill or wound Burr. Nor was there any question of his own physical courage, which he had proved dozens of times during and after the war. In the duel itself, conducted on almost exactly the same spot in Weehawken where his son had died, Hamilton threw away his own shot, as he had resolved to do. He fired into a tree four feet to Burr's left and far above his head.

Burr had no such intentions. He took careful aim. The ball from his pistol hit Hamilton at the top of his right hip, ricocheted through his liver, and lodged between the bottom two vertebrae of his back. Hamilton dropped to the ground, paralyzed from the waist down. As a student of anatomy, he immediately knew his wound would be fatal. He lingered for thirty-one hours in excruciating pain, surrounded by his friends and family.

His death created a national sensation. In addition to detailed accounts of the duel, many newspapers carried extensive reflections on Hamilton's role in the War of Independence, his transcendent performance as secretary of the treasury, and his extraordinarily dramatic life. Burr, meanwhile, still vice president, fled to Georgia in the face of a murder charge, which was later dropped.

Hamilton's funeral in New York was an elaborate affair, the largest ceremony of its kind in the city's history up to that time. Thousands of people crowded the streets, stunned by the sudden death of their most prominent citizen. His burial took place in the courtyard of Trinity Church, at the corner of Broadway and Wall Street. The engraving on the stone reads, in part:

FOR
The PATRIOT of incorruptible INTEGRITY
The SOLDIER of approved VALOUR
The STATESMAN of consummate WISDOM
He died July 12th 1804. Aged 47.

New Yorkers wore black armbands for a month afterward.

Before the interview with Burr, Hamilton had composed not only his rationale for going through with the duel, but also a short letter to be given to his wife in the event he was killed.[5]

This letter, my very dear Eliza, will not be delivered to you, unless I shall first have terminated my earthly career; to begin, as I humbly hope from redeeming grace and divine mercy, a happy immortality.

If it had been possible for me to have avoided the interview, my love for you and my precious children would have been alone a decisive motive. But it was not possible, without sacrifices which would have rendered me unworthy of your esteem. I need not tell you of the pangs I feel, from the idea of quitting you and exposing you to the anguish which I know you would feel. Nor could I dwell on the topic lest it should unman me.

The consolations of Religion, my beloved, can alone support you; and these you have a right to enjoy. Fly to the bosom of your God and be comforted. With my last idea, I shall cherish the sweet hope of meeting you in a better world.

Adieu best of wives and best of Women. Embrace all my darling Children for me.

Ever yours,

AH

PART II

Albert Gallatin
1761–1849

FIGURE 14. Statue of Albert Gallatin, by James Earle Fraser. The statue overlooks the north plaza of the Department of the Treasury, Washington, D.C., and was dedicated in 1947.

CHAPTER 15

Choosing the New World

Albert Gallatin, an immigrant from Geneva, filled the same role for presidents Thomas Jefferson and James Madison that Alexander Hamilton, an immigrant from St. Croix, had filled for George Washington. As secretary of the treasury from 1801 to 1813, Gallatin dominated public financial affairs. But he went far beyond that field and into foreign policy, military strategy, and the development of the American West.[1]

As a member of the House from 1795 to 1801, he was the first powerful congressman who lived on the western side of the Appalachian Mountains. When Jefferson made him secretary, Gallatin also became the first cabinet member from the West among the twenty appointed up to that time in any department. He did more than any other federal official to oversee settlement and economic growth in the West, and to turn America's public lands into a force for the public good. This was his signature contribution, as financial modernization had been Hamilton's.[2]

Hamilton and Gallatin were political enemies, but they had many things in common. Both had lost their parents by the age of nine. In their teens, both emigrated to North America and later married into prominent New York families. Both had brilliant intellects, a quick facility with numbers, rare administrative abilities—very rare for that time—and the capacity to outwork their contemporaries. Both opposed slavery and joined organized groups promoting manumission.

Each was a reflective person, but neither wrote an autobiography, as did Benjamin Franklin, or kept a diary and commonplace book, as did Thomas Jefferson. Each left behind thousands of pages of correspondence, pamphlets, and government reports—not the homespun musings of Franklin or the soaring phrases of Jefferson, but reams of careful, fact-based analysis ending in detailed policy prescriptions. Of the two, Hamilton possessed the more dashing personality, Gallatin the more tactful temperament, which made him more agreeable to work with than Hamilton. It also made Gallatin an easy man to underestimate, a miscalculation he recognized and often used to his advantage.

At about 5'10" and 150 pounds, Gallatin was three inches taller than Hamilton and twenty-five pounds heavier. With his gawky frame, oversized nose, and early baldness, he lacked Hamilton's good looks and appeal to women. Nor could he match Hamilton's way with words, either on paper or at the podium. Almost nobody could. "I was destitute of eloquence," Gallatin recalled, "and had to surmount the great obstacle of speaking in a foreign language [that is, English] with a very bad pronunciation." Although he came to the United States before he was twenty, his heavy French accent stayed with him for the rest of his life.[3]

Henry Adams, the ablest early analyst of this generation of statesmen, captured well the unusual roles of both Hamilton and Gallatin. Only the two of them, Adams wrote, needed to be studied by "persons who wish to understand what practical statesmanship has been under an American system." Adams, himself the grandson of one president and great-grandson of another, went on to say that "Washington and Jefferson doubtless stand pre-eminent as the representatives of what is best in our national character or its aspirations, but Washington depended mainly upon Hamilton, and without Gallatin Mr. Jefferson would have been helpless." The word "helpless" overstates the case, but not in the administrative sense Adams intended.[4]

Nor does Adams exaggerate Gallatin's role when he refers to Jefferson, James Madison, and Gallatin as a "triumvirate." In 1813, the Boston congressman Josiah Quincy remarked that the country had been governed for the previous twelve years by "two Virginians and a foreigner." With his quiet composure and unerring judgment, Gallatin moderated Jefferson's ideological fervor and Madison's frequent indecisiveness. Had they heeded his advice more often, both would have been more successful presidents.[5]

Abraham Alfonse Albert Gallatin was born in Geneva in 1761, four years after Hamilton's birth in the West Indies. The Gallatin family had lived in Geneva since 1510, when an ancestor from Savoy first moved there. Albert's father, an aristocratic landowner and seller of watches, died when Albert was four. His mother then took over the family business and sent her son to be raised in the household of Catherine Pictet, a well-to-do spinster. Miss Pictet was Mrs. Gallatin's best friend and a distant relative of her late husband. When Albert was nine his mother died, but by that time he had practically become the foster son of Catherine Pictet. She hired home tutors for him, then enrolled him at age twelve in the *collège* (middle school) of Geneva. At fourteen he entered the equally elite Academy of Geneva, which was almost the equivalent of a modern university.[6]

Geneva, then a city of 25,000 people, had—and still has—a unique geography: a narrow strip of land (only six square miles), thrusting deep into France like the toe of a slipper. It is surrounded by the Alps and remains a place of great natural beauty. An associate member of the Swiss Confederation in Gallatin's time, the city was cut off from Switzerland proper by Lake Geneva (225 square miles), which feeds the Rhône, one of Europe's major rivers. Geneva was not a kingdom but an independent republic, very unusual for that time, and 2,000 of its citizens had the right to vote.

The city also had a distinctive culture. Though its famous watch industry and emergent banking system made it wealthy, the local moral code still bore the stamp of the Protestant theologian John Calvin (1509–1564), the most influential person in Geneva's history. "The consequence," Gallatin recalled, "was that it became disgraceful for any young man of decent parentage to be an idler. All were bound to exercise their faculties to the utmost." Here lay the roots of his future mania for work, which rivaled Hamilton's.[7]

The stern religion of Calvin forbade Genevans to wear jewelry or even to use carriages in the city, and Gallatin followed a frugal regimen for his entire life. But he believed that Calvin's greatest legacy was his emphasis on free schooling, which made Geneva's residents some of the best-educated people in Europe. The philosophers Voltaire and Rousseau (a native Genevan) lived in or near the city during Gallatin's youth. Their writings, though sometimes banned for religious reasons, stimulated high-level thought and analysis. These circumstances made the studious Gallatin a much more sophisticated young man than most others who were emigrating to the United States. At the Academy of Geneva, he finished first in his class in mathematics, in Latin translation, and in "natural philosophy," the traditional term for the natural sciences.[8]

By the time Gallatin graduated from the academy, he had grown restless within the strict home of his foster mother and the cramped atmosphere of Geneva. He had a strong independent streak. With two classmates from the academy named Henri Serre and Jean Badollet, he resolved to leave the city and cross the Atlantic, where vast tracts of land in the United States awaited development. This was in 1780, when Gallatin was nineteen and the U.S. was fighting its war for independence. It was also the year when Lieutenant Colonel Alexander Hamilton was writing his fiancée that if the war turned out badly they might move to the republic of Geneva after their marriage.[9]

In deciding to come to America, Gallatin and his two young friends were acting on a psychological impulse rooted in a romantic dream. Unlike Hamilton's departure from St. Croix, nothing except their own imaginations was pushing them out of Geneva. It seems peculiar that Gallatin would so casually leave such a cultured city, where his ancestors had lived since 1510 and where he himself held such high social status. But he was a bold young man. Nor could he and his friends have had more than a vague idea of what life would be like in a world that remained a rural frontier. And since they knew almost no English, why go to the United States rather than to Québec, where their native French was spoken?

They were three young men in a state of rebellion moving to a place that was itself rebelling. They seemed to believe that Rousseau's notions about the moral virtues of nature might be realized in the United States—a new country where they could become rich landowners, doing well by doing good. That they had no experience as farmers and might well fail does not seem to have occurred to them. Their dreams of becoming landlords were misdirected illusions of ways to become rich.

It would take Gallatin well over a decade to realize that his gifts lay not in dealing with land and agriculture, but rather in managing money and other financial instruments—liquid capital, not illiquid land. His talents resembled those of Hamilton more than those of Jefferson and Madison, and that is what later made him so useful, so nearly indispensable, to the Virginians and the Republican Party. There had been banks in Geneva for more than a century before Gallatin emigrated, and he took their existence for granted in a way Jefferson and Madison did not.

Without telling anyone, not even his foster mother, Gallatin slipped out of Geneva with Henri Serre on April 1, 1780. Their friend Jean Badollet followed a few years later. Gallatin and Serre took along an amount of money equivalent in the early twenty-first century to about $5,000. This was enough to pay for their transatlantic crossing and perhaps to set up a small business in America before they began their grand quest for land. After four weeks' travel across France, they arrived at the port of Nantes. Still having no notion of what they were in for, they bought passage aboard the American ship *Katty*. In the largest gesture toward entrepreneurship they could afford, they purchased nine cartons of tea that they planned to sell once they arrived.

The trip to Massachusetts took seven weeks. From the fishing port of Gloucester, Gallatin and Serre made their way forty miles south to Boston, searching for employment and—rather desperately—for other French speakers. Their tea sales did not go well, and Gallatin found Boston about as puritanical as Geneva, with few opportunities for adventure or entertainment. Boston's people were preoccupied with their war with Britain, but Gallatin and Serre had no interest in becoming soldiers.

Instead, on the advice of a Bostonian named Lesdernier, who had grown up near Geneva, they set out with him by boat for Fort Gates in Machias, a tiny town 250 miles northeast of Boston. This decision amounted to still another sign of their naïveté. Machias lay five miles inland from the remote northernmost coast of Maine, which was then part of Massachusetts. Lesdernier's son was serving with American forces at nearby Fort Gates, a small outpost near the Canadian border. Gallatin and Serre had purchased some rum, sugar, and tobacco that they might sell to either soldiers or Native Americans, whom they thought would have furs to trade. They arrived in mid-October, on the brink of a harsh Maine winter. They would have sold nothing at all had the sutler at Fort Gates not paid them $100 in Continental currency for the goods they brought from Boston.

Despite dismal prospects, Gallatin and Serre remained in Machias through the winter and the following spring and summer—hoping, Micawber-like, that something would turn up. Nothing did. At Gallatin's urging, the two then returned to Boston. By this time, Catherine Pictet, his foster mother in Geneva, had traced the boys' movements and prevailed upon Genevans with friends in Boston to help them. Through this intervention, the near-penniless Gallatin and Serre were hired by Harvard College as tutors in French. Gallatin paid for his room and board at the rates offered to other Harvard tutors. Seventy students enrolled in his classes, and he spent two years in Cambridge teaching French, improving his English, and pondering his next move.

CHAPTER 16

Moving to the West

Gallatin disliked New England, both at this time and throughout his life. His dream, from the beginning, had been to set himself up as a gentleman farmer and land dealer in the trans-
Appalachian West. As he wrote years later, for all of the early
English colonists, "the most vast field of enterprise was opened
which ever offered itself to civilized men. Their mission was to
conquer the wilderness, to multiply indefinitely, to settle and
inhabit a whole continent, and to carry their institutions and
civilization from the Atlantic to the Pacific Ocean." Not to be-
little his own home city, but "the situation of Geneva was precisely the reverse of this."[1]

Gallatin's eyes, like those of many other immigrants, remained
fixed on the prize of land ownership in the American West. Almost from the beginning, he had a specific plan. As he wrote
Jean Badollet in October 1780, when he was only nineteen
and still in Maine with Henri Serre, the three of them could
grow wealthy by persuading European peasants to emigrate.

The three friends would purchase tracts of land, then pay for the peasants' trip across the Atlantic and offer them a year's support once they arrived. After that, "they would pay us half the income of the land if it raised grain, one quarter if it were in pasture, the balance continuing over ten, fifteen, or twenty years, the longer the better, at the end of which time the half or the quarter of the land would belong to them in perpetuity."[2]

This plan remained on hold for three years because the boys from Geneva had almost no money to invest in land or anything else. Gallatin's first real opportunity to pursue his dream came through a Frenchman whom he met in Boston: Jean Savary, the agent of a wealthy French merchant who was supplying wartime goods to Virginia. Savary could neither speak nor write English, and he persuaded Gallatin—who had learned the language on the fly after three years in America—to serve as his interpreter on a trip south to Richmond. There, Savary would press his principal's claims, accepting payment in the form of Virginia's public lands.

En route, Gallatin noted with interest what he called the "air of opulence" he saw in New York and Philadelphia. But he had no interest in settling in either city. He was still three years shy of age twenty-five, when he would receive a sizable inheritance from his late parents. Meanwhile, Savary might help him start toward the entrepreneurial aim he had devised at age nineteen: to buy and then rent or sell large tracts of real estate. Gallatin had decided that the best prospects lay neither in New England nor in the deep South, but in the western parts of Pennsylvania and Virginia. At that time Virginia was by far the largest state, comprising not only its present area but also today's Kentucky and West Virginia. It laid dubious claim, as well, to some northern territories that had become part of Pennsylvania in 1780.

Land speculation had already attracted thousands of Americans, including famous ones such as Robert Morris, Benjamin Franklin, and George Washington. Richmond, Baltimore, and other cities were major centers for the sale of "warrants," which were options to purchase land. Warrants for almost all undevel-

oped trans-Appalachian lands were cheap because of the difficulty of transporting crops grown in the West over the mountains to eastern markets.[3]

On their trip from Boston to Richmond, Gallatin and Savary paused in Baltimore, where Savary bought warrants for
120,000 acres in the greater Ohio River Valley. He lent Gallatin
a quarter-interest in the warrants, to be repaid when the younger man received his inheritance in a few years. This quarter-
interest represented the equivalent of about 7.5 times the area
of Gallatin's native Geneva. He was still thinking big. Some of
the land appeared to be adjacent to the Ohio River, a convenient avenue for shipping to the Mississippi and thence south
to the port of New Orleans. More of the property lay along the
Monongahela, which flows up through what is now West Virginia and meets the Allegheny River at Pittsburgh, to form the
Ohio. Like other entrepreneurs of the time, Gallatin had formed
the idea of connecting the Ohio River with the Potomac, which
flows east to the Atlantic Ocean. (He later played a major role
in planning the public roads and canals built for this purpose.)
In 1783, when he made his trip to Richmond, there were no
"artificial roads" at all west of the Allegheny Mountains.[4]

Once in Richmond, as Gallatin recalled, "I was received with
that old proverbial Virginia hospitality to which I know no parallel anywhere within the circle of my travels." Everyone he met
seemed to take an interest in him. "I was only the interpreter of
a gentleman, the agent of a foreign house that had a large claim
for advances to the State; and this made me well known to all
the officers of government and some of the most prominent
members of the legislature. It gave me the first opportunity of
showing some symptoms of talent, even as a speaker, of which I
was not myself aware." John Marshall, the future chief justice
of the United States, "though but a young lawyer in 1783, . . .
offered to take me into his office without a fee and assured me
that I would become a distinguished lawyer." [Governor] "Patrick Henry advised me to go to the West, where I might study

law if I chose, but predicted that I was intended for a states-man."[5]

Despite his budding skills as a negotiator, Gallatin failed in pressing the land claims of Savary's principal. He and Savary then spent several months in Philadelphia preparing to explore western Pennsylvania and northwestern Virginia, where they planned to buy huge tracts of land. Once they crossed the mountains, they soon discovered that most of their Baltimore warrants entitled them not to lush fields, but rather to steep hills unsuited for agriculture. (This was the fate of hundreds of other speculators exploring the wilderness.)

Gallatin still believed that Virginia held the key to his future as a landowner, and he made frequent trips to Richmond as well as to Philadelphia. In 1785, he swore allegiance to the Commonwealth of Virginia and thereby became an American citizen. By this time the Revolutionary War had ended and Gallatin was twenty-four years old. His French patron, Savary, who had less taste for frontier land speculation and was put off by the threat of violence from Indians, soon moved back to the East Coast.[6]

The Gallatin-Savary business partnership lasted an additional four years, but their personal relationship was never the same. Gallatin's closest friend, Henri Serre, the Geneva classmate with whom he had come to America, had planned to join him in Virginia once his commitment as a Harvard tutor ended. Instead, Serre sailed from the United States to Jamaica, where he died not long after his arrival, still in his mid-twenties.

So Gallatin was now on his own, but he had accumulated a great deal of knowledge about the United States. He had lived in or visited Boston, Newport, New York, Philadelphia, Baltimore, and Richmond—most of the important cities in the country, except the southern ports of Norfolk, Charleston, and Savannah. He had explored and purchased lands in western Virginia and Pennsylvania, becoming familiar with the vast wilderness that seemed to define America's future. He made frequent trips east, especially to Richmond and Philadelphia, and northward as well. Once, his arrival in the Connecticut Valley surprised some of his Harvard friends, who had read newspaper reports of his death from Indian scalping. His foster mother in Geneva heard the same rumor, and asked Thomas Jefferson, then U.S. minister to France, to confirm or rebut the report. She had written Gallatin a long series of reproachful letters about his "vanity" and "indolent ways"—ironic criticism, since his character was the very opposite on both counts.[7]

In 1786, Gallatin came into the bulk of his inheritance. His foster mother sent him, through a draft on Robert Morris's company in Philadelphia, one-fourth of his legacy, a sum equivalent in the early twenty-first century to about $65,000. During the depressed 1780s, this was a significant amount of money. Gallatin used part of it to buy larger tracts of land. He decided to live on a scenic 400-acre plot of what he thought to be fertile soil in Fayette County, Pennsylvania. The spot he chose is located in the southwest corner of the state, near its borders with Virginia and Maryland. There, Gallatin built a modest Georgian stone house that he named "Friendship Hill."[8]

The nearest significant settlement was Pittsburgh, about fifty miles to the north—a trading center with great commercial potential because of its position at the intersection of three rivers. A few years later, when wars in Europe threatened to overtake Geneva and the Swiss Confederation, Gallatin believed he might at last attract Swiss settlers to America. With them, he could establish a close community of liberty-loving farmers in what he now considered "the freest country in the universe."[9]

His plan for resettling Genevans in Pennsylvania—a refinement of what by now was a dream first developed nine years earlier—was less hare-brained than it might appear. His college friend Jean Badollet had finally joined him in America and had also settled near Friendship Hill. The likelihood of broader success in attracting Swiss immigrants may have been slim, but it was far from zero. Gallatin was thinking in the way most entrepreneurs think: not of sure things, but of plausible projects that promise a high payoff in the event of success. His strategy had been to locate his home, farms, and a few businesses midway between the Potomac and Ohio rivers. He could thereby take advantage of future water routes both to the East Coast and, via the Ohio and Mississippi rivers, to the Gulf of Mexico.

But he had made three serious mistakes, each of a type common to inexperienced entrepreneurs. First, he had been much too optimistic about the time it would take the government to construct roads and canals connecting the Potomac and Ohio rivers. And he had therefore underestimated the amount of money that would be necessary to keep his plans afloat in the meantime.[10]

His second error lay in thinking that a sufficient number of Swiss and other Europeans would emigrate as tenant farmers, rather than as direct owners. Land was so cheap in the United States that most people who could make the transatlantic passage could also afford to buy a small farm. Few were likely to accept a ticket under Gallatin's plan of renting them land in return for a large share of their agricultural output.

His third and most fundamental mistake was in overrating the fertility of his holdings at Friendship Hill. Unlike millions of other immigrants who came during the next several generations, Gallatin had little understanding of agriculture. He did not go from being a European farmer to being an American farmer. He had seldom gotten his hands dirty, sweating in the fields and tilling crops. Yet he remained convinced, as he had been when he left Geneva, that in the United States he could profit from his lands—through farming, renting, resale, or all three. He remained under the delusion that the fertility question would somehow resolve itself.

Meanwhile, he, Jean Badollet, and three other investors founded the firm Albert Gallatin & Co., still with the idea of attracting renters or buyers for portions of their lands. The partners established the town of New Geneva near Gallatin's home at Friendship Hill. They organized a company store, a boatyard on the Monongahela, and later a glass works. These ventures did not fulfill the partners' hopes, mainly because new settlers failed to show up.

The glass works—the first in America west of the Appalachians—prospered for a while, and in Gallatin's eyes it came to represent his best investment. But it suffered not only from undercapitalization, but also from inadequate supervision, since Gallatin was beginning to spend more of his time in politics. Still, he never forgot the strong promise of his glass works. After he became secretary of the treasury, he tried to establish a federal investment bank to assist similar enterprises. Owing in large part to his failure as a land developer, his ideas about capital began to evolve in a more modern direction. It took him several years to understand all this, however, and had he been less brilliant, he might have remained at Friendship Hill for the rest of his life.[11]

Gallatin's congenial disposition, superb education, and capacity for hard work made him a natural choice to represent rustic Fayette County in Pennsylvania politics. His heavy French accent put off some voters, but his obvious talents overcame this prejudice. Most other people in Fayette County had arrived recently themselves. Gallatin's political prospects, therefore, were stronger on the frontier than they would have been in Philadelphia, Boston, or any other long-settled city. In 1788, he was elected a delegate to the conference in Harrisburg called to discuss revisions to the U.S. Constitution, which the states had not yet ratified. Gallatin had reservations about the Constitution's centralizing powers, and at the conference he proposed drastic revisions that stood no chance of passing. This baptism taught him a valuable lesson about when to speak and when to keep his mouth shut—a skill Alexander Hamilton never learned, but that became one of Gallatin's strongest assets.

At that time, political partisanship in the state divided Philadelphia, the nation's largest city and soon to be its capital, from the frontier West, whose residents tended to oppose any form of centralized authority. As a delegate from the West, Gallatin took the side of the anti-Federalists, as those opposed to a strong national government were called. In the end, Pennsylvania ratified the Constitution, but, like many other states, only on the condition that it be amended—the result being the first ten amendments, the Bill of Rights.

⁂

By 1788, Gallatin had reached the age of twenty-seven and had grown almost desperate to find a wife with whom he could share his lonely existence at Friendship Hill. He found an ideal candidate in Sophie Allegre, a beautiful daughter of the Richmond landlady in whose boardinghouse he often stayed. Sophie's ancestors had been immigrant French Huguenots, and she knew enough French to converse with Gallatin in his native language. He had fallen in love with Sophie almost from the moment he met her. The problem was that he knew almost nothing about women and hadn't the faintest idea how to engage Sophie in a serious conversation about their future. He finally summoned the courage to write her a letter in which he vaguely proposed marriage. She declined to answer it, knowing that her mother, who had a low opinion of Gallatin, would balk at any such union. Gallatin continued to dither.

A breakthrough came a year later, in the spring of 1789, when Sophie visited her married sister at New Kent, thirty miles from Richmond. Gallatin, now twenty-eight, followed her there and, steeling himself, managed to stammer out a marriage proposal. Sophie's reaction amazed him. As he wrote a friend, she "did not play the coquette with me at all, but from the second day gave me her full consent." Sophie added that she would have done so earlier had he taken the trouble to ask. She "had always known that I loved her, but had been surprised not to hear from me for more than a year." Small wonder.[12]

When Sophie's mother learned of this development, she at once summoned her daughter back to Richmond. Gallatin tried to reason with Mrs. Allegre, but to little avail. "She was furious," he wrote, "refused me in the most brutal manner, and almost forbade me admission to the house." Mrs. Allegre believed that nobody who spoke with such a strong accent and had taught at Harvard could be a suitable match for Sophie. Worse, Gallatin would carry her off to a dangerous frontier, where, in Mrs. Allegre's view, he had no prospects for success. "She is a devil of a woman whom her daughter fears horribly," Gallatin wrote. "I believe, however, that I will succeed." He did, and they were married in a quiet ceremony outside Richmond. Sophie then tried to conciliate her mother: "He is perhaps not a very handsome man, but he is possessed of more essential qualities, which I shall not pretend to enumerate; as coming from me, they might be supposed partial."[13]

Gallatin's marriage was deliriously happy for him, but—as often happened in those days of frequent infections and no antibiotics—tragically short. It lasted only five months, from May to October 1789, when Sophie fell ill and died. Gallatin buried her on the crest of Friendship Hill.

Stunned, he now began to question everything he had done over the previous nine years: leaving Geneva without so much as a word to his foster mother, gallivanting about the United States, treating his late friend Henri Serre cavalierly, dawdling in his courtship of Sophie, and moving her into the wilderness. In April 1790, he wrote Catherine Pictet hinting that he might now sell his American properties and return to Geneva. But by this time the French Revolution had begun and the future of both France and Geneva was uncertain.[14]

Miss Pictet wrote back, "As for the advice you ask about your coming home and the resources you might find, I am quite embarrassed to reply." Gallatin was taken aback by this frosty answer, but he had not really wanted to leave America in the first place. So, rather than return to Europe, he submerged his grief by plunging into the public affairs of his adopted country. During the years he served in that role, his experiences as an immigrant entrepreneur—both successes and failures—shaped his most innovative proposals and policies.[15]

CHAPTER 17

Entering Politics

From the time of Sophie's death in 1789 until 1829, a period of forty years, Gallatin devoted almost all of his time and energy to public service—and phenomenal energy it turned out to be. Late in life he reflected on "that great facility of labour with which I was blessed." During the winter of 1789–1790, he represented Fayette County at the Pennsylvania convention called to revise the state constitution. His neighbors then elected him to the state House of Representatives. In that contest he won two-thirds of all votes cast. In 1791 and 1792 he was reelected without opposition. Of necessity, he began to spend less time at Friendship Hill and more in Philadelphia, which was now the capital not only of Pennsylvania but also of the United States.[1]

Gallatin quickly became a force among the sixty-nine delegates in the Pennsylvania House, even though he was in the anti-Federalist minority. Despite his agrarian orientation, he excelled in finance, and prepared by himself the entire report of the Committee on Ways and Means for 1790–1791. This achievement, he believed, "laid the foundation of my reputation. I was quite astonished at the general encomiums bestowed upon it and was not at all aware that I had done so well." Within

the Pennsylvania House, "I acquired an extraordinary influence," he recalled. "The labouring oar was left almost exclusively to me. In the session of 1791–1792, I was put on 35 Committees, prepared all the reports and drew all their bills." It is
difficult to see how he could have worked any harder, and he
was learning politics very fast.[2]

One of his reports attacked slavery as "obviously contrary to
the laws of nature, the dictates of justice . . . and natural right."
Concurrently, Gallatin joined the Pennsylvania Society for Promoting the Abolition of Slavery. He spent most of his time,
however, drafting bills on finance and taxation, trying to get
their language just right. "Absorbed by those details, my attention was turned exclusively to administrative laws and not to
legislation properly so called"—that is, he worked more on
writing bills than on getting them passed.[3]

Gallatin's special talent, a rare one much like Alexander
Hamilton's, lay less in political horse-trading and back-slapping
than in spending prodigious amounts of time framing careful
legislation that stood a good chance of passage and, once enacted, of being administered efficiently. His major successes had
to do with finance: tax plans to reduce the state's debt; the char-
tering of the Bank of Pennsylvania, with several branches (this
was the state's third bank, following the Bank of North America and Hamilton's Bank of the United States); and a general
program of frugality overseen by the Committee on Ways and
Means. Each of these measures foreshadowed Gallatin's later
policies as a congressman and as secretary of the treasury. And
each moved him, step by step, into the Jeffersonian fold opposed to Hamilton.

In 1791, still a member of the Pennsylvania House, Gallatin
had his first direct clash with the Federalists' fiscal program. At
Hamilton's behest, Congress had passed a fundraising act that

placed an excise tax on whiskey. This was the nation's initial "internal" tax under the Constitution—the first federal revenue law that was not a duty on imports. The act provided for two methods of assessing the tax—either by a levy that gradually declined according to the volume of whiskey distilled, or by a flat fee for each gallon. It therefore favored large eastern distillers, who produced in volume. They paid an average of about six cents per gallon, whereas western farmers who converted their grain to whiskey in smaller amounts were assessed nine cents—almost 40 percent of a gallon's retail value at that time.[4]

The Westerners were outraged. The whiskey trade was important to them, they argued (a little speciously), because they could transport distilled liquor to eastern markets more cheaply than bulk grain. They responded to the new law with uniform belligerence. Often they refused to pay the tax at all.[5]

While the Whiskey Bill was being debated in Congress, Gallatin spoke often in the Pennsylvania legislature, condemning the tax. At one point he proposed a state law that would have declared unconstitutional any act by Congress taxing goods sent from one state to another. This radical proposal went nowhere, and Gallatin learned another important lesson about how far he could push his ideas in public. After Congress passed the Whiskey Act and President Washington signed it, the fight moved from legislative chambers into the countryside.[6]

Westerners in nearly all states containing trans-Appalachian settlements had long been leery of a whiskey tax. Pennsylvania itself had levied such a tax, only to repeal it after rancorous opposition from the western counties. The idea of a federal tax on whiskey struck Westerners as little short of outrageous. Trans-Appalachian residents of Pennsylvania and every other affected state tended to be suspicious of any federal authority at all over their working lives. By the 1790s, they had accumulated specific quarrels with the national government: it furnished them with insufficient protection from Indian attacks, which were on the rise especially in Pennsylvania; and it failed to guarantee their rights to ship goods south on the Mississippi River, the Louisiana Territory then being the property of Spain.

In such a context, the Whiskey Act seemed a slap aimed directly at them. Frontier farmers from Georgia, the Carolinas, Maryland, Virginia, and Pennsylvania called meetings to protest the tax, and hounded the hapless revenue officers sent out to collect it. In 1792, Gallatin served as clerk at a meeting of "Whiskey rebels" held at Pittsburgh. This, he later wrote, was "my only political sin," because he did so little to defuse his constituents' fury. The fight persisted for several months, and in 1794 flared into a potential insurrection against the federal government.[7]

In 1793, the Pennsylvania legislature elected Gallatin to the U.S. Senate, where he would serve alongside Robert Morris of the state's eastern faction. Also in 1793, he married again, this time choosing Hannah Nicholson, the daughter of James Nicholson, a prominent New Yorker. Nicholson was a wealthy former naval officer and a powerful member of the anti-Schuyler/Hamilton faction in New York politics. He and Hamilton had once come close to fighting a duel.

Gallatin's courtship of Hannah Nicholson again showed his ineptitude in affairs of the heart; but this time he succeeded with a little help from his friends. During the spring of 1793, after a long legislative session, his Pennsylvania confidant Alexander James Dallas proposed that he and Gallatin take a brief vacation to New York. Dallas was yet another immigrant and future secretary of the treasury—a tall, suave native of Jamaica. In New York City they visited the home of Commodore Nicholson and his wife, an heiress whose father had emigrated to New York from Bermuda.

In addition to a son, the Nicholsons had four daughters. One was married to a U.S. senator from Georgia and another later married a congressman from Maryland. Mrs. Dallas, playing matchmaker for Gallatin, invited Hannah, an unmarried Nicholson daughter, for a sailing trip up the Hudson to Albany. On this voyage, Gallatin, now thirty-two years old, became enamored of Hannah, who was twenty-seven and on the verge of spinsterhood.[8]

After a brief return to Philadelphia, Gallatin went back to New York, bent on pursuing her. As he wrote his friend Jean Badollet, Hannah was "neither handsome nor rich, but sensible, well-informed, good-natured, and belonging to a respectable and very amiable family, who, I believe, are satisfied with the intended match." Gallatin did not feel the ardent sexual attraction for Hannah that he had for Sophie Allegre, but there was no question of his affection for her. Recalling that he had erred in dithering for so long in his courtship of Sophie, he took swift action. He wrote Commodore and Mrs. Nicholson that they must have understood "the object of my late journey to your city and of my behaviour whilst there." He then asked their permission to ask Hannah to marry him. "I love Miss Nicholson and wish no greater happiness than to be forever united to her."[9]

In a carefully phrased letter, Commodore Nicholson replied that the family had no objection "to your intention of endeavoring to gain our child's hand, for which purpose you have our consent." Nicholson made clear, however, that Hannah's financial expectations depended on the partition of her Bermuda grandfather's estate. He reminded Gallatin that there were four other Nicholson children with whom Hannah would divide the inheritance. "So until the death of her mother," Hannah's "maintenance must depend solely upon you. These reflections we flatter ourselves will have their full weight upon you both." After long discussions between Gallatin and Hannah over what she might expect in Fayette County—a frontier with which she was entirely unacquainted—she consented to the marriage. To soften the prospect of life in the wilderness, Gallatin pointed out that he had been elected to the U.S. Senate and that they would spend much of their time in Philadelphia, the national capital.[10]

———

Gallatin well knew his own social limitations. He had left Geneva as little more than a boy and had then lived mostly in backwoods America. "Thence, although I feel no embarrassment with men," he wrote Hannah, he still felt "awkwardness in mixed companies which will forever prevent a man from becoming a party in the societies where he mixes." He might have made progress during his time in the state legislature, "but I felt no wish of doing it." Therefore, Hannah would have to take a remedial hand: "You must polish my manners, teach me how to talk to people I do not know, and how to render myself agreeable to strangers." Gallatin had repeatedly been elected to represent his constituents, and later became known as a splendid conversationalist. But here he was referring to women, who did not vote and in whose company he had spent little time.[11]

His marriage to Hannah was not as dazzling a leap up the social ladder as Hamilton's to Elizabeth Schuyler had been, but it was still very big. Gallatin acquired powerful political connections not only in New York, but also in Georgia and Maryland, through Hannah's sisters who married politicians from those states. Then, too, Hannah's young brother, James W. Nicholson, became Gallatin's business partner and helped to manage his Pennsylvania properties for the next thirty-five years. Membership in the large and welcoming Nicholson family remained a great personal comfort to the orphaned Gallatin for the rest of his life. Eventually he and Hannah had six children, two boys and four girls. The Nicholsons also introduced him to John Jacob Astor, with whom he formed a close friendship.[12]

A month after his marriage, which took place in November

1793, Gallatin assumed his seat in the U.S. Senate, where he immediately began a strong opposition to Hamilton's fiscal program. He introduced resolutions requiring Hamilton to present a full accounting of all Treasury operations since 1789—a drastic demand. Soon, however, petitioners from Pennsylvania challenged his eligibility for the Senate on grounds that he was an immigrant who had not been an American citizen for the requisite nine years before his election. This was true, although at the time the issue was not wholly clear. The lead petitioner pointed out that "one of the ancient Republics made it death for an alien to intermeddle in their politics."[13]

Battling hard to keep his seat, Gallatin was able to put forward only a feeble argument: that he had briefly served in the Revolutionary War during 1780 while he lived in Maine as a twenty-one-year-old, and he deserved citizenship from that date. He had gone out on one patrol, but, as he admitted years later, "As I never met the enemy, I have not the slightest claim to military service." At the end of February 1794, by a straight party vote of 14 to 12, the Federalist-controlled Senate expelled him. Robert Morris, Pennsylvania's other senator, came under heavy pressure and voted with the majority although he had promised to remain neutral. At the time, Gallatin's banishment seemed a major setback to his political career. Once he left the Senate, nothing came of his resolutions for a five-year accounting by Hamilton, which the Republicans had believed might yield bountiful political returns.[14]

He and Hannah then moved west to Friendship Hill, where she developed no affection whatever for the frontier. It took several days of hard travel over the mountains from Philadelphia even to reach Fayette County. And as much as Gallatin loved Friendship Hill, he had chosen a poor place to earn a decent living and raise a family. He and his friend Jean Badollet had idealized the Pennsylvania frontier, taking too hopeful a view of the pace of its economic development. Badollet, who turned out to have a streak of stubbornness, remained there for the next eighteen years, but Gallatin decided to establish a second residence on the eastern seaboard. He kept most of his western lands, including Friendship Hill, and sold other holdings to Robert Morris. He and Hannah then spent a good deal of time in Philadelphia and also in New York City, where she felt very much at home.

During the early 1790s, the simmering Whiskey Rebellion in Pennsylvania came to full boil. Despite Gallatin's efforts to pacify the rebels, they attacked individual collectors and set fire to the barns of farmers who complied with the tax. In July 1794, 500 armed men gathered near Pittsburgh and began threatening all manner of mayhem—firing shots into the air, interfering with the courts, robbing the mails, and planning an assault on federal property in Pittsburgh. It was the first serious domestic challenge to the national government under the Constitution, and was met by decisive action.[15]

Urged on by Hamilton, President Washington sent a force of about 12,500 militiamen into western Pennsylvania—an overwhelming display of federal power. Hamilton himself traveled from the capital in Philadelphia as a civilian observer. As he wrote Angelica Church, his sister-in-law, "A large army has cooled the courage of those madmen & the only question seems to be how to guard best against the return of the phrenzy . . . Twas very important there should be no mistake in the management of the affair." The militia arrested about twenty rebels, two of whom were convicted of treason and sentenced to hang. Washington, concluding that the proper lesson had been taught and learned, commuted these sentences. But Gallatin always regarded the incident as an gross overreaction by the federal government. It confirmed his worst suspicions about Hamilton, whom he came to think of as a tool of wealthy Easterners unconcerned with the West.[16]

Despite Gallatin's expulsion from the Senate in February

1794, his absence from Congress in Philadelphia did not last long. In November 1794, having now been a citizen for nine years, he won election to the U.S. House of Representatives. He took his seat in 1795, a year after his banishment from the Senate and just after Hamilton's departure from the Treasury. And he quickly became a major force in the House.

CHAPTER 18

Becoming Jeffersonian

After the resignation of Jefferson as secretary of state in 1793, he and his allies had begun to formulate a plan to gain control of the national government. More than any other event, the fight over the Jay Treaty with Britain gave them the ammunition they needed. Gallatin's arrival in Congress in 1795 therefore came at a pivotal moment. The Jeffersonians were in open revolt against the Federalists, not only over Hamilton's economic program but now over the Jay Treaty as well.

The treaty did avert a possible war with Britain and open some Caribbean ports to American exports. But it did not stop British intrigues with Indians impeding westward expansion, or—most important—impressment of American seamen into the Royal Navy. In 1796 the Republicans, furious over the treaty's apparently pro-British outcome, held the first party caucus in U.S. history. Meanwhile, the Federalists were beginning to split into warring factions led by Hamilton on one hand and John Adams on the other.

It was at this juncture that Gallatin took his place as the leading Republican expert on finance in Congress. He knew more about the subject than any other senator or representative in his party, and probably more than any other Republican at all. Not only did he have a gift for mathematics and the patience to study complex financial reports; he also had gained valuable experience with finance in the Pennsylvania legislature. As Madison wrote Jefferson in 1796, "Gallatin is a real Treasure . . . He is sound in his principles, accurate in his calculations and indefatigable in his researches."[1]

Jefferson, as he made clear in his reply to Madison, persisted in his belief that Hamilton had deliberately cast the Treasury's reports on the national finances "into forms which should be utterly undecypherable. I ever said he did not understand their condition himself, nor was able to give a clear view of the excess of our debts beyond our credits, nor whether we were diminishing or increasing the debt." Jefferson went on to say, somewhat inconsistently, that the "accounts of the U.S. ought to be, and may be, made, as simple as those of a common farmer, and capable of being understood by common farmers." Madison knew better, and Gallatin much better.[2]

In the elections of 1794, the Republicans had gained control of the House. Gallatin would therefore start his career in the House as a member of the majority—and, for both Jefferson and Madison, he would be a uniquely useful colleague in the party they were building.

———

Hamilton's fiscal program had long been the bane of the Republicans, and Gallatin proved to be the ideal weapon of attack. In 1796, after only a year in Congress, he published *A Sketch of the Finances of the United States*. This document, despite its modest title, is the length of a small book, and replete with detailed numbers on federal income and expenditures. Its text is also full of relentless assaults on Hamilton, on his successor, Oliver Wolcott, and even on President Washington. Gallatin names none of these men, but any informed reader could easily identify them as his targets. Here, perhaps more than in any other single document of the era, one can see in high relief the differences in the two American schools of thought about a wide variety of issues.[3]

A strong moral tone runs through Gallatin's *Sketch*. He presents in full particulars the orthodox Republican conviction that a national debt has no legitimacy and that it produces endless mischief: corruption of public morals, an excessive military establishment, and a financial class favored by the government—in short, the same British system that had caused the colonists to revolt in the first place. Gallatin argues that Hamilton's fiscal plan had led to lavish federal spending and a deliberate increase in the national debt. The document also expresses, almost perfectly, the Jeffersonian position on military affairs and other issues besides finance. Because it so thoroughly foreshadows the policies followed later by the Jefferson and Madison presidential administrations, the contents of the *Sketch* merit a close look.[4]

Gallatin begins with about thirty pages explaining how the U.S. Treasury obtains and spends its income. He includes insightful commentary on the problems of finance in a new nation, but omits any applause for how Hamilton's programs met those problems. For example, Gallatin presents federal income figures for the year 1795 without mentioning the dismal prospects of earlier years. For 1795, Gallatin summarizes this way:

Federal receipts for 1795

Duties on imports and tonnage	$5,810,000
Internal duties	410,000
Postage of letters	30,000
Dividend on bank stock	160,000
Total	$6,410,000

Gallatin did not have fully accurate figures for the years 1790–1793, but for 1794 he knew that federal receipts had totaled $5.4 million. Receipts for 1795, therefore, were 19 percent higher than for the preceding year, and—as Gallatin would have known if he'd had the exact numbers, rather than approximations—four times the amount of federal receipts for 1790. Yet

Hamilton receives no accolades for shaping an economic climate in which revenues grew so fast in so short a time. Nor does Gallatin dwell on the advantages accruing to American exports and shipping from the war that began between Britain and France in 1793.[5]

In his *Sketch,* Gallatin recognizes the inconvenient dependence of the United States Treasury on revenues from British imports. But he then tries to demonstrate that the American economy was in worse condition in 1796 than it had been when Hamilton took office in 1789—the national debt having increased from about $75 million to $85 million. Both the U.S. economy and federal receipts had grown so much faster than the debt during this period, however, that Gallatin would have a hard time convincing an unbiased audience that the country was worse off. As a historical document, the *Sketch* is useful primarily as a long synopsis of the way Jeffersonians viewed recent events, and as a precursor to the policies that would follow under a government they led.

In the two main parts of his *Sketch,* Gallatin's version of recent history was less effective than his outline of potential new policies. In the first, less constructive part, he elaborates at length on major mistakes he attributes to Hamilton's original plan and to the general conduct of the Washington administration. By far the worst error, he argues, lay in Hamilton's insistence on the assumption of state debts. Gallatin retells the story of this bitter fight for the purpose of arguing that the national debt should have been much less than it was. The interest on the debt constituted "an unnecessary expense, arising from an unnecessary assumption of debt, and which must continue till the debt itself is discharged."[6]

Gallatin next takes up military expenditures for both land and naval forces. He complains about the excessive cost of federal efforts to diminish the dangers of Indian attacks. This criticism seems odd coming from a representative of western Pennsylvania, the source of a steady drumbeat of complaints about insufficient help for defense against the Indians. Then, too—and here Gallatin's partisanship becomes clear from his choice of words alone—he argues that the country's naval armament "seems to be rather an object of parade than of real utility."[7]

At that time, the Washington administration was building six heavy frigates, the most famous being the Constitution, known as "Old Ironsides." In 1794, Madison had written to Jefferson that "every consideration first rendering [the frigates] unwise, now renders them absurd." In his Sketch two years later, Gallatin questions the appropriateness of even having a navy. He suggests that the funds to build the frigates would be better spent "in laying the foundation for a real navy by the purchases of timber, materials, &c., and by preparing all those things which time alone can procure." Under such a plan, however, there would be no existing ships as a deterrent to war. And during the many months required to build them, American ports and commercial ships at sea would remain unprotected.[8]

Next in his Sketch, making a much stronger argument, Gallatin objects to the government's disproportionate response to the Whiskey Rebellion. "The call of about 15,000 militia and the expenditure of twelve hundred thousand dollars for the purpose of suppressing mobs and riots" wildly overshot the mark of what was necessary. One-fifth of those resources would have been plenty. Gallatin contrasts this incident with the more moderate measures taken to quell Shays's Rebellion in Massachusetts—another taxpayers' revolt that had occurred eight years earlier than the Whiskey Rebellion, during the depression years of 1786–1787.[9]

This comparison was a good rhetorical ploy, but the two episodes were not very similar. During Shays's Rebellion, which began as a protest over money owed to veterans of the Revolution, over the scarcity of hard money, and over mortgage payments, several people were killed, many wounded, and two hanged by the government. A force of 4,000 militiamen dealt with an insurrection that threatened a federal arsenal as well as the government of Massachusetts. The Shays affair occasioned Jefferson's famous comment that "a little rebellion now and then is a good thing. The tree of liberty must be refreshed from time to time with the blood of patriots and tyrants. It is it's [*sic*] natural manure." Jefferson was in Paris as minister to France at the time, and his view differed markedly from that of his fellow Virginians, Washington and Madison. The real significance of Shays's Rebellion was to demonstrate that the Articles of Confederation were too feeble a foundation on which to build a viable national government. The episode marked a milestone on the road to the Constitutional Convention of 1787.[10]

Gallatin's *Sketch* next turns to Hamilton's funding and assumption plans. Gallatin acknowledges that some kind of funding was essential, but complains that by funding the debt at par Hamilton had paid four times its market value. As for assumption of the states' debts, Gallatin reargues its alleged faults in copious detail: it need not have been done at all; part of the total was funded "at the rate of one hundred for one"; and "the depreciation of the paper money" issued by individual states amounted to "the only taxes raised upon the people during the war." Here he seems to be saying that people who accepted state-issued paper money at face value had voluntarily helped to pay for the Revolution. This would have been a nice argument, were it not for the mass of protests against the rapid depreciation of state currency and the Constitution's subsequent outlawing of state issuances altogether.[11]

Each of these points had long since been settled, but they still rankled in the minds of many Republicans, and a more radical critique of the Federalists was on the rise. One of the Republicans' core tenets held that *any* national debt amounted to a national curse. France's huge debt, they contended (accurately), had played a big role in bringing on the French Revolution in 1789 because it required new taxes; and Hamilton's plans for dealing with the American debt smacked too much of the hated English system, with all its financial corruption. In the view of almost all Republicans, the Americans had fought their War of Independence against just this kind of system. The inescapable fact remained, however, that in doing so the new nation had incurred an enormous debt.

Gallatin's *Sketch* acknowledges that the war had been expensive. But it concedes nothing to Hamilton's establishment of U.S. creditworthiness—the ingenuity of his making federal bonds attractive to investors at home and abroad. Gallatin even objects to the sale of securities to foreign investors. It "had some dazzling temporary effect," but it also increased the "acquisition of wealth to the speculators in stock alone, and not to the nation." Far from being rescued, the country was worse off because it now had to pay the interest on bonds purchased by foreigners. This kind of reasoning was either naïve on Gallatin's part or, more likely, a partisan attack on the Federalists—using any argument that might persuade readers.[12]

The harshest words in the *Sketch* are reserved for Hamilton's assumption of state debts. Gallatin here tries to turn on its head Hamilton's claim that assumption would cement the bonds of national union. "Experience," Gallatin argues, had "shown that the additional debt laid upon the Union by the assumption, so far from strengthening government, has created more discontent and more uneasiness than any other measure." New federal taxes had been levied (actually almost none except the whiskey tax) to pay the interest on assumed state bonds; and the returns had gone to "some influential characters whose wish was to increase and perpetuate the debt." In other words, Hamilton had abetted the schemes of evil men to take advantage of the assumption plan, and perhaps had even engineered the schemes himself.[13]

Still hammering assumption as "that fatal measure," Gallatin asserts that if the national government had to interfere with state debts at all, Hamilton should never have funded them at par value. He should have assumed only $11 million of the state debts, rather than the full $22 million. Again, Gallatin did not address the deleterious effects such a step would have had on the nation's creditworthiness. Much as Madison had done in the original debates, Gallatin goes into detail about how a plan of his own for discharging state debts could have been worked out.[14]

He next turns to the Bank of the United States, and here he departs altogether from Jefferson's across-the-board opposition to banks. On the contrary, Gallatin argues, banks are essential, especially in a new country located far from capital markets and with little gold and silver of its own. Rather than objecting to banks per se—he had been familiar with them in Geneva before he emigrated, and in the state legislature had helped to charter the Bank of Pennsylvania—he finds fault with the way Hamilton capitalized the Bank of the United States. He implies that Hamilton's aim was to facilitate illegitimate stock-jobbing by his friends and supporters along the eastern seaboard, at the expense of the West. This was a standard objection to Hamilton's policies, raised by many Republicans.[15]

In practice, Gallatin goes on to say, the Washington-Hamilton administration had borrowed too much from the Bank of the United States. It had paid excessive interest rates and had spent too freely, thereby increasing the potential corruption inherent in public borrowing. Thus, the Jeffersonians' fears about the bank have "in some instances been justified, that the bank might become a political engine in the hands of government." Here Gallatin was on firmer ground. Hamilton had indeed used the Bank of the United States for purposes—large loans to the federal government, for example—that his original *Report on a National Bank* forbade but that the law passed by Congress permitted.[16]

Heaping on still more scorn, Gallatin maintains that because seven years had elapsed between the end of the war in 1783 and Hamilton's *Report on Public Credit* in 1790, there had actually been no financial emergency. Provisions for the debt "were already in a great measure cured by the exertions of private industry. The funding of the debt was therefore attended with no immediate evil, except that arising from the taxes necessary to pay the interest." Gallatin here seems to be assuming that the 1780s had been a prosperous decade and that the national debt would somehow have taken care of itself. It was a curious and wholly specious argument, but the rewriting of recent history was then, and of course still is, a commonplace in politics.[17]

Gallatin further contends that the new bond issues sponsored by Hamilton had no purpose—that funding the public debt, rather than extinguishing it, was an illegitimate policy. Even before the creation of the Bank of the United States, existing banks had been issuing enough paper money, "and the increase in circulation they produce [is] in general fully sufficient for the demands of the country." The additional currency issued by the Bank of the United States constituted a needless drain on the precious specie essential to back it up. Yet again, Gallatin was presenting standard Republican criticism—in this case again incorrect—of Hamilton's program.[18]

Who could doubt, he writes, that the debt had weakened the Union more than "any other internal cause? It is a lamentable truth that the Americans, although bound together by a stronger government, are less united in sentiment than they were eight years ago"—that is, in 1788. What was now needed was removal of all unnecessary taxation and of other conditions that divided the American people. Of these, the public debt stood at the top of the list. "It requires no argument to prove, it is a self-evident truth that, in a political point of view at least, every nation is enfeebled by a public debt." The debt hurt the United States in almost every way. "We would not be much exposed to the wanton attacks, depredations, or insults of any nation was it not known that our revenue and resources are palsied by an annual . . . five millions of dollars"—the amount necessary to pay interest on the debt.[19]

What, then, was Gallatin's overall solution? The answer could hardly be simpler: abolish the debt. In summarizing the details of his solution, Gallatin shifts from partisan argument to a sounder and more objective analysis of the American situation. He notes that the federal government must continue to obtain most of its revenues from imposts, but proposes that it now augment its income through sales of western lands. This was an index of his own preoccupation with development in the West, where the government owned tens of millions of acres.

As Gallatin describes the national situation, "There are at present but two species of wealth of a general nature in the United States, viz., lands and capital employed in commerce. It has already been stated that in proportion to our population we were one of the first commercial [trading] nations. It cannot be denied that we are by far the first agricultural nation. It must be acknowledged that we are not yet a manufacturing nation. Our capital in commerce is great; our capital in lands is immense; it can hardly be said that we yet have any capital in manufactures. Taxes must be raised from that fund which can afford to pay"—that is, first through imposts, then through land sales. Meanwhile, the federal government should practice extreme frugality, notably in defense expenditures. There was no pressing need for either a standing army or a substantial navy. Land sales in fact began in 1796, but they never yielded the large revenues that both Hamilton and Gallatin had hoped for.[20]

Gallatin's sweeping indictment of Hamilton's program, however exaggerated, reflects sincere indignation. The Republicans actually believed that the Federalists were betraying Revolutionary ideals. The *Sketch* is best read not only as a partisan tract but also as a call to restore the principles of the Revolution and, above all, to extinguish the national debt. This goal was not merely a financial tenet of the Republicans, but a moral one as well: a pillar of their anti-British and anti-corruption ideology.[21]

In writing his *Sketch*, Gallatin was refreshing the memories of any Jeffersonians who might have forgotten the particulars of how Hamilton and the Federalists had worked their trickery. And he was showing the way out by specifying alternative and plausible policies. That he disdained the spectacular success of Hamilton's program was a mere detail—a trait common to all partisan documents. The *Sketch* appeared in 1796, a general-election year. In addition to what were certain to be hotly contested congressional contests, Jefferson had become a candidate to succeed Washington as president of the United States.

Gallatin's *Sketch* was an attack by one immigrant financial theorist on the program of another. Each had proved himself the preeminent economic expert within one of the two emerging political parties: Hamilton for the Federalists, Gallatin for the Republicans. It was not a coincidence that each team was headed by an immigrant economic thinker. The ideas of both men about the movement of capital across nations and oceans, and about integrating the United States into transatlantic credit markets, were shaped by their own experience of mobility and migration.[22]

By the time he wrote his *Sketch* in 1796, Gallatin had become so thoroughly caught up in American politics that he was hardly less concerned than Hamilton about achieving Fame. His best route forward would be as the leading authority on finance in a Jefferson presidential administration. That ambition would be realized, but not quite yet.

CHAPTER 19

The Climb to Power

In the election of 1796, the Federalists regained control of the House and kept their large majority in the Senate. In the presidential election, Jefferson lost a close race to John Adams, who had been vice president under Washington. Before the passage of the Twelfth Amendment in 1804, the winning candidate became president and the second-place finisher vice president. Once in office, Vice President Jefferson was almost never consulted by Adams. He did, however, participate actively in government. He presided over the Senate during a tumultuous four years, built an opposition party, and planned another run for the highest office.[1]

After the Adams administration took over in March 1797, James Madison left the House of Representatives and went home to Montpelier, his Virginia plantation, much as Jefferson had retired to Monticello in 1793. Many of the duties of House Republican leadership then fell on Albert Gallatin, who was only thirty-two years old at the time. He worked long hours not only as a congressman, but also as one of the linchpins of Jefferson's plan to oust the Federalists from power.

While Gallatin paid attention to politics, his agents and associates in western Pennsylvania looked after his business affairs, and consistently mismanaged them. As he wrote a friend in 1798, "I am a bad farmer, and have been unfortunate in some mercantile pursuits I had embraced." Gallatin believed he was no better off financially than he had been a dozen years earlier, in part because the bankruptcy of Robert Morris deprived him of the third installment of payment for the sale of his lands. It was a tribute to Gallatin's generous temperament that he remained on at least outwardly cordial terms with Morris, whose vote had earlier cost him a seat in the U.S. Senate and whose bankruptcy now cost him a good deal of money. "The fact is," he went on in the 1798 letter to his friend, "I am not well calculated to make money,—I care but little about it, for I want but little for myself, and my mind pursues other objects with more pleasure than mere business." Certainly national politics at this time was more exhilarating than a hardscrabble life on the Pennsylvania frontier.[2]

The Adams administration (1797–1801) proved ineffective from the start. Adams's talents, though formidable, were those of a lawyer and constitutional theorist, not an administrator or—most clearly—a party leader. Neither he nor Alexander Hamilton possessed anything like Thomas Jefferson's gifts as a politician: the abilities of quiet persuasion and behind-the-scenes orchestration of a nationwide movement; the unfailing sense of when to speak and when to keep quiet; the knack for being all things to all voters. Then, too, Adams spent an inordinate amount of his time not at the capital in Philadelphia, but at his home in Quincy, Massachusetts. Nor did Adams get along well with Hamilton. Each behaved badly toward the other, often conspicuously so. Both should have known better, and their chronic bickering did credit to neither man. It damaged their party, their personal stature, and the country as a whole.[3]

Albert Gallatin took an active role in Congress during the Adams presidency. He peppered the new secretary of the treasury, Oliver Wolcott Jr., with constant barbs and demands for information. Wolcott, Hamilton's longtime protégé and successor, was the scion of an old Connecticut family. He had served first as auditor and then as comptroller at the Treasury, before President Washington appointed him head of the department. As secretary from 1795 to 1800, Wolcott followed Hamilton's financial policies and often sought his counsel. A first-rate administrator, he ran a tight ship, but in a deteriorating political situation. Wolcott was never asked to play the broad role in government that Hamilton had performed.

This was true during both the remainder of Washington's second term, which ended in March 1797, and the presidency of Adams. During those periods, much of what Albert Gallatin said and did in the House—establishing stronger legislative oversight of the Treasury and issuing a constant stream of demands for reports—made the new secretary's life miserable. After five years' service, Wolcott resigned in 1800, a presidential-election year. Adams took other steps to reduce Hamilton's influence, finally shifting the membership of his cabinet, which for almost four years had been heavily influenced by Hamilton. Adams remarked at the time that Hamilton "was a bastard and as much a foreigner as Gallatin." There seemed to be more prejudice against immigrants in New England than in other sections of the country.[4]

During the Quasi-War with France (1798–1800), the Republicans, with Gallatin as their chief spokesman in Congress, opposed expenditures on either the army or the navy. They retained their hatred of the British, even as they later denounced Napoleon's betrayal of the ideals of the French Revolution. In Congress, Gallatin opposed military action against France or even preparation for it. For this, he suffered consistent attacks on his immigrant origins, his heavy French accent, and even his loyalty to the United States.

In 1797, in a barb aimed directly at Gallatin, the Federalist congressman John Allen of Connecticut said on the House floor that the nation "had reason to wish that foreign intercourse, so far as it related to importing intriguing foreigners, had long ago ceased." A few months later, as relations with France continued to worsen, Gallatin spoke against having American warships protect convoys of merchant ships. Again, Congressman Allen assailed him: "Is this the language of an American who loves his country? No, sir, it is the language of a foreign agent." These were harsh words from the Federalist side, and they were as baseless as similar assaults on Hamilton's immigrant origins had been.[5]

By the late 1790s, most naturalized voters were gravitating toward the Republicans, whose democratic rhetoric appealed to them. To slow this process, the Federalist-controlled Congress passed the Naturalization Act of 1798, which increased to fourteen years the period before immigrants could become citizens—and therefore voters. This law was changed many times in the future, shortening the required period of residence.[6]

Taking steps that were of more immediate hazard to the nation, Congress passed and the president signed three Alien and Sedition Acts. These laws, which cleared the Senate easily but the House by very narrow margins (52 to 48 on the original reports), provided for the deportation of aliens whom the president deemed dangerous, and imposed severe penalties for criticizing the government. Jefferson believed that the Alien Act was designed in part to threaten the status of Albert Gallatin.[7]

In significant measure, the larger goal of the acts was to silence opposition journalists. Both the Republicans and the Federalists were still sponsoring newspapers that churned out scurrilous bombast on each side of every party controversy. Many of these journals were edited by talented British and Irish immigrants. Editors of Republican papers, who were winning the battle for public opinion, found themselves among the primary targets of the Federalist laws.[8]

The Republicans responded swiftly to the Alien and Sedition Acts. Vice President Jefferson drafted the Kentucky Resolution of 1798 for the legislature of that state, while James Madison wrote a similar Virginia Resolution. In both cases, their authorship remained secret. Jefferson composed the Kentucky Resolution in the form of a legal pleading. He used potent language that he took care to repeat in several places, much as he had done in the Declaration of Independence. Politicians in Kentucky softened the rhetoric a bit, but it remained explosive. Each Alien and Sedition Act, Jefferson wrote, "is not law, but is altogether void, and of no force." Coming from the vice president of the United States, these were remarkably strong words.[9]

Madison, who was not a lawyer by profession but nevertheless a capable legal thinker, took a milder and less formal tone. But the message of both resolutions—that states could annul federal laws—foreshadowed the nullification doctrines used later by secessionists: both New Englanders before and during the War of 1812, and Southerners from the 1820s until the Civil War. The Alien and Sedition laws threatened a disastrous partisan split that reflected badly on the behavior of both Federalists and Republicans.[10]

The Federalists had inflicted severe political damage on themselves by passing the laws in the first place. In particular, they had offended immigrant voters and radicalized a whole corps of Republican journalists, who now redoubled their efforts. And the Kentucky and Virginia resolutions did not enhance the legacies of Jefferson and Madison except among their most ardent admirers. Had Jefferson's authorship been disclosed, it is possible that he would not have won the presidential election of 1800. As the sitting vice president of the United States, he had not only written a scorching denunciation of administra-

tion policy. He had also called for a de facto constitutional revolution in the way acts of Congress were to be enforced.[11]

Gallatin was no more deterred by attacks on his immigrant origins through the Alien Act than Hamilton had been by earlier
assaults. As the Quasi-War with France continued into the election year of 1800, Gallatin wrote still another long denunciation of Federalist fiscal policy, similar to his *Sketch* of 1796. Titling his 1800 piece *Views of the Public Debt, Receipts and
Expenditures of the United States,* he noted that during most of
the Adams administration, the federal government had received
more funds than it spent. Following a wise policy, Gallatin
wrote, it had managed to reduce the national debt by almost
$3.6 million. But then, during its last year in office, the adminis-
tration had lavished so much money on military preparations
for war with France that the debt had grown by about $5 mil-
lion. The Republicans valued American national honor no less
than the Federalists, but both Jefferson and Gallatin were appalled by these new military outlays. They continued to see the
French as a lesser threat than the British, whom they still detested. It is conceivable that if the funds had been spent to gird
the nation against Britain rather than France, their objections
might have been less strenuous. But their later policies, once in
executive power, usually augured against military expenditures
as a principle in itself.

The chief foreign-policy task of American government from
1793 until 1812 was to avoid being whipsawed by Britain and
France during their struggle against each other. In retrospect, it
is clear that although the United States often took advantage of
economic opportunities afforded by the war, there was no way
to escape the larger dilemma. Gallatin, initially as Republican
leader of the House, then as secretary of the treasury, could not
have avoided spending enormous amounts of time dealing with

the problems posed by threats from both the British and the French.[12]

The administration of John Adams and then those of presidents Jefferson and Madison searched constantly for a solution to the quandaries of neutrality. They used every possible means: diplomacy, boycotts, embargoes, the arming of American merchant ships, and naval action. Within the United States, war fever ebbed and flowed—directed against France, then against Britain, and sometimes, implausibly, against both at the same time. Throughout this long period, Gallatin remained almost as involved in diplomacy as he was in economic policy: first in measures attempting to avert war with either country, then in trying to pay for the War of 1812 against Britain, and finally in negotiating the treaty ending that war. Gallatin's surviving correspondence for the twenty-two years of war between Britain and France contains thousands of letters and messages about foreign policy as well as public finance.

In the middle of this period, at the time of the presidential election of 1800, the national capital moved to Washington, D.C. The shift from Philadelphia to the Potomac completed the final step in the bargain over debt assumption that Hamilton had struck with Jefferson and Madison at their famous dinner party in 1790. During November 1800, President John Adams took up residence in the Executive Mansion. (It was not called the White House until 1811.) He then moved out four months later, having lost his bid for reelection. Adams did not attend Jefferson's inauguration, instead departing in a bitter mood at four o'clock in the morning without so much as a word to his successor.

Two months earlier, in January 1801, Gallatin had written a long letter to his wife, describing the primitive conditions in the new capital. Knowing that Hannah preferred living in a city and had little use for rural settings, Gallatin gave a candid warning: "Our local situation is far from being pleasant or even convenient. Around the Capitol are seven or eight boarding-houses, one tailor, one shoemaker, one printer, a washing-woman, a pamphlets and stationery shop, a small dry-goods shop, and an oyster house. This makes the whole of the Federal city as connected with the Capitol." There were a few suitable private houses on Capitol Hill, and Gallatin hoped to move his family into one of them. Eventually he did, to the great advantage not only of his wife and children, but also of his own working routine. But the unappealing conditions in the D.C. area as a place to live made it hard to recruit good civil servants. The government was sometimes forced to pay higher salaries than would have sufficed in Philadelphia.[13]

About three-quarters of a mile to the east of the Capitol, Gallatin wrote his wife, was the Potomac River, with "a wharf graced by not a single vessel," and, near the river, a small cluster of ramshackle buildings. A large swamp separated the Potomac from Capitol Hill, and also blocked easy passage from the Capitol to the president's house. In between these two new buildings there was supposed to be a "causeway (called the Pennsylvania Avenue)." But the fetid swamp made things so unpleasant that "not a single house intervenes or can intervene without devoting its wretched tenant to perpetual fevers."[14]

Slightly better conditions prevailed a little farther west. About a mile and a half from the Executive Mansion was the old Maryland settlement of Georgetown, situated on higher ground. "But *we* are not there; the distance is too great for convenience from thence to the Capitol; six or seven of the members have taken lodgings at Georgetown, three near the President's House, and all the others are crowded in the eight boarding-houses near the Capitol." In Conrad and McMunn's boardinghouse, Gallatin shared a room with a Massachusetts congressman and paid "at the rate, I think, including attendance [at meals], wood, candles, and liquors, of 15 dollars per week. At table, I believe, we are from twenty-four to thirty," and were it not for the wives of two boarders, we "would look like a refectory of monks." Gallatin went on to assure Hannah that he would never again allow politics to separate him so long from his family.[15]

Knowing her husband's obsessive work habits, Hannah replied with some skepticism. "Remember that it is *intended* to be the last time that you will have anybody but your own family for roommates, and this delightful thought must and will console you. Ah! Albert! how often have you expressed this to your poor wife, but no matter. I feel myself more determined this time than ever I did before, and I think this will have some influence on future arrangements." Neither of the Gallatins knew, however, that he was about to become secretary of the treasury, a post that would cause annual summer separations of at least two months. Nor that a diplomatic assignment a decade later would take him to Europe without Hannah for more than two years.[16]

Many other prominent government men, including Thomas Jefferson, the vice president and soon-to-be president-elect, lived in the same Washington boardinghouse as Gallatin. Conversation focused on the recent presidential contest. The balloting had gone on from April through October 1800, since in those days each state had the power of deciding when to vote. After the final tally, the Republican electors held a majority of 73 to 65 against the Federalists. Each elector was entitled to two votes, but the Republicans had inadvertently cast the same number of votes for Jefferson and for his running mate, Aaron Burr. The resulting 73-to-73 tie, under a constitutional provision, forced the decision into the House of Representatives.

At that time, Virginia had nineteen congressmen, Massachusetts fourteen, and Pennsylvania thirteen, while the less populous Georgia, Tennessee, and Delaware had one each. Yet according to the Constitution, each state, regardless of its size, could cast only a single vote in choosing the president when the

Electoral College produced no majority. The votes of nine of the existing sixteen states would be necessary to name a winner. The Federalists, who had kept their majority in the elections of 1798, still controlled the House as lame ducks. The Republicans had moved back into power in 1800, but the new Congress would not take office until March, along with the new president—whoever he turned out to be.[17]

In this convoluted and precarious situation, there was high potential for extraordinary damage to the country. Some knowledgeable people even predicted a civil war if the Federalists conspired to make Aaron Burr president. That possibility also crossed the mind of Albert Gallatin, who was working almost around the clock as the House floor leader for Jefferson. To complicate matters further, the coy Burr declined to issue a clear statement deferring to Jefferson. In consequence, the House debated and voted in an atmosphere of intense anxiety for seven days, from February 11 to 17, 1801. During one twenty-hour session, many congressmen slept on the floor of the Capitol building.

In thirty-five consecutive ballots, Jefferson received eight of the required nine state votes. Burr received six. Delegations from the remaining two states, Vermont and Maryland (two congressmen each), were split, and so their states could cast no vote. Jefferson himself proposed in letters to Madison and to James Monroe that if Burr won the election through Federalist support, then a national convention to amend the Constitution should be called. "I may aver," Gallatin wrote years later, "that under no circumstances would that plan have ever been resorted to or approved by the Republican party."[18]

Among the many ironies in what came to be called the "Revolution of 1800" was Alexander Hamilton's role in making his old foe Jefferson president. Hamilton had first weakened John Adams's candidacy by exacerbating the split in the Federalist Party. Then he had supported Jefferson over Aaron Burr, whom he knew to be an unscrupulous opportunist. "There is no doubt," he had written Oliver Wolcott in December 1800, "but that upon every virtuous and prudent calculation Jefferson is to be preferred. He is by far not so dangerous a man and he has pretensions to character." A month later, as the deadlock continued, Hamilton urged James Bayard, another Federalist and Delaware's sole congressman, to reject Burr, "the most unfit man in the U.S. for the office of President. Disgrace abroad and ruin at home are the probable fruits of his elevation . . . For Heavens sake my dear Sir, exert yourself to the utmost to save our country from so great a calamity."[19]

Bayard complied and cast a blank vote. In addition, the Federalist congressmen from Vermont, Maryland, and South Carolina declined to vote in their caucuses. These measures reduced Burr's vote by two states and increased Jefferson's by two, making him the winner by 10 to 4. The episode had been a real crisis in the young Republic's history, and it might have ended in catastrophe. To avoid a repetition, in 1804 the states ratified the Twelfth Amendment to the Constitution, which provided for the separate election of president and vice president.

The Revolution of 1800 was not an agrarian movement directed against cities, although the new president still believed in the superior virtues of rural life. Instead, the election reflected a class-based movement that involved most of the white population and looked toward democratic rights for larger numbers of people. Most of the "middling sort" within the nation, including not only farmers but also urban craftsmen, mechanics, and tradesmen, were drawn to these goals, as were most immigrants. Each of these groups had already become less deferential toward their "betters," including the monied interests represented by what were now called High Federalists.[20]

During the early years under the Constitution, it had been essential to seduce those monied interests away from individual states and toward the federal government. Hamilton had judged this tactic necessary in order to fund the huge debt. But once he had accomplished that goal, public sentiment gravitated more strongly away from even an attenuated version of the British class structure, with its traditions of aristocracy and privilege.

The speed and extent of the change may be measured by the radically different party alignments in Congress before and after Jefferson became president. In the election of 1798, about 43 percent of winning candidates for the House of Representatives were Republicans. Eight years later, in the election of 1806, that number shot up to 83 percent. During the same period, the Senate changed from a 22–10 Federalist majority to a 28–6 Republican majority. Never again in American history has there been such a drastic swing in the makeup of Congress.[21]

Even so, like most social movements, Jeffersonianism evolved from deep roots. Part of the initial justification of the Revolution of 1775, after all, had been to preserve the rights of Englishmen against unreasonable policies by the Crown—the Englishmen in question being the colonists themselves. Jefferson's brand of republicanism, therefore, cannot be equated with the more ragtag and leveling movement that swept Andrew Jackson into power in 1828. Jefferson, Madison, and Gallatin, like their Federalist counterparts, were "gentlemen" in the eighteenth-century sense of the word. By contrast, prominent American politicians of the near future, such as Jackson, Sam Houston, and Abraham Lincoln, were not gentlemen and did not aspire to be.

CHAPTER 20

Debt, Armaments, and Louisiana

When Jefferson took office on March 4, 1801, every informed person knew he was going to name Gallatin secretary of the treasury, even though the immigrant Genevan had been re-elected to Congress. There were no other plausible candidates for the post. As Jefferson put it, Gallatin was "the only man in the United States who understands, through all the laberinths that Hamilton involv'd it, the precise state of the Treasury, and the resources of the Country."[1]

Gallatin was originally intending to retire from politics and move to a large city after his term in Congress expired in 1803. He had planned, somewhat vaguely, to become a lawyer. He wrote his sister-in-law, "As a political situation [compared to Congress], the place of Secretary of the Treasury is doubtless more eligible and congenial to my habits, but it is more labori-ous and responsible than any other." Perhaps it would be better to study law, settle in Philadelphia or New York, and earn more money to support his family. Instead he chose to remain in poli-tics, having little idea of quite how laborious and responsible his duties were about to become.[2]

Many insiders were not certain that the Senate would confirm Gallatin for the Treasury. He had been a relentless partisan during his years in Congress, and even some Republican senators remained suspicious of his immigrant background. At Gallatin's request, Jefferson therefore delayed the appointment until May 1801, when both houses of Congress were in recess. After the legislature reconvened, the Senate confirmed Gallatin as secretary in January 1802. By then, he had moved out of his boardinghouse and, with Hannah and their young children, into one of the few decent homes located on Capitol Hill.[3]

His office at the Treasury was about twenty minutes away by carriage, next door to the Executive Mansion. But the thrifty Gallatin seldom took a carriage. He usually walked to work, often carrying an umbrella during the six hottest months of the year, to shield himself from the broiling Washington sun. Living conditions in the new capital city, remained primitive for the entire period the Gallatin family spent in Washington. Gallatin's usual routine was to divide his time between the Treasury, the Capitol, and his own house, which lay only about 150 yards from the Capitol. For the next twelve years, the Gallatins' home served as a convenient place for him to confer with Republican leaders in Congress.[4]

Once in office, Jefferson, Gallatin, and secretary of state Madison worked closely as a team. Of the three, Gallatin at age forty was the youngest, most energetic, and most active in administering the government. Jefferson was fifty-eight, Madison fifty, and both had chronic health problems. As they took over from the Federalists in 1801, the triumvirate had two major goals and a series of well-specified policies to carry them out. Their first goal was the one common to all incumbent parties: to retain power and increase their percentage of the vote in elections at all levels. The second was to reduce and perhaps extinguish the federal debt.[5]

As one of several means to this second goal, slashing the size

FIGURE 15. Albert Gallatin in his third year as secretary of the treasury, 1803, looking a good deal better-groomed than he usually did. This is an engraving made for sale to the public, adapted from a portrait by Gilbert Stuart.

of the federal government appealed to Jefferson, but Gallatin managed to cool his ardor a bit. The secretary persuaded Jefferson that since the total number of civilian employees stood at only about 2,500, a drastic reduction was impracticable for a growing nation of 5.5 million people. Jefferson nonetheless did cut several hundred federal employees. Against Gallatin's advice, he also replaced most appointed Federalist officeholders with Republicans.

When the Republicans took power, Gallatin had suggested that appointments to federal offices be strictly merit-based. Political affiliation should play no part in staffing the civil service. Yet this is not what happened. Nor did Jefferson appoint appreciably fewer educated, wealthy, or "connected" persons than his predecessor had done. The common man did not suddenly ascend to high appointed office. Nor, later on, did Jefferson accept Gallatin's suggestion that the government might benefit from the addition of female talent. "The appointment of a woman to office," Jefferson wrote, "is an innovation for which the public is not prepared, nor am I."[6]

Both Gallatin and Jefferson tried to convert incumbent Federalist officeholders to the Republican cause, with some apparent success. But the sincerity of these sudden changes of heart is open to question. Many other Federalists were fired or forced to resign. There was no wholesale expulsion of political opponents in 1801, as there would be in 1829 under Andrew Jackson and the spoils system, but Jefferson did reshape the government along partisan lines. The famous conciliatory statement from his first inaugural address—"We are all republicans: we are all federalists"—did not guide his removals and appointments.[7]

In 1803, Gallatin made the only personally related patronage appointment of his career, recommending his old classmate Jean Badollet for a position as surveyor of the Ohio Territory. Badollet was a mercurial character, but for Gallatin the friendship remained an emotional link to his early life in Geneva. In 1804 Gallatin arranged for Badollet to take a more important post as register of the new land office in Vincennes, capital of Indiana Territory. Badollet remained in Vincennes for the rest of his life. He wrote frequent, long, and agitated letters to Gallatin about the evils of slavery and the difficult conditions on the frontier.[8]

Gallatin, Madison, and Jefferson were intent on extinguishing the national debt and maintained that goal throughout the entire time they held power. Jefferson's own fierce opposition to debt constituted one of the many paradoxes in his complex character. Like his frequent denunciations of slavery during a lifetime in which he owned a total of more than 600 slaves (seldom more than 200 at once), his constant attacks on indebtedness seemed inconsistent with his personal habits of living high on borrowed money. He dressed modestly and cultivated an image of frugality. But he spent lavishly on wines, books, furniture, and other goods that made Monticello a showcase of conspicuous consumption. For most of his adult life, Jefferson owed large sums to a variety of creditors in the United States and Britain. His frequent sales of slaves and his famous transfer of 6,500 books to the Library of Congress brought in substantial sums of money to pay his personal debts. On the larger question of the national debt, however, there was no ambiguity. Jefferson viewed it as a moral issue, a curse to be abolished forthwith.[9]

To accomplish that aim, he and Gallatin emphasized three policies: reduce both taxes and spending, impose tighter control over specific appropriations, and thwart the growth of a standing army and a strong navy. They sought to avoid what they regarded as grievous flaws in the British and European traditions: monarchy, luxury, rigid class structures, financial corruption, military adventurism, and a heavy tax burden. Understandably but in large part inaccurately, they equated Hamilton's fiscal program and the Federalist philosophy of government with the British and Continental systems. Gallatin himself, unlike Jefferson, did live frugally. A Federalist senator once commented that Gallatin was so tightfisted as to be "very inattentive and negligent of his person and dress. His linen is frequently soiled and his clothes tattered."[10]

Jefferson and his followers held the presidency from 1801 until 1825, but they never undermined the foundation Hamilton had laid for the nation's economic future. Early in his first term, Jefferson instructed Gallatin to expose "the blunders and frauds of Hamilton." Gallatin began his quest with enthusiasm. But in the end he is reported to have told a disappointed Jefferson that "Hamilton made no blunders, committed no frauds. He did nothing wrong."[11]

Gallatin guided the legislative campaigns for all of the Republicans' chief domestic strategies. He had a warm relationship with the House Committee on Ways and Means, a body that he had helped to found and that remained crucial to his plans. The committee was now led by his good friend John Randolph of Roanoke, a brilliant but sometimes eccentric Virginian. The second-ranking member was Hannah Gallatin's cousin Joseph Hopper Nicholson of Maryland. In cooperation with these two congressmen, Gallatin easily secured the administration's first policy: legislation providing for reduction—and in most cases abolition—of internal federal taxes, including the hated excise on whiskey.[12]

He also steered the Committee on Ways and Means toward reducing federal expenditures, and won relatively easy approval there as well. He had less success with the administration's policy of empowering the Treasury to discipline other departments on how they spent their appropriations. The strict controls Gallatin requested met with intense objections from both the secretary of war and the secretary of the navy (a new cabinet post established in 1798). Each argued that he needed flexibility to shift money from one use to another as needs changed during the fiscal year.[13]

Gallatin regarded the abolition of the national debt as his principal assignment. He succeeded in securing tax cuts, but he had no intention of reducing import duties, which remained the chief source of federal income. With total receipts from all sources now exceeding $10 million per year, he proposed an annual earmark of $7.3 million from import duties toward payment of principal and interest on the debt. Under that plan, he calculated that the entire debt, which stood at just over $83 million in 1801, could be discharged within sixteen years.

Leaving aside the wisdom of a rigid determination to erase the debt, this was not an unreasonable plan. It could be done because Gallatin had inherited a fiscal situation much less daunting than the one Hamilton had faced in 1790. Hamilton had been compelled to invent ways for the nation to survive with a debt-to-income ratio of 46 to 1. For Gallatin, the initial ratio was only 8.3 to 1. And during most of his time in office, he made significant progress in reducing the debt.[14]

Gallatin's influence on Jefferson persisted at a high level from the start. He never hesitated to make clear to the president where he disagreed with him or thought corrections should be made. Often these adjustments pertained to translating Jefferson's sometimes romantic ideology into practical policies. Jefferson himself, accustomed to being out of power, wanted to unite the country behind his own vision as soon as possible. He was a poor public speaker but an inspired writer who tended to embellish his case on whatever issue lay at hand. (His original draft of the Declaration of Independence contained unduly inflammatory passages.) It was left to others, principally Gallatin but sometimes Madison as well, to tone down the president's rhetoric. If issued publicly in unedited form, some of Jefferson's written statements would have made it difficult for the new administration to govern.[15]

For example, Jefferson had always been suspicious of the general-welfare clause of the Constitution, which Hamilton had used in several of his successful legislative strategies. (Article I, Section 8, gives Congress the power to "lay and collect Taxes, Duties, Imposts, and Excises, to pay the Debts and provide for the common Defence and general Welfare of the United States.") In the draft of a message to Congress, Jefferson proposed an amendment to remove this clause. Gallatin convinced him to omit the recommendation, which, had it passed, likely would have caused very significant problems for future generations.[16]

In 1802, when the president drafted his first message to Congress and asked for Gallatin's advice, the secretary responded with additions and corrections running to about 3,500 words, the equivalent of ten printed pages. Parts of these "Notes on President's Message" sought to educate Jefferson further on the nation's financial condition and how it had evolved. Jefferson had drafted a passage noting that federal revenues had increased "in nearly the same ratio" as the population. Gallatin pointed out that they had actually grown much faster, and explained the complex reasons: the country's wealth and income had increased more rapidly than the population; and the consumption of imported goods (on which the government received duties of about 20 percent) had grown faster in populous urban areas than in rural ones, where consumers spent less on imports. Both of these two circumstances, Gallatin pointed out, were owing "principally to our *neutrality* during the war [between Britain and France]; an evident proof of the advantages of peace notwithstanding the depredations of the belligerent powers." The carrying trade had drawn more people, including immigrants, to American ports than to the countryside.[17]

Gallatin's approach to the public budget, and especially his drive to cut military and naval expenses, was predicated on the nation's remaining at peace and attracting immigrants from Europe. He believed that these circumstances offered unique opportunities for the United States: to rid itself of the national debt, to protect its citizens from heavy taxation, and to solidify the ongoing American effort to create a new kind of country.

As Gallatin wrote Jefferson at the start of the new administration in March 1801, "We can save but thousands" through economies in the civil government, yet "hundreds of thousands" by cutting funds for the army and navy. For the Jeffersonians, the existing debt and the Federalists' habit of borrowing were not mere ideological fixations, and Gallatin himself was no mindless budget-cutter. Instead, the elimination of the debt and the habit of heavy public spending symbolized the Republicans' resolve to avoid the British and European traditions of corruption and militarism. For Gallatin, the United States still represented a fragile experiment, just as it had for Alexander Hamilton.[18]

The difference was that Hamilton believed the country to be more vulnerable militarily than Gallatin did. Gallatin was convinced that the United States, protected by the barrier of the Atlantic Ocean, could avoid the chronic warfare that had plagued Europe for centuries and corrupted its governments. In November 1801, he wrote Jefferson that "pretended tax-preparations, treasure-preparations, and army-preparations against contingent wars tend only to encourage wars." Like other Republicans but more so than most, he rejected the Old World's traditions of heavy military expenditures and preparation for war—which, he believed, often led to actual war.[19]

From the moment the Jefferson-Madison-Gallatin team assumed office in 1801, they were in agreement that military expenditures should be cut as much as possible. Gallatin's proposals to Congress provided for the barest minimum of funds for the War Department and for deep cuts in the navy's budget. He achieved most of his aims, but only in the face of seething opposition, particularly from the navy. The maintenance of existing warships was expensive and construction of new ones even more so. The very idea of having a navy had been controversial since the navy's temporary abolition after the War of Independence.

In 1793, Britain and France had gone to war with each other and started threatening American commerce. In response, and at President Washington's request, Congress voted in 1794 to authorize a modest shipbuilding program. In the House of Representatives, the measure passed by the thin margin of 46 to 44, an index of the Jeffersonians' opposition to a larger naval program. But events of the 1790s made it clear that the new nation needed at least some maritime protection against threats from the British and French. Both countries had forces of almost 200 ships, including dozens of large "ships of the line," the counterparts of modern battleships. In 1799 Hamilton had suggested that the United States needed a much bigger navy: "six Ships of the line Twelve frigates and twenty four sloops of War." His proposal failed, but by 1800 the United States had completed the construction of six frigates, comparable to modern destroyers or small cruisers.[20]

These six ships—at that time the largest and best of their class in the world—were the USS *Constitution, Constellation, United States, President, Congress,* and *Chesapeake.* George Washington himself chose the names of all but the *Chesapeake.* Several of the frigates proved useful during the Quasi-War with France, capturing numerous French merchantmen. In 1799 and 1800, the *Constellation,* in the first significant victories by an American-built ship in the history of the U.S. Navy, defeated two French frigates in ship-to-ship duels.[21]

Gallatin had opposed naval expenditures during his years in the House of Representatives and continued to do so as secretary of the treasury. After sending his initial messages to Congress for cutting the budgets for the army and navy, he succeeded in getting his program passed, but only after some concessions to the navy. Nearly everyone connected with the navy and the American merchant marine regarded both Gallatin and Jefferson as implacable foes of American sea power.[22]

Jefferson much preferred inexpensive small gunboats to oceangoing ships, and proposed to build them not at existing shipyards but at the Washington Navy Yard on the Potomac. Almost all U.S. naval experts emphatically opposed and derided the gunboat plan, and their objections proved correct. Later, during the War of 1812, these vessels proved to be ineffectual. In most ship-to-ship battles, each side fired hundreds of shots that found their mark. But a single ball from a British warship could blow an American gunboat out of the water. This situation pointed up an irony of both the Jefferson and Madison administrations: the desire to minimize military expenditures on the one hand and an equally strong determination to uphold the nation's honor on the other.[23]

The first episode of clashing standards came early in Jefferson's first term. It involved the "pirate" states along the Barbary Shore of North Africa—Algiers, Tripoli, Tunis, and Morocco. Ships from these states began seizing American merchant vessels in the Mediterranean, along with those of all other trading nations that refused to pay annual bribes ("tributes").[24]

Britain, France—and, under presidents Washington and Adams, the United States as well—had paid tributes in return for the Barbary states' leaving their merchant ships alone. Jefferson, however, saw the issue as a moral one and refused further payments. Against Gallatin's advice, he dispatched several American warships to the Barbary Shore, including three of the six frigates built over his own objections during the 1790s. Once in the Mediterranean, they upheld American honor during what came to be called the First Barbary War. Patrols by these American ships lasted, off and on, from 1801 to 1805. The Barbary conflict later gave rise to the phrase "shores of Tripoli" in the Marine hymn. It also produced the first native-born American hero of the seas, Stephen Decatur, and increased the country's sense of nationhood.[25]

—◆◆◆—

Nevertheless, from the start of his time as secretary, Gallatin opposed military expenditures, not only in the abstract, but also on questions such as protecting U.S. ships at sea. As he saw it, even though Barbary pirates—and, more importantly, British and French naval vessels and privateers—might prey on American merchant ships, the U.S. oceangoing sector as a whole remained large and prosperous. It still dominated the carrying trade of cargoes sold to both France and Britain in their war against each other. Much of this trade was in the form of agricultural exports or reexports—goods landed in the United States and then shipped abroad. Most American exports and reexports went to Britain and its Caribbean colonies.[26]

A lesser volume could reach France and its continental allies because of the British navy's blockade of Europe. Gallatin, always looking ahead, warned Jefferson that if peace between Britain and France should come (as it did, temporarily, for fourteen months during 1802–1803), "our enormous carrying trade of foreign articles must be diminished," with a consequent "decrease of *revenue.*" At several points, both before and after the temporary suspension of the war in 1802, Napoleon was able to mount a credible threat to cross the English Channel and invade Britain itself.[27]

When the war resumed in 1803, American revenues went back up and the public debt continued to decline. Whereas it had been $83 million in 1801, it stood at only $45.2 million in 1812, before the United States declared war on Britain. This was a reduction of about 46 percent since 1801, an impressive achievement by any standard. The debt would have dropped even further had it not been for the Louisiana Purchase of 1803, which occasioned the only public borrowing during Jefferson's presidency. Gallatin, a Westerner, was not only willing to spend public money to acquire Louisiana; he was also prepared to pay for military mobilization if that proved necessary to prevent its falling into hostile hands. The Louisiana Purchase proved to be a revealing litmus test of Gallatin's thinking about the nation's future.

The situation in Louisiana involved not only the United States and France, but Spain and Britain as well. In the settlement ending the Seven Years War in 1763, France had ceded to Spain its territorial claims west of the Mississippi River and to Britain those east of the Mississippi. In 1800, France regained possession of the Louisiana Territory west of the Mississippi through a secret treaty with Spain. By 1803, the French treasury was burdened by the expense of Napoleon's renewed land battles in Europe and his preparations to invade Britain. Meanwhile, France was losing revenues from its Caribbean sugar islands because of interdictions by the British navy.

Most significantly, the failure of Napoleon to overturn Toussaint L'Ouverture's revolution against French rule in Saint-Domingue (Haiti) made it too expensive for him to continue his adventures in the Western Hemisphere. This meant, in turn, that he could no longer defend Louisiana. Napoleon also wanted to strengthen the United States in every way possible as a future naval power against Britain. He was therefore readier to make a deal over Louisiana than the Americans realized.[28]

At that time, the great jewel of the Louisiana Territory—an area so vast that nobody knew its full extent—was the port of New Orleans. American trappers, commercial farmers, and craftsmen living in the West relied on free transit down the Mississippi River and the "right of deposit" at New Orleans for exporting their goods. Through the years, Spain had alternately withdrawn these rights and then granted them again. The Republicans wanted a final settlement of these issues, through any practical means.[29]

In 1801, the Jefferson administration learned about the secret treaty delivering Louisiana to France. In 1802, the matter became urgent when the Spanish administrator of New Orleans, who remained in control pending the transfer of governance to France, revoked the right of deposit still again. This maneuver posed the threat of a real crisis involving not only Spain and France, but also Britain. Jefferson still detested the British, but saw that they might be a potential ally of the United States in regaining the right of deposit. Because New Orleans was essential to western development, both Jefferson and Gallatin regarded the city as the single most important key to the material progress of the United States.[30]

The Jefferson-Madison-Gallatin trio thereupon decided to try to resolve the issue through the simple device of purchasing New Orleans. Secretary of state Madison instructed Robert Livingston, the American minister to France, to begin negotiations. By 1803, the talks having come to nothing, Jefferson dispatched James Monroe to Paris to assist the sixty-six-year-old Livingston.[31]

Four days before Monroe's arrival in Paris, the French astounded Livingston by presenting an offer to sell not just New Orleans, but the entire Louisiana Territory. Napoleon's minister of finance proposed to Livingston and Monroe that the United States acquire the vast Territory for a price of $15 million. The two Americans had been authorized to offer $2 million and to negotiate up to $10 million for just the city of New Orleans and its surrounding lands. The exact dimensions of the Louisiana Territory were not known, but its acquisition would at least double the size of the United States. After two weeks of haggling over price, Monroe and Livingston accepted the offer, gambling that their superiors in the United States would support them. The treaty was dated April 30, 1802, and signed in Paris on May 2. Its text reached Washington on July 14.[32]

The Louisiana Purchase—one of the epochal events of American history—derived from a confluence of four circumstances: the successful Haitian Revolution, which induced Napoleon to dispose of Louisiana; the war between Britain and France, which strained the treasuries of both nations; the U.S. government's creditworthiness, established by Hamilton in the 1790s and confirmed by Gallatin during his first two years in office; and the "Revolution of 1800," which put Jefferson, Gallatin, and other westward-looking Republicans in power.

Almost all Federalists opposed the acquisition, Alexander Hamilton being one of the few exceptions. Pessimistic about the likelihood of a purchase, Hamilton wrote in a newspaper article that the government should "seize at once on the Floridas and New-Orleans, and then negociate." Once the Louisiana Purchase had gone through, Hamilton attributed the success "to a fortuitous concurrence of unforeseen and unexpected circumstances, and not to any wise or vigorous measures on the part of the American government." The chief circumstance, he added, was "the courage and obstinate resistance made by [Saint-Domingue's] black inhabitants."[33]

The combination of these diverse elements confers on the Louisiana Purchase—which was easily the highlight of Jefferson's eight-year presidency—an aura not only of singular good luck, but also of canny American opportunism. As Robert Livingston put it, "We have lived long but this is the noblest work of our whole lives . . . [T]he United States take rank this day among the first powers of the world."[34]

Albert Gallatin played three important roles in the Louisiana Purchase. Before Monroe's departure for France, he made it a point to go on record about the constitutionality of buying New Orleans. Jefferson was proving to be extremely hesitant to proceed without a constitutional amendment authorizing the purchase of additional lands for the United States. Seeing that such a course would delay and perhaps scuttle the whole New Orleans project, Gallatin responded immediately. In a long and vigorous letter to the president, Gallatin used a loose-construction argument much like Hamilton's in 1791, when Jefferson had opposed the Bank of the United States. This time Jefferson gave in, and the transaction moved forward.[35]

Gallatin also directed the Treasury Department's financing of the $15 million payment for Louisiana. In a complicated transaction, the Treasury issued $11.25 million in 6 percent bonds, redeemable at not less than $3 million per year beginning fifteen years after the date of the treaty. Napoleon's government—which in May 1803 faced a resumption of its war with Britain after fourteen months of peace under the Treaty of Amiens—

had no intention of waiting fifteen years to begin receiving payment of the principal. So the French sold the American bonds for cash to two leading banks, Hope & Co. in Amsterdam and Baring Brothers in London. The Treasury had already sent some of the bonds to Baring Brothers, and Gallatin's close work with Sir Alexander Baring began one of the warmest friendships of his life. To make up the remainder of the total $15 million price, the Treasury reimbursed in cash $3.75 million owed by French debtors to U.S. creditors living in the United States. It was fortunate for the Jefferson administration and the nation that Gallatin, a sophisticated immigrant from Europe unfazed by dealing in such gigantic sums, was secretary of the treasury during this complex negotiation.[36]

Even with all the good luck, the Louisiana Purchase nearly misfired when the House of Representatives took up the issue of actually paying Napoleon $15 million. This total exceeded the government's annual revenues at the time by about 40 percent. In a bid to block the purchase, an almost unanimous phalanx of Federalists joined numerous Republicans led by John Randolph of Roanoke. Randolph, a former Gallatin ally and one of the most powerful members of Congress, was an extreme advocate of states' rights and of limits on the U.S. Constitution. The final action to authorize payment to Napoleon squeaked through on a vote of 59 to 57. A tie cannot be broken in the House, as it can in the Senate by the vice president. So a switch of one vote out of the 116 cast would have killed the Louisiana Purchase.[37]

Gallatin played a third role in the Louisiana adventure through his part in planning the expedition led by Meriwether Lewis and William Clark. As early as 1801, Jefferson had discussed a western expedition with Lewis, an army officer then serving as his personal secretary. In 1802, a year before Napoleon offered to sell Louisiana, Gallatin had championed to Jefferson and others an exploration reaching across the entire continent to the Pacific Coast. Gallatin wanted to discover the best route to the Far West. He also wished to acquire as much information as possible about the region's topography, its Native American population, the potential for expanding the nation's fur trade, and the use of Pacific ports.[38]

Both Jefferson and Gallatin were thinking in the long term about settlement of the West—about its control by the United States and the prevention of new alliances between British agents and Indian tribes. The long series of preparations for a possible expedition got under way in 1802. At that time, nobody in the United States had any idea that the nation was about to acquire the Louisiana Territory. The Lewis and Clark expedition itself consumed two years, from 1804 to 1806.

In 1805, after months of arduous travel, the expedition reached the headwaters of the Missouri, the longest river in North America (2,464 miles). At that point, three rivers flow together to form the Missouri, and the explorers named them the Jefferson, the Madison, and the Gallatin. The small town that came into being at this confluence, Three Forks, is located in Gallatin County, Montana. There is also a Gallatin Range in the Rocky Mountains, a Gallatin Canyon, and a Gallatin National Forest of 2.1 million acres, which borders Yellowstone National Park.[39]

FIGURE 16. Thomas Jefferson at the start of his second presidential term, in a portrait by Gilbert Stuart, 1805. By now sixty-two years old, Jefferson had begun to lose some of his former vigor.

FIGURE 17 *(opposite, top)*. Portrait of James Madison, by Gilbert Stuart, 1804. Though sometimes indecisive after he became president in 1809, Madison was perhaps the most profound thinker of all the founders. At the start of Jefferson's second term in 1805, he was fifty-four years old and serving as secretary of state.

FIGURE 18 *(opposite, bottom)*. Portrait of Albert Gallatin, age forty-four, by Rembrandt Peale, 1805. Gallatin, then secretary of the treasury, bore the heaviest administrative load of the triumvirate, much as Hamilton had done during the Washington administration.

CHAPTER 21

Developing the West

Gallatin's preoccupation with Louisiana grew out of the same deep impulse about land that had motivated his emigration from Geneva in 1780. It also comported with his own purchase of public lands in Virginia and Pennsylvania and his efforts to develop the area around Friendship Hill. His dominant idea of how the United States should evolve centered around settlement of the West. This too would require financial innovation, and the frugal Gallatin was willing to spend ample federal funds for the surveying, clearing, and sales of western lands.

Without the availability of cheap land, neither Gallatin himself nor millions of other immigrants who came before and after him would have crossed the Atlantic at all. A hundred years before he arrived, Pennsylvania had been founded on the basis of a land grant by the English Crown to William Penn and his community of Friends. The Quakers, who were persecuted in England for their religious beliefs, in 1681 acquired the rights to large tracts in what became Pennsylvania. They developed their new colony on both religious and commercial principles, and many Quaker merchants in Philadelphia became wealthy international traders. Other Friends carved out prosperous farms east of the Appalachian Mountains. A very few settled west of the mountains a generation before Gallatin's arrival in 1780.[1]

From the colonial period until well into the nineteenth century, everything seemed up for grabs in North America. Vast, seemingly unlimited tracts of land were sold at low prices or given away by the royal, colonial, state, and finally federal governments. Everyone wanted the best land, and neither the first colonists nor the pioneers pressing across the frontier had much compunction about dispossessing Native Americans or one another. Sometimes they resorted to outright murder. The westward movement constituted a great epic, romanticized in countless American novels and films. But in many details it was a brutal story.[2]

When the United States declared its independence in 1776, four years before Gallatin's arrival, most white settlement did not reach very far beyond the eastern seaboard. Under the Articles of Confederation, several states with extensive western claims ceded their lands to the U.S. government: New York in 1780, Virginia in 1781, Massachusetts in 1784, Connecticut in 1786. When the Americans won their War of Independence, they received, under the Treaty of Paris (1783), all British-claimed lands east of the Mississippi River and south of the Great Lakes. This large area, whose boundaries remained a little imprecise, became known as the Northwest Territory, being north and west of the Ohio River. (Under British rule, it had been called the Indian Reserve.) It comprised the present states of Ohio, Indiana, Illinois, Michigan, Wisconsin, and parts of Minnesota.

Laws to organize the Northwest Territory for future development—passed in 1784, 1785, and 1787—were collectively the most important legislative acts of the Confederation Congress. They provided for future disposition of the Territory, and later were adapted as patterns for the development of public lands across the country. The Ordinance of 1784, drafted mostly by Thomas Jefferson, laid the basic groundwork. A year later, the

Land Ordinance of 1785 specified a procedure for surveying the public domains: division of new lands into "townships" of thirty-six square miles (six by six, laid out in patterns running due east, west, north, and south). Each of the square miles comprised 640 acres, a "section" that could be sold to settlers or other buyers. The third major law, the Northwest Ordinance of 1787, prohibited slavery in the Territory and established the pattern for the admission of new states into the Union. Both of these provisions were crucial for the future development of the nation.

The Northwest Territory, like Louisiana and other large tracts acquired later on, amounted to a bonanza of incalculable value to the federal government and the country as a whole. Even before Gallatin became secretary of the treasury in 1801, he saw more clearly than most American statesmen that the public lands were by far the government's most valuable asset. Further, he perceived that land could be used for many different purposes, including the raising of money. Like Hamilton, he believed—too optimistically in the short term, as it turned out—that the western lands could be converted to liquid capital.

Land nonetheless became the keystone of U.S. economic growth, because of North America's rich soil and abundant natural resources. Those assets alone, of course, cannot account for the long U.S. record of sustained economic progress. Many lavishly endowed countries, both old ones (Russia) and new (Congo), have never approached the long-term growth record of the United States.[3]

By contrast, some meagerly endowed countries (Japan, Switzerland) have taken their places among the richest nations in the world, through the education of their people and the quality of their products. In the United States, governments and private entrepreneurs combined these strategies, adding value to the nation's natural resources. Forests became lumber, plywood, and paper; oil became gasoline and petrochemicals; iron ore and coal became steel, which in turn became bridges, cars, and skyscrapers.[4]

A pattern of systematic development also characterized American agriculture. In the year 1800, 74 percent of the American labor force worked on farms. (The figure today is under 1.4 percent.) There were prosperous tobacco and rice plantations in the South, but most farmers and their families—which is to say most Americans—grew crops primarily for their own consumption. By the time Gallatin arrived, they had long since begun to barter with one another, and to buy and sell produce in significant quantities. Some specialization of crops had already started. This shift from subsistence to commercial agriculture—including the slave-based tobacco, rice, and (later) cotton economies—contributed to the inauguration of American capitalism on a broad scale.[5]

Even so, the four economic factors of production—land, labor, capital, and entrepreneurship—were out of balance in the United States. There was a superabundance of land and a healthy spirit of entrepreneurship, but a scarcity of labor and a severe lack of capital. In 1791, Alexander Hamilton had noted in his *Report on the Subject of Manufactures* this "very peculiar situation, the smallness of [the Americans'] population compared with their territory [and] the constant allurements to emigration from the settled to the unsettled parts of the country." The shortage of labor put a big premium on inventions and other ways to mechanize work. In addition, real wages climbed to much higher levels than those in Europe, a difference that encouraged continuous immigration.[6]

Hamilton had also mentioned in his *Report* "a deficiency of pecuniary capital." In the United States, far more than in most other countries, policymakers such as Hamilton, Gallatin, and others sought to solve this shortage by making land do the work of money. Between 1781 and 1867, a colossal endowment of two billion acres accrued to the federal government through the Northwest Territory, the Louisiana Purchase, and other big acquisitions, not counting Alaska. When any new state joined the Union, its public lands became federal property. The only exception was Texas, which insisted on keeping its lands as a condition of statehood.[7]

By the last quarter of the twentieth century, the government had disposed of about half of its land endowment. Of the one billion acres it had sold or given away, a quarter of the total went to citizens, and another quarter to settlers under the Homestead Act of 1862. Eleven percent more went to railroad companies or to states for the construction of railroads. States received an additional 7 percent for the support of common schools. The remainder went for a variety of uses such as veterans' bounties and the drainage of swampland.[8]

All together, sales and donations of federal lands provided both the government and chosen recipients with a convenient substitute for cash and credit—a way to convert one factor of production into another. Even down to the present day, Americans have made more fortunes from the appreciation of land than from any other source. They have often lost money during periodic busts in real estate, but they have earned much greater sums during the long and steady rise in land values.

Albert Gallatin supervised the first major organized sales of public lands from the federal government to the public. During his thirteen years as secretary of the treasury, the number of land offices grew from four to eighteen. At these offices, settlers and other buyers paid for their land—often on installment plans—and received title to it. From 1801 to 1812, the Treasury sold four million acres, not an immense total but an impressive start nonetheless.[9]

Managing the land offices was not a simple task. Widespread speculation in the North, South, and West had been an established American tradition since the seventeenth century. One of Gallatin's aims was to change this tradition and distribute the public lands not to monied investors but to actual settlers. Problems abounded, however. Official surveys, which were expensive and difficult, had to be completed before new sales could proceed efficiently. In many areas, settlers had already moved into the new territories and begun to farm public lands not as owners but as squatters—and they, in turn, attracted more squatters. (Gallatin referred to them as "intruders.") Squatters were hard to dislodge, and their continuing presence made it complicated to sell the property they occupied. This was not so much a problem in the neatly gridded Ohio Territory as in lands farther south: Kentucky, Tennessee, and particularly the Mississippi Territory, which included Alabama and had once been claimed by the colony of Georgia.[10]

Then there was the issue of pricing. Gallatin, even more than Hamilton before him, wanted to use public land sales to increase federal revenues and minimize taxes. Neither secretary had much success. Low prices were necessary to attract most settlers, but cheap land would also encourage speculators, the more so when it was sold on credit, as it often was. On the other hand, if prices were set too high, all categories of purchasers would become discouraged. New settlement would stagnate and less money would accrue to the Treasury. In 1804 Gallatin proposed a price of $2 per acre for Ohio lands. Congress reduced the minimum to $1.64 per acre, a tremendous bargain for purchasers.[11]

Gallatin himself still owned tracts in Ohio, Virginia, and Kentucky, some of them dating back to the warrants he and Jean Savary had purchased in Baltimore during the 1780s. His extensive personal experience with public lands gave him an advantage that his three predecessor secretaries of the treasury—and most of his successors as well—did not have. He well understood the variety of issues involved in administering the vast territories now under federal control.

One overarching problem was clear: there were not nearly enough courts, lawyers, or surveyors to resolve the various problems of pricing, squatters, and conflicting claims by different people for the same lands. Possibilities for corruption flourished, even among those who administered the land offices.

Jared Mansfield, surveyor general under Gallatin, reported that speculators routinely engaged in "Jobbing, Pettyfogging, Fakery . . . everything except labour and industry." To Gallatin's distress, Mansfield himself bought lands that had been returned to the public domain through forfeiture of payment—not an illegal practice by Mansfield, but one that created the appearance of impropriety. Other officials were even bolder, and attempts to police their illegal activities raised major problems. The U.S. government was not big enough or sufficiently well organized to control the situation.[12]

Nobody knew this better than Gallatin. He had so many other responsibilities as secretary of the treasury that he badly needed help. That help finally came in 1812, when Congress established the General Land Office. Still under the Treasury (where it remained until the creation of the Department of the Interior in 1849), the General Land Office took charge of managing the public domain. It thereby lifted from Gallatin's shoulders one of his most bothersome duties.

The orderly development and implementation of land policy was a tribute to Gallatin's administrative skills, even though he did not raise much money through sales. It was remarkable— indeed, a minor miracle—that he kept as tight a rein as he did over such a raucous, confusing, and strident set of issues while he fulfilled so many other duties. Almost everything could have gone wrong in land policy: too much speculation, rampant public corruption, lack of control over squatters, too rapid a western migration, and chaos in organizing new territory. But nothing of much significance did go wrong. Instead, under Gallatin's guidance, the administration of the Northwest Territory, the Louisiana Purchase, and the Mississippi Territory remained turbulent but under sufficient control.[13]

Acquiring and administering so much public land led to the question of how best to develop it. This was part of the larger issue of economic growth in the country as a whole. As secretary of the treasury, Gallatin paid more attention to it than did Jefferson or Madison. A confirmed nationalist, he was also more willing than his Virginia colleagues to invest federal money for western development.[14]

Despite the Republicans' strict constructionist doctrines, a few of them saw at least some need to spend public revenues on roads and canals—then called "internal improvements." This issue became one of Gallatin's preoccupations, and he took a much more advanced position than most other Republicans. In 1802, he proposed a federally funded road that would cross the Appalachian Mountains and provide a link between the coastal states and the country's interior. This would fulfill a dream hatched twenty years earlier in his decision to settle at Friendship Hill, near both the Potomac and Ohio rivers. A "National Road," as it came to be called, would stretch from the Potomac, which flows into the Atlantic, to the Ohio, which meets the Mississippi and flows to New Orleans and the Gulf of Mexico. The new road would provide western producers much cheaper access to eastern, southern, and foreign markets.[15]

Jefferson had mentioned this proposal in his Annual Message to Congress in 1802. Then, in his Second Inaugural Address of March 1805, he took the idea a step further. He noted that federal revenues could be "applied in time of peace to rivers, canals, roads, arts, manufacturers, education, and other great objects." Gallatin had discussed these matters many times with Jefferson—and finally, with great difficulty, had dissuaded his chief from the idea that appropriations for such purposes required an amendment to the Constitution. He also took issue with Jefferson's notion that each region of the country should receive federal assistance in proportion to its population. To Gallatin, that view made little sense. The purpose of most roads and canals was to develop new, underpopulated areas, not merely to improve existing ones.[16]

In 1807, believing that the time had come for more decisive action, Gallatin caused the Senate to request from him a plan for a thorough development of the nation's infrastructure. In April 1808, he delivered his *Report on Roads and Canals*, a long document he had worked on for nearly a year. It contained sweeping proposals for federal assistance, the total cost aggregating $20 million—a gigantic sum for that time. Here Gallatin was pushing against traditional Republican dogma that opposed strong federal initiatives.[17]

Gallatin urged that the expense be paid through automatic annual appropriations of $2 million for ten years. This strategy would avoid annual battles in Congress over questions such as which regions should get how much money. Hamilton had used the same device in 1790, when he had persuaded Congress to reserve a large percentage of customs duties for interest payments on the national debt. Gallatin himself had done something similar in 1801, by inducing Congress to set aside annual payments for retirement of the principal on the debt.[18]

The annual $2 million he now proposed in his *Report* would promote four specific systems of internal improvements:

1. "Great canals, from north to south, along the Atlantic Coast." Here Gallatin had in mind saltwater canals that would cut through Cape Cod in Massachusetts; through the Delaware peninsula, which impeded water-borne commerce between New York and Philadelphia; through the Chesapeake peninsula, which blocked direct routes from northern ports to Baltimore and thence to Washington; and through the Dismal Swamp of Virginia and North Carolina. Taken together, the new canals would much shorten the time necessary to move cargoes up and down the Atlantic Coast. Gallatin also called for an even bigger north-south project: "a great turnpike road from Maine to Georgia." The proposed turnpike was the most expensive of all his proposals and the most difficult from an engineering viewpoint.

2. "Communications between the Atlantic and Western waters." In 1808, east-west transportation in the United States still proceeded mostly by oxcarts making their laborious way up and down high hills on primitive roads, where there were any

roads at all. The Appalachian Mountain barrier, which runs more than a thousand miles from Canada in the North to Alabama in the South, had yet to be penetrated. This problem blocked development of the West, and Gallatin was determined that the Republicans remedy it. He himself had to endure the ordeal of getting over the mountains every time he made a trip between the east coast and Friendship Hill.

3. "Communications between the Atlantic waters, and those of the great lakes, and river St. Lawrence." Here the goal was the same: opening up the West. And again the means would mainly be canals. In the back of Gallatin's mind lay the British model of using efficient inland water transportation for economic development. Britain's extraordinary system of interconnected rivers and canals, together with its well-developed coastal ports, had been fundamental to its rise as the world's leading manufacturing country.

4. "Interior canals" connecting seaports (Boston, Philadelphia, Baltimore, Charleston) with towns fifty or so miles inland. Here, too, Gallatin saw canals as the least costly way to increase American manufacturing and commerce. He did not believe that an integrated system of canals could be built without federal assistance.[19]

In the text of his *Report,* Gallatin presented cost estimates for every project. With his customary thoroughness, he gave his best projection: $4.8 million for the turnpike from Maine to Georgia, $2.2 million for a "great inland navigation opened the whole way by canals from the North [Hudson] River to Lake Ontario," and an additional $1 million for a "canal around the falls and rapids of Niagara." These two canals would connect the port of New York, via the Hudson River, with Lake Ontario, Lake Erie, Lake Huron, and Lake Michigan. Such a system, like the Maine-to-Georgia turnpike, might stimulate spectacular economic growth.[20]

In all, Gallatin's *Report on Roads and Canals* well captured his vision of national development. He was thinking in the same grand—and, for that time, grandiose—way Hamilton had done in his 1791 *Report on the Subject of Manufactures,* although Gallatin laid heavier emphasis on the West. In the years after 1791, Congress had taken only minimal action on Hamilton's *Report,* and much the same happened with Gallatin's *Report on Roads and Canals.* Both were eminently sensible, though flawed, and both encountered ideological resistance.

Each plan was also ahead of its time and a little too expensive. Hamilton's proposals ran up against barriers of technology, management expertise, and inadequate federal income. Gallatin's dream for internal improvements depended on money that he thought would be ready at hand but instead went toward national defense, particularly the War of 1812. And even without the war, states'-rights factions within his own party would likely have prevented anything more than token expenditures. Many strict constructionists among the Republicans insisted that the Constitution prohibited federal spending on internal improvements. In 1816, after the war, the House of Representatives passed a modest internal-improvements bill by the narrow margin of 86 to 84. The Senate endorsed it as well, but James Madison vetoed it on constitutional grounds.[21]

Nevertheless, the visions of both Hamilton and Gallatin ultimately materialized. The Erie Canal, built with New York State funds between 1817 and 1825, opened the West in exactly the way Gallatin had pictured in his plan of 1808. He had preferred Lake Ontario as the western canal terminus because it lies much closer to the Hudson River than Lake Erie does. But the engineering expertise of the time was not up to the feat of constructing a canal that would raise and lower boats around the imposing precipice at Niagara Falls.

Neither Hamilton nor Gallatin could have foreseen what turned out to be the most efficient instrument for penetrating the Appalachian barrier: the steam railroad. Developed in England during the 1820s, the railroad soon became the key to economic development in the United States and other countries. Beginning in the late 1820s, the Baltimore and Ohio Railroad pierced the Appalachians. Soon, in a burst of competition that lasted for decades, it was followed by three other "trunklines," each with numerous branches: the Erie Railroad, the New York Central, and the great Pennsylvania Railroad, the last of which turned out to be one of the most important organizations for economic development in U.S. history. By the 1850s, all four of these systems reached far into the nation's interior, eliminating the mountain barrier once and for all. Eventually, every goal in Gallatin's 1808 *Report on Roads and Canals* was met, in one way or another. In classic American fashion, the accomplishment came not primarily through federal funds, but through ad hoc combinations of state, local, private, and federal investment in canals and especially railroads.[22]

The one big project whose construction began during Gallatin's tenure as secretary was the National Road, which he first proposed in 1802 and for which he pushed hard. It linked Cumberland, Maryland, on the Potomac River with Wheeling, Virginia (now West Virginia), on the Ohio. Most Jeffersonians opposed this kind of federal activity on ideological grounds, but in this case Gallatin outsmarted them. He figured out a way to have the road built with revenues from the sale of public lands in Ohio—once again finding ingenious ways to move money. Jefferson wavered when politicians tried to redirect parts of the road, but Gallatin urged the president to go ahead. If he did not, Gallatin wrote him in 1808, "we will infallibly lose the State of Pennsylvania at the next election."[23]

Arguments over federal expenditures for internal improvements continued for many years, and proponents of federal expenditures usually lost. Andrew Jackson's veto of the Maysville (Kentucky) Road Bill of 1830 and James K. Polk's similar refusal to sign the Rivers and Harbors Bill of 1846 confirmed traditional constitutional opposition. Even so, as the nineteenth century progressed, the government extended Gallatin's National Road farther and farther west. In the twentieth century, it became U.S. Highway 40, stretching across the continent from Atlantic City, New Jersey, to San Francisco. Part of its original route through Maryland now parallels Interstate 68, a section of which is called the National Freeway in honor of the original National Road.

Within the Jefferson-Madison-Gallatin circle, Gallatin had by far the highest enthusiasm for federal expenditures on internal improvements. On most other issues (slavery and banks being the major exceptions), the three shared similar attitudes. Throughout their collaboration, Gallatin remained the most practical and least ideological of the three—the one least reluctant to implement policies often regarded by Jefferson and occasionally by Madison as unconstitutional.

That the Virginians asserted unconstitutionality on a wide variety of issues is apparent in another matter they seldom mentioned: slavery. Jefferson, Madison, and every other important southern politician of this generation—and the next two as well—believed that slavery had to be protected from interference by the national government. The U.S. Constitution remained the rock on which they relied. And they were reluctant to interpret it loosely on any issue, lest slavery be the next such issue.

During the thirty years preceding Jefferson's inauguration as president, slavery had become a more contentious question throughout the Atlantic world. England in effect abolished it in 1772, and Scotland in 1778. Vermont, during its brief period as a republic, forbade slavery in its constitution of 1777. In 1783, a court ruled that the Massachusetts constitution of 1780, written by John Adams, had made slavery illegal there. In 1780, the Pennsylvania legislature passed an act for gradual emancipation, and other states followed with similar acts: New Hampshire (1783), Connecticut and Rhode Island (1784), New York (1799), and New Jersey (1804). In 1782, Virginia softened its firm law of 1726 so as to permit the freeing of slaves at the master's death through last will and testament or by deed of manumission. In 1807, Congress forbade the importation of slaves from abroad, effective January 1, 1808.

Few of these American measures were truly radical, but they seemed to point toward a less harsh future for slaves. At the same time, paradoxically, southern resistance to change started to increase. The government of Virginia, for example, began to rethink its 1782 law softening the rules of manumission and to pass legislation making slavery more severe.

In 1793, Eli Whitney's invention of the cotton gin initiated a gradual but fateful change in the economics of slave-based agriculture. Planters began to shift from decreasingly profitable crops and toward cotton. Over the next sixty-eight years, cotton became a cash bonanza for southern growers and for northern brokers, shippers, and insurers. In part because Congress had stopped the importation of slaves in 1808, the extraordinary returns from cotton increased the value of slaves already living in the United States. A vast internal market in human beings therefore arose and lasted for five decades. An estimated one million enslaved persons, their price steadily rising, were sold by their owners in such states as the Carolinas, Maryland, Delaware, and Virginia. The purchasers were mostly cotton planters moving into the Deep South and the emerging Southwest: Alabama, Mississippi, Louisiana, Arkansas, and Texas.[24]

This economic shift had barely begun during the administrations of Jefferson and Madison, but its outlines were becoming clear. Both presidents tended to think in the long term, and neither of them failed to see and to dread where it all might lead. As slaveholding planters, each struggled with the question throughout his adult life. Each opposed slavery in thought but not in deed. Both remained tied to it by personal economic interest and by the stiffening political climate of Virginia. In almost every year from 1792 through 1808, the state enacted legislation that tightened the screws of slavery in one way or other, sometimes brutally.[25]

In 1806, Virginia repealed most of the manumission law it had passed in 1782, and made the granting of freedom through a last will and testament much harder. It also required that any slave freed after May 1, 1806, leave the state within a year or revert to enslaved status. In 1791, the wealthy Virginian Robert Carter III had begun freeing all of his 452 slaves by "deed of gift"—the largest voluntary manumission in American history. And George Washington, who died in 1799, had stated in his will that his slaves should be freed upon the death of his wife.

But had either Jefferson or Madison become an active abolitionist or even arranged for the freedom of his slaves, his political position within Virginia would have become a good deal more complicated. Right up until the time of their deaths—Jefferson's in 1826, Madison's in 1836—neither man was able to work out a satisfactory way to resolve his own possession of slaves. Each spoke in favor of emancipation but did essentially nothing. Each placed his hopes on an impractical plan for colonization of black Americans, a plan that would have amounted to their mass expulsion from the United States.[26]

During the years in which the Jefferson-Madison-Gallatin trio led the federal government, slavery remained a pervasive but often suppressed issue. Gallatin, as an immigrant, had no emotional ties to Pennsylvania or any other state comparable to the deep connection his two colleagues felt for Virginia. Gallatin was not a member of the planter class and had always opposed slavery. As he wrote William Henry Harrison in 1809, "This is a subject on which I differ in opinion from many valuable friends." He lacked Jefferson and Madison's aversion to the idea of a pliant Constitution and a strong federal government that might (as it eventually did) mount a direct attack on slavery.[27]

Often, therefore, Gallatin found himself trying to persuade the Virginians, and Jefferson in particular, that the Constitution permitted wide discretionary latitude. On major issues such as the Bank of the United States, the Louisiana Purchase, and federally funded internal improvements, it was always Gallatin who urged quick action, rather than deferrals based on potential unconstitutionality. For Gallatin, as for Hamilton, the Constitution was not a constraining document in the way it was for Jefferson and Madison.

———

In 1810, Gallatin emulated Hamilton's 1791 *Report on the Subject of Manufactures* by making his own suggestions to Congress on the same subject. Gallatin's *Report on Manufactures* proposed a bold federal loan program to assist fledgling American makers of a wide variety of products. Like Hamilton, he recommended against using the customary European method of promoting domestic manufactures through high protective tariffs. Unlike Hamilton, Gallatin did not urge that bounties be paid to domestic producers. But the goals behind both documents were the same: to diversify the American economy beyond an agricultural/commercial base and to increase the interdependencies among sections of the country. Manufacturing regions would sell to agricultural areas, and vice versa. Their internal trading would form a tighter economic and political union among the states. Gallatin's *Report on Manufactures* is full of the kind of language Hamilton had used, recognizing and underscoring the unique opportunities available in America to enterprising individuals, including immigrants.

As immigrants themselves, both Hamilton and Gallatin saw how much the United States differed from most nations. As Gallatin's *Report* expressed it, America's economic development owed much of its success to "the absence of those systems of internal restrictions and monopoly which continue to disfigure the state of society in other countries." He was struck, as perhaps only a native European could be, that "no law exists here, directly or indirectly, confining man to a particular occupation or place, or excluding any citizen from any branch." Instead, unfettered opportunity remained open in "every species of trade, commerce, art, profession and manufacture." The usual European barriers—tight systems of licenses, guilds, apprenticeships, and export controls—did not dominate the U.S. economy.[28]

As Gallatin went on to say, "The progress of America has not been confined to the improvement of her agriculture, and the rapid formation of new settlements and States in the wilderness; but her citizens have extended their commerce through every part of the globe." With proper assistance from the federal government, the same achievement could be gained in manufacturing. American freedoms "must ultimately give in that branch, as in all others, a decided superiority to the citizens of the United States over the inhabitants of countries oppressed by taxes, restrictions and monopolies."[29]

Gallatin was convinced that the only real barrier to a burst of development in manufacturing was a shortage of liquid capital. Traditional banks, except for their purchases of government bonds, lent money for the short term, seldom beyond three months. But manufacturing concerns needed much more time than this to develop products, build factories, and tool up for larger-scale outputs.

During the 1790s, Gallatin had seen at first hand the importance of investment capital when he and his partners set up their glass works in Pennsylvania. That venture would undoubtedly have become more prosperous if long-term developmental loans had been available. More than any other episode, this one taught him that real progress in U.S. manufacturing was going to require additional capital. But it seemed easier to move money across the Atlantic Ocean—even in huge amounts, as in the Louisiana Purchase—than across the Allegheny Mountains. Gallatin sold his glass works in 1806, but his personal twelve-year experience with the venture underlay his ideas about how to stimulate manufacturing.

In his *Report on Manufactures* of 1810, he proposed that a $20 million federal loan program be set up to meet this kind of entrepreneurial need, much as he had recommended that $20 million be appropriated for internal improvements. Gallatin contemplated in his *Report* a special kind of investment bank—not unlike a modern venture capital firm—that would lend a total of $2 million per year over a period of ten years. Entrepreneurs with promising plans would compete for the loans and would pay interest in the conventional way. The loan program would therefore be self-liquidating. In modern jargon, his program would be called "micro-financing."

What made the idea especially practical was that most manufacturing remained small in scale and did not require huge amounts of money. No industry at this time had giant factories. Even the great textile mills of New England—the first large-scale manufacturing operations in the United States—lay twenty-five years in the future. But even small start-up factories needed some support. Existing banks were not supplying it; and the corporate form of organization, the other best method for aggregating capital, required a special legislative charter for each venture. In Gallatin's time, legislatures granted charters mostly to public-purpose corporations such as turnpikes, canals, and banks.[30]

In the short term, little came of Gallatin's 1810 *Report on Manufactures,* as had been true of Hamilton's *Report on the Subject of Manufactures* nineteen years earlier. Among other problems, the War of 1812 soon intervened, destroying the surplus in federal revenues that Gallatin had anticipated would be available. So his plans for the development of manufacturing went the same way as his plans for internal improvements. In both cases, however, Gallatin had exhibited a compelling vision of the American economy's long-term potential, just as Hamilton had done earlier. And his recommendations for federally assisted manufacturing had been a most un-Jeffersonian kind of proposition.[31]

One issue the Jefferson-Madison-Gallatin triumvirate did agree on was reduction of military expenditures. That policy persisted through Gallatin's tenure in the Treasury Department right up until the War of 1812. In the minds of the three leaders, military cutbacks would decrease the national debt and solidify Republican Party principles. Jefferson, Madison, and Gallatin all recognized that lasting peace between the United States and other nations was an essential prerequisite for these goals. As they correctly argued, monarchical governments in Britain and continental Europe had been fighting wars for centuries, as a matter of routine. In these countries, the glorification of war became manifest in the way military leaders were granted not only honors, but lavish gifts of lands, palaces, and money.

Then, too, the enormous overseas empires of Britain, France, Holland, Spain, and Portugal had been built mostly through exploration and discovery, followed by settlement, and then military conquest of indigenous peoples. The United States itself had originated in this way. In turn, those conquests brought the colonial powers into frequent overseas competition with one another over the control of new territories. The French and Indian War in North America (1754–1763) had broadened into the almost worldwide Seven Years War in Europe and South Asia. The Napoleonic Wars, though not of colonial origin, embroiled almost all the colonies of Britain, France, Spain, and Holland.

By contrast, the ideology of republicanism—both the lowercase "r" generic and the capital "R" of the Jeffersonians—underscored the discontinuity wrought by the American Revolution. "We the People" of republicanism differed altogether from the royal "We" of monarchy. In 1783, the world had regarded with incredulity the quiet retirement of George Washington to Mount Vernon after his victory over the British. No important conquering general, with the sole exception of Cincinnatus in Roman times, had ever done this before. Many had become kings and established hereditary dynasties that still ruled most of Europe. In Gallatin's time, Napoleon Bonaparte was only the latest military commander to follow this route. Napoleon crowned himself emperor and installed his relatives as heads of state in several countries.

Among the American founders, some—Washington, Adams, Hamilton—believed that the new United States would have to retain enough military power to defend itself. During the 1790s, they sought to provide for the common defense by maintaining a small army and encouraging state militias. They also authorized the construction of a modest navy, comprising mainly six elite frigates that could afford at least some protection of the long American coastline.

Other founders—Jefferson, Madison, and later Gallatin—opposed anything more than a token army and navy. Only in the event of war, they believed, should the United States spend significant funds on national defense. Since there had been no declared wars during the 1790s, almost none of the Jeffersonians saw a need for more than minimal military spending. They wished to maintain the capacity to mobilize if war should come, but meanwhile wanted to keep only a skeleton of actual forces.[32]

The problem with this strategy, as the triumvirate discovered, was that mobilization took far longer than they anticipated. And when it did become necessary, it required taxes and other obligations that did not appeal to the American people. Here, again, the personal experiences of Washington and Hamilton during the Revolution contrasted with those of Jefferson and Madison: they knew what it was like to be on the battleground, fighting an underfunded war against the British (Washington served for eight years, and Hamilton for six). Jefferson and Madison, who lacked that experience, tended to think more in terms of abstract political principles than of the nation's continued vulnerability, let alone of specific military strategies. Jefferson, as many of his writings show, believed that the United States could avoid wars almost altogether and remain morally superior to Europe.

Gallatin had no useful experience in war and little interest in military affairs. He had arrived in America in 1780, just a few months before Hamilton wrote from Washington's headquarters that the fighting had reached a crossroads—that the Continental Army "is now a mob, rather than an army, without clothing, without pay, without provision, without morals, without discipline." Being a young man of peace, Gallatin felt no urge to don the uniform. As a congressman in 1794, he regarded the Federalists' military response to the Whiskey Rebellion as a gross overreaction. And in 1798, he viewed the Quasi-War with France as something of an absurdity. Gallatin's main concerns stayed focused on the trans-Appalachian West. He would have been happy to turn his back on Europe and potential wars altogether. Near his home at Friendship Hill, Indians sometimes remained a threat, but the remnants of hostile French and British forces in the West were gradually being neutralized or evicted through diplomatic means.[33]

Except for the Barbary incident that began in 1801, the nation achieved peace during Jefferson's first term, at a time when Britain and France remained at war (apart from the fourteen-month interlude during the Peace of Amiens in 1802–1803). The American economy flourished: in further settlements of the trans-Appalachian West, in continued growth of the population, and especially in the maritime carrying trade, which benefited tremendously from the European war. And with the Louisiana Purchase, the administration had brought off a pivotal achievement. Overall, Jefferson's first term was one of the most successful of all presidential administrations, down to the present time.

In cabinet discussions during this period, Gallatin usually took the lead, as Hamilton had done under Washington ten years earlier. Also like Hamilton, he was a superlative administrator who assumed many tasks performed today by the White House chief of staff. Of the three most powerful men in the government, only Gallatin was willing to spend the hot summer months in Washington. Jefferson and Madison took frequent trips to their up-country plantations and spent most of every summer there. It took at least one and sometimes two days of hard riding for the mail to reach Monticello or Montpelier, Madison's home, and an equal time to return. "Grumble who will," Jefferson wrote Gallatin in 1801, "I will never pass those [summer] months on tide-water." In aggregate, Jefferson spent at least two of his eight years in office away from the capital.[34]

During his prolonged absences, he relied on Gallatin to oversee the functions of government. An onerous burden therefore fell on the secretary, made worse by the absence of Hannah and the children. After their miserable first summer's experience with the heat and humidity of Washington, Gallatin sent them to Hannah's home in New York every year after 1801, while he himself remained in the capital. During his thirteen-year tenure as secretary of the treasury, he visited New Geneva and his home at Friendship Hill only three times: in 1803, 1806, and 1810.[35]

Apart from the many tasks Gallatin undertook for the president, he brought greater administrative discipline to the Treasury Department. He also sponsored the repeal of excise taxes, while simultaneously reducing the national debt. He led Jeffersonian financial principles to a level of success many Federalists had considered impossible. Dozens of new banks appeared throughout the country, chartered by the states. Prosperity reigned.

Many more people were beginning to participate in American politics than had done so under Federalist rule. When Jefferson ran for reelection in 1804, twice as many voters went to the polls as in 1800 or 1796, even though the laws of suffrage had not changed very much. In 1804 Jefferson won 73 percent of the popular vote over the Federalist candidate, Charles Cotesworth Pinckney of South Carolina, and an Electoral College landslide of 162 to 14. The Republicans replaced Vice President Aaron Burr with George Clinton, another New Yorker.

Throughout the country, all seemed well, the future full of promise for another triumphant Jefferson administration. But Jefferson's second four years in office turned out to be far less successful than his first—in large measure because he paid insufficient attention to the advice of Albert Gallatin.

FIGURE 19. Thomas Jefferson's Monticello, one of the iconic buildings in the United States. Jefferson kept altering the design, from the start of its construction in 1768 until its completion during his presidency. The 20,000-square-foot mansion, located near Charlottesville, Virginia, was the center of a 5,000-acre plantation staffed with about 150 slaves.

MANSION OF PRESIDENT MADISON.
Montpelier Va.

FIGURE 20. Montpelier, James Madison's ancestral home, located in Virginia about thirty miles from Monticello. Originally built in 1764, the house was gradually expanded to 12,000 square feet. The surrounding plantation was a little more than 5,000 acres, staffed with about 100 slaves.

FIGURE 21. Friendship Hill, Albert Gallatin's home on 400 acres in the southwestern corner of Pennsylvania. The modest building pictured here is the "Stone House," constructed in 1822 after Gallatin returned from his assignment as minister to Great Britain. The original "Brick House" at Friendship Hill, a smaller structure built in 1789 and now coated with stucco, is attached behind the Stone House on the left side, looking much like a later addition shown here on the right side. The house and grounds, like the Hamilton Grange, are today maintained by the National Park Service. Admission to both is free. Monticello and Montpelier are owned and operated by private foundations, which charge substantial admission fees.

CHAPTER 22

Embargo and Frustration

In 1806, Lewis and Clark returned from their two-year exploration of the West, and their glowing reports on the Louisiana
Territory captured the nation's imagination. But few other
things went well from 1805 to 1809. Jefferson was almost sixty-
six when his second term ended—an old man for that time. Like
Washington during his own second term, he had become sickly
as he aged and had started to lose his earlier enthusiasm for
government. Plagued with frequent headaches and numerous
other ailments, Jefferson felt at home only at Monticello. There,
he could control his daily routine without the incessant demands that vex every chief executive.[1]

The other main source of problems during Jefferson's second
term was the deteriorating situation in foreign affairs. In 1805,
the war between Britain and France, by now in its twelfth year,
had become hotter than ever: a full-blown European land war,
as well as a fight to the death at sea. The British navy's blockade
of continental Europe squeezed ever tighter. Through a series of
official decrees called Orders in Council, the British government
began for the first time to interfere with the ships of neutral na-

tions, including the United States. In response, Congress passed a Non-Importation Act against certain British goods. This measure failed to prevent British attacks on U.S. merchant vessels bound for European ports. At the same time, Napoleon issued a set of decrees similar to Britain's Orders in Council. Thousands of American merchant ships now became fair game for Britain and France. Both nations captured hundreds of U.S. vessels, either with their warships or by using heavily armed raiders ("privateers") licensed to prey on American commerce. Gallatin's job as secretary of the treasury was about to become much more difficult.

Even worse in its effects on American public opinion, the Royal Navy's traditional practice of "impressment" now reached a new plateau. The naval equivalent of being drafted into the army, impressment was essential for maintaining the crews of Royal Navy ships. It was therefore crucial to British national security. Over the course of the war, "press gangs" rounded up well over 150,000 British men for service in the navy. Even sailors on British merchant ships were seized as a matter of routine.

Real trouble arose when British impressment spread to the American merchant marine, and even to the U.S. Navy. British sailors could earn much more money on American commercial ships than in the Royal Navy or the British merchant marine. A few American volunteers who had earlier served on ships of the Royal Navy were among the many who now deserted in favor of employment on American vessels. A larger number of young men either had emigrated from Britain or had become U.S. citizens by paying a small fee to American consuls in foreign ports. The British government, however, refused to recognize these men as American citizens unless they had been naturalized by 1783, when the Revolution ended. As a consequence, press gangs scoured British and Caribbean ports for deserters or former British citizens, in order to capture them for service in the Royal Navy. From 1792 to 1802, they impressed at least 2,400

American seamen. (About 6,000 more were seized over the next ten years.) These were large numbers at a time when the typical crew of a merchant ship was well under 100 sailors.[2]

Looking for some way out of this dilemma, Jefferson tried to negotiate with the British. The Jay Treaty of 1795 was about to expire, and the president instructed James Monroe, the American minister in London, to work out a renewal that forbade impressment. Monroe and another American diplomat, William Pinkney, engaged in tough bargaining with the British over a period of four months. On December 31, 1806, they signed a treaty that covered some trading rights but did not resolve the question of impressment. On that point, the British refused to budge. When the Monroe-Pinkney Treaty arrived in the United States, secretary of state Madison and a furious Jefferson rejected it out of hand. The president refused to submit it to the Senate for ratification, an act that severely embarrassed James Monroe.[3]

Next, Madison suggested another solution: that the U.S. agree not to permit the employment of British sailors if the British would stop impressing men from American ships. When Gallatin looked into this idea, he found—to the surprise of nearly everyone—that about 9,000 sailors on U.S. merchant ships engaged in overseas trade were British and therefore vulnerable to seizure. This was about half of all the able seamen serving on American vessels in this trade, and it made Madison's suggestion impracticable. Implementation of the policy, Gallatin wrote him, would "materially injure the navigation of the United States." So British sailors continued to serve on American ships, and impressment by the Royal Navy persisted.[4]

The American people and their government found this situation intolerable. It seemed an outrageous breach of the rights of neutral seamen, including young immigrants who intended to become U.S. citizens or had already been naturalized. Neither side in this controversy saw any room for compromise. Impressment remained a bombshell ready to go off as soon as a major incident took place.

—∞—

That incident came in June 1807, when the large British warship HMS *Leopard* encountered the smaller USS *Chesapeake* off the coast of Virginia. The *Leopard,* denied permission to search for deserters, proceeded to fire three twenty-five-gun broadsides into the *Chesapeake.* Three sailors were killed and eighteen wounded, including the American commanding officer. The British then boarded and searched the *Chesapeake.* They removed four sailors—three Americans and one Englishman—all of whom were deserters from the Royal Navy. At that time, such a step was tantamount to an act of war by Britain against the United States. The American people were appalled. "This country," wrote Jefferson, "has never been in such a state of excitement since the battle of Lexington" in 1775.[5]

In a flurry of activity led by Jefferson, Madison, and Gallatin, the government demanded an apology and return of the three Americans (the English deserter was hanged at the British naval base in Halifax). Anticipating war, the U.S. issued a call for the states to mobilize their militiamen. Britain equivocated on any apology; and, at this highest stage of its sea war against the French, announced that impressment would not only continue but would be stepped up.[6]

Gallatin, as much as he detested nearly all things military, now believed war with Britain to be inevitable. He and others recommended that Congress be called from its summer recess to an immediate special session—not necessarily to declare war, but to settle on an appropriate policy. But Jefferson refused. Gallatin wrote his wife that "the principal objection [to a special congressional session] will not be openly avowed, but it is the unhealthiness of this city." Thus did the climate of its national capital affect the country's decision for war or peace. When Congress reconvened on October 26, 1807, Jefferson asked not for war, public opinion having cooled a bit, but instead for an Embargo Act that would take American ships off the high seas altogether. As he later wrote the governor of Virginia, "The great objects of the embargo are keeping our ships and seamen out of harm's way."[7]

Jefferson's fiery rhetoric in his embargo message moved Gallatin yet again to suggest that the president tone down his language. "I would wish its general color and expression to be softened." As for the embargo itself, Gallatin opposed it more strongly than any other proposal Jefferson made during their eight years together in office. And he tried, almost desperately, to prevent it. He pointed out how much an embargo would violate Jefferson's own principles of individual freedom: "Governmental prohibitions do always more mischief than had been calculated; and it is not without much hesitation that a statesman should hazard to regulate the concerns of individuals as if he could do it better than themselves." Nor could such an embargo possibly serve its purpose. "As to the hope that it may . . . induce England to treat us better, I think it entirely groundless."[8]

Jefferson nevertheless went ahead. Congress passed the Embargo Act on December 22, 1807, six months after the *Chesapeake* incident. The act, startling in its reach, required that all foreign trade by American ships come to a halt. It specified that no American merchant vessel could leave an American port for a foreign destination and that no U.S. ship anywhere could carry goods to Britain, France, or their colonies. As Jefferson apparently saw it, the embargo's purpose was to protect American ships from capture and American seamen from impressment, while buying time for the United States to prepare for war. The government's call for the widespread activation of militiamen, meanwhile, evoked a tepid response from the states.

The most earnest apostle of "economic coercion" within the administration was secretary of state Madison, who had long believed that the U.S. government could punish Britain by depriving it of supplies from America. But there was a good deal

of confusion within the government about what economic coercion could accomplish. An embargo that applied only to U.S.
shippers was not really "economic coercion," as that term was
commonly understood. In maritime practice, an embargo was a
rare measure considered to be a short-term prelude to war. But
in 1807 the United States was nowhere near ready for war, and
Britain needed American markets for its own exports more than
it needed American supplies from American ships. Tobacco and
cotton accounted for almost half of U.S. exports to Britain, and
under the Embargo Act much of this total could still be carried
by British ships.[9]

Congress had already passed the Non-Importation Act, which
prevented British ships from delivering certain goods to American ports, but the exceptions far outnumbered the prohibited
items. Under the terms of Jefferson's embargo, British ships
could continue to trade in American ports, purchasing exports,
selling most imports, and providing, through import duties,
nearly half of the revenues of the federal government. In other
words, the biggest losers under the embargo would be *American* exporters and shippers, not the British or French governments or their own producers and traders. Overall, the embargo
amounted to a dire and self-inflicted wound to the American
economy.

Contrary to almost all expectations, the embargo continued
not for a few weeks but for fifteen months, until Jefferson was
about to leave office. During this long period, the embargo did
not even begin to accomplish its purpose. It brought untold
mischief and lawbreaking, and proved to be the biggest blunder
of Jefferson's presidency. Secretary Madison's avid enthusiasm
for the embargo persisted for about a year. It then began to
wane in the face of what Madison regarded as disloyal opposition from the New England states. Meanwhile, the administra-

tion asked Congress to increase the size of the U.S. Army from 2,800 soldiers to 30,000, but Congress refused.[10]

The embargo turned out to be a Gordian knot that Thomas Jefferson could not bring himself to cut. Throughout his long career, one of Jefferson's greatest strengths as a statesman had been his ability to avoid precipitous action and take the time to think matters through to their core principles and likely consequences. As the price of this virtue, he sometimes acted too late and failed to correct mistakes promptly. That was one reason why the lightning-quick Hamilton had so often outmaneuvered him during the early 1790s, and why Gallatin had to prod him to act immediately on such matters as the Louisiana Purchase. In the case of the embargo, Jefferson seemed to sense his error fairly early. But the issue was so complicated that the right course of action eluded him. He soon became frustrated and tried to distance himself from the entire question. The burden of implementing the embargo therefore fell on Gallatin—ironically, since the secretary had been the only cabinet member opposed to the measure and still believed it to be futile. He regarded the legislation as a colossal mistake, certain to divide the country and wound its economy.[11]

Gallatin had numerous conversations with Jefferson about the embargo and wrote him scores of communications over the months following its enactment. He informed the president that the embargo could not work in the absence of a British policy reversal, which was very unlikely and in fact never came. The embargo, Gallatin pointed out, would damage almost every element of American business: domestic shipowners, farmers whose produce made up a large part of American cargoes, and merchants and manufacturers who exported their goods. As commerce declined, smuggling by American shippers would rise. The embargo would require ever-stronger policing by the federal government, a contradiction of core Jeffersonian principles. As Gallatin put it to the president, "Congress must either invest the Executive with the most arbitrary powers and sufficient force to carry the embargo into effect, or give it up altogether." There was no doubt about which alternative Gallatin preferred.[12]

But the embargo continued, month after month, and the situation became more and more awkward. As secretary of the treasury, Gallatin himself had to enforce the law even as he watched all of his predictions come true. The Treasury's customs officers, high-ranking supervisors who collected duties and cleared ships for departure, were responsible for commercial traffic in and out of all ports. Communication between Gallatin and the seventy-odd collectors remained slow and difficult, dependent on the mails. Some of the collectors resigned in frustration. Others, threatened with mayhem, hesitated to crack down on violators, whom local juries were loath to convict. Then, too, a great deal of water-borne commerce had long operated along the border with the British colony of Canada, through Lake Champlain and the Great Lakes. Traffic on the lakes was covered by the embargo and proved even harder to police than movements out of Atlantic ports.[13]

Under these conditions, maritime smuggling spiraled out of control. Less than three weeks after the initial embargo became law in December 1807, Congress was forced by circumstances to pass a supplementary act that covered not only ships crossing the Canadian border on lakes, but even riverboats. It also imposed extremely heavy penalties for violations: forfeiture of the ship and its cargo, or a fine double the value of both. In March 1808, still a third law prohibited the export of all goods of any kind, even overland into Canada or, in the South, into Florida, which was then in the hands of Spain. This third law was a harsh and telling extension of the original act, which, in Jefferson's words, was supposed to keep American ships and seamen from harm's way. In July 1808, Gallatin wrote the president: "Nothing but force on *land* (for there the collectors have the right to seize property on shore) will put a stop to the violations."[14]

Methods of evading the embargo became ever more ingenious. Thousands of small boats carried goods into Canada across Lake Champlain and the Great Lakes. In response, Gallatin and his staff devised still more stringent regulations, until the level of detail became almost absurd. Cargoes of flour drew special attention because food was one of the great needs in Britain, Europe, and the Caribbean. But large amounts of flour had long been shipped from one U.S. port to another, and the inspectors could not be certain what their actual destination would be. Regulations required shippers of flour and similar goods to post cash bonds in steadily higher amounts—cash that they had to forfeit if the ships failed to show up at their announced destinations.

If an embargo applying to oceangoing vessels were passed in the twenty-first century, it would not be hard to enforce. The U.S. Navy and Coast Guard would simply keep American ships within their home ports or track their movements when they left. But in 1807 and 1808, of course, no radar, satellite, or other electronic tracking devices existed. It took days, weeks, and sometimes months to report on ship movements. Effective administration stood no chance of success. The government might as well have passed a law prohibiting water from running downhill.

President Jefferson, having delegated the impossible task of enforcement to Gallatin, began to retreat for longer respites at Monticello. He seemed, in this last year of his presidency, to grow less interested not only in diplomacy and the possibility of war, but also in other affairs of state. He urged Gallatin to follow a hard line in enforcing the embargo. Otherwise he distanced himself as much as possible from its consequences, which had already begun to damage his legacy.

At the end of June 1808, Gallatin wrote Hannah, his wife,

that the embargo was likely to cost the now-divided Republicans the upcoming presidential election. In July, his close friend Alexander James Dallas wrote him: "I will candidly tell you, that almost everything that is done, seems to excite disgust." Dallas predicted that another year of these conditions "would render Mr. Jefferson a more odious President, even to the Democrats, than John Adams." In August 1808, Gallatin told Jefferson: "I deeply regret to see my incessant efforts in every direction to carry the law into effect defeated in so many quarters." The embargo was hurting the Republican Party more than it was hurting the British or French. Unless some means was found "to raise the embargo before the 1st of October, we will lose the Presidential election." Jefferson urged Gallatin to secure still stronger laws of enforcement.[15]

Contemporaries argued at the time about the president's intentions, and historians have done so ever since. After all, Jefferson was a genuine American icon whose views had helped to shape the national character. But the embargo flew directly in the face of the very principles of liberty he personified. Some interpretations hold that his agrarian thinking had been altered by the American prosperity achieved when U.S. ships carried cargoes for the French and British in their long war. That war persisted, with one brief interruption, for the entirety of Jefferson's presidency. But once both countries began to prey on American ships, the earlier U.S. affluence declined. And when HMS *Leopard* fired on the USS *Chesapeake* in 1807, the game was up.[16]

During the fifteen months of the embargo, which was not repealed until the very last week of Jefferson's time in office, the president seemed to develop an isolationist position based on his idealism about the American experiment in republican government. The economic corollary of taking the United States out of harm's way was an extreme conception of American self-sufficiency: its need for neither imports nor exports. The economic term for this kind of policy is "autarky," and for Jefferson it mirrored the kind of self-sufficiency he had achieved at Monticello.

—∞∞—

There, on his mountaintop retreat, all necessary provisions and goods were grown or manufactured on-site. Agricultural autonomy was matched by industrial autonomy. Carpenters, joiners, brickmasons, farmers, vintners—and Jefferson himself as architect during the continuous remodeling of Monticello—created a self-sufficient community. But to project this small-scale autarky onto a national economy, even one as diverse and innovative as that of the United States, could hardly have been less realistic, the more so because Monticello's economy depended on slave labor.[17]

In February 1808, a little over two months after passage of the first Embargo Act and thirteen months before the official end of his presidency, Jefferson wrote James Monroe that "my longings for retirement are so strong that I with difficulty encounter the daily drudgeries of my duty." And the next month, in another letter to Monroe: "For myself I have nothing further to ask of the world than to preserve in retirement so much of their esteem as I have fairly earned, and to be permitted to pass in tranquillity, in the bosom of my family and friends, the days which yet remain to me." But Jefferson's presidency still had a year to run. His responses to Gallatin's constant entreaties about what to do next were brief and dismissive: you know the situation and I don't; you have my proxy; you decide; hold firm to principle, but set the rules for enforcement yourself.[18]

The likely truth was that Jefferson had grown too weary to attend to public affairs. Now past sixty-five, he was plagued with health problems, emotionally drained, and bedeviled with the intricacies of European diplomacy. He had lost much of his popularity and was finding it difficult to continue as chief executive. After forty years of dedicated public service, he had finally had enough. So he made himself a virtual cipher with respect to the embargo.[19]

Jefferson's behavior created a further predicament for Gallatin because the terms of the legislation permitted the president to make exceptions for individual ships on particular voyages. As might have been expected, a deluge of applications poured in. The president intervened at unpredictable moments, but he remained largely unavailable to adjudicate these applications, causing Gallatin still more trouble. On the broader question of the embargo, Gallatin wrote Jefferson in November 1808, "I think that we must (or rather that you must) decide the question absolutely, so that we may point out a decisive course either way to our friends." But the president did almost nothing.[20]

Whatever the cause of Jefferson's behavior, the consequences were severe. American exports declined from $108 million in 1807 to $22 million in 1808, a drop of 80 percent; imports fell by a little less but still by more than half, from $139 million to $56 million. From 1808 to 1809, federal revenues plummeted from $17 million to $7.8 million. The public's alienation mounted not only in the New England states, where the Jeffersonians' popularity had seldom been high, but in every port city in the nation. John Randolph of Roanoke, Jefferson's former ally, wrote at the end of Jefferson's second term, "Never has there been any Administration which went out of office and left the nation in a state so deplorable and calamitous." James Madison managed to win the election of 1808 by a comfortable margin, but much of the country's animosity continued into his presidency.[21]

How serious an error was the embargo? In 2006 a poll of ninety scholars, who were asked to enumerate the worst of all presidential mistakes, ranked it at number seven. (James Buchanan's dithering during the four years before the Civil War ranked number one.) The results of such polls vary with the times and must be used with great caution. But in many polls about American presidents, Jefferson is often ranked at number four, behind only Lincoln, Washington, and Franklin D. Roosevelt. And the name of no other chief executive ranked among even the top seven appears on the top ten list of presidential mistakes.[22]

The obvious irony of the months from June 1807 to March 1809 was that Jefferson, the nation's best-known apostle of liberty and minimal government, had created their precise opposite. The embargo imposed the most rigorous and prolonged economic restrictions on the liberties of white Americans up to that time, and the strongest peacetime restrictions down to the present day. Jefferson apparently expected voluntary compliance with the embargo, and it seems likely that he believed his fellow citizens to be as idealistic as he himself was. He had allowed his ideas about how Americans should behave to overwhelm the obvious fact that the embargo was a draconian and unreasonable measure, certain to fail.[23]

CHAPTER 23

Dispiriting Diplomacy

The commercial and political trap set for the United States by the Napoleonic Wars did not disappear with the end of Jefferson's presidency. His successor, James Madison, proved to be a weak and indecisive executive until his final two years in office. The first six years of Madison's presidency seemed to contrast with his earlier achievements: as a delegate at the Constitutional Convention, as author of many of *The Federalist Papers,* and as Republican leader in Congress. But the contrast may have been more apparent than real. Madison was one of the most perceptive and original political thinkers the United States has ever produced. As many of his arguments at the Philadelphia Convention of 1787 and in *The Federalist Papers* suggest, he believed that Congress, and not a strong chief executive, should be the core of American government.

Barely five feet four and weighing about a hundred pounds, Madison lacked the commanding physical presence of his two Virginia predecessors, Washington and Jefferson. "Little Jemmy" was a first-rate political philosopher, but a second-tier executive and administrator. Like Jefferson, and even more so like

John Adams, who regularly spent several months at a time in Massachusetts, Madison often absented himself from the capital city. He much enjoyed retreating to Montpelier, his large plantation in the hills of Virginia, about thirty miles from Jefferson's home at Monticello.

Madison had intended to appoint Albert Gallatin secretary of state, a slightly more prestigious though less demanding post than secretary of the treasury. Gallatin deserved, wanted, and expected this appointment, but his candidacy suffered because of his role as the embargo's chief enforcer. Over the years, he had also made numerous enemies through his stringent financial controls over public expenditures. Then, too, there were objections from important members of Congress about making a "foreigner" the nation's chief diplomatic officer. An informal tally of votes in the Senate found seventeen members opposed to Gallatin's confirmation, ten in favor, and seven undecided.[1]

The new president therefore bypassed him and appointed Robert Smith, who had been secretary of the navy under Jefferson. In collaboration with his powerful brother, Senator Samuel Smith of Maryland, Robert Smith had long been an opponent of Gallatin. Both Smiths had expressed frequent and sometimes nasty objections to the treasury secretary's efforts to reduce naval appropriations.

Madison's elevation of Robert Smith to a post Gallatin had wanted displeased him immensely. Not only was Smith an irritation; he was unqualified to be secretary of state, as every informed person well knew. Madison had caved to complaints about Gallatin's foreign origins and to political pressure led by Smith's brother, and the president soon had cause to regret his decision. Once in office, Robert Smith proved not merely an incompetent secretary of state, but a disastrous one. Years later, John Quincy Adams wrote in a private memoir that if Gallatin rather than Smith had been appointed in 1809, "it is highly probable that the war [of 1812] with Great Britain would not have taken place." This may overstate the case, but of Smith's poor qualifications there can be no doubt.[2]

⁕

By the fall of 1809, Gallatin's morale had reached one of its lowest points ever. He had felt defeated in his effort to prevent the enactment of Jefferson's embargo in 1807, then at having to enforce a law he regarded as foolish and oppressive. Nor could his family life have been happy at this time. In 1808, his infant daughter died—a third such personal tragedy, two other small daughters having perished in 1802 and 1805. Although childhood deaths were not uncommon in this era, these emotional blows to Albert and Hannah Gallatin were hard to bear. Two sons and a fourth daughter survived, but the Gallatins lost three of their six children.

In his professional life, the embargo and its successor laws made it impossible for Gallatin to continue paying off the national debt, which remained his greatest ambition. With the sole exception of the Louisiana Purchase in 1803, the federal government was spending more than it was taking in. And now Madison's appointment of Robert Smith seemed the last straw. Gallatin wanted to resign from the cabinet, but reluctantly decided to stay.

In November 1809, he sent a revealing letter to Jefferson, to whom he felt closer than to Madison and who was now in his eighth month of retirement. "I do not pretend," the secretary wrote, "to step out of my own sphere and to control the internal management of other Departments"—even though as a member of the triumvirate he had often done just that. But Gallatin now felt his voice was heeded less, his old influence reduced. "I cannot, my dear sir, consent to act the part of a mere financier . . . to become a contriver of taxes, a dealer of loans, a seeker of resources for the purpose of supporting useless baubles, of increasing the number of idle and dissipated members of the community, of fattening contractors, pursers, and agents, and of introducing in all its ramifications that system of patronage, corruption, and rottenness which you so justly execrate."[3]

Coming from the level-headed and self-effacing Gallatin, these were strong words. When Jefferson's tenure ended in March 1809, Gallatin had wished either to leave the government or to become secretary of state. Now his frustration boiled over. His letter to Jefferson seemed to question whether the Revolution of 1800 still applied. In response, Jefferson and Madison did everything they could to mollify him. Madison, having appointed a remarkably undistinguished cabinet, needed Gallatin's talents not only as head of the Treasury but as an all-around adviser on diplomacy, military affairs, and government in general.

As secretary of the treasury, Gallatin was still locked in a permanent battle with his Republican enemies in the Senate, known as "the Invisibles" and led by Senator Samuel Smith of Maryland, Secretary Robert Smith's brother. In addition, he had long been under constant attack on nearly all subjects by a related group of Republicans, the "Philadelphia Junto." Its most vocal spokesman, William Duane, who had succeeded Benjamin Franklin Bache as editor of the influential *Aurora,* maligned Gallatin mercilessly. Duane, who became a powerful political force in his own right, would continue to do so in the future, calling him a "Frenchified Genevan." Jefferson and Madison seemed unable to stifle Duane's relentless attacks on Gallatin.[4]

Besides these handicaps, Gallatin had been forced to administer the successor bills to the embargo. First came the Non-Intercourse Act of 1809, passed three days before Madison's inauguration as president. This bill repealed the embargo, but reenacted its provisions for ships destined for Britain or France. It was a more enforceable measure than the embargo but still unpopular among merchants, commercial farmers, and especially shippers. All continued to blame Gallatin and the Republican Party for their troubles.

After two years under the feckless Non-Intercourse Act, amid constant debate within the government about what to do next,

Congress passed still a third measure. This law went under the
name of Macon's Bill No. 2, a revision of a bill reported out of
the House Foreign Relations Committee, chaired by Nathaniel
Macon of North Carolina. Macon, an extreme proponent of
states' rights, had long fought against federal powers of all
kinds. He had opposed the Constitution of 1787 as ceding too
much power to the central government, and he detested the U.S.
Navy. The first measure reported out of Macon's committee
was passed by the House but killed by the Senate. A revised bill
made it through both houses, even though Macon himself voted
against it and many senators attacked it ruthlessly. In 1810,
President Madison signed it into law, despite his own reservations. The farce that had begun with the embargo was now entering its most dangerous phase.[5]

Macon's Bill No. 2 authorized the president to restore trade
with Britain and France if they ceased to interfere with American shipping. If only one of the two nations complied, the boy-
cott of the other could continue. Viewed from the American
perspective, Macon's Bill No. 2 appeared to be a clever way to
play the two great powers off against each other. Viewed by the
more experienced diplomats of London and Paris, it seemed a
naïve ploy by an ambitious but impotent would-be player on
the international stage. The Americans possessed hundreds of
first-rate cargo ships—but without a powerful navy to protect
them, these ships remained at the mercy of British and French
men-o'-war and privateers.

In Macon's Bill No. 2, Napoleon saw a delicious opportunity
to tweak the British. He sent a message to Washington agreeing
to the terms of the bill, even though he had no intention of implementing his agreement. (On the same day he sent his message, he told his ministers as much and made plans to confiscate
American property in France.) French warships and privateers
continued to capture American merchant vessels. The British,
angered at this newest evidence of apparent Republican favoritism toward the French, grew even more intransigent toward the
United States. So the Americans lost all around. Henry Adams

later wrote that Macon's Bill No. 2 "has strong claims to be considered the most disgraceful act on the American statute-book ... The imagination can scarcely conceive of any act more undignified, more cowardly, or, as it proved, more mischievous."[6]

As federal overseer of all maritime commerce, Gallatin faced the same impossible task in 1810 that had bedeviled him for three years. His voluminous correspondence with customs collectors at all major ports, and with presidents Jefferson and Madison alike, shows rising discontent as the embargo gave way to the Non-Intercourse Act and finally to Macon's Bill No. 2. The problem seemed to have no solution and no end.

Wars between the British and French had been proceeding off and on since 1754, seven years before Gallatin's birth in Geneva. Why should anyone expect an end to the two countries' animosity toward each other—or, as a corollary, any settlement of America's maritime grievances toward both? In the end, Macon's Bill No. 2 turned out to be yet another fruitless American attempt to come to grips with the chaos of the Napoleonic Wars—a way-station on the road to America's own War of 1812 against Britain.

CHAPTER 24

The Fate of the Bank

Meanwhile, Gallatin found himself in the middle of a frustrating fight on still another front: an internal battle over renewal of the Bank of the United States. Its twenty-year charter, secured by Alexander Hamilton in 1791, would expire in 1811. Many Republicans, including Jefferson, opposed the existence of all banks and of this one in particular. Shortly after the Louisiana Purchase of 1803, Jefferson had written Gallatin that the secretary's proposed new branch of the bank at New Orleans was out of the question: "This institution is one of the most deadly hostility existing against the principles and form of our Constitution ... What an obstruction could not this bank of the United States, with all its branch banks, be in time of war? It might dictate to us the peace we should accept, or withdraw its aids. Ought we then to give further growth to an institution so powerful, so hostile?"[1]

In response, Gallatin explained why "I am extremely anxious to see a bank at New Orleans." As Hamilton had done in his *Report* to Congress a dozen years earlier, Gallatin tried to communicate in elementary terms the wisdom of having a Bank of the United States. As he wrote Jefferson, it would continue to facilitate the nation's financial affairs through several advantages not fully available through state banks:

1st. A safe place of deposit for the public [that is, federal] moneys.

2nd. The instantaneous transmission of such moneys from any one part of the continent to another, the Bank giving us immediately credit at New York, if we want it, for any sum we may have at Savannah or any other of their offices, and *vice versa*.

3rd. The great facility which an increased circulation [of currency] and discounts [loans or redemption of loans and of other banks' notes] give to the collection of revenue.[2]

Gallatin could have written a much longer list—mentioning, for example, that the bank issued Jefferson's own paycheck and those of all other federal employees; that the bank evened out balance-of-payments issues with other nations; that in the event of war the bank would be crucial as a means of financing mobilization; and that its very existence made the operation of the Treasury Department much easier. Gallatin knew Jefferson well, however, and did not want to oversell an institution the president would always despise. In the end, a reluctant Jefferson gave in and signed the bill creating another branch of the bank at New Orleans. But he did not let the occasion pass without complaining yet again about the likely unconstitutionality of the entire enterprise.

The Bank of the United States never ceased to be a target of controversy, and its enemies lay in wait until its charter expired and they might kill it. Early in 1808, the bank's stockholders petitioned Congress to begin considering an early renewal of the twenty-year charter. The Senate asked for Gallatin's advice. The secretary, sensitive to Jefferson's hostility as well as to attacks from other quarters, replied that his report should come after the presidential election, "at the next session of Congress." He submitted his report about a year after it had been requested, and, not coincidentally, one day before Jefferson left office. In his report, Gallatin urged the bank's recharter. Congress did nothing, and an additional year passed. Early in 1810, the House agreed to consider a recharter bill. But, preoccupied with other matters and not eager for a premature fight, Congress still again took no action on the bank.[3]

Finally, in January 1811, as the original charter was about to expire, both the House and Senate were forced to address the issue. Once more, Gallatin strongly endorsed recharter. President Madison did not share Jefferson's intense aversion to all banks, but neither did he come forward with robust support. Like Jefferson, Madison had argued against the original charter in 1791, when Hamilton had proposed it.

In 1811, both houses of Congress were evenly divided over recharter. Most Federalists supported Gallatin, but by now their numbers were reduced, and the Republicans had split along several fault lines. It was not an issue that pitted agrarian interests against mercantile ones, as might be expected. Nor did the sections of the country line up as North versus South, or East versus West. Powerful Senate Republicans, such as William Harris Crawford of Georgia (a future secretary of the treasury and presidential candidate), supported recharter. In the House, so did numerous other Jeffersonians from both the South and the West.

Opposing recharter were two groups of Republicans having little in common with each other. Many "Old Republicans," such as Senator William Branch Giles of Virginia, still believed the bank to be an unconstitutional extension of federal power. To them, Gallatin as secretary of the treasury had not behaved with sufficient partisanship. The other group of hostile Republicans were businessmen with an entrepreneurial turn of mind. They wanted state-chartered banks of their own and the freedom to operate without oversight from the Bank of the United States. The different reasons for opposition were reflected by actions taken by the legislatures of five states. Such disparate states as Massachusetts, Pennsylvania, and Virginia instructed their U.S. senators to vote against recharter.

By 1811, individual states had granted corporate charters to eighty-eight banks, up from three in 1791. Many states taxed these new banks, owned shares in them, or both. For some states (Pennsylvania and Delaware in particular), the income from shares or taxation of banks brought in a substantial proportion of all state revenues—50 percent for Pennsylvania during the years 1801–1805. Almost all of these eighty-eight banks issued their own currency. Their notes circulated locally and became worth less of their face value the farther away from home consumers tried to spend them. The situation was altogether different from the one that modern consumers have long been accustomed to: a single national currency.[4]

Some Federalists owned stock in state banks and did not support recharter. Both they and the larger number of Republicans who owned shares of state banks had two forceful reasons for wanting the Bank of the United States undone. First, their own banks could take over the profitable business done by the bank and its many regional branches, such as holding substantial deposits of federal money and lending to the national and state governments. Second, in the event the Bank of the United States was abolished, state banks would be freed of the regulations it imposed on them. As Hamilton had intended, the bank fulfilled numerous functions of a central bank analogous to today's Federal Reserve System. Those functions included serving as lender of last resort to federal and state governments, issuing currency accepted everywhere at its face value, and providing some oversight of state banks.[5]

———

The crucial tool of regulation was this: the bank's power to require payment in gold or silver from state banks in return for those banks' notes. The Bank of the United States could thereby exert some control over the reserve assets of the state banks and limit inflationary trends resulting from unfettered issuance of their own currencies. In all, the Bank of the United States had been a resounding success for twenty years—everything Hamilton had predicted it would be, and more. If not quite indispensable to Gallatin and the Treasury, the Bank of the United States was not far from it.[6]

In the political climate of 1811, however, the bank's near-indispensability and its long record of brilliant success did not guarantee its recharter. American politics did not work that way then, and has seldom done so since. In 1811, congressional supporters of easy credit objected to the bank's regulatory powers, however modest they were. The vigorous young congressman Henry Clay of Kentucky, for example, saw the bank as an inconvenient obstacle to the ambitions of bankers in his home state and in the West generally. Even some urban New England Federalists turned their backs on recharter. In the fight for public opinion, it was far easier for the bank's diverse opponents to conjure up fears about it than for supporters to defend its record.

Among the many ironies in this situation, the Bank of the United States was not a federal agency, but a profit-making institution. The bank remained as Hamilton had designed it in 1791, except that by 1802 the government's one-fifth stake in its total shares of stock had all been sold to private investors. But that did not prevent a chorus of objections about excessive federal power. A petition from eighty residents of Pittsburgh asserted that the Bank of the United States "held in bondage thousands of our citizens who dared not to act according to their consciences from fear of offending the British stockholders and Federal directors." The facts, however, were that British stockholders had no influence, and there were no federal directors on the bank's board.[7]

Even so, British investors' ownership of a large proportion of bank stock proved to be a valuable piece of ammunition. Had not the Revolution been fought against the British? Had not

HMS *Leopard* fired broadsides into the USS *Chesapeake?* Had not the Embargo Act, the Non-Intercourse Act, and Macon's Bill No. 2 been directed primarily against the British? How could any loyal citizen support the continuance of an institution whose stock had gravitated from American to British investors? It did not seem to matter that British stockholders could not vote on the election of bank directors or exercise any influence whatsoever on the bank's affairs. Nor did it make any difference to the bank's opponents that the inflow of British funds helped the U.S. national economy. As often happens in politics, slogans had become stronger than facts.

The most important rationalization against the bank's recharter was its alleged unconstitutionality—an idea restated so many times since 1791 that it seemed to have become true by endless repetition. "Old Republicans" in Congress used this argument constantly. So, too, did certain business interests throughout the country. Their real aim was to open banks of their own, chartered by the states and unregulated by any quasi-national authority.[8]

Against the powerful but mixed coalition of opponents to the bank stood most of the merchant and shipping interests in port cities. Gallatin's allies in the House and Senate, who represented both agrarian and urban regions, also supported recharter. Had President Madison taken a firmer stand, their cause would have been much strengthened and the recharter assured. But to Gallatin's great frustration, the president simply waffled.[9]

On January 24, 1811, after less than three weeks' debate in the House, the motion for the bank's recharter was put off "indefinitely" by vote of 65 to 64. Eleven congressmen did not vote at all. For most of them, their consciences would have required a yes vote, whereas their constituents preferred a no. Seven arranged to be absent from Washington, and four others declined to vote at all.

In the Senate, Gallatin presented a draft bill and an enthusiastic recommendation for the recharter. In an ingenious proposal, he suggested a large increase of capital through the issuance of more bank stock. He reasoned that in the event of war with Britain—very likely at this point—the Bank of the United States would be in a position to lend the federal government as much as $40 million (an enormous sum for that time) and thereby minimize additional taxes. His supporters presented the bill on February 5, 1811. After two weeks' debate—during which Gallatin was attacked for suggesting policies Hamilton had sponsored during the 1790s—the Senate voted 17 for, 17 against. Vice President George Clinton, a political enemy of both Gallatin and Madison, then broke the tie by voting no. Thus died the Bank of the United States.

In its subsequent breakup, the money that had to be paid to foreign shareholders drained about $7 million from the United States—a substantial loss of liquidity at what turned out to be a very untimely moment. The bank's eight branches were purchased by local investors in the cities where they operated (Boston, New York, Baltimore, Washington, Norfolk, Charleston, Savannah, and New Orleans). Most were reopened under new state charters. The main office in Philadelphia, including the grand headquarters building, was sold to Stephen Girard, a wealthy immigrant from France who was already the bank's largest shareholder. He continued to operate the Philadelphia business as a sole proprietorship called "Stephen Girard's Bank."[10]

Meanwhile, the number of state-chartered banks exploded: from 88 (in 1811) to 208 (in 1815) to 246 (in 1816). Most issued their own currency, subject to almost no regulation. Many retail transactions turned into sessions of haggling over the value of banknotes offered in payment or given in change. The value of notes from different banks (there were more than 800 by 1840) varied widely, giving rise during the 1830s to thick pamphlets and guidebooks about what their currencies were worth. Some of these guidebooks were updated in weekly editions.[11]

For Gallatin, the failure of the bank's recharter amounted to

a personal affront by James Madison and a staggering professional setback. In March 1811, Gallatin wrote a furious letter
to the president stating that "your present Administration is de-
fective, and the effects, already sensibly felt, become every day
more extensive and fatal. New subdivisions and personal factions, equally hostile to yourself and the general welfare, daily
acquire additional strength. Measures of vital importance have
been and are defeated; every operation, even of the most simple
and ordinary nature, is prevented or impeded." Because things
could not continue in this way, "a radical and speedy remedy has become absolutely necessary." Gallatin concluded that
whatever that remedy might be, it would not involve his own
continuance in office. Therefore, "I beg leave to tender you my
resignation."[12]

Madison, now trapped in a dilemma of his own making, at
last took action. He fired the current secretary of state, Robert
Smith, who together with his brother, Senator Samuel Smith,
had opposed Gallatin at every turn. The president then asked
Gallatin—whom he knew had long wanted to be secretary of
state—to sound out James Monroe for the post, and Monroe
accepted. Showing irritation but infinite patience, Gallatin then
withdrew his resignation and agreed to stay on at the Treasury.

The next year brought the War of 1812. For the preceding
decade, Gallatin had seldom asked for measures that would
raise additional revenues, and when he did Congress had generally refused. Now that Congress had stupidly killed the Bank of
the United States, the government found itself in a precarious
financial position to fight any war—let alone one so fraught
with peril as this one turned out to be.

CHAPTER 25

Financing the Wayward War

War had been a real possibility since 1807, when HMS *Leopard* attacked the USS *Chesapeake*. When it finally came in 1812, it marked the climax of many years of controversy: over sailors' rights against impressment, British capture of U.S. merchant ships, conspiracies between British agents and Indian tribes to thwart settlement of the West, and general humiliation of the United States. Those Americans who wanted war exploited the long-held popular suspicion that Britain was determined to recolonize their country. The British had no such intention, and in May 1812 even repealed some of the Orders in Council pertaining to American trade. But the news of that concession did not reach Washington until it was too late.[1]

Neither Madison nor Gallatin much wanted war, but they saw no alternative. Nor did it escape the Republicans' attention that a war would enhance Madison's prospects for reelection. The vote on his message to Congress, which almost but not quite asked for a declaration of war, showed sharp regional divisions: the Northeast was strongly against war, the South and West were mostly in favor, and the Middle Atlantic states were divided. In the Senate, the initial vote on a declaration ended in a tie. After additional debate, the margin was 19 to 13 in favor of war. In the House, the final tally was 79 for, 49 against. These were by far the closest votes in American history, down to the present time, on whether the country should go to war. Madison signed the declaration on June 18, 1812.[2]

For the British, engaged as they were in a mortal struggle with Napoleon, the American war seemed little more than an irksome sideshow. The Madison administration, including Gallatin, believed that state militiamen and the U.S. Army could easily capture strategic parts of Canada. Jefferson, in retirement, predicted that "the acquisition of Canada this year [1812] will be a mere matter of marching." Adding territory to the United States was not one of the administration's primary purposes—as opposed to that of some of the congressional "war hawks." Rather, it was to deprive the British of vital supplies from Canada and then to use the captured provinces as bargaining chips in the subsequent peace conference. Madison and his advisers believed such a conference would soon begin.[3]

They miscalculated on both points. American incursions into Canada were very badly botched; and the British, despite their preoccupation with Napoleon, were in no hurry to make peace. Instead, the Royal Navy—which in 1812 possessed a huge armada including 191 ships of the line and 245 frigates—dispatched just enough warships to blockade the U.S. east coast. Many American merchant vessels leaving port were seized by British privateers or the Royal Navy. American privateers, meanwhile, captured numerous British merchant ships. Fighting at sea spread into the North and South Atlantic and even into the Pacific, where the British tried to disrupt the large American whaling industry.[4]

The six elite U.S. frigates constructed under Federalist administrations during the 1790s—against the opposition of Gallatin and almost all other Republicans—served with marked distinction throughout the war. Several ship-to-ship engagements against British frigates ended in U.S. victories, thereby raising the American people's morale. These triumphs were dramatic but largely symbolic, doing little to break the British blockade. Much more important were the successes of Oliver Hazard Perry and other naval commanders on the Great Lakes, which prevented effective counterattacks by land from Canada. Timeless slogans soon entered American folklore: "We have met the enemy and they are ours," reported Perry. "Don't give up the ship," said the dying Captain James Lawrence, after a rare defeat of an American frigate in 1813. (His ship, the USS *Chesapeake*, in fact was given up, and taken by HMS *Shannon* to the British naval base in Halifax.) The Royal Navy's bombardment of Fort McHenry in Baltimore harbor inspired Francis Scott Key to write "The Star-Spangled Banner."

Ever since 1807, when HMS *Leopard* had first fired on the USS *Chesapeake*, Gallatin had been thinking about how to finance a potential war. He had planned almost entirely on using borrowed money and higher rates of import duties. By 1811, his first estimate of a necessary domestic bond issue of $10 million had escalated to $40 million. It also became evident to him that the 6 percent interest rate allowed by Congress would have to be increased to 8 percent, adding $800,000 to the annual interest charges on $40 million. By 1812, Gallatin's estimate of $40 million had grown to $50 million. To make matters much worse, his entire plan for borrowing had been undercut by Congress's refusal in 1811 to recharter the Bank of the United States. The bank would have been the most important single source of wartime loans to the government, exactly as Alexander Hamilton had predicted in 1791.[5]

State-chartered banks proved reluctant to buy government bonds and were of almost no help. In addition, Congress had refused most of Gallatin's requests to augment federal revenues through tariff increases and new domestic taxes. Now, on the eve of war, he proposed a 100 percent increase in tariff rates, and Congress at last complied. But since the nation was soon fighting against Britain, receipts from import duties on British goods plummeted. With reluctance, Gallatin drafted about a dozen new tax laws, and most were eventually passed.[6]

————✸————

The pivotal role of Gallatin and other immigrants in helping to pay for the War of 1812 provides another example of their crucial importance in early American finance. The six most significant players—three in the public sector, three in the private—were all immigrants. The public servants were Gallatin, who continued to serve as treasury secretary until May 1813, when Madison asked him to be one of the peace negotiators in Europe; George W. Campbell (born in Scotland), who succeeded Gallatin after his departure for Europe and served for eight months; and Campbell's own successor, Alexander James Dallas (born in Jamaica), a close friend of Gallatin. The talented Dallas performed much better than Campbell, who was physically ill during his eight months' service. But Dallas, like Campbell and Gallatin, had problems selling U.S. securities at reasonable rates. Secretary Campbell, in particular, could raise money only by marketing securities at heavy discounts and paying high interest rates.[7]

From the private sector, the three largest investors in U.S. wartime securities were three of the nation's wealthiest immigrants: the merchant and banker Stephen Girard, who had arrived from France in 1774 and who had purchased most of the outstanding shares of the Bank of the United States in 1811; the fur trader and merchant John Jacob Astor, a German who had emigrated to New York in 1784; and the financier and merchant David Parish, who had come from Germany in 1805 and settled in Philadelphia. Parish organized the largest domestic syndicate for the purchase of securities issued to pay for the war, and his two main partners were Girard and Astor. Parish first pitched his plan to Alexander James Dallas, who then recommended it to Secretary Gallatin. The secretary had already discussed the outlines of this plan with his friend John Jacob Astor. The syndicate's infusion of $16 million—of which Parish, Girard, and Astor subscribed $9.1 million—came ten months after the war began. This was in April 1813, just in the nick of time. On March 5, 1813, Gallatin had written Madison: "Dear Sir,—We have hardly enough money to last till the end of the month."[8]

In late 1813, eighteen months into the war and well after Gallatin's departure, Congress restored internal excise taxes of the kind Hamilton had instituted in the 1790s. Before he left for Europe, Gallatin had asked, in strong terms, that these taxes be reinstated. Meanwhile, the sale of Treasury bonds, potentially the major source of funds, remained a persistent problem. The war was affecting the nation's creditworthiness, both at home and abroad.

In desperation, Congress authorized the printing of federal currency notes—the first since the ratification of the Constitution. There were five separate issues from 1812 to 1815, totaling $36.7 million. This step amounted to fighting the war with printed money backed by nothing, much as the Continental Congress had done during the Revolution. Whether Gallatin would have countenanced the large issues made after his departure for Europe remains an open question. They went against his deepest principles, but the war had forced him to take similar steps even before he departed.[9]

The financial cost of the war completely upset the Republicans' plans to retire the national debt. Gallatin's single-minded pursuit of this goal had reduced the debt from a high of $86 million after the Louisiana Purchase to about $45 million at the start of 1812. But four years later, on January 1, 1816, the debt had ballooned to $127 million, almost triple the prewar figure and 53 percent higher than the Federalist peak of $83 million in 1801.[10]

Overall, the War of 1812 had many elements of a fiasco, even a farce. The British had their hands full with Napoleon, and repealed some of their offensive Orders in Council just before the Americans declared war but before the notice reached the United States. On the American side, the close vote in Congress reflected hopeless internal divisions. Neither of the warring countries showed much enthusiasm for combat, and the most spirited fighters were often the British colonists in Canada and their Indian allies. Once war was declared, U.S. Army enlistments lagged and several states balked at cooperating with the War Department. Some New England states even refused to place their militias under federal command. Both the army and the militias had poor leaders and performed abysmally in the field, especially during the early part of the war. The Royal Navy's blockade of the American coast bottled up commerce, but a good deal of illicit trading between U.S. merchants and the British army and navy went on. And the Americans' most spectacular victory—in the Battle of New Orleans under General Andrew Jackson—came after the peace treaty was signed but before word of it reached the troops.[11]

In August 1814, Britain inflicted one of the worst humiliations the United States has ever suffered: it invaded Maryland and burned part of Washington. The Treasury, the White House, the U.S. Capitol—and, incidentally, Gallatin's own house on Capitol Hill—were all put to the torch. President Madison was out of the city, but his wife, Dolley, barely escaped capture. She fled the executive mansion only a few hours before the British troops arrived. Their officers dined on the meal that had been prepared for Mrs. Madison and her guests, then set their fires and watched the White House go up in smoke.[12]

In the northeastern states, the war pushed some extremists toward nullification of federal laws and toward secession from the Union. Even before hostilities began, merchants and shippers had discussed this drastic option privately with one another. With ironic zeal, New England Federalists reread the

Kentucky and Virginia resolutions written by Jefferson and Madison in 1798, advocating state nullification of federal laws, and came close to acting on their recommendations. Business in the Northeast had suffered grievously for four years under Jefferson's embargo, the Non-Intercourse Act, and Macon's Bill No. 2. The War of 1812 augured a potentially permanent end to prosperity.

In late 1814, the issue of secession was raised at the Hartford Convention, an assembly of representatives from the five New England states. This gathering, called to discuss effective ways to protest the war and the policies of trade restriction, met during December 1814 and early January 1815. The delegates were unaware that efforts at a political settlement of the war stood on the verge of success. The peace treaty, signed on December 24, 1814, was on its way by ship to Washington, D.C., for ratification when the Hartford Convention adjourned. In American public opinion, the treaty discredited the proceedings at Hartford and all but killed what few remnants were left of the Federalist Party.[13]

The War of 1812 had lasted thirty months, from June 1812 through December 1814. By comparison, U.S. participation in World War I lasted seventeen months and in World War II forty-four months. The conflict of 1812–1815, though perhaps unavoidable, was nevertheless one of the strangest in American history.

FIGURE 22. The United States Capitol after it was burned by the British in August 1814. Other images of this scene, from different angles, show the two parts of the building completely separated from each other, with about seventy-five feet of daylight in between.

CHAPTER 26

Winning the Peace

Gallatin's role in ending the war turned out to be one of his greatest contributions to his adopted country. In all, the negotiations consumed twenty-one months. Throughout this long period, the British took a rude, dilatory, and intransigent stance toward the Americans. On the U.S. side, two members of the diplomatic team—John Quincy Adams and Henry Clay—quarreled almost constantly with each other. Without Gallatin's limitless patience toward both the British and his own colleagues, the negotiations might well have collapsed.

They began in March 1813, when Russia's representative in Washington wrote President Madison of a proposal by Czar Alexander I to serve as mediator in the war. Madison accepted the offer at once. He should have known that Britain would reject any such proposal, but the Russian offer came at the same time Gallatin told him that the Treasury was about to run out of money. On the brink of bankruptcy after less than a year's fighting, Madison wanted peace by any honorable route.

The president chose as chief negotiator John Quincy Adams, who was serving as American minister in St. Petersburg, Russia's capital. The preliminary talks would presumably begin there. The cabinet suggested a three-person delegation, and Gallatin offered to serve, taking what he thought would be a temporary leave from the Treasury. For partisan balance, Madison appointed a third member, James Bayard, a Federalist senator from Delaware—the man whom Alexander Hamilton had persuaded to abstain in the Electoral College vote of 1801 that awarded the presidency to Thomas Jefferson.[1]

Gallatin wrote his brother-in-law explaining his decision to volunteer for the peace mission. He specified two reasons, and each speaks volumes about the War of 1812: "1. The great incapacity for conducting the war, which is thereby much less efficient and infinitely more expensive than it ought to have been. 2. The want of union, or rather open hostility to the war and to the Union, which, however disgraceful to the parties concerned, and to the national character, is not less formidable and in its consequences of the most dangerous tendency." Under these circumstances, "I have made up my mind that I could in no other manner be more usefully employed for the present than on the negotiation of a peace." Anticipating a long absence, Gallatin moved Hannah and two of their children to the Nicholson home in New York. Their third surviving child, the sixteen-year-old James, accompanied his father to Europe.[2]

The voyage to St. Petersburg took ten weeks. Gallatin and Senator Bayard arrived only to find that Minister John Quincy Adams believed, correctly, that Russian mediation would be useless. Czar Alexander was fighting Napoleon in Bohemia at the time, and in any case there was little reason to think that the British would accept his good offices. A long and pointless waiting game now began, as the British did essentially nothing.

The weeks turned into months, and the American delegates passed the time as best they could. They composed a long history of the events that had led to war. They worked out their opening positions in the negotiations and the conditions under which they would accept peace. They went sightseeing around the Baltic. Gallatin wrote to ask the advice of Sir Alexander Baring in London, with whom he had become friends during the financing of the Louisiana Purchase. The London banker replied that Britain would likely undertake only direct negotiations with the United States, without Russian mediation.[3]

Meanwhile, back in the U.S., the Senate—where Gallatin still had many enemies—voted 18 to 17 against approving his credentials as envoy extraordinaire, since he was still secretary of the treasury. Madison then appointed congressman Henry Clay and Jonathan Russell, the new American minister to Sweden, to the delegation. Gallatin began to make plans for returning to Washington, but he was in no hurry. As it turned out, he remained a member of the delegation because of a law providing that a cabinet office unoccupied for six months must be declared vacant. It was at this point that George Campbell became secretary of the treasury, on the understanding that the post would revert to Gallatin upon his return.[4]

In January 1814, Gallatin and James Bayard, tired of six months' fruitless waiting in St. Petersburg, decided to go to London. At the height of the Russian winter, they undertook an icy and dangerous 1,500-mile overland trip. They managed to reach Amsterdam three months later, and in April 1814 crossed the English Channel. By the time they arrived in London, they had been absent from the United States for almost a year. Henry Clay and Jonathan Russell, meanwhile, had gone to Gothenburg, then the capital of Sweden. By letter they informed Gallatin of his reinstatement to the team, which had now swelled to five members. Gallatin replied that the entire delegation should begin talks with the British as soon as possible. He suggested London, Amsterdam, or the Hague as a meeting site. Clay and Russell rejected London, the enemy's capital, but accepted either of the Dutch cities. The British then proposed Ghent, a third city in the Low Countries, located in what is now Belgium.[5]

Three more months dragged by before negotiations began. The British then sent a group of third-tier representatives to Ghent, with instructions to do nothing without checking with their superiors in London—a formula for still more delay. The continuing procrastination, as might be expected, angered the American delegates. Henry Clay, at that time something of a hothead, periodically proposed that the talks be broken off. Even John Quincy Adams, one of the most astute diplomats in American history, considered giving up. Weeks and months continued to pass without progress. The high-living Clay would often arrive at the delegation half-drunk after an all-night poker session, just as the abstemious Adams was rising for his morning physical regimen. In this situation, Gallatin once again showed his skills to best advantage. Counseling forbearance, he held the motley American group together and gradually replaced Adams as its leader.

Gallatin believed that neither Britain nor the United States was likely to win a clear victory in the War of 1812. Had the British so chosen, they could have shifted overwhelming forces to North America after they defeated Napoleon in April 1814. They could have begun an all-out land and naval war that would have lasted for many years and inflicted a terrible toll on the United States, even if the Americans ultimately prevailed. At the negotiations in Ghent, therefore, Gallatin persuaded his team to stall after every British success in Europe or North America. The British delegation did just the opposite, and the chess match began to seem interminable. In the end, the negotiations at Ghent consumed four months.

During this period, the Americans never spoke with anyone in the British government who had real authority. But Gallatin kept in close touch with Sir Alexander Baring, who told him that after more than two decades of European war, Britain was tired of fighting. Money was short and taxes remained extremely high. Britain's greatest active soldier, the Duke of Wellington, privately advised against a major effort against the United States. (Restraint proved fortunate for the British, since in 1815 Napoleon escaped from exile in Elba, returned to France, and had to be defeated yet again, at Waterloo.)

Even so, Gallatin feared that the British would unleash their immense military power against the Americans. In August 1814 he wrote secretary of state Monroe that the British intended to make significant gains from the war: "It appears to me most likely that their true and immediate object is New Orleans. They well know that it is our most distant and weakest point, and that if captured it could not be retaken without great difficulty . . . It is now evident that Great Britain intends to strengthen and aggrandize herself in North America." Gallatin was right. A large British army sailed for America in September 1814, its mission the capture of New Orleans.[6]

With the negotiations in Ghent at a standstill, Gallatin hit on a new device to break the deadlock. He proposed that each side prepare a careful draft treaty that its government was willing to sign. The two drafts could then be compared and their common elements incorporated into an actual treaty. Relatively mild differences would be negotiated, and their resolution added to the treaty. If there were strong differences, these would be deferred for future talks after the fighting ended. Here Gallatin was assuming that both sides wanted peace but had become intransigent over a few sticking points that they could never work out at Ghent.

He proved to be correct—and at long last, his patience and wisdom were rewarded. A new document drafted along these lines was discussed by the two parties for almost a month. And on December 24, 1814, the American and British negotiators signed the Treaty of Ghent, ending the War of 1812.

Then came a final punctuation to the war's many absurdities. In January 1815, the Americans won a spectacular victory at the Battle of New Orleans—their most glorious military triumph since the Battle of Yorktown in 1781, thirty-four years earlier. The commanding general, Andrew Jackson, became the

FIGURE 23. Sketch of Albert Gallatin, 1815, by the European artist Pieter Van Huffel. It was accompanied by a caption that read: "Portrait de Monsieur Gallatin, Ministre des Etats Unis d'Amérique auprès du Congrès de Gand" ("Portrait of Monsieur Gallatin, Representative of the United States of America at the Congress of Ghent").

greatest national hero since George Washington. The Battle of New Orleans occurred after the treaty had been completed at Ghent but before news of the signing had reached the United States.

The details of the treaty changed little that would not have occurred anyway because of the end of the Napoleonic Wars. The impressment of seamen, which to the Americans had been the single biggest cause of the war, now became moot because Britain demobilized much of its navy. Secretary of state James Monroe had instructed the negotiators to leave aside the issue of impressment altogether, and the treaty's text omits any reference to it. No significant territory in Canada became part of the United States, or vice versa. With two important exceptions, the war ended in stalemate, and conditions in 1815 reverted to those that had prevailed before its start in 1812.

The first exception was the gradual resumption of normal trade relations between the two countries. This provided great relief to the American economy and a big boost to the Treasury's income from duties on British imports. The second exception was that Britain gave up its long-running endeavor to promote an Indian confederation on U.S. territory. That effort had hindered America's fur trade and, more important, had discouraged further white settlement in the West.

⸺

The Indians, therefore, were big losers in the War of 1812, just as they had been in the American Revolution thirty years earlier. For them the Treaty of Ghent was a crushing blow, the more bitter after their role in such British victories as the capture of Detroit in 1812. The war had claimed the lives of famous Indian chiefs, including the great Tecumseh, who had died in 1813 during a pitched battle in southern Ontario. He had taken his forces from their midwestern stronghold to assist the British against an American invasion. The war's end meant that without British supplies and support over the long term, what had been a formidable Indian confederation crumbled in the face of relentless white migration westward. This was the most significant substantive result of the War of 1812. Although Gallatin was more sympathetic than most whites toward Indians, he had strong feelings in favor of westward expansion and national development.[7]

Among American citizens, the war's most important psychological effect was an upturn in national morale. Despite the many comic-opera aspects of the war, the stalemate of 1815 was interpreted in most sections of the country as something close to a victory, in what came to be called "the second war of independence." Then, too, the Republicans could plausibly argue that they had fought a war against the greatest military power on earth without compromising their principles.

This claim was something of a stretch, considering the severe suppression of civil liberties during Jefferson's embargo, the sharp rise in taxation to fight the war, and the 182 percent increase in the national debt. Since the "Revolution of 1800," the Republicans' chief goals had been the extinction of the national debt, minimal taxation, the extension of civil liberties, and international peace. The embargo and the War of 1812 made a mockery of each of these goals. But in the flush of a stalemate that could be portrayed as a victory, the ironies quickly receded.

As Gallatin wrote in 1816, "The war has laid the foundation of permanent taxes and military establishments which the Republicans had deemed unfavorable to the happiness and free institutions of the country. But under our former system we were becoming too selfish, too much attached exclusively to the acquisition of wealth, above all, too much confined in our political feelings to local and State objects. The war has renewed and reinstated the national feelings and character which the Revolution had given, and which were daily lessened." This statement might have been written by Alexander Hamilton, had he still been alive in 1816. Coming from Gallatin, it smacked of after-the-fact rationalization. The war and its resolution, he went on to say, had made the people "more Americans; they feel and act more as a nation." Gallatin's upbeat temperament inclined him to look on the bright side of things, and his arduous assignments from 1801 to 1814 had almost compelled him to do so.[8]

For Gallatin and many other American statesmen, not to mention the American people as a whole, the mere avoidance of defeat offset humiliations such as the impressment of seamen and the burning of Washington, D.C. And Jackson's dramatic triumph at New Orleans provided real cause for celebration. There seems little question that the fortuitous outcome of the War of 1812 instilled a stronger sense of nationhood, however ironic that outcome may have been. In calling attention to this result, Gallatin was correct.[9]

The advantageous Treaty of Ghent represented a masterly feat of diplomacy, one of the crowning achievements of Gallatin's public career. John Quincy Adams's grandson Henry Adams called the treaty "the special work and the peculiar triumph of Mr. Gallatin." After its signing, Gallatin and his son James took a trip to Geneva, where they stayed for more than a month. It was Gallatin's first return since his departure in 1780, thirty-five years before. The city received him with enormous enthusiasm, showering him with attention and honors. He then spent several weeks in Paris, where he learned that Jackson had repelled the British invasion of New Orleans, that the U.S. Senate had ratified the Treaty of Ghent, and that Napoleon had escaped from Elba and was about to enter France. Gallatin returned to London before Napoleon's final defeat at Waterloo.[10]

The Ghent negotiating team then reassembled, charged with working out a commercial treaty with Britain. The talks began in London during May 1815, continued into July, and were very successful. The final terms reaffirmed many provisions of the Jay Treaty, which Gallatin and his fellow Republicans had attacked so vehemently in 1795, and which had been in limbo since the failure of the Monroe-Pinkney Treaty in 1807. But the passage of time had mooted the problems of both 1795 and 1807. France no longer loomed either as an ideal of the Republicans or as a military threat to the British.

The changes wrought by the Treaty of Ghent, Napoleon's defeat at Waterloo, and the subsequent Anglo-American commercial agreements demonstrated just how wrenching the wars between Britain and France from 1793 to 1815 had been for the United States. During that period the Americans had split internally over the Jay Treaty, had fought a Quasi-War with France, and then waged a real war with Britain. Almost incredibly, they had come close to declaring war on both of these two great powers at the same time.

Gallatin had been at the center of national affairs throughout this entire twenty-two-year period. When he returned from his diplomatic missions in September 1815, he and his son had not seen Hannah and the rest of the family for two years and three months.

CHAPTER 27

His Long and Useful Life

When the War of 1812 ended, Gallatin was fifty-four, seven years older than Hamilton had been when Burr's bullet killed him. But unlike Hamilton, Gallatin lived a very long life. He survived until the age of eighty-eight and continued to make major contributions to his adopted country. In 1815, President Madison asked him two different times to resume his duties at the Treasury, but Gallatin said no on both occasions. In 1816, he helped in the campaign to charter the Second Bank of the United States, replacing the bank Congress had terminated in 1811. Having learned its lesson, the legislature now acted more responsibly, and the Second Bank began its own twenty-year career in 1816.

In 1815 Madison offered Gallatin the post of minister to France. At first he declined, writing the president that his health was poor and that he could not afford the expense of living in Paris. But his feelings were ambivalent, and he spent several months trying to decide. Either he could return to Europe, where he had felt more at home than he had expected, or he could stay in the United States and go into business with his old friend John Jacob Astor. This latter opportunity, pressed on him by Astor, represented a real chance to become wealthy. Meanwhile, President Madison asked him yet again to return to his old post at the Treasury, an offer Gallatin refused immediately. In the end, after much urging from secretary of state Monroe, Europe won out. In 1816, still not sure he had made the right decision, Gallatin sailed with his family for France.

He served as the American minister in Paris for seven years, until 1823. Although the restored Bourbon monarchy formed a poor match with his republican ideals, this period turned out to be, as he later wrote, "the most pleasant of my life." The city-bred Hannah Gallatin loved Paris—the antithesis of the Pennsylvania frontier. And Gallatin himself felt relieved after years of unremitting work at the highest levels of national government. He was pleased by the slower pace of diplomatic rounds in the City of Light, a setting now much relaxed after twenty-five years of revolutionary fervor and Napoleonic upheaval. He also much enjoyed his new and hard-earned international stature. Europeans recognized him as an American statesman of the first rank, as well as the famous negotiator of the Treaty of Ghent.[1]

When Gallatin returned to the United States from Paris in 1823, he briefly became involved in presidential politics, allying himself with the Jeffersonian candidate, his friend William Harris Crawford of Georgia. Some of Crawford's supporters asked Gallatin to be his running mate. (Like Hamilton, Gallatin could have become president, having been a citizen in 1789, the year of the Constitution's adoption.) But after such a long absence abroad, he lacked political clout. He watched as the election of 1824 became even more convoluted than the Jefferson-Adams-Burr affair of 1800. In 1824, there were four major candidates, all but one of whom Gallatin knew well: Crawford, now the incumbent secretary of the treasury; John Quincy Adams, secretary of state; Henry Clay, Speaker of the House; and Senator Andrew Jackson of Tennessee, the hero of New Orleans. Gallatin had deep reservations about Jackson, whom he identified with reckless militarism. Only Crawford ran under the Republican banner, the others as independents. The first party system no longer existed, because of the collapse of the Federalists.

In the election, support among the candidates split by sections of the country. The Northeast went mostly for Adams, the Middle Atlantic and South voted mostly for Jackson, and the West was divided between Jackson and Clay. Jackson won both the popular vote (41 percent to Adams's 31 percent) and the Electoral College vote (99 to Adams's 84, Harris's 41, and Clay's 37). The Constitution, however, requires an electoral majority, rather than a plurality. So, as in 1800, the contest was thrown into the House of Representatives. There, to the extreme consternation of Andrew Jackson, Clay's supporters voted for Adams, who became president. Adams then appointed Clay secretary of state, and the legend of a "corrupt bargain" between the two began—a legend that affected the next election, in 1828.

Gallatin, meanwhile, having finally had enough of active politics, went back to his home at Friendship Hill in western Pennsylvania. Hannah and most of the children detested the place, but Gallatin had little alternative. He wrote his old friend Jean Badollet that "the impossibility of subsisting on my scanty income in one of our cities, and the necessity of attending to a valuable but mismanaged property have left me no choice, and we are all here"—back on the Pennsylvania frontier. In 1825, Badollet came for a visit to Friendship Hill, and the two boys from Geneva, now in their middle sixties, saw each other for the first time in twenty-one years.[2]

In 1826, President John Quincy Adams asked Gallatin to become minister to Great Britain, and he accepted with reluctance. Gallatin did not enjoy his sojourn in London nearly as much as his long mission in France, being put off by British arrogance and dissimulation. As always, the British took an intransigent initial position on every question. But Gallatin's patience and firmness again served U.S. interests well, and he successfully negotiated most of the issues still remaining between Britain and the United States. The big questions were

American commercial rights and the delicate issue of resolving the two countries' rival claims to the vast Oregon Territory. In the end, there was no resolution of Oregon, but an extension of existing agreements.

In November 1827, Gallatin returned to the United States and took up still other diplomatic missions: securing American acceptance of the terms he had negotiated in London, and a final settlement of the long-simmering dispute with the British about the border between New Brunswick and Maine. These tasks consumed most of the years 1828 and 1829. Gallatin then let it be known that he would accept reappointment as minister to France. But he had no standing in the new administration of Andrew Jackson and received no offer.

Under these circumstances, Gallatin at last began to pay serious attention to earning more money for the support of his family. After years of indecision and regret, he had given up on his Pennsylvania adventures. The land around Friendship Hill, he wrote his son James in 1827, "is a troublesome and unproductive property, which has plagued me all my life. I could not have vested my patrimony in a more unprofitable manner." The dreams of the nineteen-year-old immigrant who had come to make his fortune as a land baron, and of the thirty-year-old who had wanted to found a thriving community of Swiss immigrants at New Geneva, had finally withered.[3]

Gallatin himself, on the other hand, was still full of energy. In 1828, at the age of sixty-seven, he left Pennsylvania for good and moved to New York City. "I was destined," he wrote Jean Badollet, "to be always on the wing." He added, more than a little disingenuously, that "I was perfectly satisfied to live & die in retirement" beside the Monongahela River. Such a life, however, could not "be borne by the female part of my family or by children brought up in Washington and Paris."[4]

In 1829 he became president of the newly chartered National

Bank of New York, an office he held for the next seven years. John Jacob Astor had provided $750,000 for the capitalization of this bank on the condition that Gallatin be named its president. With a substantial and, at last, stable income from the bank, Gallatin began to behave like an elder statesman, dispensing advice on a variety of public affairs.

For this role, he was in exactly the right place at the right time. New York had become the nation's largest and most exciting city, and it was growing fast. When he and Hannah had married in 1793, New York's population had been about 35,000. By 1830, when he became a banker, it had grown to 200,000, and by 1850 to 500,000. No other major American city came close to this mushroom growth. Gallatin and Hannah, who was delighted to be back on her native ground, took up residence in a fine house at 57 Bleecker Street, where they lived for almost two decades.

During the 1830s, Gallatin tried to persuade the Jackson administration—which in the election of 1828 had swept into office on a tide of popular support—to recharter the Second Bank of the United States. But the campaign against the Second Bank turned even more bitter and demagogic than the one in 1811 against the first bank. And this time President Jackson vowed to "kill it" himself, which he did. In 1832, Congress passed a bill for early recharter of the Second Bank, but Jackson vetoed it. His accompanying message rehearsed all the old arguments against both the first and Second Bank: they were unconstitutional; they stifled state banks; they invited dangerous foreign stock ownership.[5]

To these familiar objections Jackson's veto added fiery statements of class conflict, portraying the bank's stockholders as greedy capitalists seeking special favors from a democratic government. Jackson's message remains to this day one of the most strongly worded and politically effective pieces of presidential rhetoric ever issued: "Many of our rich men have not been content with equal protection and equal benefits, but have besought us to make them richer by act of Congress. By attempting to

gratify their desires we have in the results of our legislation ar-
rayed section against section, interest against interest, and man
against man, in a fearful commotion which threatens to shake
the foundations of our Union." By 1836 there were enough
votes in Congress to recharter the bank on schedule, but not
enough to override a certain veto by Jackson. So the bill was
never submitted to the president, and the Second Bank of the
United States went out of existence.[6]

In consequence, from 1836 until the initial meeting of the
board of governors of the Federal Reserve System in 1914—a
period of seventy-eight years—the United States had no central
bank. This era was one of immense economic growth and, in
most years, general prosperity. But there were also an inordinate
number of panics, recessions, and depressions: in 1837, 1839–
1843 (severe), 1847–1848, 1853–1854, 1865–1867, 1873–
1877 (severe), 1882–1885, 1893–1894 (severe), 1896–1897,
1902–1904, 1907–1908 (severe), and 1910–1911. The congressional investigations that followed the Panic of 1907 ultimately
led Congress to pass the Federal Reserve Act of 1913. No consensus exists on the causes of these economic downturns. But
there is little question that a well-managed central bank would
have prevented some of them and mitigated all of them. Alexander Hamilton and Albert Gallatin, who disagreed on some
other issues, were correct in their emphatic support for a central bank.

During his twenty-year residence in New York, Gallatin chaired
numerous public-service committees, wrote influential articles
for magazines, and enjoyed the high esteem of almost everyone.
In 1831 he helped to found what is now New York University
and became president of its Council. As he wrote Jean Badollet,
"It appeared to me impossible to procure our democratic institutions & the right of universal suffrage, unless we could raise

the standard of general education & the mind of the labouring classes nearer to a level with those born under more favorable circumstances." Today, NYU has a Gallatin School of Individualized Study, a *Gallatin Review* for student publications, an Albert Gallatin Scholars program, an Albert Gallatin Lecture series, and a Gallatin Arts Festival. The university's internal "Albert" website is the basic information source for accessing online data, and is used by almost every student every week.[7]

Despite all of Gallatin's accomplishments, his immigrant origins were never forgotten—and were never far from the insults of his opponents. In 1831, during a rancorous national debate over protectionist tariffs, he accepted the chairmanship of a committee to promote freer trade, of which he had been a lifelong advocate. The committee produced a long document reminiscent of Gallatin's earlier performances, such as his 1796 *Sketch of the Finances of the United States.* The committee presented its resolution to Congress in 1832, a presidential election year in which Henry Clay, now a senator from Kentucky and an ardent protectionist, intended to challenge the incumbent, Andrew Jackson. In one of the least creditable performances of Clay's career, he took to the Senate floor and denounced Gallatin, at whose side he had negotiated the Treaty of Ghent eighteen years earlier: "Near fifty years ago Pennsylvania took him to her bosom, and warmed and cherished and honored him; and how does he manifest his gratitude? By aiming a vital blow at a system endeared to her by a thorough conviction that it is indispensable to her prosperity. [Pennsylvania was a strongly protectionist state.] He has filled, at home and abroad, some of the highest offices under this government during thirty years, and he is still at heart an alien."[8]

Aside from slavery, an issue to which it was connected, the question of protectionist tariffs versus lower ones "for revenue only" became one of the most controversial political issues of the nineteenth century. Clay's rhetoric was therefore not unusual. Here, however, he overstepped a line in bringing up Gallatin's background as an immigrant—as so many others had done before with both Gallatin and Hamilton.

—⚬∞⚬—

One of the chief accomplishments of Gallatin's late years was a pioneering series of works on Native American ethnology. During his sixties and seventies, he published two important books on this subject: *A Table of Indian Languages of the United States* (1826) and *A Synopsis of the Indian Tribes within the United States East of the Rocky Mountains and in the British and Russian Possessions of North America* (1836). The latter volume, which is 422 pages long, appeared when its author was seventy-five years old. Gallatin urged an assimilationist policy toward Native Americans, as opposed to their forced confinement on reservations. In 1842 he cofounded the American Ethnological Society and served as its first president. In 1843 he received further recognition as an elder statesman when he was elected president of the New-York Historical Society.[9]

Nor did he ignore national politics. Following the election of James K. Polk to the presidency in 1844, Gallatin opposed, in vehement terms, militarist threats of expansionism. The Polk administration's bellicose claims to the entire Oregon Territory especially troubled him. This immense area included all of the present states of Washington, Oregon, and Idaho, parts of Montana, and large portions of British Columbia. The question of its ownership threatened to spark still another war with Britain. As U.S. minister in London during the mid-1820s, Gallatin had negotiated a renewal of the joint British-American administration of this territory, and now that arrangement seemed about to fall apart.[10]

It was the Oregon Question that popularized nationalistic slogans such as "Manifest Destiny" and "Fifty-Four-Forty or Fight." Fifty-four degrees and forty minutes marked the northern latitude of the most extreme U.S. claim, which reached deep into British Columbia. The British counterclaim was 42 degrees latitude, which lay 840 miles farther south. The traditional line of 49 degrees latitude, which Gallatin had renewed in his 1820s negotiation, eventually prevailed. But the episode represented dangerous American brinksmanship.

Gallatin also opposed the Polk administration's support of the admission of Texas to the Union. This step would add another slave state, and, given its huge size, possible division into as many as five states, as the agreement between Texas and the U.S. provided. Equally galling to Gallatin, the annexation of Texas guaranteed a war with Mexico, which had never recognized the proclamation of the Lone Star Republic in 1836. Texas was admitted to the Union on December 29, 1845, and the expected war with Mexico soon followed.

In 1847, Gallatin—now eighty-six years of age—wrote a long and eloquent pamphlet, *Peace with Mexico*, of which 90,000 copies were distributed throughout the country. In annexing Texas, he argued, the nation had betrayed its original purpose "to improve the state of the world, to be the 'model republic.'" Instead, for the first time in its history, the United States had given itself over to what Gallatin called "unjust aggrandizement by brutal force," guided by "love of military fame and of false glory." In his old age, Gallatin had begun to have real doubts about the evolving character of his adopted country.[11]

Ironically, it had been the inexorable westward push of American settlement—the fulfillment of Gallatin's own long-term vision—that had brought on both the Oregon and Texas crises. National expansion, no matter where it occurs, nearly always leads to violence. The Louisiana Purchase had arisen out of the Napoleonic Wars, and the settlement of that territory had brought still more wars, with the Indians. Gallatin was never naïve about these truths, but he remained to the end a man devoted to peace.

In 1842, he wrote a lengthy letter to his close friend Sir Alexander Baring, with whom he had worked out the financing of the Louisiana Purchase and who had helped him before and during the negotiations at Ghent. "I am now in my 82d year, and on taking a retrospective view of my long career I derive the greatest consolation . . . that I ever was a minister of peace, from the fact that the twenty last years of my political life were almost exclusively employed in preventing the war [of 1812] as long as I could, in assisting in a speedy restoration of peace, and in settling subsequently as many of the points of difference as was at the time practicable." Though self-effacing, Gallatin was a proud man with much to be proud of.[12]

When the 1840s drew to a close, both Albert and Hannah Gallatin, married for fifty-five years, suffered rapidly declining health. In May 1849, Hannah died at their home in New York City, in the room next to her husband's. Three months later, Albert Gallatin, who had been an invalid for about a year, died in his own room, at the age of eighty-eight.

There were no elaborate funeral parades, but he would not have wanted a showy public spectacle. Better to have his memory honored, as it was, at meetings of the New-York Historical Society, the American Antiquarian Society, and many other nonprofit organizations. The *Daily National Intelligencer* of Washington, D.C., printed the New-York Historical Society's tribute: Gallatin's career showed that "under the glorious institutions of our happy country, merit, and merit alone, is necessary for advancement and success in all that is honorable and worthy of attainment. A young man—a foreigner—had landed upon our shores, without acquaintances, without friends—almost without a knowledge of our language—and yet, before he had attained the age of manhood, he was placed in a situation of trust."[13]

A newspaper in Mississippi echoed the same theme: "Alone and unaided, a stranger and unknown, he exalted himself to the highest point the laws of his adopted country permitted, and made his career a brilliant commentary on the perfectness

FIGURE 24. Albert Gallatin at age eighty, the elder statesman. Portrait by William Powell, 1841.

of American institutions." Philadelphia's *North American and United States Gazette* lavished praised on him: "As a diplomatist, no minister from any country, at the great courts to which he was accredited, ever sustained a higher reputation, nor were the United States ever more ably represented, anywhere, than in the person of Albert Gallatin."[14]

Gallatin had lived one of the longest, most honorable, and most productive public lives of any member of his generation. He was buried in the small cemetery of Trinity Church, at the intersection of Wall Street and Broadway—not far from the grave of Alexander Hamilton.

How fitting that these two financial experts, born across the seas, should be buried at this particular spot in what is still a city full of immigrants. Both would have been gratified by the remarkable development of the United States. Neither, however, would have countenanced the intermittent abuses symbolized by the term "Wall Street"—from the Gilded Age corruptions of the late nineteenth century to the profligacy preceding the Great Crash of 1929, to the shameless profiteering of the late twentieth and early twenty-first centuries.

Hamilton and Gallatin had helped to lay the intellectual and policy framework for the rise of the United States as a powerful engine of economic innovation. In the administrations they served, they differed from their native-born, planter-led colleagues. The two of them together had deep personal experience of rootlessness—experience with the Atlantic world and the Caribbean, experience with the national and international mobility of money. It was this kind of background, together with their own brilliance, that enabled them to envision and then to execute the responsible deployment of rootless capital in the forging of a new economy.

PART III

The Legacies

CHAPTER 28

Immigrant Exceptionalism?

Why were Robert Morris, Alexander Hamilton, and Albert Gallatin selected to oversee the nation's finances for such a long and crucial period? The answer is simple: well-informed political leaders judged them superior to native-born candidates in their ability to manage liquid capital.

During the crisis year of 1781, Robert Morris appeared to be the only logical choice for the newly created position, superintendent of finance. The national government was bankrupt and the Continental Army on the brink of disintegration. Morris had dealt with money and credit for decades, had developed invaluable mercantile contacts in the Caribbean and Europe, and had accumulated ample experience in government. There were few people like him, and even fewer willing to risk their substantial personal fortunes. That the twenty-four-year-old Alexander Hamilton was even considered for this vital post attests to the small number of plausible candidates.

Eight years later, Hamilton was appointed secretary of the treasury. Like Morris, he had worked in a merchant house as a teenager. There, he learned at first hand the language of accounting, the valuations of different national coinages and currencies, and the mechanisms of bills of exchange, which facilitated the paper transfer of money across oceans and national borders. After he became Washington's aide in 1777, at the age of twenty, he immersed himself in every financial treatise he could find. This self-training, combined with his obsession with work and his inherent brilliance, enabled him to perform with singular distinction after he became secretary of the treasury.

Albert Gallatin grew up in a European city that was already a financial center. Banks had existed in Geneva for more than a century before their first appearance in the United States, and Gallatin took their legitimacy for granted. He was born a gentleman and, unlike Morris and Hamilton, had never worked in "trade" until he emigrated to the United States and set up his glass works, boatyard, and retail store in New Geneva, Pennsylvania. Gallatin thought—mistakenly, as it turned out—that his best chance for material success was in the accumulation of land. But his real advantage lay in his gift for numbers and his ability to interpret complex financial ledgers. He shared these traits with Morris and Hamilton, but not with many others in such a small agrarian country.

That two immigrants—Robert Morris and Alexander Hamilton—were Washington's first and second choices to be secretary of the treasury shows how much their talents stood out among potential candidates. Some native-born statesmen sought the position of secretary. Robert Livingston, for example, a distinguished politician and the scion of a prominent New York family, wanted to be head of the Treasury but stood no chance of getting the post. Later on, Albert Gallatin's appointment as secretary—twice by Jefferson and twice more by Madison—suggests a continued shortage of financial ability and experience among native-born North Americans. Gallatin's two successors, George W. Campbell and Alexander James Dallas, were also immigrants.

It is not that there were no other candidates at all, especially among Federalists, many of whom were wealthy city dwellers and prominent merchants. Oliver Wolcott, Hamilton's replacement, came from an old Connecticut family and was well qualified to fill the post of secretary, which he did with distinction. But Wolcott's chief advantage was his experience as assistant to Hamilton for almost six years before succeeding him. When Jefferson became president in 1801, there were no other Republicans who came close to Gallatin as the best choice for secretary.

How did those who selected Morris, Hamilton, and Gallatin know that they were the best people for the job? Morris had long been a familiar figure in Philadelphia business circles through his connection with the Willing family, which was prominent in both commerce and politics. During the years after the formation of his partnership with Thomas Willing, Morris's rising fortune made him one of the wealthiest merchants in the colonies. In 1775, his constituents elected him to the Continental Congress, and in 1776 he began chairing its Secret Committee on Commerce. He raised large sums of money, exploited his extensive overseas connections to procure gunpowder and other munitions, and often risked his personal credit. There could have been no better choice in 1781, immigrant or native-born, for the post of superintendent of finance.

Alexander Hamilton put himself forward more aggressively than Morris had done. Even before the outbreak of war in 1775, Hamilton threw his energies into the contest for public opinion by producing two superb pamphlets supporting the muscular measures of the Continental Congress. As soon as the fighting started, he joined the army and received his commission as an artillery officer. After two years' service, he embraced Washington's invitation to become his aide-de-camp. For the next twelve years, Hamilton soaked up lessons about public finance from every available source and became known as an expert.

He also trained himself in the law, and served a term in the

Confederation Congress and as a delegate to the Constitutional Convention. Long before his nomination as secretary, he had formulated—with his characteristic audacity—specific plans for dealing with the national debt, for assuming the state debts, and for creating a Bank of the United States. Despite his youth, nobody else in the country was better prepared for the job.

Albert Gallatin lacked the early mercantile experience of Morris and Hamilton, but he had by far the best formal education of the three. After some aimless wandering after his arrival in North America in 1780, he set up his household at Friendship Hill and gained a reputation among his trans-Allegheny neighbors for intelligence and good judgment. When the issue of Pennsylvania's ratification of the Constitution arose, his constituents elected him the delegate from their region. Then they sent him to the state legislature, where he served during the session of 1790–1791 on the Ways and Means Committee, the financial hub of Pennsylvania's House of Delegates.

The next year he was placed on thirty-five different committees, and, by his own testimony, did most of the work of all thirty-five. It was during this period that Gallatin made his reputation. He rose so quickly in the esteem of his peers that the legislature elected him one of Pennsylvania's U.S. senators. After the Federalists expelled him from the Senate on the grounds of insufficient years' residence in the United States, Gallatin won election to the U.S. House of Representatives. In that body his facility with numbers, his ability to absorb complex financial data, and his zeal in attacking Hamilton's economic program made him a priceless asset to the Republican Party. Nobody else among the Jeffersonians had the expertise or the reservoirs of energy to do all of these things well. By the time Jefferson became president in 1801, Gallatin had become the only logical choice for secretary of the treasury.

Why was there such a meager pool of candidates for the offices to which Morris, Hamilton, and Gallatin were appointed? For one thing, nobody had national experience with public finance because no nation existed until 1776. The country itself had a sparse and dispersed population. Whatever background colonial and state officials had in public finance was necessarily on a small scale.

Within the colonies, the functions of managing currencies, collecting taxes, and spending on defense and public works had been performed either by British administrators serving in America or by local officials. There was a conspicuous intellectual vacuum in financial thinking on a large scale. This was especially clear from 1776 onward, in the new and independent nation. During those years, a whole series of financial arrangements—among the states, between the states and the national government, and between the United States and other countries—had to be worked out. Morris, Hamilton, Gallatin, and other immigrants plugged the many institutional holes in a multilayered system undergoing very rapid change.

Nor did anyone in either the colonies or the new nation have experience working in banks, because none had ever been established. Morris caused the founding of the modest-sized Bank of North America, which opened in 1782, and in 1784 Hamilton wrote the state charter for the Bank of New York. The Bank of the United States, chartered by Congress in 1791, dwarfed each of the three banks operating at that time, and this was a full fifteen years after the Declaration of Independence.

That so few native-born Americans in the late eighteenth century understood finance reflected both the agrarian nature of the society and a broad aversion to indebtedness. In all its forms, whether personal, business, or governmental, borrowing was widely looked on with disfavor. Among those who did understand credit—wholesalers, insurers, and others—many had no taste for public service. This was particularly true during the depressed 1780s, when most merchants had to look after their own businesses.

Then, too, by far the principal economic interest among most segments of society was *land*. It is hard to overstate the breadth and depth of this preoccupation, among both the American people and their leaders. Both Washington and Jefferson were experts in agriculture. Washington made the bold decision to shift his principal cash crop from tobacco to wheat, and Jefferson was one of the nation's authorities in the science of botany. Jefferson championed the superiority of agrarian living, and this was one of the sources of his political popularity. As late as 1858, Emerson wrote: "The first farmer was the first man, and all historic nobility rests on the possession and use of land."[1]

Albert Gallatin's own early fixation with land—and Robert Morris's disastrous real-estate speculations of the 1790s—reveal much about the extent of this cultural obsession. Here were two of the most talented financial minds of their time sinking their own capital into the least liquid of assets. As odd as it seems in retrospect, their attraction should not surprise us. Benjamin Franklin, the most versatile and widely traveled of all the founders and no gentleman by birth, indulged in widespread land speculation as well. John Adams was raised on a farm and, despite his prodigious achievements as a constitutional lawyer, disliked finance and detested banks. He never lost his deep attachment to his lands around Quincy, Massachusetts, where he spent most of his life, including much of his presidency.

During the eighteenth and early nineteenth centuries, land remained the most respected form of property not only in America, but also in Europe. The French Physiocrats of the late eighteenth century, who can lay claim to being among the earliest professional economists, believed that all wealth derived from land. Their leaders, men such as François Quesnay and the Marquis de Mirabeau, argued that agriculture could best yield what they called a *produit net*—an output of product that exceeded inputs of labor and capital. Adam Smith and other classical economists disagreed with Physiocratic doctrine in many particulars. But Smith argued in *The Wealth of Nations* that the United States would be well advised to stick to agriculture.

In most of Europe and Britain, well into the nineteenth century, the landholding aristocrats and the group just beneath them, the "landed gentry," were regarded as the natural leaders of society. They were subordinate only to royalty, who owned the most land of all.

"It is a comfortable feeling to know that you stand on your own ground. Land is about the only thing that can't fly away," says a character in Anthony Trollope's novel of 1867, *The Last Chronicle of Barset*. Certainly that was the view of most Americans of the Revolutionary generation, steeped in tradition despite their advanced political ideas. For about 250 years after 1607—the date of the first English settlement in North America—much of the best American talent gravitated toward land development and away from trade, finance, and manufacturing. This preference was most pronounced in the planter class of the South, but unmistakable in other parts of the country as well.

From the colonial period until the late nineteenth century, most immigrants also had a ravenous appetite for land—a feeling born of European deprivation confronting New World opportunity. This demand, pent up for centuries, suddenly encountered plentiful supply. The newcomers' hunger for land thrust them westward across the North American continent, where they established farms, mines, and ranches they themselves could *own*. This was the American Dream in its most elemental form, and many of those who lived it felt a double incredulity: not only toward their good luck, but also toward the backbreaking work essential to realize the dream.[2]

Abundant land is the starting place for the story of both American immigration and American economic growth. But land was not the primary basis for the innovations that came to characterize the nation's business system. Land is only one of the fundamental economic "factors of production." The others are capital, labor, and entrepreneurship. Of these four, it was expertise in the management of capital that distinguished the immigrants depicted in this book.[3]

Morris, Hamilton, and Gallatin were by no means the only immigrant financial experts who led or assisted the government from 1775 to 1816. Several of these others are mentioned earlier in this book, but it will be useful here to name some of them again and to note the dates when they came to North America.

Haym Solomon, a native of Poland, helped Robert Morris to raise funds for the War of Independence. Solomon arrived in 1772. After the fighting began, he received a death sentence for spying in British-occupied New York, but escaped from prison and made his way to Philadelphia. There he became paymaster for the American-allied French military forces from 1779 to 1783, and official broker to the office of finance during Robert Morris's tenure as superintendent. Solomon sold bonds issued by Congress, lent money to legislators and others, and invested his own funds in the war effort.

In 1789, just below Hamilton in the Treasury's hierarchy, two more of the top five officers were also immigrants. One served with dishonesty, the other with distinction. The dishonest one was assistant secretary William Duer (1743–1799), a native of Devonshire, England, who had inherited a family fortune in West Indian sugar plantations. On a trip from the Caribbean to New York in 1768 to secure supplies of lumber, Duer saw new opportunities to make money and decided to settle in the Hudson Valley. His entrepreneurial ventures included investments in land, lumber, and mercantile enterprise. Spreading himself very thin, Duer also served as a delegate to both the Continental Congress and the New York state legislature.

Duer saw no reason to separate his private business from his official duties. After Robert Morris's resignation in 1784 as superintendent of finance, Duer became clerk of the three-person board that assumed Morris's duties. Throughout his time in public service, Duer not only continued his private ventures but also exploited inside information for his own gain. The Treasury Act of 1789 forbade this practice, and Duer resigned his post as assistant secretary in March 1790. Two years later, in the midst of a financial panic that he himself precipitated, Duer lost his fortune. He spent the rest of his life in debtors' prison, where he died in 1799.[4]

The immigrant Treasury official who served with distinction was Joseph Nourse, who came from London in 1769 at the age of fifteen. During the War of Independence, Nourse served in several military staff positions. In 1779 he was appointed register (registrar) of the Board of Finance, then register of finance under Superintendent Morris in 1781, and finally register of the Treasury under Secretary Hamilton in 1789. One of his duties was to sign all important monetary instruments of the federal government. After the Treasury began to issue large amounts of new bonds, Nourse wrote his signature on thousands of debt instruments. More importantly, he kept the accounts of the Treasury, a task requiring great care and precision. Nourse has been called "America's first civil servant," and he held the post of register for thirty-eight years. In 1803 he signed all 5,071 securities issued to finance the Louisiana Purchase.[5]

George W. Campbell came with his parents from Scotland to North America in 1772. Like Gallatin, he settled in the trans-Appalachian West—in his case, Tennessee, which elected him a U.S. senator. While Gallatin was negotiating what became the Treaty of Ghent, James Madison appointed Campbell secretary of the treasury. He served for eight months during the difficult year 1814.

Alexander James Dallas, who arrived from Jamaica in 1783, succeeded Campbell as secretary and held the office for two years, from 1814 to 1816. Dallas was a close friend of Gallatin and a prominent Philadelphia lawyer. Before Gallatin's departure in 1813 for his diplomatic duties, he and Dallas helped to organize the largest single bond issue for financing the War of 1812. This was an emergency transaction, completed just as the Treasury was about to run out of money, and it brought three more immigrants to prominence in public finance.

The first of these was Stephen Girard (who came from France in 1774). In 1811, when Congress declined to renew the charter of the Bank of the United States, Girard bought most of its stock and opened "Stephen Girard's Bank" on the same site. During the financial emergency of 1814, he participated in a syndicate of investors who purchased large sums of bonds issued to conduct the war.

His partners in this transaction were John Jacob Astor (who came from Germany in 1784) and David Parish (from Germany in 1808). Parish, Gallatin, and Dallas led the effort to form the syndicate—during a time when most native-born investors, particularly in New England, refused to buy Treasury bonds even though the nation was at war. Girard, Astor, and Parish all risked their considerable fortunes to save their adopted country.[6]

Of the men on this list—Solomon, Duer, Nourse, Campbell, Dallas, Girard, Astor, and Parish—three were less formidable than the other five. William Duer betrayed his fiduciary duties. George W. Campbell was a capable senator but a poor secretary of the treasury, plagued with ill health during his eight months in office. Joseph Nourse was an excellent inspector of public accounts and well qualified for his post as register, but he was not quite a man of first-rate talents.

The other five, along with Morris, Hamilton, and Gallatin, were persons of real distinction. It would be impossible to construct a roster of native-born Americans of that time who could match these eight immigrants in their expertise at large-scale finance—or their importance to the solvency and prosperity of the national government.

Was the young United States the only country to call on foreign-born financial talent? No. From the seventeenth century down to the present, outsiders have been summoned to straighten out financial disarray in many countries. Their lack of ties to existing national interest groups has, almost by itself, made them more neutral judges of what must be done.[7]

A conspicuous early instance was the appointment of the Scottish economist John Law (1671–1729) as controller general of finances in the French government of Louis XV. The country's economy had been crippled by almost continual wars under the "Sun King" Louis XIV, and Law was viewed as a potential savior. A first-class theorist who understood the mechanism of paper money, Law accomplished a great deal: the creation of France's first central bank, an increase in foreign commerce, and the promotion of manufacturing. But Law was an inveterate risk taker (some historians think he invented the game of poker), and he unwisely engineered a consolidation of firms trading in Louisiana into one large venture called the Mississippi Company. The steep rise in that company's share prices—the "Mississippi Bubble"—led to the collapse not only of the company, but also of France's central bank. Law was removed from his position and forced to flee the country.

A second example was Jacques Necker (1732–1804), a Genevan financial theorist with wide experience in French banking. It was from Necker's copious and best-selling treatises that Hamilton and many other readers learned much of what they knew about the fundamentals of finance. In 1777, the French government of Louis XVI appointed Necker director general of finances. He made substantial strides in reforming the nation's archaic tax system and in funding France's large national debt. He also argued, successfully, that France should provide financial support to the American War of Independence.

Within the French court, Necker's reforms made him a controversial figure and a special enemy of the queen, Marie Antoinette. He resigned his post in 1781. His reforms of the tax system were then largely undone, and French finances deteriorated. By 1788 the country stood on the brink of ruin, and Necker was summoned back to office. Though a masterly financier, he proved again to be a poor court politician. Despite enthusiastic support from much of the French public, he was dismissed after less than a year, on July 11, 1789. This step played a major role in precipitating the storming of the Bastille three days later, on July 14, and the king restored Necker to his position on July 20. By then, however, it was too late to reverse the course of the French Revolution.[8]

There are many other instances in which foreigners were asked to mend a troubled nation's finances. Some individual "money doctors" became well known during the decades after 1850; and in our own time, the International Monetary Fund (IMF) has institutionalized the function. The IMF, established in 1945, has sent teams of advisers not only to developing countries, but also to nations such as the United Kingdom, which it successfully assisted in 1976. In other instances, its efforts have produced mixed results and have become controversial because of the austerity measures the IMF typically imposes as conditions for its loans.[9]

Are these examples—John Law, Jacques Necker, the money doctors, and the International Monetary Fund—comparable to the experiences of foreign-born financial experts in the United States? At bottom, no. The difference is that the Americans were not invited to come as experts. They arrived as young immigrants, intending to settle permanently in the new country. They would experience the results of their policies along with their fellow citizens. By contrast, Law, Necker, the money doctors, and the IMF staffers did their work and departed. They are more analogous to the European military officers who assisted in America's War of Independence and then returned home—soldiers such as Lafayette of France and Kosciuszko of Poland. In the realm of finance, the immigrant public servants, if not unique to the United States, were certainly exceptional during the period 1775–1816.[10]

CHAPTER 29

Comparisons and Contingencies

In the popular consciousness, and even in much academic writing, many aspects of the historical era covered by this book have come down to a dualism: between Alexander Hamilton and Thomas Jefferson as personalities, and between Hamiltonian and Jeffersonian ways of thinking. For more than 200 years, these men have prevailed as two of the most potent personal symbols in American politics. Histories, biographies, and even novels have explored the economic and political differences between Hamiltonian and Jeffersonian patterns of thought and of government.

Some of this literature, despite its merits, comes up short on several fronts. It dwells too much on the writings of Hamilton and Jefferson, and too little on what each one did when he held power. It pays too little attention to the roles of Washington, whose support was indispensable to Hamilton, and of Madison and Gallatin, Jefferson's partners in the Republican triumvirate. It tends to oversimplify issues that were far too subtle for sweeping claims that one man—Hamilton or Jefferson—had the better character, or that one was right and the other wrong; that Hamilton, for example, was an elitist and monarchist who favored the wealthy, while Jefferson fought for the interests of the poor and the "middling sort," with whom he had a special bond.[1]

When we consider the backgrounds of the two men, these characterizations would seem, at the very least, counterintuitive. At the time when they joined Washington's cabinet, Jefferson was a socially prominent forty-six-year-old Virginia planter—someone about as close to an aristocrat as a U.S. citizen could be. Hamilton, by contrast, was an unmonied, illegitimate, thirty-two-year-old West Indian immigrant who arrived 100 years after Jefferson's first North American ancestor. Hamilton believed that wealthy entrepreneurs were vital to the nation's economic success. But he was certainly no monarchist, as Jefferson and Madison ceaselessly charged during the 1790s. More to the point, Hamilton and Jefferson had different kinds of assignments within the Washington administration. Comparing them to each other is not quite an apples-and-oranges situation, but neither is it the optimal approach.

This book portrays Hamilton in a better light than Jefferson, and Madison as well. But that is primarily because the book concerns finance—by far Hamilton's strongest suit, and one of Madison's and especially Jefferson's weakest. Gallatin, as a superior economic thinker, also appears more favorably here than Jefferson and Madison.

Many historical rankings are pointless, most are highly subjective, and all must be used with great care. But it is not too much to say that if this book were about political theory, Madison would take pride of place and Jefferson or Hamilton would be ranked second. If it were about the politician's arts, Jefferson—one of the shrewdest and most inspiring politicians in American history—would easily rank first. Madison and Gallatin would come in second or third, and Hamilton a distant fourth. If it were about the art of diplomacy, Gallatin would rank first; it is impossible to picture Hamilton having the patience Gallatin showed during the prolonged negotiations over the Treaty of Ghent. Jefferson would likely have become irritable during the talks at Ghent as well; Madison, perhaps less so.

—⁂—

Often the most informative comparisons are like with like: one should ask not whether William Wordsworth was the literary peer of Jane Austen, but whether he was as good a poet as John Keats. By this standard, one should compare Jefferson not with Hamilton, but with other secretaries of state, presidents, and politicians who held primarily elective office. In all three of these categories, Jefferson fares well.[2]

Hamilton, rather than being compared to Jefferson, would be better measured against other appointed officials: against U.S. secretaries of the treasury, of whom he is widely acknowledged the greatest, and against designers of national economic strategies in other countries. This group includes such statesmen as Jean-Baptiste Colbert, the innovative controller general of finances under Louis XIV from 1665 to 1683; Charles Montagu, the British chancellor of the exchequer and chief creator of the Bank of England during the 1690s; and Jacques Necker, the learned French finance minister of the 1770s and 1780s. Hamilton studied the works and writings of all three—Necker's in particular. Once in office, he matched or exceeded the achievements of each of them.

In comparison with Hamilton, Albert Gallatin as secretary of the treasury did not meet the standard of financial wizardry his predecessor had set. But that was not necessary, because he did not have to design the basic structure. And Gallatin was a superb secretary, usually ranked second only to Hamilton. He fit what the country needed during his years in office, and he was just as useful to presidents Jefferson and Madison as Hamilton had been to Washington. Had they followed his advice as closely as Washington did Hamilton's, both could have had more successful presidencies. Jefferson would not have imposed the embargo of 1807–1809, and Madison would have supported the recharter of the Bank of the United States in 1811. It is even conceivable, as John Quincy Adams remarked, that if Madison had appointed Gallatin rather than Robert Smith secretary of state in 1809, the War of 1812 might have been avoided.[3]

Despite what would seem to be the obvious advantages of these broader comparisons, many accounts of Jefferson's life tend to demean or even demonize Hamilton, and vice versa. This is an outworn perspective. It distorts the characters not only of Hamilton and Jefferson, but of other statesmen as well, and even of American society during their era.[4]

The historical literature on the early Republic is uncommonly good, but some versions that focus on the founders tend to downplay the fluid, fast-changing circumstances in which events compelled them to act. As Kierkegaard once wrote, "Life can only be understood backwards; but it must be lived forwards." Even in the best historical writing of all kinds, it becomes tempting to assume certainty of outcomes and to minimize contingent circumstances.

The result of looking only backward—rather than also forward, from the perspectives of the participants—can be an ossification of history. In the case of the United States from 1775 to 1816, a reluctance to imagine different outcomes leads to the neglect of such phenomena as the razor-thin margins by which some of the biggest decisions were made. At worst, readers encounter versions of history in which mature, fully formed statesmen acted according to coherent, well-developed doctrines that came to bear their names. But when one returns to the original sources and reconstructs their decision making, it becomes clear that they were operating in extremely protean situations and having to make up new answers as they went along. Sometimes their answers ill accorded with the images we glean from their writings or even from their own preferences at the time. Much of history is a story of events that might well have turned out differently. As Lincoln wrote in 1864, "I claim not to have controlled events, but confess plainly that events have controlled me."[5]

So it was in the early Republic. Important events affected subsequent events—preventing, causing, and shaping particular outcomes. The authors of the Articles of Confederation, for example, wrote into that document a requirement for unanimity among all thirteen states on any structural alteration of its provisions. Had that mandate been absent from the Articles, then Rhode Island could not have blocked Congress's attempt to gain control of customs revenues in 1781. If this obstruction had not occurred, then the national government would have had a large and independent source of income no later than 1781. And in that situation, Robert Morris's financial program might have worked. The drive for a new Constitution might have been much weakened, and the Convention of 1787 might never have happened at all.[6]

So, too, during the first twenty-seven years under the Constitution, 1789–1816. Events, or the consequences of previous events, shaped public policy, which in turn shaped subsequent events and policies. During the first four years of this period, from early 1789 through late 1792, the financial predicaments inherited from the War of Independence and the Confederation period tended to dominate public affairs. Then, for the next twenty-two years (1793 to 1815) the new nation's financial and foreign policies fell under the shadow of the long war between Britain and France, and of America's own War of 1812.

The writings of the founders are so rich that putting them aside even for a moment becomes difficult, and rereading them often sways the reader first one way and then another. But the *outcomes* of the founders' battles with one another are quite clear. During the period 1789–1816, the Federalists under Washington, Hamilton, and Adams won every important fight for the initial twelve years. Then the Republicans under Jefferson, Madison, and Gallatin did the same for the next fifteen years. Throughout these twenty-seven years, there was ceaseless, fervent, and bitter conflict among the founders. The spirit of compromise had peaked at the Constitutional Convention in 1787, and did not return to that level until about 1817, by which time the Federalist Party lay in ruins.

During the Washington administration—when Hamilton served as secretary of the treasury, Jefferson as secretary of state, and Madison as de facto leader of the House—Hamilton won and Jefferson and Madison lost every battle: over funding the national debt at par, over federal assumption of state debts, over the creation of the Bank of the United States, over the building of the six frigates for the navy, and over the Jay Treaty and the use of trade sanctions against Britain. Madison and Jefferson pushed this latter policy very hard. Hamilton fought it on the grounds that the Treasury, burdened with interest payments on the colossal national debt, could not sustain the loss of revenues from tariffs on British imports.

These patterns of the founders' thinking—and of outcomes—continued unchanged for several years after the three men left office: Jefferson in 1793, Hamilton in 1795, and Madison in 1797. During the years when they were ostensibly out of power, all three remained extremely influential. Jefferson served as vice president from 1797 to 1801, and although he had little clout within the government, he continued to build an opposition party outside it.

From 1794 to 1796, the Jay Treaty dominated national politics. In the eyes of Washington and Hamilton, the success of this treaty represented the only chance to avert war with Britain and avoid a catastrophic blow to the Treasury. By contrast, for Jefferson and Madison the Jay Treaty symbolized the Washington administration's favoritism to the British at the expense of the French. For them, it provided further evidence of Hamilton's attempts to introduce British ways of corrupt government into the purified American system.

Hamilton's forces won this crucial fight, though only through the direct intervention of Washington. There was nothing inevitable about this result. Hamilton and his allies prevailed with the bare minimum of the required two-thirds vote for ratification of the treaty by the Senate (20 to 10), and a very narrow House vote of 51 to 48 for providing funds to implement its terms. The Federalists triumphed yet again in passing their ill-advised Alien and Sedition Acts of 1798, but again only by an initial 52-to-48 House vote. Thus, during each of the three Federalist presidential administrations from 1789 to 1801—two terms under Washington, one under John Adams—the Federalists won every big political fight. But they could easily have lost some of them.

The presidential election of 1800 ended in a tie between Jefferson and Aaron Burr, his running mate, threatening a constitutional crisis that was averted only with great difficulty. But once the Republicans gained control of the presidency in 1801, they won and the Federalists lost all of the important contests. The Republicans won the battle over the Louisiana Purchase— although here again, the House vote for appropriating money to pay France for the territory was tantalizingly close: 59 to 57. This vote, like the narrow margins earlier, was an index of the country's partisan rifts.[7]

The Republicans went on to score a long succession of other congressional victories: the Embargo Act in 1807, the Non-Intercourse Act in 1809, Macon's Bill No. 2 in 1810, the refusal to recharter the Bank of the United States in 1811, and the declaration of war against Britain in 1812. Many of these votes were also extremely close—against the bank recharter by 55 to 54 in the House and a tie of 17 to 17 in the Senate, broken by a negative vote by the Republican vice president. And the declaration of war in 1812 was passed with by far the narrowest margin of any in American history: an initial 17-to-17 tie in the Senate that ended in an affirmative 19 to 13; and a vote of 79 to 49 in the House.

Every one of these votes signified acute splits within the nation—sectional, economic, and cultural. After 1792, each one also reflected the financial and foreign-policy dilemmas in which the war between Britain and France had trapped the United States. Even in the contest over the bank recharter in 1811, opponents invoked the spurious issue of foreign ownership of shares as a reason to kill it.

The number of tight legislative margins on so many important issues underscores the truth that historical outcomes are contingent and far from inevitable. In 1790, the federal assumption of state debts passed the House by vote of 32 to 29, and would not have passed at all except for Hamilton's agreement to move the location of the national capital. Without that bargain, the capital would likely have remained in New York.[8]

Had the Federalists lost their shipbuilding program of 1794 rather than winning the House vote by 46 to 44, there would have been no new frigates to send to the Barbary states or to fight in the War of 1812. Similarly, had the Jay Treaty not been ratified in 1795, war with Britain would probably have come when the United States was even less prepared than it was in 1812. And had the vote to pay for the Louisiana Purchase failed rather than squeaking through the House in 1804, the history of the United States would have evolved very differently indeed.

Almost nothing that happened during these years was inevitable. As the English historian F. W. Maitland once put it, "What is now in the past was once in the future." In all of these close votes, if a few members of Congress—sometimes even one—had cast a different ballot or been struck by lightning or died of pneumonia in untimely fashion, events might have turned out in some other way. Histories of this period too often neglect this remarkable series of dramatic, touch-and-go contingencies, each of which reflected deep divisions within the country.

Then, too, a different sequence in control over the national government would likely have had negative consequences. It was uncommonly lucky for the United States that Hamilton's financial program—which rescued the nation from bankruptcy and placed it on a sound financial footing—preceded the "Revolution of 1800" and its single-minded goal of extinguishing the national debt.

A reverse sequence would have meant a firm determination not just to fund the debt through interest payments, but to retire its principal as soon as possible. In the context of the 1790s, such a policy could well have brought both financial and political adversity, if not disaster. The quick prosperity that followed Hamilton's program almost surely would not have occurred, and the depression of the 1780s might have continued. For most of the period before Gallatin took office as secretary of the treasury in 1801, American taxpayers had neither the resources nor the inclination to pay the debt's principal.

Some of the existing literature on the early national period misses these important details of the major events and contingencies from 1789 to 1816. Moreover, by taking a short-term view that stops in 1816, it subjects itself to two other potential lapses. First, it badly understates the gravity of the slavery question. This transcendent issue threatened the Union from at least 1819 onward and shattered it in 1861—only twelve years after the death of Albert Gallatin.

Second, most existing histories recognize the Republicans' adaptation of a few Federalist policies. But they neglect the long-term merging of broad economic strategies—in particular, those of Hamilton and Gallatin. That fusion came to constitute the basic capitalist framework of the American political economy during the nineteenth century and even down to the present time.

CHAPTER 30

Capitalism and Credit

In the era of Hamilton and Gallatin, the American economy was moving toward a modern capitalist system, which matured during the nineteenth century. Their policies accelerated that transition. Yet in their time, even the most sophisticated analysts were only starting to imagine how a fully industrialized capitalist economy might work. The word "capitalism" had not yet been invented. It first appeared around 1850, as an antonym for socialism. The term "capital," on the other hand, had made its debut in about 1630. The *Oxford English Dictionary* gives it this concise definition: "accumulated wealth reproductively employed."

Capital, of course, exists in almost any type of economy. But capital*ism* has distinctive traits: a full-fledged market system, the rule of law, the easy purchase and sale of property, the sanctity of contracts, the mobility of labor, the payment of wages in cash, and—crucially—the ready availability of credit. In this last element, capital*ism* goes well beyond the definition of "capital." Capitalism employs not only accumulated wealth but also "money of the mind," as credit has aptly been called.[1]

And therein lies a key difference between the way Robert Morris, Alexander Hamilton, and Albert Gallatin thought about the American economy and the way John Adams, Thomas Jefferson, and James Madison did. Credit, if managed well, holds the key to almost unlimited economic growth. If mismanaged, it can bring catastrophe: to a national economy, an industry, a company, or an individual—as it did to Robert Morris and William Duer. It also gave a great deal of trouble to Jefferson, who fell ever more deeply into debt the longer he lived.

⁂

Credit stands at the heart of all capitalist systems. It depends on faith in a better material future, as its Latin root implies (*credere*, "to believe"). Banks—regarded as essential by Morris, Hamilton, and Gallatin but often deplored by Adams, Jefferson, and Madison—lend funds far beyond the sum of their cash reserves. They "leverage" their reserves in the expectation of future repayment of loans, with regular interest payments in the meantime. This process creates credit, multiplies the amount of money in circulation, and enables economies to grow much faster. Corporations do something similar when they issue stocks and especially bonds. The value of these securities depends on the expected returns from the corporations' future earnings. Even the soundness of government bonds relies on bondholders' faith in the future viability of the government that issues them.

The essence of a capitalist system, therefore, is a strong psychological orientation toward the future. And that orientation is best expressed in the system's pervasive reliance on credit. Despite its many faults, credit-based capitalism has turned out to be the most productive economic system ever devised, by a wide margin. In *The Communist Manifesto* (which appeared in 1848, some fifty-nine years after Hamilton's appointment as secretary of the treasury), even Karl Marx and Friedrich Engels conceded that capitalism had "created more massive and more colossal productive forces than have all preceding generations together."[2]

Capitalism is not, however, the natural state of human affairs. If it were, it would have arisen thousands of years ago and spread throughout the world. Instead, it first appeared in semi-modern form in the seventeenth century, and even then only in Holland, England, and several European city-states, where a few banks had been founded even earlier (the Medici Bank in Florence, the Fuggers of Augsburg). This early form of capitalism had been around for hardly more than a century and in only a handful of places when Morris, Hamilton, and Gallatin undertook to build the American financial system.

For hundreds of years before the arrival of capitalism, farming had dominated national economies almost everywhere. In Britain and Europe, agricultural affairs were organized around landed estates and the principles of primogeniture (inheritance of the estate primarily by the eldest son), and entailment (specification of inheritance through many future generations). In North America, the abundance of land had softened the effect of these laws and traditions, even in colonial times. But in most parts of the United States in the time of Hamilton and Gallatin, many of the old traditions still endured.

Landed estates in Virginia, staffed by slaves and owned by such founders as Washington, Jefferson, and Madison, fell into this category. The major differences were that the slaves were literally owned by their masters, and the estates in America could more easily be expanded by the purchase of undeveloped adjacent tracts. The landed manors in New York owned by patroons such as Hamilton's in-laws, the Schuylers, operated in similar ways, though mostly without slaves. These great estates stood as testimony to the strength of Old World traditions.

By the early national period, however, the American economy was beginning to move in a different direction. Clear class distinctions still existed, but were weakening. The "middling sort," as they were called—urban craftsmen and clerks, proprietors of small but prosperous farms—were becoming much more numerous. It was this diverse group that provided the big Republican majorities in presidential and congressional elections after 1800.

Credit-based commerce and manufacturing were on the rise, especially after 1816. Foreign and domestic trade in goods of all kinds underpinned an "Era of Good Feelings" that lasted through most of the presidency of James Monroe (1817–1825), despite a financial panic in 1818–1819. The contentious political battles of the two previous generations seemed to go into brief adjournment. Meanwhile, however, the invention of the cotton gin in 1793 portended a vast expansion of the slave system after the War of 1812. This unexpected development enriched both planters and the northern shippers and insurers who helped to manage the credit-based export trade. But in the South it also impeded the momentum toward modern capitalism, in both agriculture and industry.[3]

From its earliest years down to the present, a capitalist system has been uncommonly difficult to organize and maintain. The appropriate balance between unfettered markets and societal restraints has never been self-evident. Nor will it ever be, because conditions change so rapidly under capitalism. As both Hamilton and Gallatin understood, too much government interference can kill a company, an industry, and even a national economy. But so can too little. Successful capitalism requires the active promotion of entrepreneurship, but also constant monitoring by government to ensure that the system does not spin out of control. Entrepreneurs, obsessed with future profits, are forever pushing the envelope, moving into gray areas and forcing government regulators to play catch-up. Business scandals have become so frequent that they must be regarded as endemic to capitalism itself, especially in finance.

Why finance? Because that is where credit is managed, where paper assets can be manipulated, and where "bubbles" originate as prices rise to insupportable levels. In the seventeenth and early eighteenth centuries, the Tulip Mania in Holland, the

Mississippi Bubble in France, and the South Sea Bubble in Britain all derived from a near-hysteria for making more and more money through buying on credit. Each of these episodes brought disgrace to numerous private citizens and public officials.

In 1792, the first of many financial bubbles struck the United States. William Duer, Hamilton's former assistant, tried to drive up the price of Bank of New York stock and other securities, while the wealthy Livingston family counter-moved to drive the prices down. This activity precipitated a run by depositors to withdraw their cash, the bank's calling-in of its loans so that it could pay its depositors, and a potential decline in the price of outstanding securities of many kinds. Hamilton took quick action to prevent a major crisis, ordering the Treasury to purchase securities and pressuring the Bank of the United States and the few other banks in existence not to call in their loans. But as long as credit remains at the heart of capitalist systems, markets will have built-in tendencies toward bubbles, and the need for rapid corrective actions will continue.

Hamilton, after all his research and experience, had come to understand credit better than any other American statesman of his time. During his final month as secretary of the treasury, he sent a thorough analysis to Congress titled *Report on a Plan for the Further Support of Public Credit* (1795). In this document—one of Hamilton's best state papers, but also one of his most historically neglected—he summarized the role of credit in the nation's growth over the preceding five years and underscored its importance for the future.

"Credit public and private is of the greatest consequence to every Country," he wrote. "It might be emphatically called the invigorating principle. No well informed man, can cast a retrospective eye over the progress of the United States, from their infancy to the present period, without being convinced that they owe in a great degree, to the fostering influence of Credit their present mature growth."⁴

Credit of every type, Hamilton continued, had played its particular role. Public credit—secured by the funding of the national and state debts and by the creation of the Bank of the United States—had created a much more hospitable business climate. Credit between merchants, augmented by loans from abroad, had delivered unprecedented prosperity to "a new Country." As a substitute for existing capital, credit "is little less useful than Gold or silver, in Agriculture, in Commerce, in the Manufacturing and mechanic arts. The proof of this needs no laboured deduction. It is matter of daily experience in the most familiar pursuits." Best of all, the new record of American prosperity could continue indefinitely.⁵

In a prescient statement, Hamilton wrote: "If the United States observe with delicate caution the maxims of Credit . . . the strong attractions which they present to foreign Capital will be likely to ensure them the command of as much as they may want in addition to their own [domestic credit]." Already, European investors had purchased large amounts of the bonds issued to fund the consolidated national debt, and had also bought stock in the Bank of the United States. Although Hamilton could not have known it, within a few years foreign investors would own a majority of both federal bonds and bank stock. This influx of capital from abroad strengthened the American economy and confirmed the efficacy of Hamilton's policies.⁶

"Credit," Hamilton concluded, "is an *intire thing*. Every part of it has the nicest sympathy with every other part. Wound one limb, and the whole Tree shrinks and decays. The security of each Creditor is inseparable from the security of all Creditors." The system, therefore, had to be managed with extreme care. Simply denouncing it because of its faults, or even its potential for occasional disaster, ignored its essential role in a growing market economy. Censure of credit could lead to its extinction, like censure of any other element integral to economic success.

"'Tis in vain to attempt to disparage Credit, by objecting to its abuses. What is there not liable to abuse or misuse?"[7]

Here, then, in his final *Report* to Congress, Hamilton foreshadowed with remarkable precision the role of credit in the long-term economic development of the United States. Just as masses of immigrants poured into the country from Europe, so did immense sums of money—foreign credit to help build the American economy.

Albert Gallatin, though initially a bit more skeptical of credit, soon came to many of the same conclusions that Hamilton reached. Even in the 1790s he supported the Bank of the United States, although Jefferson, the leader of his party, adamantly opposed it. In 1804, Gallatin advised Jefferson to open another branch of the bank in New Orleans. In 1811, he fought hard for the bank's recharter. In 1816, he championed the creation of the Second Bank of the United States. In the 1830s, he attacked Andrew Jackson's veto of the Second Bank's recharter. And in that same decade he became a banker himself.

In their promotion of these measures, Hamilton and Gallatin were departing from the prejudices against credit that had prevailed when they arrived in North America. They were defining one of the key elements in what came to be called capitalism— the system that would propel the phenomenal growth of the American economy.

CHAPTER 31

The Political Economy of Hamilton and Gallatin

For much of its history, the United States has been the quintessential capitalist nation, the one most open to entrepreneurial opportunity. It has been the country whose laws and circumstances most encouraged immigration from abroad and economic growth at home. These are the legacies of the American Revolution and of economic policies forged by Hamilton, Gallatin, and the other immigrants mentioned in this book.

Taken together, their policies added up to a hothouse for the germination of business. The plants of private enterprise did the actual growing and made up the final harvest. But without the hothouse, and without close attention to the provision of plentiful sunlight, warmth, and moisture, the harvest could never have been so bountiful.[1]

How is this framework—this hothouse for economic growth—best understood, and how is it related to the careers of Hamilton and Gallatin? As a rough guide, imagine four broad categories of government participation in a capitalist economy:

1. laissez-faire, with minimal intervention by any government;
2. frequent, uncoordinated intervention in mostly free markets by governments at all levels: city, county, state, and national;

3. systematic government guidance of private decision making, coming mostly from the top—that is, the national level;

4. thorough government management and decision making for the whole economy, entirely from the top.

The record throughout American history has hovered around category two. This is one of the salient constants of the nation's existence. The American experience has shifted around within this category, but has never left it for long. The country has spent no time at all in category one (laissez-faire) or category four (thorough national management). And only during periods of major war (1861–1865, 1917–1918, 1941–1945) has it taken up even temporary residence in category three. Category two—frequent but uncoordinated intervention in mostly free markets—has been the American way of public economic management.[2]

During the years that Hamilton and Gallatin served as secretary of the treasury, their ideological differences often overshadowed their areas of agreement. The same is true of their writings and of many historical studies of their lives. These studies are often based heavily on their polemics, which were composed mostly for partisan purposes. But in retrospect it is clear that their official *actions* reveal a shared general preference for category two and for a variety of specific policies.[3]

Once the Republicans assumed executive power in 1801, outside pressures pushed the Jefferson-Madison-Gallatin triumvirate toward category two. The Napoleonic Wars, the Louisiana Purchase, the embargo of 1807–1809, and the War of 1812 compelled the Republican governments to become more "energetic" in the Hamiltonian sense. The frequency and extent of federal involvement in economic affairs after 1800 far exceeded the level idealized by Republicans during the 1790s.

Later, in the years following 1816, events interacting with periodic swings in the national temper resulted in a compromise between the ideas of Hamilton on the one hand and those of Gallatin on the other. Gallatin favored minimal encroachment by governments at all levels, and therefore gravitated toward category one. But he never advocated anything approaching systematic laissez-faire. Even if he had been so inclined, which he was not, his wish to develop the West required active management of the public lands and support of internal improvements at federal expense. Similarly, Hamilton's energetic and coordinated policies sometimes tended toward category three, but never reached it. Nor did he advocate it, any more than Gallatin championed laissez-faire.[4]

Hamilton and Gallatin disagreed, of course, on how to manage the debt, on appropriate levels of taxation, and—at least rhetorically—on the proper role of government itself. But the single biggest difference lay in their sense of the country's national security. Hamilton came to North America in 1772 as the clouds of war against Britain were beginning to gather. He had a military frame of mind from the start. For the remaining thirty-two years of his life, first the independence and then the continued safety of his adopted country remained at risk from foreign threats. He was determined to defend the country against these threats.

Gallatin, by contrast, disliked all things military. When he arrived in 1780, he had no wish to become involved in the Revolutionary War. Once he took office in 1801 as secretary of the treasury, he opposed Jefferson's military action against the Barbary pirates, most of the trade sanctions against Britain and France, the embargo of 1807–1809, and any buildup of military forces until the last minute, even in 1812. Once the outcome of the War of 1812 ended external threats, Gallatin's strong disposition toward peace prevailed for the remaining thirty-four years of his life.

These disparate attitudes of Hamilton and Gallatin led to different visions of the geography of the country's defense. Hamilton, preoccupied with preserving independence against

European threats, looked eastward, toward Europe. In 1790, in a very telling comment, he wrote of British Canada as being on "our left" and Spanish possessions, which then included New Orleans, as being on "our right." Such a vision was possible only if he was facing east, toward Europe. Hamilton saw the importance of western development and was prepared to seize New Orleans even during the Quasi-War with France, long before the Louisiana Purchase. But he did not see the future of the trans-Appalachian West as clearly as Gallatin did. Gallatin was less worried about threats from abroad, and looked consistently not toward the Atlantic but toward the West. Even so, both he and Hamilton were economic nationalists, and their shared viewpoint toward the country's development overshadowed their different attitudes toward national defense. Both believed that military effectiveness depended on economic strength.[5]

Because of their economic nationalism, they both advocated federal aid for internal improvements—which in their time included roads, canals, rivers, and harbors. Here Gallatin departed from the preferences of his Virginia colleagues. Jefferson gave mixed signals on the issue, whereas Madison usually opposed it. One of Madison's final acts as president in 1817 was to veto a modest internal-improvements bill passed by Congress.

During the 200-odd years after the publication of Gallatin's *Report on Roads and Canals* in 1808, internal improvements came to include railroads, highways, and airports as well. Throughout this long period, the relative role of governments at different levels remained controversial, as it was when Gallatin wrote his original *Report*. Federal aid ebbed and flowed according to party politics, the need to supplement private capital, and the question of whether national, state, or local government had primary responsibility.[6]

Both Hamilton and Gallatin wanted to promote American manufacturing, and each wrote an insightful report on how that should be done. Hamilton favored bounties—subsidies designed to persuade specific manufacturers to produce desired goods—but Gallatin did not. Bounties, though they could be very effective and had been so in Europe, lent themselves to political favoritism. In the context of America's determination to avoid the corruption of the Old World, Gallatin had the better of this argument. The more important point was that both he and Hamilton were thinking of how best to develop a diversified national economy.

In one of the most revealing of all the views they held in common, both strongly supported the Bank of the United States. Each expended herculean efforts on its behalf, and each had memorable disagreements with Thomas Jefferson, not only about this bank but about all banks. Hamilton, with President Washington's support, was able to establish the Bank of the United States in 1791 and to make it an immediate success. Gallatin, without similar support from President Madison, could not get its charter renewed in 1811—to the great detriment of the nation's financial situation as the War of 1812 began. Madison realized his mistake and in 1816 signed the bill creating the Second Bank of the United States.

Hamilton and Gallatin were also united in their opposition to slavery. They made no secret of their hostility to the peculiar institution, and both joined societies to promote manumission. Each might conceivably have done a bit more in the emerging fight; but as secretary of the treasury in administrations headed by slaveholding presidents, they were not in advantageous positions.

Although Hamilton probably had the stronger antislavery feelings of the two, Gallatin—like Jefferson and Madison—lived long enough to face real concerns about civil war. Threats of disunion over slavery had preceded the Missouri Compromise of 1820, a complicated measure designed to maintain the legislative balance between slave and free states. In 1819 and 1820, the arguments in both the House and Senate caused a constitutional crisis. Thomas Jefferson, by then seventy-seven years old, wrote in 1820 to a friend, "This momentous question, like a fire bell in the night, awakened and filled me with terror." The country had "the wolf by the ear . . . Justice is in one scale and self-preservation in the other. I considered it at once the knell of the Union."[7]

The issue of disunion also arose over the related question of high protective tariffs, which many northern states supported but most of the South opposed. Why, the Southerners asked, should they pay higher prices for imported goods just to support the development of northern industry? Congress passed the first broad and explicitly protective tariff in the nation's history in 1816, to forestall a sudden influx of cheap imports from Britain after the War of 1812. The goal was to keep prices favorable for the new American manufacturers who had sprung up during the war. The tariff levels of 1816, though not extremely high, went beyond what either Hamilton or Gallatin would likely have recommended. Yet the effects of these tariffs promoted the kind of economic diversification that Hamilton had aimed for in his 1791 *Report on the Subject of Manufactures* and Gallatin in his own *Report on Manufactures* of 1810.[8]

The long-term prominence of protectionism in national politics turned out to be an issue nobody in 1816 could have predicted. In 1828, Congress passed a bill with such high levels of protection that it became known in the South as the "Tariff of Abominations." Legislation of 1832 reduced these levels, but not by enough to satisfy most southern political leaders, particularly in South Carolina. In November 1832, that state passed an Ordinance of Nullification negating both tariffs, its logic relying on the Kentucky and Virginia resolutions written in 1798 by Jefferson and Madison. Congress responded with the Force Bill, authorizing President Andrew Jackson to take military action against the state, which he was quite prepared to do. At the same time, Congress enacted a conciliatory lower tariff, and South Carolina thereupon repealed its Ordinance of Nullification on March 11, 1833.

A month before the repeal, while the crisis still loomed, Gallatin wrote Jean Badollet, his old Geneva friend and classmate:

"The present state of our national politics is extremely discouraging." Gallatin, now seventy-two years old, went on to say that the really "dangerous questions," such as slavery and protective tariffs, which arose from "our complex, half consolidated, half federalistic form of government," should be avoided wherever possible. "The acts of S. Carolina are outrageous and unjustifiable. The difficult part for our Government is how to nullify nullification and yet to avoid a civil war." The tortured syntax throughout Gallatin's letter reflected the intractable nature of the problems he was describing.[9]

When serving as secretary of the treasury, Hamilton and Gallatin had been nationalists—more so than Jefferson, Madison, and other founders. Although these others were revolutionaries against Britain, they remained more tied to their native states than were immigrants who had no hereditary American state.[10]

A fusion of many of Hamilton's and Gallatin's policies found expression in an economic program that came to be called the "American System"—the fullest program for national economic development since Hamilton's *Reports* of 1790–1791. In speeches and legislative bills beginning in 1815 and continuing for two decades, Henry Clay and many others sketched out blueprints for the establishment and then continuation of the Second Bank of the United States, for federal aid to build roads and canals, for development of the West, and for the encouragement of manufactures through high levels of tariff protection. On each of these goals except for the high protective tariffs, the American System mirrored the policies of both Hamilton and Gallatin. It was aimed not only at encouraging economic growth, but also at promoting harmony in a country becoming rife with sectional discord.[11]

Under the provisions of the American System, the industrializing Northeast and Middle Atlantic states would secure new markets for their manufactures in the South. The South would keep its international market for cotton, which constituted more than half of all American exports in the decades before the Civil War. It would also supply the cotton textile mills that were beginning to burgeon in New England. The South would purchase fewer imports from Europe and more products made in America. The salient aspect of the American System was that it did consist of a nationwide *system*, not just a convenient marriage of unrelated policies.

Most advocates of the American System were committed nationalists, determined to tie the Union together economically and prevent it from splitting apart over the slavery issue. Yet those advocates and their entire generation failed in this effort. The institution of slavery was too ingrained in the economy and social structure of the South and too widely condoned in much of the North. It was a moral issue, a curse that could never be offset by countervailing economic forces, no matter how well designed.

The American System as a full-blown industrial policy was never implemented to the degree that its supporters envisioned. It required a more powerful national government than most American voters were prepared to accept. There was too much protectionism in it—and, in its support of a national bank and of federal aid to internal improvements—a little too much of both Hamilton and Gallatin for the temper of the times. From 1829 to 1861, when the Civil War began, Andrew Jackson and most of his successors in the White House opposed the American System.[12]

Much of its apparatus survived, however, both before and especially after the Civil War. During the rest of the nineteenth century, federal aid continued in the form of substantial land grants to railroads, to homesteaders, and to states for the purpose of subsidizing education. Just as important, individual cities and states stepped into the breach with their own assistance programs to banks, canals, and railroads. By 1890, a century after Hamilton's financial program had set the small and precarious American economy on a firm foundation, the United

States was leading every other nation in the world in the production of both agricultural and manufactured goods.

———

So the dream of an integrated, diversified, and booming economy—the aspiration of Hamilton, Gallatin, and many other immigrant nationalists—eventually came true. Robert Morris, who had grown up in England, Hamilton in St. Croix, Gallatin in Geneva, Haym Solomon in Poland, Alexander James Dallas in Jamaica, Stephen Girard in France, John Jacob Astor and David Parish in Germany—all had emigrated from their homelands with open minds, fresh eyes, and a flair for finance. All, in both the public and private sectors, took the profound personal step of uprooting themselves because they believed that they might achieve a better future in North America. And that is what they did, both for themselves and for the United States.

Notes

1. In this book the word "immigrant" will appear many times. During the eighteenth century, however, the words "alien," "foreigner," and "newcomer" were much more common. The *Oxford English Dictionary* reports that the pioneering American historian Jeremy Belknap was one of the first to use "immigrant" and its cognates in print. In his *History of New Hampshire* (1792), vol. 3, preface, 6, Belknap wrote: "There is another deviation from the strict letter of the English which is found extremely convenient in our discourses on population . . . The verb *immigrate* and the nouns *immigrant* and *immigration* are used without scruple in some parts of this volume." The use of "immigrant" appears to have become frequent only after the heavy transatlantic movements of people to North America. After the onset of mass immigration to the United States, which began in the 1840s, the term became routine. A useful discussion is Donna Gabaccia, "Nations of Immigrants: Do Words Matter?" *The Pluralist* 5 (2010), 5–31.

On institutions and actions, see Richard R. John, "Why Institutions Matter: Rewriting the History of the Early Republic," *Common-Place* (2008), www .common-place.org/vol-09/no-01/john/ (accessed 12/27/11).

2. The high quality and volume of recent research on the political economy of the 1790s and on Hamilton himself are quite striking. As the endnotes for Part I of this book will indicate, it includes works by many scholars, such as Douglas A. Irwin, Robert E. Wright, Howard Bodenhorn, David J. Cowen, Jeffrey L. Pasley, Gautham Rao, Max M. Edling, and especially Richard Sylla and Ron Chernow.

3. The sixth immigrant cabinet member was James McHenry, who was born

in Ireland in 1753, came to North America in 1771, became a close friend of Alexander Hamilton, and served as secretary of war under presidents Washington and John Adams. The number sixty for the period 1789–1839 does not double- or triple-count the many appointees who held more than one cabinet post at different times or in different presidential administrations. It does, however, include attorneys general and two postmasters general. The precise dating of full cabinet status for these offices is not a settled issue among historians.

4. The first of the two immigrant secretaries after 1815 was William J. Duane, who was born in Ireland and brought to the United States as a child. He served as secretary from May 29, 1833, to September 22, 1833, and then was fired by Andrew Jackson for his refusal to withdraw federal funds from the Second Bank of the United States. The second secretary was W. Michael Blumenthal, who was born in Germany in 1926, fled the Nazi regime and went to Shanghai with his parents in 1939, and moved to the United States in 1947. He served under President Jimmy Carter from January 23, 1977, to August 4, 1979. Two of the sixty-seven, both of them native-born, were secretary twice, serving nonconsecutive terms.

These kinds of statistics can, of course, be misleading, and one has to look beneath them to consider who the secretaries were and under what circumstances they served. But even after making every allowance for distortion, the comparison of 78 percent versus 1 percent continues to speak for itself.

5. These percentages are estimates based on the available data. Almost 100,000 people immigrated to the United States during the 1790s, but this was a small total compared to what happened fifty years later. See Hans-Jürgen Grabbe, "European Immigration to the United States in the Early National Period, 1783–1820," in Susan E. Klepp, ed., *The Demographic History of the Philadelphia Region, 1600–1860* (Philadelphia: American Philosophical Society *Proceedings* 133, 1989), 190–214.

Mass immigration did not begin until the 1840s. In 1823, the year Albert Gallatin returned to the United States after his seven years as minister to France, 1,100 Irish and 183 Germans emigrated to the United States. In 1849, the year Gallatin died, 159,398 Irish and 60,235 Germans emigrated. The Census of 1850, taken after a decade in which several hundred thousand Irish and an almost equal number of Germans entered the country, reported the percentage of immigrants in the total population as 9.6.

After extremely high immigration from southern and central Europe during the late nineteenth century, the total reached 13.6 percent of the population in 1900 and 14.7 percent in 1910, the historic high. By 1970 that number had dropped to 5.4 percent, but since 2000 it has ranged from 10.4 percent immigrants to about 14 percent, some of whom are undocumented and ineligible for public office. See U.S. Bureau of the Census, *Historical Statistics of the United States, Colonial Times to the Present* (Washington, DC: Government Printing Office, 1975), I, 106; and Roger Daniels, *Coming to America: A History of Ethnicity and Immigration in American Life,* 2nd ed. (New York: HarperPerennial, 2002), 410.

6. John Adams had two ancestors dating from 1620. He was a direct descendant of John and Priscilla Alden, who came over on the *Mayflower*. Benjamin Franklin's maternal grandfather, Peter Folger, settled in Watertown, Massachusetts, in 1635; Josiah Franklin, Benjamin's father, emigrated from England to Boston in 1683. James Madison's great-great-grandfather, John Maddison [*sic*], gained the rights to 600 acres of Virginia land in 1653, but he may have come to North America before that. George Washington's great-grandfather, John Washington, was born in Lancaster, England, and emigrated to Virginia in 1659. Jefferson's maternal great-grandfather, William Randolph of Warwickshire, came to Virginia in 1672. His paternal great-grandfather, also named Thomas Jefferson, arrived in Virginia during the 1670s, having spent some time in St. Kitts after emigrating from England.

7. Even in the absence of Census figures, it is clear that the percentage of immigrants during the early years of the Republic cannot begin to account for their prominence in financial affairs. Suppose we concede that Robert Morris, as superintendent of finance under the Articles of Confederation, and Hamilton and Gallatin, as secretaries of the treasury, were the three most influential financial policymakers in early U.S. history. Let us then assume that during their combined years in office, non-African foreign-born residents averaged 5 percent of the population. Under these suppositions, then the mathematical odds against immigrants' being the three most influential financial officers in the early Republic are 5 percent multiplied by 5 percent multiplied by 5 percent—or 8,000 to one. That is, .05 × .05 × .05, or 0.000125, one eight-thousandth. Even if the white immigrant population was as high as 10 percent, which it almost surely was not, the odds are still prohibitive: 1,000 to one.

8. George Washington owned the most land—about 8,000 acres by the 1790s, mostly around Mount Vernon; Jefferson's plantations at and near Monticello totaled about 5,000 acres; Madison's at his family's home, Montpelier, which is located thirty miles from Monticello, also about 5,000 acres; Monroe at Highlands (later called Ash Lawn), which is very near Monticello, 550 acres, in addition to 4,400 acres Monroe owned at Oak Hill in northern Virginia. All of these plantations were staffed primarily by slaves.

9. The aphorism by Emerson is from his essay "Wealth," in *The Collected Works of Ralph Waldo Emerson*, vol. 6: *The Conduct of Life*, ed. Joseph Slater, Douglas Emory Wilson, and Barbara L. Packer (Cambridge, MA: Harvard University Press, 2004), ch. 3. The six banks chartered by Virginia had an average capital of more than $1 million, versus $301,000 for the Massachusetts banks, $379,000 for the New York banks, and $485,000 for the Pennsylvania banks. This difference reflects several factors, one of which was the number of attempts by entrepreneurs to open new banks, another the relative ease of getting a charter bill through a state legislature. The total capitalization of Virginia banks in 1837 was $6.7 million, of Massachusetts banks $37.1 million, of New York banks also $37.1 million, of Pennsylvania banks $23.8 million. See John Joseph Wallis, "The Other Foundings: Federalism and the Constitutional Structure of American Government," in Douglas A. Irwin and Richard Sylla, eds., *Founding Choices: Ameri-*

can Economic Policy in the 1790s (Chicago: University of Chicago Press, 2011), ch. 6. A key element of most bank charters was the provision for limited liability among the shareholders, who did not have to risk their entire personal fortunes as they would have in banks organized as partnerships. When the United States was created, Virginia had ranked first among the thirteen states in population, and New York fifth. In the Census of 1840, the populations of the four states mentioned were as follows: New York, 2.4 million; Pennsylvania, 1.7 million; Virginia, 1.0 million; Massachusetts, 738,000.

10. For an analysis of the kinds of people who emigrated to the United States, see Marilyn C. Baseler, *"Asylum for Mankind": America, 1607–1800* (Ithaca, NY: Cornell University Press, 1998).

11. William Faulkner, *Light in August* (New York: Random House, 1932), 241. Faulkner's context here is not the Revolutionary period but the years after the Civil War: the movement of reformers from the North into the South to help assist former slaves. The speaker is Joanna Burden.

1. ST. CROIX AND TRAUMA

1. Hamilton to William Jackson, Aug. 26, 1800, enclosed in a letter to James McHenry, Aug. 27, 1800, in *The Papers of Alexander Hamilton,* ed. Harold Syrett et al. (New York: Columbia University Press, 1961–1978), vol. 25, 88. This well-annotated collection, which contains twenty-seven volumes totaling more than 16,000 pages, is by far the best single source on Hamilton's life, and is hereafter cited as *Hamilton Papers.* There are many other examples of Hamilton's sense of unfair criticism, such as his remarks in the New York Assembly, Feb. 15, 1787, ibid., vol. 4, 73; and his long letter to William Hamilton, his uncle in Scotland, May 2, 1797, ibid., vol. 21, 77–78.

2. Hamilton's biographers differ on the date of his birth. The most thorough modern chronicler is Ron Chernow, whose *Alexander Hamilton* (New York: Penguin, 2004) puts the birthdate at 1755. Other important biographies published since 1950 include John C. Miller, *Alexander Hamilton: Portrait in Paradox* (New York: Harper, 1959), a perceptive and readable book; Broadus Mitchell, *Alexander Hamilton,* 2 vols. (New York: Macmillan, 1957, 1962), an analysis by an economic historian, condensed into *Alexander Hamilton: A Concise Biography* (New York: Oxford University Press, 1976); Jacob Cooke, *Alexander Hamilton: A Profile* (New York: Hill and Wang, 1967), a well-informed book full of psychological arguments written by a co-editor of Hamilton's Papers; James Thomas Flexner, *The Young Hamilton: A Biography* (Boston: Little, Brown, 1978), an insightful treatment of Hamilton's life into his twenties; Forrest McDonald, *Alexander Hamilton* (New York: Norton, 1979), a combative book especially strong on the economics of Hamilton's achievement and a bit too critical of the Jeffersonian opposition; Noemie Emery, *Alexander Hamilton: An Intimate Portrayal* (New York: Putnam, 1982), which is good on psychological insights; and Rich-

ard Brookhiser, *Alexander Hamilton, American* (New York: Free Press, 1999), a brief, well-written, and sympathetic interpretation.

3. The comment by Hamilton's sister-in-law is quoted in Robert Henderson, *Hamilton I, 1757–1789* (New York: Mason Charter, 1976), 246.

4. *Hamilton Papers*, vol. 1, 3; Esmond Wright, "Alexander Hamilton, Founding Father," *History Today* 7 (1957), 182–189; Emery, *Alexander Hamilton,* 36.

5. Chernow, *Alexander Hamilton,* 27–28, contains a fairly full discussion of Hamilton's paternity. Chernow comes to no conclusion, and none is possible without DNA evidence. He hints, without quite saying, that he believes Hamilton and Stevens to have been half-brothers.

6. Mitchell, *Alexander Hamilton: A Concise Biography,* 12.

7. *Hamilton Papers,* vol. 1, 8; Chernow, *Alexander Hamilton,* ch. 2.

8. *Hamilton Papers,* vol. 1, 14, 24.

9. Ibid., 4.

10. Ibid., 34–37.

2. NEW YORK AND PROMISE

1. *The Papers of Alexander Hamilton,* ed. Harold Syrett et al. (New York: Columbia University Press, 1961–1978), vol. 1, 40–41; vol. 20, 456; vol. 26, 307 (hereafter cited as *Hamilton Papers*); Ron Chernow, *Alexander Hamilton* (New York: Penguin, 2004), 38, 695, 725.

2. *Hamilton Papers,* vol. 1, 80; Chernow, *Hamilton,* ch. 2; Noemie Emery, *Alexander Hamilton: An Intimate Portrayal* (New York: Putnam, 1982), 27–28; Jacob Cooke, *Alexander Hamilton: A Profile* (New York: Hill and Wang, 1967), 7–9; Nathan Schachner, "Alexander Hamilton Viewed by His Friends: The Narratives of Robert Troup and Hercules Mulligan," *William and Mary Quarterly* 4 (1947), 203–225.

3. The literature on the Revolution and its origins is rich, varied, and extraordinarily copious. Here is a sample of standard works: Bernard Bailyn, *The Ideological Origins of the American Revolution,* enlarged ed. (Cambridge, MA: Harvard University Press, 1992), the foundational book on the subject of its title; Bernhard Knollenberg, *Origin of the American Revolution, 1759–1766* (New York: Macmillan, 1960), which shows the importance of British measures even before the Stamp Act; Douglas Leach, *Roots of Conflict: British Armed Forces and Colonial Americans, 1677–1763* (Chapel Hill: University of North Carolina Press, 1986), which covers colonial objections to British military authority over almost a century; Fred Anderson, *Crucible of War: The Seven Years' War and the Fate of Empire in British North America, 1754–1766* (New York: Knopf, 2000), which is especially vivid on military history; Alan Rogers, *Empire and Liberty: American Resistance to British Authority, 1755–1763* (Berkeley: University of California Press, 1974), whose title explains itself; Pauline Maier, *From Resistance to Revolution: Colonial Radicals and the Development of American Op-*

position to Britain, 1765–1776 (New York: Random House, 1973), an analysis of how protest evolved into war; Robert Middlekauf, *The Glorious Cause: The American Revolution, 1763–1789* (New York: Oxford University Press, 2005), a conventional synthesis of much prior scholarship; Gordon S. Wood, *The American Revolution: A History* (New York: Modern Library, 2002), a brief but rich interpretation; Max M. Edling, *A Revolution in Favor of Government: Origins of the U.S. Constitution and the Making of the American State* (New York: Oxford University Press, 2003), which uses a comparative analysis to argue that the nationalists among the founders were concerned with protecting the new Republic from military threats; T. H. Breen, *The Marketplace of Revolution: How Consumer Politics Shaped American Independence* (New York: Oxford University Press, 2004), which emphasizes the role of the market more than that of the founders; Gary B. Nash, *The Unknown Revolution: The Unruly Birth of Democracy and the Struggle to Create America* (New York: Viking, 2005), which focuses on the contributions of common folk; and Jack Rakove, *Revolutionaries: A New History of the Invention of America* (Boston: Houghton Mifflin Harcourt, 2010), which portrays both the best-known and some lesser-known founders. The quotations are from a letter John Adams wrote to Hezekiah Niles, Feb. 13, 1818, in *The Works of John Adams, Second President of the United States: With a Life of the Author, Notes and Illustrations*, ed. Charles Francis Adams (Boston: Little, Brown, 1856), vol. 10, 282–283.

4. John Brewer, *The Sinews of Power: War, Money and the English State, 1688–1783* (New York: Knopf, 1989); see also Eliga H. Gould and Peter S. Onuf, eds., *Empire and Nation: The American Revolution in the Atlantic World* (Baltimore: Johns Hopkins University Press, 2005), a book containing essays on both the effects of the Seven Years War—the larger conflict that began with the French and Indian War—and on aspects of the Revolution itself.

5. The standard accounts are Edmund S. and Helen M. Morgan, *The Stamp Act Crisis: Prologue to Revolution* (Chapel Hill: University of North Carolina Press, 1953); Maier, *From Resistance to Revolution*; and Peter D. G. Thomas, *British Politics and the Stamp Act Crisis: The First Phase of the American Revolution* (New York: Oxford University Press, 1975). There was a great deal of opposition to the Stamp Act in Britain as well, especially by merchants who sold exports to the colonies. During the time when it was in effect, most colonies did not implement the act. It did, however, affect the export economy, where American ships could not deliver goods in British imperial ports because their clearances were not on stamped paper. Parliament repealed the Stamp Act in 1766 but accompanied repeal with the unwise Declaratory Act, which insisted that Parliament could pass whatever laws it wished relating to the colonies, including tax laws.

6. *A Full Vindication . . .* is in *Hamilton Papers*, vol. 1, 45ff. The quoted passage is on p. 55.

7. *Hamilton Papers*, vol. 1, 81ff. The quoted passage is on p. 122. For a brief exegesis, see Richard Brookhiser, *Alexander Hamilton, American* (New York: Free Press, 1999), 162.

3. WAR AND HEROISM

1. *The Papers of Alexander Hamilton,* ed. Harold Syrett et al. (New York: Columbia University Press, 1961–1978), vol. 1, 182, 195–196 (hereafter cited as *Hamilton Papers*); Ron Chernow, *Alexander Hamilton* (New York: Penguin, 2004), 83–86.

2. Other Washington aides were also talented, of course; they would not have been chosen if they weren't. Two in particular, Tench Tilghman and John Laurens, were almost as important to Washington as was Hamilton; and Robert Hanson Harrison, the senior aide, perhaps more so. See Jacob Cooke, *Alexander Hamilton: A Profile* (New York: Hill and Wang, 1967), 13–15.

3. On the routine at Washington's headquarters, see ibid., 12–16; James Thomas Flexner, *The Young Hamilton: A Biography* (Boston: Little, Brown, 1978), 136–158; John C. Miller, *Alexander Hamilton: Portrait in Paradox* (New York: Harper, 1959), 21–42; and Chernow, *Alexander Hamilton,* 86–90.

4. Hamilton to Laurens, April 1779, *Hamilton Papers,* vol. 2, 34–35. John ("Jack") Laurens was the son of Henry Laurens, president of the Continental Congress. Noemie Emery, *Alexander Hamilton: An Intimate Portrayal* (New York: Putnam, 1982), 38–39, suggests that the headquarters atmosphere promoted by Washington may have fulfilled not only Hamilton's vision of a wholesome family life, but also Washington's. Hamilton sometimes professed a lack of affection for Washington and implied that the general's advances of friendship to him were not welcome, but he was very likely protecting his sense of independence. See Hamilton to Philip Schuyler, Feb. 18, 1781, *Hamilton Papers,* vol. 2, 563–564. Chernow, *Alexander Hamilton,* 88–89, 153, 290, 479, 499–500, and 600 contains useful material on the Hamilton-Washington relationship.

5. *The Farmer Refuted,* in *Hamilton Papers,* vol. 1, 157–158.

6. Flexner, *The Young Hamilton,* 137; Cooke, *Alexander Hamilton,* 15–16.

7. On Lafayette's view of Hamilton as a foreigner, see Flexner, *The Young Hamilton,* 238.

8. Ibid., 137, 321. See also Cecelia M. Kenyon: Hamilton always "put country first, self second," which was not necessarily a sacrifice but a "fulfillment of . . . deepest desires." Kenyon, "Alexander Hamilton: Rousseau of the Right," *Political Science Quarterly* 73 (1958), 174. Hamilton did take a short time off in 1780, to get married. But he soon returned to duty.

9. Hamilton to Washington, Nov. 22, 1780, *Hamilton Papers,* vol. 2, 509. On the larger theme, see the classic essay by Douglass Adair, "Fame and the Founding Fathers," which is most easily accessible in Trevor Colbourn, ed., *Fame and the Founding Fathers* (New York: Norton, 1974), 3–36. This book contains several other powerful essays on the subject of its title.

10. Hamilton to McHenry, Feb. 18, 1781, *Hamilton Papers,* vol. 2, 569.

11. Chernow, *Alexander Hamilton,* 160–164.

12. Ibid., 164–166.

13. Emery, *Alexander Hamilton,* 33–37, 75–76.

14. Hamilton to Washington, March 1, 1782, *Hamilton Papers,* vol. 3, 5. Con-

gress later waffled on the issue of half-pay for officers, going back and forth several times before resolving it at less expense to the government.

4. LOVE AND SOCIAL STATUS

1. Hamilton to John Laurens, Jan. 8, 1780, *The Papers of Alexander Hamilton*, ed. Harold Syrett et al. (New York: Columbia University Press, 1961–1978), vol. 2, 255 (hereafter cited as *Hamilton Papers*).

2. Hamilton to Laurens, April 1779, *Hamilton Papers*, vol. 2, 37.

3. Caroline V. Hamilton, "The Erotic Charisma of Alexander Hamilton," *Journal of American Studies* 45 (2011), 1–19. Abigail Adams is quoted in Page Smith, *John Adams*, 2 vols. (New York: Doubleday, 1962), vol. 2, 907.

4. Hamilton to Elizabeth Schuyler, March 17, 1780, *Hamilton Papers*, vol. 2, 286–287; Tilghman is quoted in Ron Chernow, *Alexander Hamilton* (New York: Penguin, 2004), 129.

5. Hamilton to Margarita Schuyler, Feb. 1780, *Hamilton Papers*, vol. 2, 269–270; Tilghman's diary is quoted in James Thomas Flexner, *The Young Hamilton: A Biography* (Boston: Little, Brown, 1978), 277.

6. Chernow, *Alexander Hamilton*, 136.

7. Hamilton to Laurens, June 30, 1780, *Hamilton Papers*, vol. 2, 347–348.

8. Hamilton to Elizabeth Schuyler, August 1780, *Hamilton Papers*, vol. 2, 398–399. On Hamilton's attitude toward wealth for its own sake, see Richard Brookhiser, *Alexander Hamilton, American* (New York: Free Press, 1999), 185–186.

9. Schuyler's letter to his daughter is quoted in Chernow, *Alexander Hamilton*, 136–137.

10. The biographies of Hamilton by Chernow, Cooke, and Emery are the strongest in their delineation of Elizabeth. Cooke goes so far as to say, "Hamilton's leap from the fringes of St. Croix's plantation society to the inner circles of the New Jersey and New York squirearchy required more agility than all the other accomplishments for which history has honored him" (p. 7). After Hamilton's death, Eliza carefully preserved his large collections of papers and negotiated with the Library of Congress for their permanent custody. She also promoted the first important biography, a multivolume work written at her constant urging by their son John Church Hamilton. On Eliza, see Chernow, *Alexander Hamilton*, 3, 146, 148–149, 203–207, 367, and 643; on Angelica Church, ibid., 133–134.

11. *Hamilton Papers*, vol. 3, 82–83.

12. Paul Finkelman, "Alexander Hamilton, Esq.: Founding Father as Lawyer" (Review of Julius Goebel Jr., and Joseph H. Smith, eds., *The Law Practice of Alexander Hamilton*, 5 vols. [New York: Columbia University Press for William Nelson Cromwell Foundation, 1964–1981]), *American Bar Foundation Research Journal* 229 (1984), 235–236: "The Hamilton practice manual is an incredible piece of work. Portions of it should be assigned to all first-year law students so

they can get a sense of continuity with past law students, stand in awe at this genius, and gain a greater appreciation for the comparative simplicity of the Federal Rules."

13. Hamilton to Laurens, Aug. 15, 1782, *Hamilton Papers,* vol. 3, 145.

14. Hamilton to Lafayette, Nov. 3, 1782, *Hamilton Papers,* vol. 3, 191–192; Flexner, *Young Hamilton,* 379; Emery, *Alexander Hamilton,* 83; Cooke, *Alexander Hamilton,* 38; Finkelman, "Alexander Hamilton, Esq.," 240.

15. Nathan Schachner, "Alexander Hamilton Viewed by His Friends: The Narratives of Robert Troup and Hercules Mulligan," *William and Mary Quarterly* 4 (1947), 235. Hamilton explained his reasons for defending Tories in a prolix (5,000-word) essay, "A Letter from Phocion to the Considerate Citizens of New-York on the Politics of the Day" (New York: Printed by Samuel Loudon, 1784), *Hamilton Papers,* vol. 3, 483ff.

16. Hamilton to Washington, April 8, 1783, *Hamilton Papers,* vol. 3, 317–321.

17. "The Continentalist," No. 6, July 4, 1782, *Hamilton Papers,* vol. 3, 106.

5. THE ROOTS OF HIS THINKING

1. This is not to say that the American situation in the 1780s was the same as in the 1770s. The basic problem of the 1770s was moving toward independence, fighting the war, and trying to finance it. After the victory at Yorktown in 1781, the chief problems were finance, statecraft, and securing the Constitution of 1787 and its ratification.

2. Drew R. McCoy, *The Elusive Republic: Political Economy in Jeffersonian America* (Chapel Hill: University of North Carolina Press for the Institute of Early American History and Culture, 1980), 76, 90–93.

3. A good summary and analysis of the broad economic issues of this period is Ben Baack, "Economics of the American Revolutionary War," EH.Net Encyclopedia, ed. Robert Whaples, Nov. 13, 2001 (updated Aug. 5, 2010). See eh.net/encyclopedia/article/baack.war.revolutionary.us (accessed 6/15/11).

4. The condition of the American economy during the 1780s has long been controversial. Some historians have argued that the period was not so bad—see, for example, Merrill Jensen, *The New Nation: A History of the United States during the Confederation* (New York: Knopf, 1950), which itself was a revision of the long-held view that the 1780s was a critical decade full of peril for the nation's future; E. James Ferguson, *The Power of the Purse: A History of American Public Finance, 1776–1790* (Chapel Hill: University of North Carolina Press for the Institute of Early American History and Culture, 1961); and Edwin J. Perkins, *American Public Finance and Financial Services, 1700–1815* (Columbus: Ohio State University Press, 1994). The contrary view—of the 1780s as a time of economic depression—is set forth, among other places, in the well-documented and authoritative work of Gordon Bjork, "The Weaning of the American Economy: Independence, Market Changes, and Economic Development," *Journal of*

Economic History 24 (1964), 541–560; of John J. McCusker and Russell R. Menard, *The Economy of British North America, 1607–1789* (Chapel Hill: University of North Carolina Press for the Institute of Early American History and Culture, 1985), ch. 17; and of Roger H. Brown, *Redeeming the Republic: Federalists, Taxation, and the Origins of the Constitution* (Baltimore: Johns Hopkins University Press, 1993).

5. Hamilton to James Duane, Sept. 3, 1780, *The Papers of Alexander Hamilton,* ed. Harold Syrett et al. (New York: Columbia University Press, 1961–1978), vol. 2, 406 (hereafter cited as *Hamilton Papers*). Part of the problem of supplying the army was not just a shortage of money. It was also an ideological suspicion—harbored by many colonists—of all professional armies, including their own. Most Americans much preferred citizen militias. On the aversion to regular armies, see Charles Royster, *A Revolutionary People at War: The Continental Army and American Character, 1775–1783* (Chapel Hill: University of North Carolina Press for the Institute of Early American History and Culture, 1979); E. Wayne Carp, *To Starve the Army at Pleasure: Continental Army Administration and American Political Culture, 1775–1783* (Chapel Hill: University of North Carolina Press, 1984); and John R. Nelson Jr., *Liberty and Property: Political Economy and Policymaking in the New Nation, 1789–1812* (Baltimore: Johns Hopkins University Press, 1987), 10.

6. The value of American exports and imports, in pounds sterling, was as follows: for 1770 (before the Revolution), 1.02 million in exports, 1.93 million in imports; for 1780, 18.6 *thousand* in exports, 825 thousand in imports; for 1790, 1.04 million in exports, 3.26 million in imports. *Historical Statistics of the United States: Colonial Times to 1970,* 2 vols. (Washington, DC: Government Printing Office, 1975), vol. 2, 1176.

7. At times the issue seemed even more divisive than the problem of slavery, although slavery itself was connected to the question of proportionate domestic taxation *within* northern and southern states. See Robin L. Einhorn, *American Taxation, American Slavery* (Chicago: University of Chicago Press, 2006).

8. The biggest danger still came from the British, French, and Spanish empires, all with remaining claims of land in North America and none wishing to encourage colonial revolutions except as a means of gaining advantage over another empire.

9. Hamilton to Laurens, June 30, 1780, *Hamilton Papers,* vol. 2, 347–348. Although Hamilton could not know it, something similar would happen in the nineteenth and twentieth centuries in the Spanish colonies of Central and South America and in the former Asian and African colonies of Britain and France. Soon after independence, they began to fight civil wars or wars against one another. Nor was Hamilton the only founder who saw the possibility of continued threats from abroad. So did John Adams and others. For an exploration of Adams's ideas and related themes about how the United States should protect itself from European interference in the Western Hemisphere, see Eliga H. Gould, *Among the Powers of the Earth: The American Revolution and the Making of a New World Empire* (Cambridge, MA: Harvard University Press, 2012). More

generally, see Max M. Edling, *A Revolution in Favor of Government: Origins of the U.S. Constitution and the Making of the American State* (New York: Oxford University Press, 2003).

10. Hamilton to Elizabeth Schuyler, August [n.d.] 1780, *Hamilton Papers*, vol. 2, 398–399.

11. Hamilton to Elizabeth Schuyler, Sept. 6, 1780, ibid., 422.

12. Gloria Main, "Forum: Toward a History of the Standard of Living in British North America," esp. "The Standard of Living in Southern New England, 1640–1773," *William and Mary Quarterly* 45 (1988), 124–134; and John J. McCusker, "Comment," ibid., 167–170.

13. Hamilton to Duane, Sept. 3, 1780, *Hamilton Papers*, vol. 2, 400–417. This letter is about 7,000 words long, or about twenty-three pages in a book of average size today.

14. Ibid.

15. Ibid.

16. Ibid. For a general comment on the nationalists' program in these years, see E. James Ferguson, "The Nationalists of 1781–1783 and the Economic Interpretation of the Constitution," *Journal of American History* 56 (1969), 241–261.

17. The "Continentalist" essays are printed in *Hamilton Papers*, vols. 2 and 3. All important biographies and other secondary sources on Hamilton emphasize their importance. See, for example, Robert James Parks, *European Origins of the Economic Ideas of Alexander Hamilton* (New York: Arno Press, 1977), 42–43.

18. "The Continentalist," No. 5, April 18, 1782, *Hamilton Papers*, vol. 3, 775–782.

19. Ibid.

20. Ibid.

6. ROBERT MORRIS, HAMILTON, AND FINANCE

1. Hamilton to Duane, Sept. 3, 1780, *The Papers of Alexander Hamilton*, ed. Harold Syrett et al. (New York: Columbia University Press, 1961–1978), vol. 2, 408–409 (hereafter cited as *Hamilton Papers*).

2. The two best biographies are Clarence L. Ver Steeg, *Robert Morris: Revolutionary Financier* (Philadelphia: University of Pennsylvania Press, 1954), an exhaustively researched work of scholarship; and Charles Rappleye, *Robert Morris: Financier of the American Revolution* (New York: Simon and Schuster, 2010), which covers more ground than Ver Steeg's book and is more colorfully written. See also Ellis Paxson Oberholtzer, *Robert Morris, Patriot and Financier* (New York: Macmillan, 1904); and Eleanor Young, *Forgotten Patriot: Robert Morris* (New York: Macmillan, 1950).

3. After a celebration aboard one of his ships, Morris Sr. was returning to shore in a small boat. When the ship's guns fired the traditional salute, he was hit by the cotton wadding in front of the gunpowder—and seriously wounded even

though the cannonball had been removed before the gun was fired. He died three days later.

4. Thomas M. Doerflinger, "Commercial Specialization in Philadelphia's Merchant Community, 1750–1791," *Business History Review* 57 (1983), 20–49, draws a vivid portrait of the city's economic vitality during Morris's years as a businessman, although he does not mention Morris himself. The author's thesis is that the common portrayal of all colonial merchants as generalists conflicts with the facts in Philadelphia. The best source on Thomas Willing, which also covers the Morris-Willing partnership, is Robert E. Wright, "Thomas Willing (1731–1821): Philadelphia Financier and Forgotten Founding Father," *Pennsylvania History* 63 (1996), 525–560. See also Burton Alva Koonkle, *Thomas Willing and the First American Financial System* (Philadelphia: University of Pennsylvania Press, 1937).

5. This half-brother, Thomas Morris, gave Robert Morris many headaches in the years to come. Thomas dissipated all good will by his erratic behavior in both America and Europe, where the firm sent him as a business agent.

6. On the rapid evolution of business in Philadelphia, see Thomas Doerflinger, *A Vigorous Spirit of Enterprise: Merchants and Economic Development of Revolutionary Philadelphia* (Chapel Hill: University of North Carolina Press, 1986).

7. Hamilton to Morris, April 30, 1781, *Hamilton Papers*, vol. 2, 604ff.

8. Ibid., 604–606.

9. Ibid., 606–607.

10. Hamilton estimated that before the war the thirteen colonies had contained approximately "thirty millions of Dollars, of which about eight might have been in Specie." Both the colonial and then the national traditions of extremely low taxation, however, made comparisons with Europe problematic. Thus, in the United States, "where the people have been so little accustomed to taxes, it may be doubted whether it would be possible to raise the same proportion of revenue." Ibid., 609–610.

11. Ibid., 608–610.

12. Ibid., 617.

13. Ibid., 618.

14. Ibid., 617–618, 621ff.

15. Ibid., 635.

16. A national debt, Hamilton went on to say to Morris, "will also create a necessity for keeping up taxation to a degree which without being oppressive, will be a spur to industry; remote as we are from Europe and shall be from danger, it were otherwise to be feard our popular maxims would incline us to too great parsimony and indulgence. We labour less now than any civilized nation of Europe, and a habit of labour in the people is as essential to the health and vigor of their minds and bodies as it is conducive to the welfare of the State" (ibid). For praise and criticism of Hamilton's statement and a history of the debt that ends with a polemic against modern deficits, see John Steele Gordon, *Hamilton's Blessing: The Extraordinary Life and Times of Our National Debt* (New York: Walker, 1997).

17. Morris to Hamilton, May 26, 1781, *Hamilton Papers,* vol. 2, 645.

18. Ibid., 646; Morris to Washington, May 29, 1781, *The Papers of Robert Morris,* ed. E. James Ferguson et al. (Pittsburgh: University of Pittsburgh Press, 1978–1999), vol. 1, 96 (hereafter cited as *Morris Papers*).

19. Donald F. Swanson, "The Origins of Hamilton's Fiscal Policies," University of Florida Monographs (Gainesville: Winter 1963), *Social Sciences* 8, 36ff. The paper money issued by Pennsylvania retained its value better than that of any other state.

20. Later, Gouverneur Morris served as a delegate to the Constitutional Convention of 1787, then as minister to France and as a U.S. senator from New York. Meanwhile, he was constantly entreated by his friends, including George Washington, to bring his runaway libido under better control. To their dismay, he did not follow this advice. See William Howard Adams, *Gouverneur Morris: An Independent Life* (New Haven, CT: Yale University Press, 2003); and Richard Brookhiser, *Gentleman Revolutionary: Gouverneur Morris, the Rake Who Wrote the Constitution* (New York: Free Press, 2003).

21. Solomon (sometimes spelled "Salomon") died in January 1785 and left few surviving papers. He is the subject of a fair amount of unreliable literature, including novels and children's books that portray him as more of a hero than he actually was. Nevertheless, his contributions to the financing of the war were significant, as becomes clear in the many references and communications to him in the *Morris Papers.* Morris usually refers to him as "the broker." For brief and reliable accounts of Solomon's career, see James H. Peeling, "Hyam Salomon," *Dictionary of American Biography* (New York: Scribner, 1928–1936); Leo Hershkowitz, "Hyam Salomon," in Michael Berenbaum and Fred Skolnik, eds., *Encyclopedia Judaica,* 2nd ed. (Detroit: Gale Cengage, 2007), 697–698; and Edgar J. McManus, "Haym Salomon," *American National Biography Online,* www .anb.org.

22. A "Bank of Pennsylvania" had been established in 1780, funded principally by Morris himself, who invested 10,000 pounds sterling of his own money. It was not a bank in the usual sense of the term, but rather a device for helping to administer funds for the military. The Bank of North America superseded it, but neither institution rose to the status of a central bank. The Hamilton-Morris correspondence about the bank (and banks in general) can be followed in the *Hamilton Papers* and the *Morris Papers,* both of which are very well indexed and annotated. The similarity of Morris's program to that of Hamilton ten years later is ably delineated in Ver Steeg, *Robert Morris: Revolutionary Financier.*

23. In addition to his duties in finance, Morris as acting Agent of Marine took a major role in naval matters during most of the War of Independence. The United States had a tiny navy, but this was only one of many maritime concerns for a country so actively involved in sea trade. For an account of one time-consuming episode involving Morris, see Stephen Tallichet Powers, "Robert Morris and the Courts-Martial of Captains Samuel Nicholson and John Manley of the Continental Navy," *Military Affairs* 44 (1980), 13–17. An episode very revealing of the nature of Morris's business is recounted in Mary A. Y. Gallagher, "Private Interest

and the Public Good: Settling the Score for the Morris-Holker Business Relationship, 1778–1790," *Pennsylvania History* 69 (2002), 179–209, an article that goes well beyond the limits implied in its title.

24. Rappleye, in *Robert Morris,* devotes most of a chapter to this episode ("Yorktown," 253–277). See also Victor L. Johnson, "Robert Morris and the Provisioning of the American Army during the Yorktown Campaign of 1781," *Pennsylvania History* 5 (1938), 7–20.

25. The dollar amounts requested and received for 1782 appear in Ben Baack, "Forging a Nation State: The Continental Congress and the Financing of the War of American Independence," *Economic History Review* 54 (2001), 639–656, which contains a wealth of other information about financing the Revolutionary War. Morris's letters to the three state governors are in *Morris Papers,* vol. 3, 414–415.

26. *Morris Papers,* vol. 3, 476.

27. Ibid., vol. 6, 282.

28. Ibid., vol. 6, 631.

29. Ibid., vol. 7, 574.

30. Ibid., vol. 9, appendix 3, 697–698.

7. THE CONSTITUTION

1. For a thorough analysis, see Edward Countryman, *A People in Revolution: The American Revolution and Political Society in New York, 1760–1790* (Baltimore: Johns Hopkins University Press, 1981).

2. Hamilton to Jay, July 26, 1783, *The Papers of Alexander Hamilton,* ed. Harold Syrett et al. (New York: Columbia University Press, 1961–1978), vol. 3, 416–417 (hereafter cited as *Hamilton Papers*). On the gradual evolution of ideas about the division of authority between the states and the national government, see Alison L. LaCroix, *The Ideological Origins of American Federalism* (Cambridge, MA: Harvard University Press, 2010). On fiscal issues and the Constitution, see Roger H. Brown, *Redeeming the Republic: Federalists, Taxation, and the Origins of the Constitution* (Baltimore: Johns Hopkins University Press, 1993), which emphasizes resistance to state taxes and the weakness of the Confederation government.

3. Madison's Notes, Jan. 29, 1783, *Hamilton Papers,* vol. 3, 247.

4. See *Hamilton Papers,* vol. 3, 420–426, for his resolution, which runs to about 2,500 words.

5. The Address of the Annapolis Convention, Sept. 14, 1786, *Hamilton Papers,* vol. 3, 686ff.; the quotation is on p. 689. Virginia, New York, Pennsylvania, New Jersey, and Delaware sent commissioners to Annapolis. Massachusetts, New Hampshire, Georgia, and Rhode Island appointed commissioners, but they failed to show up. Connecticut, Georgia, South Carolina, and Maryland (even though the meeting was in Annapolis) appointed no commissioners. The meetings lasted only four days, Sept. 11–14, 1786.

6. In the great adventure at Philadelphia of drafting the Constitution, Hamilton did not play a leading part. Another immigrant, the brilliant legal scholar James Wilson of Scotland, did play such a part—perhaps second only to that of James Madison. Wilson served as a delegate from Pennsylvania and helped to compose the original draft of the Constitution. George Washington later appointed him a member of the first Supreme Court.

7. The relationship between slavery and the Constitution is a very controversial topic. Eminent constitutional scholars such as Bernard Bailyn and Gordon Wood have tended to downplay the relationship, primarily (and here I must simplify what would otherwise be an unduly complex discussion) because they have been concerned more with ideology than with institutions. The contrary case—that slavery lay at the heart of the compromises that permitted the Constitution to be written, ratified, and enforced—is ably argued in such books as Robin L. Einhorn, *American Taxation, American Slavery* (Chicago: University of Chicago Press, 2006), a remarkably original interpretation; George William Van Cleve, *A Slaveholders' Union: Slavery, Politics, and the Constitution in the Early Republic* (Chicago: University of Chicago Press, 2010), which is especially strong on legal issues; and David Waldstreicher, *Slavery's Constitution* (New York: Hill and Wang, 2009). Pages 161–168 of the latter book concisely summarize the evolution of the debate and provide an ample bibliography. One of the most zealously argued cases against the founders, particularly Jefferson, who was minister to France in 1787 and not a delegate to the Constitutional Convention but who often wrote about slavery, is Paul Finkelman, *Slavery and the Founders: Race and Liberty in the Age of Jefferson* (New York: M. E. Sharpe, 1996).

8. The bill of which this clause was a part failed to pass, receiving eleven votes of the unanimous thirteen required to change any part of the Articles' framework. See Einhorn, *American Taxation, American Slavery,* 162–169, which clearly explains the taxation and representation issues.

9. Ibid.

10. Ibid. Hamilton is quoted in Joseph J. Ellis, *Founding Brothers: The Revolutionary Generation* (New York: Knopf, 2000), 201. The quoted phrases in the Constitution occur, respectively, in Article 1, Section 2; Article 4, Section 2; and Article 1, Section 9.

11. Constitutional Convention Speech on a Plan of Government, Philadelphia, June 18, 1787, *Hamilton Papers,* vol. 4, 223–224.

12. Ibid.

13. Ron Chernow, *Alexander Hamilton* (New York: Penguin, 2004), 234. It is conceivable, though very unlikely, that Madison altered his drafts so as to paint a less favorable picture of Hamilton. Madison turned strongly against Hamilton during the 1790s, and he often revised his notes during the forty-nine years between the Philadelphia Convention of 1787 and his death in 1836, after which the notes were published. Madison's most sympathetic biographer, Irving Brant, cites instances in which Madison altered the historical record—even primary sources, including a few of his letters to Jefferson. On the other hand, notes taken by the Clintonian delegate Robert Yates of New York, parts of which are quoted

here, tend to confirm Madison's account of Hamilton's remarks of 1787. See *Hamilton Papers*, vol. 4, 195–201.

14. As the historian Gordon Wood, who is no fan of Hamilton but remains one of the keenest analysts of the Convention, has put it, "Hamilton's outrageous suggestion of a president and senate for life was his tactical effort to make the Virginia Plan seem more moderate than in fact it was. That is why Hamilton tried to lump it in with the rival New Jersey Plan, which only involved amending the old Articles of Confederation, as 'pork with little change of the sauce.'" See Wood, review of Andrew Burstein and Nancy Isenberg, *Madison and Jefferson* (New York: Random House, 2010), in *The New Republic*, April 7, 2011, 25. Other scholars have made a similar argument, as Chernow notes in *Alexander Hamilton*, 234.

15. Hamilton to Washington, July 3, 1787, *Hamilton Papers*, vol. 4, 223–224.

16. The sample size of fifty-five is perhaps too small to be statistically robust. Even so, it is noteworthy that in addition to Robert Morris and Hamilton, another financially sophisticated immigrant who signed was Thomas Fitzsimons, who had emigrated from Ireland in 1760 and had been active during the 1780s as a director of the Bank of North America. Some delegates who did not sign, such as George Wythe of Virginia, might conceivably have signed had they not already left Philadelphia. Wythe supported the Constitution at his state's ratifying convention.

17. Hamilton's essays are printed in *Hamilton Papers*, vol. 4, 287–717. Apart from the original text, a good representative of the immense secondary literature is David Epstein, *The Political Theory of the Federalist* (Chicago: University of Chicago Press, 1984). Hamilton also invited Gouverneur Morris and William Duer to participate. Morris declined because of other commitments. Duer wrote two essays that were not included in the collected papers. See Chernow, *Alexander Hamilton*, 246–250.

18. On newspaper support for the Constitution, see Jeffrey L. Pasley, *"The Tyranny of Printers": Newspaper Politics in the Early Republic* (Charlottesville: University Press of Virginia, 2001), 43.

19. Hamilton, speech at the New York Ratifying Convention, Poughkeepsie, June 17, 1788, *Hamilton Papers*, vol. 5, 102. In the very large literature on the nature and history of nationalism, Hamilton's thoughts and feelings are effectively captured by Isaiah Berlin's definition of the term: "the belief in the overriding need to belong to a nation; in the organic relationships of all the elements that constitute a nation; in the value of our own simply because it is ours; and, finally, faced by rival contenders for authority or loyalty, in the supremacy of its claims." See "Nationalism: Past Neglect and Present Power," in Berlin, *Against the Current: Essays in the History of Ideas* (New York: Viking, 1980), 342, 345.

20. Chernow, *Alexander Hamilton*, 286–288; Charles Rappleye, *Robert Morris: Financier of the American Revolution* (New York: Simon and Schuster, 2010), 454–455. In their accounts of Washington's offer to Morris, both authors rely on George Washington Parke Custis, *Recollections and Private Memoirs of Washington* (Washington, DC: W. H. Moore, 1857), written by Washington's step-

grandson. So the evidence is thin and inconclusive, as it often is in matters of appointments offered and declined, and there seems to be no better evidence to the contrary. Madison had earlier reported to Jefferson that the leading candidates for secretary of the treasury were Hamilton, John Jay, and Robert Livingston of New York, who, Madison added, wanted the job but would not get it. See Madison to Jefferson, May 27, 1789, in James Morton Smith, ed., *The Republic of Letters: The Correspondence between Thomas Jefferson and James Madison, 1776–1826* (New York: Norton, 1995), vol. 1, 613. A month later he informed Jefferson that of the candidates, "Hamilton is most talked of." Madison to Jefferson, June 30, 1789, ibid., 622. Madison went on to say that members of Congress "are disqualified" from the post, but Robert Morris was not chosen as senator from Pennsylvania until September 1789, several months after his conversation with Washington.

21. On debtors' prisons and changing attitudes toward private debt in general, see Bruce H. Mann, *Republic of Debtors: Bankruptcy in the Age of American Independence* (Cambridge, MA: Harvard University Press, 2003).

8. NEW GOVERNMENT, OLD DEBT

1. The chief exceptions were the large loan in 1803 for the Louisiana Purchase, and heavy taxes imposed during wartime, the Civil War in particular.

2. Congress passed the Tariff Act two months before the creation of the Treasury Department and Hamilton's appointment as secretary. Washington signed the measure on July 4, 1789. Duties were raised periodically during the 1790s and early 1800s because of the need for increased revenue. It is difficult to attach a precise percentage to the overall tariff because general import duties, which started at 5–10 percent, were supplemented by much higher duties on specific items. For a fuller explanation, see Douglas A. Irwin, "Revenue or Reciprocity? Founding Feuds over U.S. Trade Policy," in *Founding Choices: American Economic Policy in the 1790s*, ed. Irwin and Richard Sylla (Chicago: University of Chicago Press, 2011), 100–105.

3. Many historians and biographers have commented on Hamilton's conception of his role as secretary. See, for example, Ron Chernow, *Alexander Hamilton* (New York: Penguin, 2004), 287–297.

4. Hamilton to Morris, April 30, 1781, *The Papers of Alexander Hamilton*, ed. Harold Syrett et al. (New York: Columbia University Press, 1961–1978), vol. 2, 604–605 (hereafter cited as *Hamilton Papers*). On some of the sources of Hamilton's ideas, see Robert J. Parks, *European Origins of the Economic Ideas of Alexander Hamilton* (New York: Ayer, 1977), 75–91. Parks notes that "Gale's theory of interest [Samuel Gale, *An Essay on the Nature and Principles of Public Credit* (London, 1786), 4–5, 9] is similar to the peculiar theory advanced by Hamilton . . . Gale theorized that the value of a given quantity of money was determined by [what modern economists would call] its velocity ('circulating

force'), rather than by the ratio of the quantity of money to the quantity of goods. But the rate of interest was not related to the value of money, because interest was a comparison between capital and returns, both of which were in terms of money." For additional speculations about the influence on Hamilton of other writers, see the editors' extensive commentary in *Hamilton Papers*, vol. 6, 51–69. The most powerful single influence was likely Jacques Necker (sometimes spelled "Neckar"), the French finance minister, who was a native of Geneva. See Donald F. Swanson and Andrew P. Trout, "Alexander Hamilton, 'the Celebrated Mr. Neckar,' and Public Credit," *William and Mary Quarterly* 47 (1990), 422–430. Some, but by no means all, of the ideas of both Robert Morris and Hamilton seem to echo the arguments of Sir James Steuart, a prominent British writer who represented the chief foil against whom Adam Smith composed *The Wealth of Nations*. Steuart, however, was much more a mercantilist than either Hamilton or Morris.

5. Broadus Mitchell, *Alexander Hamilton: The National Adventure, 1788–1804* (New York: Macmillan, 1962), 357–358. The best source on the vital customs service and related issues is Gautham Rao, "The Creation of the American State: Customhouses, Law, and Commerce in the Age of Revolution" (Ph.D. diss., University of Chicago, 2008).

6. Jefferson's feelings are expressed in many places, perhaps most fully in his long letter to George Washington of May 23, 1792. See *The Papers of Thomas Jefferson* (Princeton, NJ: Princeton University Press, 1990), ed. Charles T. Cullen, vol. 23, 535–540.

7. Quoted in Jacob Cooke, *Alexander Hamilton: A Profile* (New York: Hill and Wang, 1967), 74–75.

8. Gerald Stourzh, *Alexander Hamilton and the Idea of Republican Government* (Stanford: Stanford University Press, 1970), 39, 82–83. Of the large literature on Hamilton, this book is a neglected classic.

9. Hamilton, speech at the New York Ratifying Convention, June 25, 1788, *Hamilton Papers*, vol. 5, 80–81.

10. Jefferson to Madison, Dec. 20, 1787, in *The Republic of Letters: The Correspondence between Thomas Jefferson and James Madison, 1776–1826*, ed. James Morton Smith (New York: Norton, 1995), vol. 1, 512–514. Max M. Edling, in *A Revolution in Favor of Government: Origins of the U.S. Constitution and the Making of the American State* (New York: Oxford University Press, 2003), shows how the nationalists construed the Constitution as enabling the new United States to protect its interests in a world of warring powers. Edling perhaps overstates his case, but he adds a dimension to the long-running debates over the views of Hamilton, who worried constantly about this question, and Jefferson, who was less concerned with it.

11. Of the many students of Hamilton's state building, one of the most insightful is James Willard Hurst, the leading scholar of American legal history. Hurst's vast body of work concentrates on economic policymaking through the shaping of the legal system. His comments on Hamilton are worth quoting:

First, his concern was almost exclusively with promoting overall capacity to produce goods and services. Conversely, he showed almost no concern with the quantity or quality of consumer satisfactions . . . His official recommendations dealt with the condition of the factors of production appraised as wholes—the labor supply, the available stock of investment capital, the sum of farm production . . . Aptly for his prime interests, he focused his analysis of public policy on what he termed "aggregate" concerns of commerce and industry . . . He stands almost alone through the nineteenth century—John Quincy Adams and Henry Clay the only notable competitors among public men—for the reach of his ambition to deal with economic aggregates . . . The third salient characteristic of his approach to law and the economy was his pioneering effort to contrive a socially desirable allocation of functions among government, the dispersed market of Adam Smith, and an elite cadre of investment and entrepreneurial talent. Underlying his interest in a tripartite division of economic management was the premise that creative talent and energetic will were chronically in short supply.

Hurst goes on to argue that "Jacksonian democracy and Whig theft of Jacksonian symbols submerged public policy attention to Hamilton's entrepreneurial elite. The turbulent growth of big business after the Civil War either diverted attention from government's potential positive roles in economic development or fostered laissez-faire fictions which denied legitimacy to government intervention while ignoring subsidies to business hidden in tax structures and behind façades of inadequate public regulation." Hurst, "Alexander Hamilton, Law Maker," *Columbia Law Review* 78 (1978), 508–510.

12. In Britain by the time of the expensive Seven Years War (1756–1763), critics had argued that the huge national debt might actually bankrupt the nation. The philosopher David Hume, after reviewing the pros and cons, concluded that "it must, indeed, be one of these two events; either the nation must destroy public credit, or public credit will destroy the nation." Hume's good friend Adam Smith agreed. So did Thomas Jefferson and his followers. On the other hand, many writers in Britain and elsewhere took a more flexible approach. Credit, they argued, was essential for the routine conduct of business, and certainly for long-term investment. Consumer borrowing was usually a bad idea, but businesses obviously needed credit—to carry their inventories and to give the businesses time to grow. Farmers required credit as well, to tide them over from the planting season to the harvest and sale of their crops. See, in general, Julian Hoppit, "Attitudes to Credit in Britain, 1680–1790," *Historical Journal* 33 (1990), 305–322; and Bruce H. Mann, *Republic of Debtors: Bankruptcy in the Age of American Independence* (Cambridge, MA: Harvard University Press, 2002). Hume is quoted in Parks, *European Origins of the Economic Ideas of Alexander Hamilton,* 75. Ironically, one of Hume's most devoted readers was Hamilton, who agreed with most of Hume's principles but not this one.

13. See the early chapters of Stephen Mihm, *A Nation of Counterfeiters: Capitalists, Con Men, and the Making of the United States* (Cambridge, MA: Harvard University Press, 2007).

14. E. James Ferguson, *The Power of the Purse: A History of American Public Finance* (Chapel Hill: University of North Carolina Press for the Institute of Early American History, 1961), 330–333.

15. The serious concerns about internal peace and national defense raised by Hamilton and other delegates at the Constitutional Convention are developed at length in David C. Hendrickson, *Peace Pact: The Lost World of the American Founding* (Lawrence: University Press of Kansas, 2003). On Hamilton's own thinking about how to balance the capacity for waging war with the maintenance of personal liberty within the new nation, see Karl-Friedrich Walling, *Republican Empire: Alexander Hamilton on War and Free Government* (Lawrence: University Press of Kansas, 1999).

16. Accounts of Hamilton's general approach to the American public debt include the following authoritative sources: the extensive notes by the editors of *Hamilton Papers*, vol. 6, 51–68; Richard Sylla, "Financial Foundations: Public Credit, the National Bank, and Securities Markets," in Irwin and Sylla, *Founding Choices*, 61–68; Ferguson, *Power of the Purse*, chs. 13–15; Max M. Edling, "'So Immense a Power in the Affairs of War': Alexander Hamilton and the Restoration of Public Credit," *William and Mary Quarterly* 64 (2007), 287–326; Swanson and Trout, "Alexander Hamilton, 'the Celebrated Mr. Neckar,' and Public Credit"; and Robert E. Wright, *One Nation under Debt: Hamilton, Jefferson, and the History of What We Owe* (New York: McGraw-Hill, 2008). Of the Hamilton biographies, those by Broadus Mitchell and Forrest McDonald are the most perceptive on Hamilton's fiscal program.

9. THE FIGHT OVER THE DEBT

1. Hamilton, *Report Relative to a Provision for the Support of Public Credit*, Treasury Department, Jan. 9, 1790, in *The Papers of Alexander Hamilton* (New York: Columbia University Press, 1971–1978), ed. Harold Syrett et al., vol. 6, 51–96 (hereafter cited as *Hamilton Papers*). The comment about "the price of liberty" is on p. 69. The *Report*'s length is about 40,000 words, the equivalent of 130 pages in a book of average size today.

2. Then, for eventual (very long-term) extinguishment of the entire national debt, Hamilton suggested a "sinking fund"—the setting aside, each year, of an unspecified amount of money toward repayment of the principal. Because the debt was so immense, this idea had only symbolic importance at the time, but for political reasons it was important to include the provision for a sinking fund. For a fuller and slightly different take, see Donald F. Swanson and Andrew P. Trout, "Alexander Hamilton's Hidden Sinking Fund," *William and Mary Quarterly* 49 (1992), 108–116.

3. Specific details of Hamilton's *Report* are ably analyzed in many sources.

The best analyses of his plan have come from modern financial historians, who understand the technical sophistication of what he was doing better than either his contemporaries or other analysts over the 180 years following 1790 were able to appreciate. The works of Richard Sylla, Robert E. Wright, Donald F. Swanson, Andrew P. Trout, and Forrest McDonald stand out in this literature.

4. Richard Sylla, "Financial Foundations: Public Credit, the National Bank, and Securities Markets," in *Founding Choices: American Economic Policies in the 1790s*, ed. Douglas A. Irwin and Richard Sylla (Chicago: University of Chicago Press, 2011), 73. The income numbers for the years 1789 through 1793 derive from Sylla's remarkable discovery of documents in the Van Eeghen collection at the University of Amsterdam. Van Eeghen & Co. were Dutch investors apparently performing due diligence on the prospects of the new United States, and Sylla comments that the listed figures "I surmise were created by the Treasury for the information of Congress at the time" (p. 73, note 3). These numbers, if they exist in the United States, have apparently not yet been discovered.

For 1789 and 1790, I have used the estimate of $74 million for the debt. The official debt figures begin in 1791. As of January 1 of each year, they were as follows: 1791, $75.5 million; 1792, $77.2 million; 1793, $80.4 million; 1794, $78.4 million; 1795, $80.7 million. See www.treasurydirect.gov/govt/reports/pd/histdebt/histdebt.htm, 1791–1849 (accessed 10/24/11).

5. I have calculated debt-to-income ratios here primarily because both the numerator and denominator are established and determinate hard numbers. In macroeconomic theory, a better index would be debt as a percentage of gross domestic product (GDP). But GDP is an invention of the twentieth century and can only be estimated for the years in question. Those estimates also show a very sharp drop in the relative burden of the debt after the implementation of Hamilton's program. Measured by estimates in nominal GDP, the approximate percentage of debt to nominal GDP was 31 in 1790, 18 in 1795, 15 in 1800, 6 in 1810, and 12 in 1815, the last number reflecting the financial impact of the War of 1812. See Douglas A. Irwin, "Revenue or Reciprocity? Founding Feuds over Early U.S. Trade Policy," in Irwin and Sylla, *Founding Choices*, 104, 115.

6. Hamilton, *Report Relative to a Provision for the Support of Public Credit*, in *Hamilton Papers*, vol. 6, 73.

7. Madison's objections are recorded in *Debates and Proceedings of the Congress of the United States* (Washington, DC: Gales and Seaton, 1834–1856), vol. 11, 1192–1196. His apparent changes of mind are contentious issues among historians. See, for example, Gordon S. Wood, "Is There a 'James Madison Problem'?" in Wood, *Revolutionary Characters: What Made the Founders Different* (New York: Penguin, 2006), ch. 4, esp. 152–156 and the endnotes, 290–294.

8. Hamilton, "The Continentalist," No. 6 (July 4, 1782), in *Hamilton Papers*, vol. 3, 102.

9. The Hamilton-Madison split has long intrigued historians, many of whom attribute the change to Madison's growing alliance with Jefferson. There can be little question that both Jefferson and Madison were upset that Hamilton's funding plan—and especially the assumption of state debts—would enrich persons

whom they thought of as "speculators," many of whom had come into the South and bought up old certificates of state debts. For the precise extent of these purchases, state by state, see Whitney K. Bates, "Northern Speculators and Southern State Debts: 1790," *William and Mary Quarterly* 19 (1962), 30–48.

Recent research suggests that an equally important origin of the split between Madison and Hamilton lay in a shift in Hamilton's attitude toward Britain. In *Federalist* No. 11 (1788), Hamilton had criticized Britain harshly. But once he became secretary in 1789, he realized that Britain's heavy exports to the United States provided a rich harvest of customs duties indispensable to his financial program. Meanwhile, Madison and Jefferson remained militantly anti-British, a stance that divided national politics during the 1790s and eventually helped to bring on Jefferson's Embargo of 1807 and "Mr. Madison's War" of 1812. See Michael Schwarz, "The Great Divergence Reconsidered: Hamilton, Madison, and U.S.-British Relations, 1783–89," *Journal of the Early Republic* 27 (2007), 407–436; and Ron Chernow, *Alexander Hamilton* (New York: Penguin, 2004), 304–306.

10. Manning proposed instead that Congress redeem "Domestick Securityes" at full face value only for original holders of the debt. Others would receive only 40 percent of the face value. Quoted in Ruth Bogin, "'Measures So Glareingly Unjust': A Response to Hamilton's Funding Plan by William Manning," *William and Mary Quarterly* 46 (1989), 317, 322, 329.

11. The congressman was Joshua Seney, quoted in Donald F. Swanson and Andrew P. Trout, "Alexander Hamilton, Conversion, and Debt Reduction," *Explorations in Economic History* 29 (1992), 423. Hamilton's sentence is from his *Report Relative to a Provision for the Support of Public Credit*, in *Hamilton Papers*, vol. 6, 90–91. This particular option was not adopted, although it well illustrates what Hamilton was trying to do.

12. As modified by Congress, the final law would permit the debt to be paid in twenty-four years. See Swanson and Trout, "Alexander Hamilton's Hidden Sinking Fund," 112–113.

13. It is likely that Hamilton's thinking about the interest rate (and other aspects of his fiscal plan as well) owed more to the widely circulated writings of the French theorist and finance minister Jacques Necker than to any British theorist or particular minister—William Pitt the Younger, for example, the architect of Britain's financial management during this period. Necker had suggested that a debt with a high interest rate should be brought under control via the conversion of outstanding bonds to new ones carrying a lower interest rate. Hamilton called this a "re-loan," and it constituted a vital part of his overall plan. See Donald F. Swanson and Andrew P. Trout, "Alexander Hamilton, 'the Celebrated Mr. Neckar,' and Public Credit," *William and Mary Quarterly* 47 (1990), 422–430.

14. Another option Hamilton put before potential buyers included partial payment of interest through federally owned "Western" lands (in the present Midwest), at twenty cents per acre. These territories had become the property of the federal government through a series of crucial laws passed during the 1780s, and

even after settlers purchased vast acreages, large portions remained federal property as new states were carved out of them.

15. In his words, the five classes were:

I. Those who were for providing for the general debt exclusively of the particular debts on the basis of the subsisting contracts.
II. Those who were for providing separately for the general debt on the principle of a discrimination between original holders and alienees [those to whom holders had alienated (sold) their instruments of credit].
III. Those who were for providing separately for the general debt without that discrimination at arbitrary rates of interest inferior to the stipulated rules.
IV. Those who were for providing for the general debt on the basis of the subsisting contracts and for assuming the particular debts upon an equal provision.
V. Those who were for providing for the general debt at arbitrary rates of interest inferior to the stipulated rates and for assuming the state debts upon an equal provision.

Of these categories, Hamilton regarded the second and fifth as the most difficult for him to manage. See "The Defence of the Funding System" (in *Hamilton Papers*, vol. 19, 2–5), an unpublished 25,000-word explanation Hamilton wrote in July 1795, the year he left the cabinet.

16. On the value Hamilton attached to his youthful experience managing the Cruger enterprise, see Jacob Cooke, *Alexander Hamilton: A Profile* (New York: Hill and Wang, 1967), 4.

17. E. James Ferguson, *The Power of the Purse: A History of Public Finance* (Chapel Hill: University of North Carolina Press, 1961), 310–312. Ferguson goes on to note that New York and Pennsylvania took no strong position either way.

18. Hamilton, "The Defence of the Funding System," July 1795, *Hamilton Papers*, vol. 19, 43ff.

19. The exact details of the compromise remain unknowable, since the only first-hand account comes from Jefferson and he devotes little space to it. Also, he wrote his account two years after the fact. It appears in Jefferson, *The Papers of Thomas Jefferson*, ed. Julian P. Boyd (Princeton, NJ: Princeton University Press, 1965), vol. 17, 205–208. See also Chernow, *Alexander Hamilton*, 326–331; and Ralph Ketcham, *James Madison: A Biography* (New York: Macmillan, 1971), 308–310.

For differing scholarly views, see Jacob E. Cooke, "The Compromise of 1790," *William and Mary Quarterly* 27 (1970), 524–525, which questions several details and places the compromise within a broader context. In response to Cooke, see Kenneth R. Bowling, "Dinner at Jefferson's: A Note on Jacob E. Cooke's 'The Compromise of 1790,'" *William and Mary Quarterly* 28 (1971); the same issue of this journal contains a rebuttal by Cooke. Certainly there was more to the resolution of the issue than the dinner alone. For one thing, Hamilton apparently agreed to make financial concessions to Virginia. For another, there were more than three possibilities for the location of the national capital (that is, sites other than New York, Philadelphia, and what became Washington, D.C.), and congressional supporters of each potential location had to be mollified by Hamilton and Madison. The basic bargain, however, was as I have represented it in the text. For expanded explanations, see Kenneth R. Bowling, *The Creation of Washington, D.C.: The Idea and Location of the American Capital* (Fairfax, VA: George Washington University Press, 1991); and Bob Arnebeck, *Through a Fiery Trial: Building Washington, 1790–1800* (Lanham, MD: Madison Books, 1991).

20. This complex outcome is summarized in many places, but not always very clearly. Three of the best explanations are Forrest McDonald, *Alexander Hamilton* (New York: Norton, 1979), 163–188; Richard Sylla, "Public Credit, the National Bank, and Securities Markets," in Irwin and Sylla, *Founding Choices*, 66–68; and Markus Claudius Cachia-Riedl, "Albert Gallatin and the Politics of the New Nation" (Ph.D. diss., University of California, Berkeley, 1998), 17–20.

21. Ibid. (all three sources).

22. Hamilton, "The Defence of the Funding System," July 1795, *Hamilton Papers*, vol. 19, 4–5.

10. THE BANK OF THE UNITED STATES

1. The original headquarters of the Bank of the United States was Carpenters' Hall on Chestnut Street, where the First Continental Congress had met in 1774. The grand building that later housed the bank was completed in 1797.

A sample of good secondary sources on the state of thinking about money and banking at this time includes E. James Ferguson, *The Power of the Purse: A History of Public Finance* (Chapel Hill: University of North Carolina Press, 1961); Bray Hammond, *Banks and Politics in America from the Revolution to the Civil War* (Princeton, NJ: Princeton University Press, 1957), chs. 1–8; Fritz Redlich, *The Molding of American Banking: Men and Ideas* (New York: Johnson Reprint Corporation, 1968; orig. pub. 1947), chs. 1–2; George David Rappaport, "The Sources and Early Development of Hostility to Banks in Early American Thought" (Ph.D. diss., New York University, 1970); Robert E. Wright, *Origins of Commercial Banking in America, 1750–1800* (Lanham, MD: Rowman and Littlefield, 2001); and Howard Bodenhorn, "Federal and State Commercial Banking in the Federalist Era and Beyond," in *Founding Choices: American Economic Policy in the 1790s*, ed. Douglas A. Irwin and Richard Sylla (Chicago: University of Chicago Press, 2011), 151–176.

2. Two more banks, both very small, were founded during the year of Hamilton's *Report* and the next year: the Bank of Maryland, which began doing business in Baltimore in 1790; and the Bank of Providence, Rhode Island, established in 1791. The combined capital of these two banks was $700,000, as compared to the $10 million that Hamilton's *Report* recommended for the Bank of the United States. See Hammond, *Banks and Politics in America*, 144.

3. Samuel Paterson to Hamilton, Feb. 1791, *The Papers of Alexander Hamil-*

ton, ed. Harold Syrett et al. (New York: Columbia University Press, 1961–1978), vol. 8, 19 (hereafter cited as *Hamilton Papers*). Paterson was a bookseller and auctioneer.

4. *Second Report on the Further Provision Necessary for Establishing Public Credit (Report on a National Bank)*, Dec. 13, 1790, *Hamilton Papers*, vol. 7, 305–341. The quoted passage is on p. 307. One of the best sources on the Bank is David Cowen, *The Origins and Economic Impact of the First Bank of the United States, 1791–1797* (New York: Garland, 2000).

5. *Hamilton Papers*, vol. 7, 308. On Hamilton's five-to-one reserve requirement, see Hammond, *Banks and Politics in America*, 132–140, which emphasizes specie reserves.

Since the closing decades of the twentieth century, reserve requirements have become ever more difficult to enforce as financial innovations have created new kinds of instruments backed by only tiny reserves. Today the "fractional reserve" system permits far higher leverage, closer to twelve-fold; and during the early twenty-first century, inept regulators allowed some institutions routinely to multiply it to thirty-fold and beyond. This huge increase in "leverage"—which for unregulated instruments such as credit default swaps became so high as to be almost incalculable—was one of the major causes of the financial meltdown of 2008.

6. *Hamilton Papers*, vol. 7, 310. The rebuttal of potential objections appears mostly on pp. 310–320. On the total capital of existing banks by the time the Bank of the United States opened its doors, see Hammond, *Banks and Politics in America*, 144.

7. *Hamilton Papers*, vol. 7, 321–332, 331, 335. This last requirement, the $50,000 limit, was often exceeded by large amounts in loans to the federal government, even in the 1790s, but only after authorization by Congress.

8. Ibid., 333. Congress passed the legislation recommended in this *Report* with less controversy than that which attended his other reports.

9. Jefferson to Washington, Feb. 15, 1791, *Jefferson Papers*, ed. Julian P. Boyd (Princeton, NJ: Princeton University Press, 1974), vol. 19, 275–280. Ralph Ketcham, *James Madison: A Biography* (New York: Macmillan, 1971), 321.

10. Hamilton's response to Washington was delivered within a week after it had been requested: "Opinion on the Constitutionality of an Act to Establish a Bank," Feb. 23, 1791, *Hamilton Papers*, vol. 8, 97–134; the passages relevant to this paragraph are on pp. 99–101.

11. Ibid., 99–101. The word "mean," like all words quoted in this book, is in the original.

12. Ibid., 103.

13. Ibid. On Hamilton's drafting of the constitution of the Bank of New York, see Hammond, *Banks and Politics in America*, 65, 142–143.

14. *Hamilton Papers*, vol. 8, 110.

15. Ibid.

16. Ibid., 124.

17. Ibid., 132.

18. In 1819, John Marshall wrote for the Court, "Let the end be legitimate, let it be within the scope of the constitution, and all means which are appropriate, which are plainly adapted to that end, which are not prohibited, but consistent with the letter and spirit of the constitution, are constitutional." This wording closely parallels sections of Hamilton's letter to Washington about the Bank of the United States.

As Hamilton had predicted, the bank earned handsome profits not only for private investors, but also for the federal government. During its first ten years of operation (1792–1802), the bank returned $1.2 million to the Treasury in the form of dividends and sales of government shares to the public. This was about 2.5 times as much as the income from the sale of public lands during the same period. Considering that the initial investment in the bank was $2 million, the government received a return of almost 58 percent during that decade. See Carl Lane, "'A Positive Profit': The Federal Investment in the First Bank of the United States, 1792–1802," *William and Mary Quarterly* 54 (1997), 601–612.

19. Robert E. Wright, "Thomas Willing, 1731–1821: Philadelphia Financier and Forgotten Founding Father," *Pennsylvania History* 63 (1996), 525–560.

20. On state taxation, see Max M. Edling and Mark D. Kaplanoff, "Alexander Hamilton's Fiscal Reform: Transforming the Structure of Taxation in the Early Republic," *William and Mary Quarterly* 61 (2004), 713–744.

21. Apart from Hamilton's own account, which is treated in Chapter 13 below, one of the fullest expositions of the Reynolds affair is in Ron Chernow, *Alexander Hamilton* (New York: Penguin, 2004), 362–370.

22. Bodenhorn, "Federal and State Commercial Banking in the Federalist Era and Beyond," 158–173; Peter L. Rousseau and Richard Sylla, "Emerging Financial Markets and Early U.S. Growth," *Explorations in Economic History* 42 (2005), 1–26.

11. DIVERSIFYING THE ECONOMY

1. Hamilton, *Report on the Subject of Manufactures*, Dec. 5, 1791, in *The Papers of Alexander Hamilton*, ed. Harold Syrett et al. (New York: Columbia University Press, 1961–1978), vol. 10, 293, 294 (hereafter cited as *Hamilton Papers*). The italics are in the original. For a general view of attitudes and activities in American manufacturing during the period from colonial times until about 1830, see Lawrence A. Peskin, *Manufacturing Revolution: The Intellectual Origins of Early American Industry* (Baltimore: Johns Hopkins University Press, 2003).

2. Jefferson, *Notes on the State of Virginia*, ed. William Peden (Chapel Hill: University of North Carolina Press, 1955), 164–165. Jefferson finished the initial version of this book in 1781 and published it privately and anonymously in Paris in 1784. The first edition in the English-speaking world appeared in 1787, from a London publisher.

3. Douglas A. Irwin, "The Aftermath of Hamilton's 'Report on Manufac-

tures,'" *Journal of Economic History* 64 (2004), 804–806; Hamilton, *Report on the Subject of Manufactures*, 291.

4. *Report on the Subject of Manufactures*, 252.

5. Ibid., 255, 256.

6. Ibid., 233, 263.

7. Ibid., 264–265.

8. Ibid., 233, 254.

9. Digges to Hamilton, April 6, 1792, *Hamilton Papers*, vol. 11, 242–244. It is not entirely clear from Digges's letter whether the 18 or 20 craftsmen he had induced to leave had departed from Ireland or England; apparently, Ireland enforced the law less stringently.

10. Ibid.

11. Barbara M. Tucker, *Samuel Slater and the Origins of the American Textile Industry, 1790–1860* (Ithaca, NY: Cornell University Press, 1984); Barbara M. Tucker and Kenneth H. Tucker, *Industrializing America: The Rise of Manufacturing Entrepreneurs in the Early Republic* (New York: Palgrave Macmillan, 1995), ch. 4. On the movement of technology from Britain to America, see Doron S. Ben-Atar, *Trade Secrets* (New Haven, CT: Yale University Press, 2004), which traces attitudes and laws from the late colonial period to about 1830.

12. Ibid. (all three sources). See also James L. Conrad, Jr., "'Drive That Branch': Samuel Slater, the Power Loom, and the Writing of America's Textile History," *Technology and Culture* 36 (1995), 1–28; Caroline F. Ware, *The Early New England Cotton Manufacture* (New York: Macmillan, 1931); and Charles Rappleye, *Sons of Providence: The Brown Brothers, the Slave Trade, and the American Revolution* (New York: Simon and Schuster, 2006).

13. Tucker, *Samuel Slater and the Origins of the American Textile Industry, 1790–1860*. The Hamilton quotation is from *Report on the Subject of Manufactures, Hamilton Papers*, vol. 10, 330. In his *Report*, Hamilton noted with approval that cotton mills and other factories could employ women and children and thereby add to the factory workforce. British manufacturers did this as a matter of course, and Slater did it in his own mill, recruiting entire families. Child labor became one of the banes of the early industrial revolution and persisted as a problem well into the twentieth century, in a way Hamilton did not anticipate.

14. *Report on the Subject of Manufactures*, 267, 281, 290.

15. These changes are proposed in Hamilton's *Report on the Subject of Manufactures* and are presented in useful tabular form in Irwin, "The Aftermath of Hamilton's 'Report on Manufactures,'" 812.

16. Ibid. (both sources).

17. Hamilton, *Report on the Subject of Manufactures*, 299. The discussion of bounties goes on for several pages in the *Report*, as Hamilton considers and attempts to refute all arguments against them.

18. Ibid., 283. The strongest advocate of the Society for the Establishment of Useful Manufactures was Tench Coxe, one of Hamilton's assistants in the Treasury Department. Coxe also helped to draft the *Report on the Subject of Manufactures*. See Jacob E. Cooke, "Tench Coxe, Alexander Hamilton, and the En-

couragement of Manufactures," *William and Mary Quarterly* 32 (1975), 370–392. Most accounts accord Coxe a smaller role in the *Report* than does Cooke's.

On the premature aspects of the Society for the Establishment of Useful Manufactures, see Stanley Elkins and Eric McKitrick, *The Age of Federalism* (New York: Oxford University Press, 1993), 262–263, 279–280. It did not help matters that William Duer, who had been assistant secretary of the treasury, was closely associated with the society. Duer had been forced out of his post at the Treasury because of his insider trading. Then, too, the funding of the society coincided with the financial panic of 1792, for which Duer was largely responsible. For an interpretation of the society as Hamilton's attempt to force a top-down development of manufacturing controlled by the federal government, see Andrew Shankman, "'A New Thing on Earth': Alexander Hamilton, Pro-Manufacturing Republicans, and the Democratization of the American Political Economy," *Journal of the Early Republic* 23 (2003), 323–352.

19. Joseph A. Schumpeter, *History of Economic Analysis* (New York: Oxford University Press, 1954), 199.

20. James Willard Hurst, "Alexander Hamilton, Law Maker," *Columbia Law Review* 78 (1978), 509–513.

21. For this before-and-after portrait and for numerous other insights about Hamilton and the U.S. financial system, all scholars of the early Republic are much indebted to Richard Sylla. In addition to other citations in this chapter, see Sylla, "U.S. Securities Markets and the Banking System, 1790–1840," *Federal Reserve Bank of St. Louis Review* 80 (1998), 83–93; Sylla, "Financial Systems and Economic Modernization," *Journal of Economic History* 62 (2002), 277–292; Sylla, "Hamilton and the Federalist Financial Revolution, 1789–1795," *New-York Journal of American History* (2004), 32–39; Sylla, Robert E. Wright, and David J. Cowen, "Alexander Hamilton, Central Banker: Crisis Management during the U.S. Financial Panic of 1792," *Business History Review* 83 (2009), 61–86; and Sylla, "Financial Foundations: Public Credit, the National Bank, and Securities Markets," in Douglas A. Irwin and Richard Sylla, eds., *Founding Choices: American Economic Policy in the 1790s* (Chicago: University of Chicago Press, 2011), 59–88. See also Richard Brookhiser, *Alexander Hamilton, American* (New York: Free Press, 1999), 120.

22. For a good discussion of corporations, including the numbers cited here, see Robert E. Wright, "Rise of the Corporation Nation," in Irwin and Sylla, *Founding Choices*, 217–258.

23. Like nearly all aspects of Hamilton's career, his contribution to American economic growth is the subject of a large and often controversial literature. The historian Joyce Appleby, in *Capitalism and the New Social Order,* makes an interesting argument that this release of energy derived from Jeffersonian individualism, and that the Federalist mindset as exemplified by Hamilton and others was too upper-class in orientation to cause a broad release of energy throughout American society. She is more charitable to Hamilton's contributions in her book *The Relentless Revolution: A History of Capitalism* (New York: Norton, 2010),

174. Even stronger deemphases on the Hamiltonian contribution are John R. Nelson Jr., *Liberty and Property: Political Economy and Economic Policymaking in the New Nation, 1789–1812* (Baltimore: Johns Hopkins University Press, 1987); and Carey Roberts, "Alexander Hamilton and the 1790s Economy: A Reappraisal," in Douglas Ambrose and Robert W. T. Martin, eds., *The Many Faces of Alexander Hamilton* (New York: New York University Press, 2006), 211–230.

My own reading of the evidence is closer to that of most scholars of the Hamilton economic program. E. A. J. Johnson, *The Foundations of American Economic Freedom: Government and Enterprise in the Age of Washington* (Minneapolis: University of Minnesota Press, 1973), presents a powerful argument for the sophistication and success of the Hamiltonian program. Drew R. McCoy, *The Elusive Republic: Political Economy in Jeffersonian America* (Chapel Hill: University of North Carolina Press, 1980), posits a modern, technology-oriented, interdependent Hamiltonian capitalism against a Jeffersonian ideal of agrarianism mixed with household manufactures, leading to a household autarky of the type Jefferson himself tried to create at Monticello. One of the broadest analyses of some of the issues at stake here is Gordon S. Wood, *The Radicalism of the American Revolution* (New York: Knopf, 1991), Part III.

Most important of all are the many recent books and articles on Hamilton by authors such as Richard Sylla, Doron Ben-Atar, Robert Wright, Douglas A. Irwin, and David Cowen. These scholars tend to employ modern finance theory and new research (such as Wright's identification of who purchased the federal bonds issued after Congress enacted Hamilton's funding and assumption program), to fill out the excellent portraits of Hamilton's work drawn by the biographers who focus on his financial innovations: John C. Miller, Broadus Mitchell, and Forrest McDonald.

24. Appleby, *Capitalism and a New Social Order,* 76. The best estimate of what is now called "growth of gross domestic product per capita" is on the order of at least 1 percent per year during the 1790s, as compared to estimates of zero at worst and 0.3 to 0.5 at best per year during the colonial period. Numbers for the 1770s, 1780s, and early 1800s remain less clear. See Irwin and Sylla, eds., "Introduction," *Founding Choices,* 4.

25. Hamilton's achievements in these areas are well documented in many of the essays in Irwin and Sylla, eds., *Founding Choices;* Gerald Stourzh, *Alexander Hamilton and the Idea of Republican Government* (Stanford, CA: Stanford University Press, 1970); Gautham Rao, "The Creation of the American State: Customhouses, Law, and Commerce in the Age of Revolution" (Ph.D. diss., University of Chicago, 2008); Frederick A. L. Dalzell, "Taxation with Representation: Federal Revenues in the Early Republic" (Ph.D. diss., Harvard University, 1993); and Ron Chernow, *Alexander Hamilton* (New York: Penguin, 2004). On the dysfunctional British system and the legal aspects of changes wrought after independence, see Daniel Hulsebosch, *Constituting Empire: New York and the Transformation of Constitutionalism in the Atlantic World, 1664–1830* (Chapel Hill: University of North Carolina Press, 2009).

26. Leonard D. White, *The Federalists: A Study in Administrative History* (New York: Macmillan, 1948), 125–126.

27. Theodore Roosevelt, *New York* (London: Longmans, Green, 1891), republished in *The Works of Theodore Roosevelt,* 20 vols. (New York: Charles Scribner's Sons), vol. 10, 485.

12. TENSIONS AND POLITICAL PARTIES

1. Hamilton, *The Federalist* No. 9, *Independent Journal,* Nov. 21, 1787, available at www.constitution.org/fed/federa09.htm (accessed 9/23/11).

2. *Federalist* No. 10, *Daily Advertiser,* Nov. 22, 1787, available at www .constitution.org/fed/federa10.htm (accessed 9/23/11).

3. *California Democratic Party v. Jones,* 530 U.S. 567, 592.

4. Hamilton to Edward Carrington, May 26, 1792, *The Papers of Alexander Hamilton,* ed. Harold Syrett et al. (New York: Columbia University Press, 1961–1978), vol. 11, 427 (hereafter cited as *Hamilton Papers*). Carrington, a Virginian nine years older than Hamilton, had been a lieutenant colonel during the Revolution, serving as General Nathanael Greene's quartermaster and as an artillery commander at the siege of Yorktown. He was later a delegate to the Confederation Congress, and then, under the new Constitution, was appointed by Washington as a U.S. marshal in Virginia. In the last sentence of the quotation, I have added parentheses around the numbers for greater clarity.

5. Madison is quoted in Charles Rappleye, *Robert Morris: Financier of the American Revolution* (New York: Simon and Schuster, 2010), 340. Hamilton to Carrington, May 26, 1792, *Hamilton Papers,* vol. 11, 429.

6. Hamilton to Carrington, May 26, 1792, *Hamilton Papers,* vol. 11, 427–428.

7. Ibid.

8. Michael Schwarz, "The Great Divergence Reconsidered: Hamilton, Madison, and U.S.-British Relations, 1783–89," *Journal of the Early Republic* 27 (2007), 407–436.

9. Hamilton to Carrington, May 26, 1792, *Hamilton Papers,* vol. 11, 428–430.

10. Ibid., 440, 441, 442.

11. Ibid., 429, 440, 441, 442.

12. Jefferson to Washington, May 23, 1792, *Papers of Thomas Jefferson,* ed. Charles T. Cullen (Princeton, NJ: Princeton University Press, 1990), vol. 23, 535–540 (hereafter cited as *Jefferson Papers*).

13. Ibid.; Robert E. Wright, *One Nation under Debt: Hamilton, Jefferson, and the History of What We Owe* (New York: McGraw-Hill, 2008), ch. 6.

14. Washington to Hamilton, July 29, 1792, *Hamilton Papers,* vol. 12, 129–133; Hamilton to Washington, Aug. 18, 1792, ibid., 228–258; Washington to Hamilton, Aug. 26, 1792, ibid., 276–277; Washington to Jefferson, Aug. 23, 1792, *Jefferson Papers,* ed. John Catanzariti, 1990, vol. 24, 317.

15. Hamilton to Washington, Sept. 9, 1792, *Hamilton Papers,* vol. 12, 347–

350; Jefferson to Washington, Sept. 9, 1792, *Jefferson Papers,* vol. 24, 351–359. The spelling and punctuation are as in the originals. Jefferson's passion on these issues is also reflected in the length of the letter he wrote Washington. It is more than twice as long as that of Hamilton, who usually composed far longer documents than his opponents.

In Hamilton's letter to Edward Carrington of May 26, 1792, he had addressed many of the charges against him (charges which he omitted from his letter to Washington):

> I am told that serious apprehensions are disseminated in your state as to the existence of a Monarchical party meditating the destruction of State & Republican Government . . . I assure you on my *private faith* and *honor* as a Man that there is not in my judgment a shadow of foundation of it.
>
> As to the destruction of State Governments, the *great* and *real* anxiety is to be able to preserve the National from the too potent and counteracting influence of those Governments. As to my own political Creed, I give it to you with the utmost sincerity. I am *affectionately* attached to the Republican theory. I desire *above all things* to see the *equality* of political rights exclusive of all *hereditary* distinction firmly established by a practical demonstration of its being consistent with the order and happiness of society.
>
> As to State Governments, the prevailing byass of my judgment is that if they can be circumscribed within bounds consistent with the preservation of the National Government they will prove useful and salutary. If the States were all of the size of Connecticut, Maryland or New Jersey, I should decidedly regard the local Governments as both safe & useful. As the thing now is, however, I acknowledge the most serious apprehensions that the Government of the U States will not be able to maintain itself against their influence.
>
> Hence a disposition on my part towards a liberal construction of the powers of the National Government and to erect every fence to guard it from depredations, which is, in my opinion, consistent with constitutional propriety . . .
>
> I said, that I was *affectionately* attached to the Republican theory. This is the real language of my heart which I open to you in the sincerity of friendship; & I add that I have strong hopes of the success of that theory; but in candor I ought also to add that I am far from being without doubts. I consider its success as yet a problem . . .
>
> On the whole, the only enemy which Republicanism has to fear in this Country is in the Spirit of faction and anarchy. If this will not permit the ends of Government to be attained under it—if it engenders disorders in the community, all regular & orderly minds will wish for a change—and the demagogues who have produced the disorder will make it for their own aggrandizement. This is the old Story.
>
> If I were disposed to promote Monarchy & overthrow State Govern-

ments, I would mount the hobby horse of popularity—I would cry out usurpation—danger to liberty &c. &c—I would endeavour to prostrate the National Government—raise a ferment—and then "ride in the Whirlwind and direct the Storm."

Hamilton Papers, vol. 11, 443–444.

16. Hamilton to John Jay, Dec. 18, 1792, *Hamilton Papers,* vol. 13, 338.

17. The resolutions are printed in *Jefferson Papers,* ed. John Catanzariti, 1993, vol. 25, 294–296. For the emotional toll on Hamilton of the repeated attacks and intrigues against him, see Ron Chernow, *Alexander Hamilton* (New York: Penguin, 2004), 422–430.

18. Hamilton to Edward Carrington, May 26, 1792, *Hamilton Papers,* vol. 11, 439. Hamilton, as he went on to say, judged Madison and Jefferson to *"have a womanish attachment to France and a womanish resentment against Great Britain . . .* In France he [i.e., Jefferson, who had spent the years 1784–1789 in Paris] saw government only on the side of its abuses. He drank deeply of the French Philosophy, in Religion, in Science, in politics. He came from France in the moment of a fermentation which he had had a share in exciting . . . He came here [as secretary of state] probably with a too partial idea of his own powers, and with the expectation of a greater share in the direction of our councils than he has in reality enjoyed." On the general issue of anti-British feeling, see Lawrence A. Peskin, "Conspiratorial Anglophobia and the War of 1812," *Journal of American History* 98 (2011), 647–669, which includes an analysis of the phenomenon during the late eighteenth century, as well as during the years immediately preceding the War of 1812.

19. Americanus No. II, Feb. 7, 1794, *Dunlap and Claypool's American Daily Advertiser* (Philadelphia), *Hamilton Papers,* vol. 16, 13. The American government's heavy dependence on import duties levied on British goods has been recognized by many historians of this period, but its overwhelming significance has often not been sufficiently emphasized. Two exceptions are Jerald A. Combs, *The Jay Treaty: Political Background of the Founding Fathers* (Berkeley: University of California Press, 1970), 40–44; and Douglas A. Irwin, "Revenue or Reciprocity? Founding Feuds over Early U.S. Trade Policy," in Irwin and Richard Sylla, eds., *Founding Choices: American Economic Policy in the 1790s* (Chicago: University of Chicago Press, 2011).

20. Washington to Hamilton, Feb. 2, 1795, *Hamilton Papers,* vol. 18, 247–248. Again all nonstandard spellings, including "wch," are in the original. In a reply the next day, Hamilton wrote:

My particular acknowledgements are due for your very kind letter of yesterday. As often as I may recall the vexations I have endured, your approbation will be a great and precious consolation.

It was not without a struggle, that I yielded to the very urgent motives, which impelled me to relinquish a station, in which I could hope to be in any degree instrumental in promoting the success of an administration under your direction; a struggle which would have been far greater, had I supposed that the prospect of future usefulness was proportioned to the sacrifices to be made.

Whatsoever may be my destination hereafter, I entreat you to be persuaded (not the less for my having been sparing in professions) that I shall never cease to render a just tribute to those eminent and excellent qualities which have been already productive of so many blessings to your country.

Ibid., 253. In the parenthesis to this last sentence, Hamilton likely had in mind his self-maintained personal distance from Washington, dating back to their close relationship and occasional quarrels during their service together in the Continental Army from 1777 to 1781.

21. Jefferson to Madison, Sept. 21, 1795, in James Morton Smith, ed., *The Republic of Letters: The Correspondence between Jefferson and Madison, 1776–1826* (New York: Norton, 1995), vol. 2, 898.

22. Hamilton, "The Defence of the Funding System," unpublished, July 1795, *Hamilton Papers*, vol. 19, 24. A thorough analysis of Hamilton's attitude toward foreign affairs is John Lamberton Harper, *American Machiavelli: Alexander Hamilton and the Origins of U.S. Foreign Policy* (Cambridge: Cambridge University Press, 2004).

23. For the texts of the essays and editorial commentary, see *Hamilton Papers*, vol. 18, 475ff. On Hamilton and the issues involved in the Jay Treaty, see Harper, *American Machiavelli*, chs. 10–13.

24. Jefferson to Madison, Sept. 21, 1795, *Republic of Letters*, vol. 2, 897. Jefferson's letter contains very strong words about the Jay Treaty: "A bolder party-stroke was never struck. For it is certainly an attempt of a party which finds they have lost their majority in one branch of the legislature [the House] to make a law by the aid of the other branch, and of the executive, under color of a treaty, which shall bind up the hands of the adverse branch from ever restraining the commerce of their patron-nation [Britain]."

25. *Hamilton Papers*, vol. 18, 477–479.

26. David Hackett Fischer, *Albion's Seed: Four British Folkways in North America* (New York: Oxford University Press, 1989), 842. Here "the North" is defined as New England and the Middle Atlantic region.

27. On the Washington-Madison split, see Stuart Leibiger, *Founding Friendship: George Washington, James Madison, and the Creation of the American Republic* (Charlottesville: University Press of Virginia, 1999), 207–209.

28. Todd Estes, *The Jay Treaty Debate, Public Opinion, and the Evolution of Early American Political Culture* (Amherst: University of Massachusetts Press, 2006). On the details of the treaty's preparation, Samuel Flagg Bemis, *Jay's Treaty: A Study in Commerce and Diplomacy* (New York: Macmillan, 1923), is still useful. See also Combs, *The Jay Treaty;* and Bradford Perkins, *The First Rapprochement: England and the United States, 1795–1805* (Philadelphia: University of Pennsylvania Press, 1955).

29. Gordon S. Wood, in his otherwise excellent *Revolutionary Characters:*

What Made the Founders Different (New York: Penguin, 2007), titles his chapter on Hamilton "Alexander Hamilton and the Making of a Fiscal-Military State," and repeats the characterization in *Empire of Liberty: A History of the Early Republic, 1789–1815* (New York: Oxford University Press, 2009). A more fully developed argument appears in Max M. Edling, *A Revolution in Favor of Government: Origins of the U.S. Constitution and the Making of the American State* (New York: Oxford University Press, 2003). Edling does not single out Hamilton in quite the way Wood does, but attributes the goal of a strong nation-state to the nationalists ("Federalists," as they were called in the 1780s before the rise of the party system) who attended the Constitutional Convention, and to those who secured the ratification of the Constitution in the states. Other scholars have mentioned the "fiscal-military state" in similar arguments about Hamilton, as if the point were self-evident. The phrase "fiscal-military state" was popularized by John Brewer's seminal book, *The Sinews of Power: War, Money, and the English State, 1688–1783* (London: Routledge, 1989), and subsequently applied to other European countries. See, among many examples, Jan Glete, *Spain, the Dutch Republic and Sweden as Fiscal-Military States, 1500–1660* (London: Routledge, 2002); and Christopher Storrs, ed., *The Fiscal-Military State in Eighteenth-Century Europe* (Farnham, U.K.: Ashgate, 2009), which contains essays on Austria, Britain, France, Prussia, Russia, and Sardinia. Philip Harlig and Peter Mandler, "From 'Fiscal-Military State' to Laissez-Faire State, 1760–1850," *Journal of British Studies* 32 (1993), 44–70, amends the argument about Britain by carrying it into the nineteenth century.

For the United States, the idea and reality of a "fiscal-military state" simply do not fit the political economy of the early Republic. They apply much more aptly to the vast American national security state as it began to evolve 145 years later, when World War II began. As Max M. Edling's own work shows, they apply better to the war with Mexico (1846–1848) and subsequent acquisitions of territory than to Hamilton's time, and even then are based primarily on the high credit rating of the United States in international capital markets. See Edling, "When Johnny Comes Marching Home . . . from the Bank: War and Finances in America, from the U.S.-Mexican War to the Present," *Common-Place* (2008), 1–8, www .common-place.org/vol-09/no-01/edling/ (accessed 1/13/12). See also Edling, "The Problem of American State Formation: Politics of Taxation and the Creation of the Federal Government," Working Paper no. 01013 (Jan. 1998), Harvard University International Seminar on the History of the Atlantic World. Here, Edling's data show that even in times of peace (Britain in 1790; the United States in 1793, after Hamilton's program was in place), the central government's burden on British taxpayers was roughly seven times what it was on the Americans (pp. 16–17).

30. Joyce Appleby, *Capitalism and a New Social Order: The Republican Vision of the 1790s* (New York: New York University Press, 1984), 76. Richard R. John, *Spreading the News: The American Postal Service, from Franklin to Morse* (Cambridge, MA: Harvard University Press, 1995), chs. 1–2.

31. Benjamin Franklin had begun his career as a boy in a printing shop and

then—wholly atypical of most printers—had grown rich from his writings, especially *Poor Richard's Almanack*. He had retired in his forties to devote himself to science and public service. Jeffrey L. Pasley, *"The Tyranny of Printers": Newspaper Politics in the Early American Republic* (Charlottesville: University Press of Virginia, 2001), chs. 1–3 and 7. As Pasley points out, the contrast between working class and gentlemen in the printing trade was less true in the South, where, because of the agrarian dominance of the region, educated men had fewer opportunities and more of them gravitated to journalism. Then, too, during and after the 1790s, southern newspapers earned substantial amounts of money by publishing advertisements for the return of runaway slaves. On newspapers generally, see also Carol Sue Humphrey, *The Press of the Young Republic, 1783–1833* (Westport, CT: Greenwood Press, 1996).

32. Pasley, *"The Tyranny of Printers,"* ch. 3. John Adams's famous translation of and commentary on *Discourses on Davila*—political essays in part critical of the French Revolution—originally appeared in Fenno's *Gazette*.

33. Freneau also attempted, without much success, to build a subscription-by-mail business. In Virginia, James Madison himself promoted this effort, and on occasions when the papers did not arrive in the mail, many subscribers complained to him rather than to Freneau. Pasley, *"The Tyranny of Printers,"* 63–66.

34. Ibid., 74. This episode may have contributed to Jefferson's resignation from the State Department in December 1793.

35. Ibid., 63–72.

36. For a sprightly analysis by a twentieth-century broadcaster, see Eric Burns, *Infamous Scribblers: The Founding Fathers and the Rowdy Beginnings of American Journalism* (New York: Public Affairs, 1996).

37. Benjamin Franklin had died in 1790 at the age of eighty-four, and Bache—a well-educated favorite of his grandfather—inherited the modern printing shop and equipment that Franklin had purchased with him in mind. When Bache wrote to some of his grandfather's friends for advice, announcing his intention to publish a newspaper, he received discouraging replies. As Robert Morris told him, "Some of your friends here are rather sorry for your intention . . . They seem to entertain the opinion that you might be more honorably & more lucratively employed by the Printing of Books." But Bache went ahead. He soon earned the nickname "Lightning Rod Junior" after one of Franklin's most famous inventions. Three good sources on Bache and his career are Pasley, *"The Tyranny of Printers,"* ch. 4 (the quotation from Morris is on p. 82); James Tagg, *Benjamin Franklin Bache and the Philadelphia Aurora* (Philadelphia: University of Pennsylvania Press, 1991); and Jeffery A. Smith, *Franklin and Bache: Envisioning the Enlightened Republic* (New York: Oxford University Press, 1990).

38. As his hostile tone against the administration mounted, Bache was twice physically attacked, the second time by John Fenno Jr., whose father Bache had condemned in print. Pasley, *"The Tyranny of Printers,"* 97.

39. Quoted in Pasley, *"The Tyranny of Printers,"* 88. The same epidemic killed John Fenno, the editor of the *Gazette of the United States*.

13. THE DECLINE

1. Most historical accounts take a dim view of James Callender. A partial exception is Michael Durey, *"With the Hammer of Truth": James Thomson Callender and America's Early National Heroes* (Charlottesville: University Press of Virginia, 1990), the most thorough biography.

2. Ron Chernow, *Alexander Hamilton* (New York: Penguin, 2004), 537–542.

3. See *The Papers of Alexander Hamilton*, ed. Harold Syrett et al. (New York: Columbia University Press, 1961–1978), vol. 21, 121–267 (hereafter cited as *Hamilton Papers*), for the full account, along with the editors' comments. The Reynolds affair is also treated fully in Chernow, *Alexander Hamilton*, chs. 19, 21, and 30.

4. *Hamilton Papers*, vol. 21, 238–240.

5. Ibid., 239–240.

6. Ibid., 250.

7. Ibid., 250–251.

8. Ibid., 251.

9. Ibid.

10. Ibid., 252.

11. Ibid., 253. Hamilton mentions $1,000 in two payments. He made additional payments of at least $100.

12. Hamilton's old roommate and friend Robert Troup commented that Hamilton's "ill-judged pamphlet has done him inconceivable harm." Both he and Webster are quoted in Chernow, *Alexander Hamilton,* 535. On the possible similarity of Maria Reynolds and Rachel Faucett, see Jacob Cooke, *Alexander Hamilton: A Profile* (New York: Hill and Wang, 1967), 183.

13. *Hamilton Papers,* vol. 21, 261. The point about Hamilton's sense of honor is well argued in Andrew S. Trees, *The Founding Fathers and the Politics of Character* (Princeton, NJ: Princeton University Press, 2004), ch. 2.

14. Chernow, *Alexander Hamilton,* 534, 542–544.

15. Callender is quoted in *Hamilton Papers*, vol. 21, 139–140; Madison to Jefferson, Oct. 20, 1797, ed. James Morton Smith, *The Republic of Letters: The Correspondence between Jefferson and Madison* (New York: Norton, 1995), vol. 2, 993.

16. Adams is quoted in Cooke, *Alexander Hamilton*, 176, 183.

17. When the Jefferson-Hemings relationship is supposed to have begun, he was in his mid-forties, she in her mid-to-late teens. Other presidential sexual scandals included Grover Cleveland's likely paternity of a child (he was a bachelor practicing law in Buffalo at the time); Warren G. Harding's alleged affair with Nan Britton, who published a book after Harding's death asserting that he had fathered her child (Harding did have affairs, but likely none with Nan Britton); and John F. Kennedy's many alleged liaisons while he was president, publicly disclosed after his death.

18. Manning J. Dauer, *The Adams Federalists* (Baltimore: Johns Hopkins University Press, 1953), though out of date in some respects, shows Adams's short-

comings as a party leader and how he allowed his supporters either to drift into the Jeffersonian camp or to keep taking their cues from Hamilton, by default.

19. On Hamilton, Adams, the army, and the quasi-war, see John Lemberton Harper, *American Machiavelli: Alexander Hamilton and the Origins of U.S. Foreign Policy* (New York: Cambridge University Press, 2004), 191–247.

20. The critique of Adams was published as "Letter from Alexander Hamilton, Concerning the Public Conduct and Character of John Adams, Esq. President of the United States," Oct. 24, 1800, *Hamilton Papers,* vol. 25, 169–178ff.

21. On Philip Hamilton's duel, see *Hamilton Papers,* vol. 26, 237.

22. Hamilton to Morris, Feb. 27, 1802, *Hamilton Papers,* vol. 25, 544. Hamilton went on to say, "Every day proves to me more and more that this American world was not made for me"—an even stronger measure of his depression.

23. Hamilton to Tobias Lear, Jan. 2, 1800, *Hamilton Papers,* vol. 24, 155.

24. Adams is quoted in John Ferling, *John Adams* (New York: Henry Holt, 1992), 394.

14. THE DUEL

1. As one might expect of such a dramatic episode, there are many accounts of the duel. Here I have relied mostly on the evidence presented by the editors of *The Papers of Alexander Hamilton,* ed. Harold Syrett et al. (New York: Columbia University Press, 1961–1978), vol. 25, 235–349 (hereafter cited as *Hamilton Papers*). See also Ron Chernow, *Alexander Hamilton* (New York: Penguin, 2004), 680–719. Thomas Fleming, *The Duel: Alexander Hamilton, Aaron Burr, and the Future of America* (New York: Basic Books, 1999), is a colorful popular account. More scholarly are W. J. Rorabaugh, "The Political Duel in the Early Republic: Burr v. Hamilton," *Journal of the Early Republic* 15 (1995), 1–23; and Joanne B. Freeman, "Dueling as Politics: Reinterpreting the Burr-Hamilton Duel," *William and Mary Quarterly* 53 (1996), 289–318.

2. Two years after that, in 1799, Burr himself challenged John Church, the husband of Eliza Hamilton's sister Angelica. Church had evidently commented that Burr had accepted a bribe from a land company. In this case the duel occurred, but after the first shots by both men missed, Church apologized and the duel ended.

3. In the large literature on Burr, one of the most insightful interpretations is Gordon Wood's essay "The Real Treason of Aaron Burr," in Wood's book *Revolutionary Characters: What Made the Founders Different* (New York: Penguin, 2006), ch. 8. In 1807 Burr was tried for treason in connection with a scheme involving a separation of western lands from the United States. He was acquitted. Wood's title alludes to that trial, but he goes on to say that "Burr was a traitor not to his country but to his class." That is, unlike Washington, Hamilton, Jefferson, Madison, and other founders, Burr put his own interests first and those of his country second.

4. After the duel, these written thoughts were retrieved from a safe-deposit

box and published in the *New York Evening Post,* the newspaper Hamilton had founded; see *Hamilton Papers,* vol. 26, 278–280. See also Chernow, *Alexander Hamilton,* 694–697, 700–704.

5. *Hamilton Papers,* vol. 26, 293.

15. CHOOSING THE NEW WORLD

1. In Part II of this book I have benefited much from the primary sources re-produced in the long biography by Henry Adams, *The Life of Albert Gallatin* (Philadelphia: Lippincott, 1879), which contains the entire texts of numerous let-ters to and from Gallatin and excerpts from many more. Adams also edited three thick volumes of Gallatin's papers, mostly dealing with his public life: *The Writings of Albert Gallatin* (Philadelphia: Lippincott, 1879; rpt. New York: Antiquar-ian Press, 1960). *Selected Writings of Albert Gallatin,* ed. E. James Ferguson (In-dianapolis: Bobbs-Merrill, 1967), has also been indispensable. Together these five volumes contain full texts or long excerpts of almost all of Gallatin's important papers. The full collection is deposited at the New-York Historical Society and includes additional personal correspondence of friends and family members to and from Gallatin.

Of the biographical and other analytical materials on Gallatin, the most useful are Raymond Walters Jr., *Albert Gallatin: Jeffersonian Financier and Diplomat* (New York: Macmillan, 1957), a fine work of scholarship half the length of Henry Adams's more discursive biography; Markus Claudius Cachia-Riedl, "Al-bert Gallatin and the Politics of the New Nation" (Ph.D. diss., University of Cali-fornia, Berkeley, 1998), a superior piece of work; and Nicholas Dungan, *Gallatin: America's Swiss Founding Father* (New York: New York University Press, 2010), a brief volume that captures Gallatin's character about as well as anything else written about him. Alexander Balinky, *Albert Gallatin: Fiscal Theories and Poli-cies* (New Brunswick, NJ: Rutgers University Press, 1958), is an economist's in-teresting evaluation that I characterize briefly in Part III of this book.

2. As Gallatin himself recalled, "The principal questions in which I was en-gaged related to constitutional construction or to the finances. Though not quite so orthodox in the first subject as my Virginia friends (witness the U. States Bank and internal improvements) [Gallatin supported the former, unlike Jefferson and Madison, and promoted the latter more than they did] I was opposed to any usurpation of powers by the General Government." Gallatin, fragment of an au-tobiographical sketch, in Gallatin, *Selected Writings of Albert Gallatin,* ed. Fer-guson, 12. One might argue that DeWitt Clinton did more to open the West, through his promotion of the Erie Canal. But Clinton was not a federal official, the canal was a project of the State of New York, and it did not fully open until 1825.

3. Ibid., 12. Gallatin wrote these lines in 1849, shortly before his death at the age of eighty-eight. For a physical description of Gallatin, see William Dunlap, *Diary* (New York: New-York Historical Society, 1930), vol. 2, 384. Dunlap was a contemporary painter and dramatist.

4. Only Hamilton and Gallatin, Adams judged, "have had at once the breadth of mind to grapple with the machinery of government as a whole and the authority necessary to make it work efficiently for a given object; the practical knowledge of affairs that enabled them to foresee every movement; the long apprenticeship which allowed them to educate and discipline their parties; and finally the good fortune to enjoy power when government was still plastic and capable of receiving a new impulse." Adams, *Life of Albert Gallatin,* 267–268. In his writings generally, Adams tended to be more generous in his judgments of Gallatin than of Jefferson. But see also the similar conclusions of Rozann Rothmann, "Political Method in the Federal System: Albert Gallatin's Contribution," *Publius* 1 (Winter 1972), 123–141; and Jay C. Heinlein, "Albert Gallatin: A Pioneer in Public Administration," *William and Mary Quarterly* 7 (Jan. 1950), 64–94.

5. Adams, *Life of Albert Gallatin,* 269, and, for many other references to the "triumvirate," *passim.* The quotation from Josiah Quincy appears ibid., 470. Quincy served in the House of Representatives from 1805 until 1813. He was mayor of Boston from 1823 to 1828, and president of Harvard University from 1829 to 1845.

6. Walters, *Albert Gallatin,* 1–2.

7. Gallatin to Eben Dodge, Jan. 21, 1847, *Selected Writings of Albert Gallatin,* ed. Ferguson, 4.

8. Walters, *Gallatin,* 3–7; Dungan, *Gallatin,* 15.

9. Where not otherwise noted, the following account in this chapter of Gallatin's move to America and his early experiences there is best documented in Walters, *Gallatin,* chs. 1–2; in the early pages of Adams, *Life of Gallatin;* in Dungan, *Gallatin,* ch. 2; and in Edwin G. Burrows, "'Notes on Settling America': Albert Gallatin, New England, and the American Revolution," *New England Quarterly* 58 (1985), 442–453, which contains long passages of letters Gallatin wrote to Jean Badollet and other friends in Geneva during his first three years in North America.

16. MOVING TO THE WEST

1. Gallatin to Eben Dodge, Jan. 21, 1847, in *Selected Writings of Albert Gallatin,* ed. E. James Ferguson (Indianapolis: Bobbs-Merrill, 1967), 4–5.

2. Gallatin to Jean Badollet, Oct. 29, 1780, "'Notes on Settling America': Albert Gallatin, New England, and the American Revolution," ed. Edwin G. Burrows, *New England Quarterly* 58 (1985), 444.

3. The second-largest state, and—if one counts all its claimed territory—perhaps the largest, was Georgia, which then included the present states of Alabama and Mississippi, in addition to other areas. But Georgia had far fewer people and much less influence than Virginia.

4. Leonard D. White, *The Jeffersonians: A Study in Administrative History, 1801–1829* (New York: Macmillan, 1951), 475.

5. Nicholas Dungan, *Gallatin: America's Swiss Founding Father* (New York:

New York University Press, 2010), 35. Dungan is quoting a letter from Gallatin to his friend William Maxwell written many years later, in 1848.

6. Gallatin himself had mixed feelings about Native Americans. Their presence and periodic alliances with British fur traders inconvenienced the westward movement of U.S. settlers. Meanwhile, however, Gallatin became fascinated with their culture—an interest he pursued avidly late in his life.

7. Quoted in Raymond Walters Jr., *Albert Gallatin: Jeffersonian Financier and Diplomat* (New York: Macmillan, 1957), 22.

8. Walters, *Gallatin*, 17–23. Gallatin's property was on land once claimed by Virginia, and it is possible that when he made his original purchases he believed himself to be buying Virginia land.

9. Quoted in Walters, *Gallatin*, 16. See also Dungan, *Gallatin*, 37–38. The following paragraphs combine information from Gallatin's letters and papers with material from the Adams, Walters, and Dungan biographies.

10. Gallatin's ambitions to become a large landowner still ran high, and his speculative impulses had not diminished. See Henry Dater, "Albert Gallatin— Land Speculator," *Mississippi Valley Historical Review* 26 (1939), 21–38. Dater overstates his case here, but not by much.

11. James O'Hara, who emigrated from Ireland to North America in 1772, organized the Pittsburgh Glass Works in 1797, which prospered in the early nineteenth century using the same strategy Gallatin had envisioned—shipping products down the Ohio and Mississippi Rivers, as well as to local and eastern markets. O'Hara died in 1819 and the works were leased to a succession of operators for the next two generations. He and his partners were better capitalized, and they succeeded where Gallatin's group failed. (This is not the same company as the giant Pittsburgh Plate Glass, which was founded in 1883.) For the early history of the Pittsburgh Glass Works, see Richard Wade, *The Urban Frontier: The Rise of Western Cities, 1790–1830* (Cambridge, MA: Harvard University Press, 1959), 48.

12. Quoted in Walters, *Gallatin*, 23.

13. Quoted ibid., 24.

14. Gallatin to Catherine Pictet, April 7, 1790, printed in Henry Adams, *The Life of Albert Gallatin* (Philadelphia: Lippincott, 1879), 75.

15. Pictet to Gallatin, July [n.d.] 1790, ibid.

17. ENTERING POLITICS

1. Gallatin to Jean Badollet, Sept. 3, 1836, *The Correspondence of John [Jean] Badollet and Albert Gallatin, 1804–1836*, ed. Gayle Thornbrough (Indianapolis: Indiana Historical Society, 1963), 323.

2. Gallatin, fragment of an autobiographical sketch, *Selected Writings of Albert Gallatin*, ed. E. James Ferguson (Indianapolis: Bobbs-Merrill, 1967), 8–10. Gallatin's program for Pennsylvania at this time in many ways paralleled Hamilton's for the federal government, the aim of both being to put public finance on a

sound footing. The main difference was circumstantial: Pennsylvania could provide foreseeably for the full payment of the principal of its debt, whereas the federal government could only pay the interest on its own. So their policies necessarily differed. See Markus Claudius Cachia-Riedl, "Albert Gallatin and the Politics of the New Nation" (Ph.D. diss., University of California, Berkeley, 1998), 27–30; and Gallatin's own recollections of his aims, printed in Henry Adams, *The Life of Albert Gallatin* (Philadelphia: Lippincott, 1879), 85–87.

3. Gallatin, fragment of an autobiographical sketch, *Selected Writings of Albert Gallatin,* ed. Ferguson, 8–10. The excerpt from the resolution on slavery is quoted in Raymond Walters Jr., *Albert Gallatin: Jeffersonian Financier and Diplomat* (New York: Macmillan, 1957), 376.

4. See Thomas P. Slaughter, *The Whiskey Rebellion: Frontier Epilogue to the American Revolution* (New York: Oxford University Press, 1986).

5. Ibid.

6. A perceptive interpretation of Gallatin's attitude toward the whiskey tax as it related to his larger political philosophy can be found in Edwin G. Burrows, *Albert Gallatin and the Political Economy of Republicanism, 1761–1800* (New York: Garland, 1986), 309–376. Burrows covers Gallatin's role in the controversy over a period of four years, from beginning to end.

7. Slaughter, *The Whiskey Rebellion;* Gallatin, Speech in Pennsylvania House of Representatives, Jan. 3, 1795, in *The Writings of Albert Gallatin,* ed. Henry Adams (Philadelphia: Lippincott, 1879), vol. 3, 7.

8. Walters, *Gallatin,* 52–53.

9. Quoted in Nicholas Dungan, *Gallatin: America's Swiss Founding Father* (New York: New York University Press, 2010), 51, 53–54.

10. Commodore Nicholson's letter is quoted ibid., 54.

11. Gallatin to Hannah Gallatin, Aug. 23, 1793, printed in Adams, *The Life of Albert Gallatin,* 103.

12. Three of the Gallatins' four daughters died in infancy.

13. Walters, *Gallatin,* 13.

14. Ibid., 59–63.

15. Richard H. Kohn, "The Washington Administration's Decision to Crush the Whiskey Rebellion," *Journal of American History* 59 (1972), 567–584.

16. Hamilton to Angelica Church, Oct. 23, 1794, in *The Papers of Alexander Hamilton,* ed. Harold Syrett et al. (New York: Columbia University Press, 1961–1978), vol. 27, 340; Jacob E. Cooke, "The Whiskey Insurrection: A Re-Evaluation," *Pennsylvania History* 30 (1963), 316–364.

18. BECOMING JEFFERSONIAN

1. Madison to Jefferson, Jan. 31, 1796, *The Republic of Letters: The Correspondence between Thomas Jefferson and James Madison,* ed. James Morton Smith (New York: Norton, 1995), vol. 2, 917.

2. Jefferson to Madison, March 6, 1796, ibid., 922.

3. Gallatin, *A Sketch of the Finances of the United States,* in *The Writings of Albert Gallatin,* ed. Henry Adams (Philadelphia: Lippincott), vol. 3, 69–206.

4. Ibid., 146–150 and *passim.*

5. From this total in Gallatin's table he deducts $40,000 for bounties to fisheries from imports and tonnage, to yield a net revenue of $6,370,000 (ibid., 97). At this time the signs for dollars and cents were not commonly used. Instead, phrases such as "100 dollars and 25/100ths of a dollar" were employed for what we would now call $100.25. Vestiges of this practice appear today on the "amount" line of personal checks.

6. Gallatin, *Sketch of the Finances,* 103.

7. Ibid., 104.

8. Madison to Jefferson, March 9, 1794, *The Republic of Letters,* ed. Smith, vol. 2, 835; Gallatin, *Sketch of the Finances,* 104.

9. Gallatin, *Sketch of the Finances,* 104–105. The actual number of militiamen was closer to 12,500, but the difference was not important.

10. Thomas Jefferson to William Stephens Smith, Nov. 13, 1787, online at www.monticello.org/site/jefferson/tree-liberty-quotation (accessed 5/3/12). Full accounts may be found in David Szatmary, *Shays' Rebellion: The Making of an Agrarian Insurrection* (Amherst: University of Massachusetts Press, 1980); and Leonard S. Richards, *Shays' Rebellion: The American Revolution's Final Battle* (Philadelphia: University of Pennsylvania Press, 2002).

11. Gallatin, *Sketch of the Finances,* 121–129.

12. Ibid., 146.

13. Ibid., 131. Gallatin goes on to say that assumption benefited some states at the expense of others, which was true enough; but he also says that the states themselves could have handled their own debts, which was not true—at least not without the kinds of taxation Gallatin and the Jeffersonians abhorred. The most lucrative source of income by far, which was duties on imported goods, was not available to the states after 1789, when the Constitution went into effect.

14. Ibid., 133.

15. Specifically, Gallatin wrote: "A demand was created for six millions of dollars in that species of [Bank of the United States] stock, which, added to one million of dollars in different species purchased in the same year (1791) by the commissioners of the sinking fund, was sufficient to raise the price of the whole debt, consisting of six per cent. stock, to its nominal value." Ibid., 133–134.

16. Gallatin also reiterated the original objection "that Congress had not, by the Constitution, a power to incorporate any public bodies, created a serious opposition to this measure, and has left many enemies to the institution." Here he was reminding partisans of one of the big reasons they had opposed the Bank of the United States in the first place. Ibid., 135–136.

17. Ibid., 144.

18. Ibid., 145.

19. Ibid., 145–150. In the ellipsis, Gallatin writes "annual defalcation of five millions," by which he means inappropriate use of funds by Hamilton as a fiduciary, not the modern equivalent of "embezzlement." His only point is that the

debt was too high in the first place, and his use of the word "defalcation" here was misleading.

20. Ibid., 147, 165–168.

21. On the Republicans' dread that the Revolution had been betrayed by Hamilton's policies, see Lance Banning, *The Jeffersonian Persuasion: Evolution of a Party Ideology* (Ithaca, NY: Cornell University Press, 1978).

22. At this time, Gallatin had not studied finance to the extent Hamilton had. Yet he did understand the theory well. In 1879, Henry Cabot Lodge referred to Gallatin as a "theorist." See Lodge, "Albert Gallatin," *International Review* 7 (1879), 264.

19. THE CLIMB TO POWER

1. The election of 1796 remains the only one in American history in which candidates from opposing parties won the two top offices. The idea of "running mates" had not yet matured, though many people understood that Thomas Pinckney of South Carolina was the Federalists' second choice and Aaron Burr of New York the Republicans'. In the Electoral College, Adams received 71 votes, Jefferson 68, Pinckney 59, Burr 30. The remaining votes were split among eight other candidates.

2. Gallatin to Lewis F. de Lesdernier, May 15, 1798, *The Writings of Albert Gallatin*, ed. Henry Adams (Philadelphia: Lippincott, 1879), vol. 1, 15.

3. Most biographies of Adams blame Hamilton. See David McCullough, *John Adams* (New York: Simon and Schuster, 2001), and John F. Ferling, *John Adams: A Life* (Knoxville: University of Tennessee Press, 1992). More balanced is Manning J. Dauer, *The Adams Federalists* (Baltimore: Johns Hopkins University Press, 1953).

4. The fullest source on Wolcott is George Gibbs, *Memoirs of the Administrations of Washington and John Adams, Edited from the Papers of Oliver Wolcott, Secretary of the Treasury*, 2 vols. (New York, printed for the subscribers, 1846). These volumes contain an abundance of letters that Wolcott exchanged with Hamilton, his father (who was serving in the Senate during part of the period), and numerous other officials. See also Neil Alexander, "Connecticut Order, Mercantilistic Economics: The Life of Oliver Wolcott, Jr." (Ph.D. diss., University of Tennessee, Knoxville, 1988); and Robert Jay Dilger, "Oliver Wolcott Jr.: Conspirator or Public Servant?" *Connecticut Historical Society Bulletin* 46 (July 1981), 78–85.

Adams is quoted in James McHenry to Hamilton, June 2, 1800, in *The Papers of Alexander Hamilton*, ed. Harold Syrett et al. (New York: Columbia University Press, 1961–78), vol. 24, 558 (hereafter cited as *Hamilton Papers*).

5. Markus Claudius Cachia-Riedl, "Albert Gallatin and the Politics of the New Nation" (Ph.D. diss., University of California, Berkeley, 1998), 108, 118, 120, 121.

6. In the early twenty-first century, the waiting period for naturalized citizenship was five years, with many exceptions such as for spouses of citizens.

7. See Jefferson to James Madison, April 26, 1798, and Feb. 26, 1799, in *The Republic of Letters: The Correspondence between Jefferson and Madison, 1776–1826,* ed. James Morton Smith (New York: Norton, 1995), vol. 2, 1042, 1100.

8. On newspapers of this period, see Jeffrey L. Pasley, *"The Tyranny of Printers": Newspaper Politics in the Early Republic* (Charlottesville: University Press of Virginia, 2001); and Marcus Daniel, *Scandal and Civility: Journalism and the Birth of American Democracy* (New York: Oxford University Press, 2009).

9. For the texts of the Kentucky and Virginia resolutions as finally passed, see www.constitution.org/cons/kent1798.htm and www.constitution.org/cons/virg 1798.htm (accessed 4/3/11). Jefferson had drafted the Kentucky Resolution for the legislature of North Carolina, but one of his political allies shifted it to Kentucky with his assent.

10. Madison was a capable legal thinker. See Mary Sarah Bilder, "James Madison: Law Student and Demi-Lawyer," *Law and History Review* 28 (2010), 389–449.

11. Standard secondary sources include James Morton Smith, *Freedom's Fetters: The Alien and Sedition Laws and American Civil Liberties* (Ithaca, NY: Cornell University Press, 1956), a careful study; and William J. Watkins Jr., *Reclaiming the American Revolution: The Kentucky and Virginia Resolutions and Their Legacy* (New York: Palgrave Macmillan, 2004), which presents a pro-Republican interpretation. The Kentucky and Virginia resolutions were submitted to other state legislatures as well, none of which passed them. The Sedition Act expired at the end of the Adams administration in 1801, and the other laws were modified in various ways. When Jefferson became president, he pardoned all ten of the persons (many of them Republican journalists) whom the Federalists had successfully prosecuted under the laws. The issue of whether Jefferson would have been elected in 1800 had his composition of the Kentucky Resolution been known is raised and answered with the phrase "probably not" by Garry Wills in *James Madison* (New York: Times Books, 2002), 50.

12. Among the many good sources covering this dilemma for part or all of its duration, two of the fullest are Stanley Elkins and Eric McKitrick, *The Age of Federalism: The Early Republic, 1788–1800* (New York: Oxford University Press, 1993); and Gordon S. Wood, *Empire of Liberty: A History of the Early Republic, 1789–1815* (New York: Oxford University Press, 2009).

13. Albert Gallatin to Hannah Nicholson Gallatin, Jan. 15, 1801, printed in Henry Adams, *The Life of Albert Gallatin* (Philadelphia: Lippincott, 1879), 252–253. On living conditions in Washington, Gallatin later wrote Jefferson that his "best clerk next to the principal, and who had twelve hundred dollars, has left me to take one thousand in Philadelphia . . . Under the present circumstances of this place, we must calculate on paying higher all the inferior offices, principally clerks, than in Philadelphia." Gallatin to Jefferson, Sept. 18, 1804, *Writings of Albert Gallatin,* ed. Adams, vol. 1, 208.

14. Albert Gallatin to Hannah Nicholson Gallatin, Jan. 15, 1801, printed in Adams, *Life of Albert Gallatin,* 252–253. See also James Sterling Young, *The*

Washington Community, 1800–1828 (New York: Columbia University Press, 1966).

15. Albert Gallatin to Hannah Nicholson Gallatin, Jan. 15, 1801, quoted in Richard Mannix, "Albert Gallatin in Washington, 1801–1813," *Records of the Columbia Historical Society* (Washington, DC: 1971/1972), Book 48, 61.

16. Hannah Nicholson Gallatin to Albert Gallatin, Feb. 5, 1801, ibid., 65.

17. There are many accounts of this famous election, which was even more complicated than my summary here suggests. Three of the best are John Ferling, *Adams vs. Jefferson: The Tumultuous Election of 1800* (New York: Oxford University Press, 2004); Susan Dunn, *Jefferson's Second Revolution: The Election Crisis of 1800 and the Triumph of Republicanism* (Boston: Houghton Mifflin, 2004); and Edward J. Larson, *A Magnificent Catastrophe: The Tumultuous Election of 1800, America's First Presidential Campaign* (New York: Free Press, 2007).

18. On Jefferson's idea of a Constitutional Convention, see Raymond Walters Jr., *Albert Gallatin: Jeffersonian Financier and Diplomat* (New York: Macmillan, 1957), 129n.

19. Hamilton to Oliver Wolcott, Dec. 16, 1800, in *Hamilton Papers*, vol. 25, 257; Hamilton to James A. Bayard, Dec. 27, 1800, ibid., 275–277; see also Hamilton to Bayard, Jan. 16, 1801, ibid., 319–320. Hamilton's overall role is summarized in Ron Chernow, *Alexander Hamilton* (New York: Penguin, 2004), 630–639.

20. That this was the essence of the "Revolution of 1800" is strongly argued in Wood, *Empire of Liberty*. See also two books by Joyce Appleby: *Capitalism and a New Social Order: The Republican Vision of the 1790s* (New York: New York University Press, 1984); and *Inheriting the Revolution: The First Generation of Americans* (Cambridge, MA: Harvard University Press, 2000). Christopher Clark, like Appleby, presents a bottom-up view of the origins of American capitalism in his book *Social Change in America: From the Revolution through the Civil War* (New York: Ivan Dee, 2006). James Horn, Jan Ellen Lewis, and Peter S. Onuf, eds., *The Revolution of 1800: Democracy, Race, and the New Republic* (Charlottesville: University of Virginia Press, 2002) is a useful collection of sixteen essays on a variety of social and political topics. Some of the essayists suggest that the Revolution of 1800 harmed certain elements of society. James Sidbury, for example, points out that the Louisiana Purchase and the end of the overseas slave trade promoted the U.S. internal market for slaves—a market that developed as white-owned plantations moved westward, breaking up very large numbers of slave families.

21. An exception might be made for the Civil War, when Southern senators and congressmen left the Capitol. But even then, the split between Democrats and Republicans did not change this much. The numbers cited cannot be precise, because party identifications were not firm. See Kenneth C. Martis, *The Historical Atlas of Political Parties in the United States Congress, 1789–1989* (Englewood Cliffs, NJ: Prentice-Hall, 1989). The very large literature on the ideological

and societal changes behind these voting patterns is well delineated in Wood, *Empire of Liberty*, which also contains an ample bibliography of other works on the subject.

20. DEBT, ARMAMENTS, AND LOUISIANA

1. Richard Mannix, "Albert Gallatin in Washington, 1801–1813," *Records of the Columbia Historical Society* (Washington, DC: 1971–1972), book 48, 67. Jefferson is quoted in Raymond Walters Jr., *Albert Gallatin: Jeffersonian Financier and Diplomat* (New York: Macmillan), 141.

2. Gallatin to Maria Nicholson, March 12, 1801, printed in Henry Adams, *The Life of Albert Gallatin* (Philadelphia: Lippincott, 1879), 275.

3. After Hannah and the children joined Gallatin in the new capital city, the family lived briefly in Georgetown and then in a house near the Executive Mansion, before moving to Capitol Hill, which Hannah believed to be a healthier spot. See Mannix, "Albert Gallatin in Washington, 1801–1813," 69.

4. Ibid.

5. On the building and sustaining of the Republican Party, see the old but still useful works by Noble E. Cunningham Jr.: *The Jeffersonian Republicans: The Formation of Party Organization, 1789–1801* (Chapel Hill: University of North Carolina Press, 1957); and *The Jeffersonian Republicans in Power: Party Operations, 1801–1809* (Chapel Hill: University of North Carolina Press, 1963).

6. Adams, *Life of Gallatin*, 279; Jefferson to Gallatin, Jan. 13, 1807, in *The Writings of Albert Gallatin* (Philadelphia: Lippincott, 1879), ed. Henry Adams, vol. 1, 328. The social and educational status of Adams's and Jefferson's appointees is analyzed statistically in Sidney H. Aronson, *Status and Kinship in the Higher Civil Service: Standards of Selection in the Adams, Jefferson, and Jackson Administrations* (Cambridge, MA: Harvard University Press, 1964).

7. Carl E. Prince, "The Passing of the Aristocracy: Jefferson's Removal of the Federalists, 1801–1805," *Journal of American History* 57 (Dec. 1970), 563–575; Markus Claudius Cachia-Riedl, "Albert Gallatin and the Politics of the New Nation" (Ph.D. diss., University of California, Berkeley, 1998), 159–192. See also Noble E. Cunningham, *The Process of Government under Jefferson* (Princeton, NJ: Princeton University Press, 1978); and the still useful Leonard D. White, *The Jeffersonians: A Study in Administrative History, 1801–1829* (New York: Macmillan, 1951). Jefferson's view on partisan appointments, as contrasted with Gallatin's more meritocratic approach, is the theme of Jay C. Heinlein, "Albert Gallatin: A Pioneer in Public Administration," *William and Mary Quarterly* 7 (1950), 64–94, a strongly pro-Gallatin argument.

8. On Badollet, see *The Correspondence of John [Jean] Badollet and Albert Gallatin, 1804–1836*, ed. Gayle Thornbrough (Indianapolis: Indiana Historical Society Publications, 1963). About 90 percent of the material in this 372-page collection consists of letters and other documents Badollet sent to Gallatin. Badollet's annual salary in Vincennes, $500, was the equivalent of about $7,200

in the early twenty-first century, but these numbers aren't really comparable; a federal position of similar responsibility would likely pay at least $100,000 today.

9. For a thorough discussion, see Herbert Sloan, *Principle and Interest: Thomas Jefferson and the Problem of Debt* (New York: Oxford University Press, 1995). Jefferson sold these books to the Library of Congress in 1815 for $23,950, a sum equivalent in the early twenty-first century to about $285,000. See www .loc.gov/exhibits/jefferson/jefflib (accessed 4/27/11). His chronic indebtedness was mostly his own fault, but not entirely, since he had inherited additional debts when his wife's father died. But at the time of his own death in 1826, he still owed a great deal of money, the payment of which required the sale of almost all his slaves and of a second large collection of books he had accumulated since 1815.

10. The senator was William Plumer of New Hampshire, quoted in Richard Mannix, "Albert Gallatin in Washington," 76.

11. It might be argued that the Jeffersonians did undermine the Bank of the United States, refusing to recharter it in 1811. But they reinstituted the bank in 1816.

The Jefferson-Gallatin exchange about Hamilton is recounted in Ron Chernow, *Alexander Hamilton* (New York: Penguin, 2004), 647. Its source is not a public document, but a comment attributed to Gallatin in a biography of Hamilton written by his son James, and is therefore not necessarily reliable. Nonetheless, it is true that although Gallatin disagreed with Hamilton's program and often criticized it, he did not regard Hamilton as dishonest. Also, Gallatin reported his exchange to James Hamilton in the 1830s, by which time he was in his seventies and had little reason to be unfair to Hamilton. The same generosity of spirit toward Hamilton was not shared by John Adams, Jefferson, or Madison when they themselves were in their old age.

12. Gallatin, ever mindful of reducing the national debt, favored a delayed repeal of the whiskey excise, but Congress followed Jefferson's wish to end it quickly, and it was repealed in 1802. Overall, Gallatin was more hesitant to abolish internal taxes than was either the president or Congress.

13. Raymond E. Walters Jr., *Albert Gallatin: Jeffersonian Financier and Diplomat* (New York: Macmillan, 1957), 149.

14. For the national debt through the years, see www.treasurydirect.gov/govt/ reports/pd/histdebt/histdebt.htm (accessed 1/2/11).

15. In 1776, the committee appointed to write the Declaration of Independence, and then Congress itself, had softened Jefferson's draft to make many passages less fiery, an action that displeased Jefferson more than a little. At the insistence of delegates from Georgia and South Carolina, a long, provocative, and far-fetched passage that appeared to blame slavery on King George III was deleted altogether.

16. Jefferson's proposal for an amendment eliminating the general-welfare clause came in his message of 1806. See *Writings of Albert Gallatin,* ed. Adams, vol. 1, 320.

17. Ibid., vol. 1, 63, 64. Gallatin's comments on Jefferson's draft message of 1802 appear in full on pp. 63–76.

18. This conviction about the unique nature of the United States is evident throughout Gallatin's writings and in his conduct as secretary of the treasury. For an elaboration, buttressed by figures comparing Gallatin's estimates of federal expenditures, amounts appropriated by Congress, and amounts actually spent for the three years 1802–1804, see Cachia-Riedl, "Albert Gallatin and the Politics of the New Nation," 217–225. In nearly every year except 1802, when Britain and France were at peace and American ships in less danger of capture at sea, military and naval expenditures exceeded Gallatin's estimates. In 1804 the navy spent nearly twice what Gallatin had believed to be necessary.

19. Gallatin to Jefferson, Nov. 16, 1801, printed in Adams, *Life of Gallatin,* 270–271.

20. Ian W. Toll, *Six Frigates: The Epic History of the Founding of the U.S. Navy* (New York: Norton, 2006); Hamilton to Jonathan Dayton, n.d. [Oct.–Nov. 1799], in *The Papers of Alexander Hamilton,* ed. Harold Syrett et al. (New York: Columbia University Press, 1961–1978), vol. 23, 599–604 (hereafter cited as *Hamilton Papers*).

21. Toll, *Six Frigates.* At the suggestion of secretary of war Henry Knox, the frigates were built in different shipyards stretching from New Hampshire to Virginia. This decision by the Federalists assisted the economies of six ports in six states, and it had obvious political as well as military implications. During the Revolutionary War, the victories of John Paul Jones were fought with ships such as the USS *Bonhomme Richard,* built in France.

On the conflict with France, one of the most thorough sources remains Alexander DeConde, *The Quasi-War: Politics and Diplomacy in the Undeclared War with France, 1797–1801* (New York: Scribner, 1966).

22. Alexander S. Balinky, "Albert Gallatin, Naval Foe," *Pennsylvania Magazine of History and Biography* 82 (1958), 293–304.

23. Jefferson remained enamored of cheap gunboats throughout his presidency, despite persistent opposition. In 1807 he wrote a letter to Gallatin insisting that 200 be built. The gunboats were so ineffective that, as Henry Adams later remarked, "Mr. Jefferson was a great man, and like other great men he occasionally committed great follies, yet it may be doubted whether in the whole course of his life he ever wrote anything much more absurd than this letter." Adams, *Life of Gallatin,* 353.

24. Frank Lambert, *The Barbary Wars: American Independence in the Atlantic World* (New York: Hill and Wang, 2005), covers the history of U.S. relations with the Barbary states from 1783 through the Madison administration.

25. When Jefferson was minister to France during the 1780s, he had tried hard to deal reasonably with the Barbary states, as had John Adams, then minister to Britain. Neither had been successful. Decatur, not John Paul Jones, was the first American-born naval hero; the latter, who had been a prominent U.S. commander during the Revolutionary War, was an adventurer born in Scotland who served not only in the American but also in the Russian navy. On the Barbary Wars and

their effect on U.S. culture, see Robert Allison, *The Crescent Obscured: The United States and the Muslim World, 1776–1815: The Legacy of the Barbary Wars* (New York: Oxford University Press, 1995).

26. Reexports, which amounted to a very substantial percentage of all shipments sent from the United States, were designed to avoid mercantile restrictions on direct shipments in American vessels from the country or colony of origin. They were goods landed in America, taxed as imports, and then shipped elsewhere. To the extent that the carrying trade involved reexports, it employed thousands of American sailors and pumped large amounts of money into the economy. But it did not contribute commensurately to federal revenues, because of drawbacks (refunds) of import duties that had been paid when the goods for reexport had originally been landed in American ports. In 1806, Gallatin reported to Congress that the carrying trade accounted for $300,000 of total federal revenues of $11.5 million. Cachia-Riedl, "Albert Gallatin and the Politics of the New Nation," 347.

27. Ibid., 217–225; *Writings of Gallatin*, ed. Adams, vol. 1, 64.

28. The revolution that gave birth to Haiti was a complex affair. It involved Spain and Britain as well as the large French colonial population, which included some free blacks along with masses of enslaved persons. The revolution began in earnest in 1791 and did not officially end until 1804. In 1802, L'Ouverture was deceived by a French expeditionary force with which he had made peace. He was taken to France under promise of safety and executed by Napoleon's government. The French, who had attempted to restore slavery in Haiti, were then defeated again and expelled permanently. In the large literature on the origins of Haiti's independence, one of the best analyses is Laurent Dubois, *Avengers of the New World: The Story of the Haitian Revolution* (Cambridge, MA: Harvard University Press, 2004).

The Napoleonic Wars had a brief respite from March 1802 until May 1803, under the Treaty of Amiens. But neither Britain nor France did much demobilization during this period. Napoleon feverishly built ships and began to mass troops for a possible cross-Channel invasion.

29. For example, Spain had closed the Mississippi to navigation in 1784—a serious blow to Americans living in the West—then restored it for three years under the Treaty of San Lorenzo, negotiated in 1796 by Thomas Pinckney. Before Jefferson became president in 1801, Spain had extended the right of deposit, but only informally. Here matters stood when Spain conveyed Louisiana to France in 1800.

30. Many books treat the Louisiana Purchase. Three of the best syntheses are Alexander DeConde, *This Affair of Louisiana* (New York: Scribner, 1976); Jon Kukla, *A Wilderness So Immense: The Louisiana Purchase and the Destiny of America* (New York: Knopf, 2003); and Peter J. Kastor, *The Nation's Crucible: The Louisiana Purchase and the Creation of America* (New Haven, CT: Yale University Press, 2004).

31. Both Monroe and Livingston were political heavyweights. Monroe was a Revolutionary War veteran, former governor of Virginia, former congressman,

and member of Jefferson's inner circle. Livingston, the scion of a great New York political family, had been a member of the Continental Congress's Committee of Five, which drafted the Declaration of Independence. The other four members of the committee were Benjamin Franklin, John Adams, Roger Sherman, and Jefferson himself, who did most of the work. Livingston had then served as chancellor (chief legal officer) of New York, and in 1789 had sworn in George Washington as the nation's first president.

32. See DeConde, *This Affair of Louisiana;* Kukla, *A Wilderness So Immense;* and Kastor, *The Nation's Crucible.* In addition, see Irving Brant, *James Madison: Secretary of State, 1800–1809* (Indianapolis: Bobbs-Merrill, 1953), 132–134; and Ralph Ketcham, *James Madison* (New York: Macmillan, 1971), 417–422. Authorities differ on whether the timing of the French offer was four days before Monroe's arrival or one day afterward.

33. Hamilton, writing as "Pericles" in the *New York Evening Post,* Feb. 8, 1803, *Hamilton Papers,* vol. 26, 82–85, 129–131. Most Federalists' opposition to the Louisiana Purchase centered on the future empowerment of the West at the political expense of the East; the likelihood that slavery would be extended westward; and what they believed to be a certainty that the Jeffersonians would have fought any such transaction on constitutional grounds, had the Federalists still been in power.

34. Livingston's comment, made at the signing in 1803, is engraved in stone over the entrance to the Louisiana state capitol in Baton Rouge.

35. Gallatin to Jefferson, Jan. 13, 1803, printed in Adams, *Life of Gallatin,* 320–321. See also *Writings of Albert Gallatin,* ed. Adams, vol. 1, 111–114; and Gallatin to Jefferson, Sept. 5, 1803, urging that the United States take immediate possession of New Orleans, lest Spain reassert its former claims (ibid., 153–154).

36. Some sources report the amount of $11.5 million in securities, but the original treaty specifies $11.25 million. See www.archives.gov/exhibits/american _originals/louistxt.html (accessed 8/11/11). Some of the securities went to the American minister in Paris for delivery to the French; the rest, directly to Baring Brothers.

Because of the details of payment, the total outlay for Louisiana was not $15 million, but about $23.5 million—much as a person today buying a house priced at $500,000 might put up $50,000 cash and then pay off a 6 percent mortgage for the remaining $450,000 over fifteen years. Because of interest payments, the total outlay of cash would therefore be far more than the original price of the house.

37. In 1806 John Randolph, a brilliant man who seemed to become more eccentric with each passing year, broke permanently with Jefferson. His unpredictability on almost any issue became a major annoyance in the administrations not only of President Jefferson but also of his successors, James Madison and James Monroe.

38. See, for example, Gallatin to Jefferson, April 13, 1803, *Writings of Gallatin,* ed. Adams, vol. 1, 120–122.

39. Of the ample literature on the Lewis and Clark expedition, one of the best

general treatments is James P. Ronda, *Finding the West: Explorations with Lewis and Clark* (Albuquerque: University of New Mexico Press, 2001). Stephen Dow Beckham et al., *The Literature of the Lewis and Clark Expedition: A Bibliography and Essays* (Portland, OR: Lewis and Clark College, 2003), catalogues and comments on the enormous body of work.

21. DEVELOPING THE WEST

1. This paragraph and the next three draw on Thomas K. McCraw, "American Capitalism," in McCraw, ed., *Creating Modern Capitalism* (Cambridge, MA: Harvard University Press, 1997), 303–304.

2. Paul W. Gates, *History of Public Land Law Development* (Washington, DC: Public Land Law Review Commissions, 1968); Malcolm Rohrbough, *The Land Office Business: The Settlement and Administration of American Public Lands* (New York: Oxford University Press, 1968); Rohrbough, *Trans-Appalachian Frontier: People, Societies, and Institutions, 1775–1850*, 3rd ed. (New York: Oxford University Press, 2008; orig. pub. 1978).

In American historiography, much of the romance of western settlement began to yield with the rise of the "new Western history." One of the best exemplars for the trans-Mississippi West is Patricia Nelson Limerick, who has written two books summarizing this approach. See Limerick, *The Legacy of Conquest: The Unbroken Past of the American West* (New York: Norton, 1987); and Limerick, *Something in the Soil: Field-Testing the New Western History* (New York: Norton, 2000), a collection of essays covering both the nineteenth and twentieth centuries.

3. McCraw, "American Capitalism," 306.

4. Ibid. See also Gavin Wright, "The Origins of American Industrial Success, 1879–1940," *American Economic Review* 80 (1990), 651–688.

5. The origin of mass capitalism in the United States is a contested issue among scholars. Two good sources on how the debate has unfolded are Winifred Barr Rothenberg, *From Market-Places to a Market Economy: The Transformation of Rural Massachusetts, 1750–1850* (Chicago: University of Chicago Press, 1992); and Joyce Appleby, *Inheriting the Revolution: The First Generation of Americans* (Cambridge, MA: Harvard University Press, 2000). See also Allan Kulikoff, *The Agrarian Origins of American Capitalism* (Charlottesville: University Press of Virginia, 1992); Christopher Clark, *The Roots of Rural Capitalism: Western Massachusetts, 1780–1860* (Ithaca, NY: Cornell University Press, 1990); and Gordon S. Wood, "Inventing American Capitalism," *New York Review of Books,* June 9, 1994, 44–48.

6. Hamilton, *Report on the Subject of Manufactures,* Dec. 5, 1791, in *The Papers of Alexander Hamilton,* ed. Harold Syrett et al. (New York: Columbia University Press, 1961–1978), vol. 10, 233 (hereafter cited as *Hamilton Papers*). See, generally, John J. McCusker and Russell R. Menard, *The Economy of British America, 1607–1789* (Chapel Hill: University of North Carolina Press, 1985);

Curtis P. Nettels, *The Emergence of a National Economy, 1775–1815* (New York: Holt, Rinehart and Winston, 1962); Douglass C. North, *American Economic Growth, 1790–1860* (Englewood Cliffs, NJ: Prentice-Hall, 1960); and Farley Grubb, "U.S. Land Policy: Founding Choices and Outcomes, 1780–1802," in Douglas A. Irwin and Richard Sylla, eds., *Founding Choices: American Economic Policy in the 1790s* (Chicago: University of Chicago Press, 2011), 259–290.

7. *Hamilton Papers*, vol. 10, 233; Allen G. Bogue, "Land Policies and Sales," in Glenn Porter, ed., *Encyclopedia of American Economic History* (New York: Scribner's, 1980), 588–589; Stanley Lebergott, "The Demand for Land: The United States, 1820–1860," *Journal of Economic History* 45 (1985), 181–212.

8. Under the Homestead Act, the land was not sold but was given away to settlers in quarter-sections (160 acres), provided they would promise to live on and develop the land for at least five years. In the twentieth century, laws increased the allowable grants to 320 acres for farming dry lands (1909) and 640 acres for ranching (1916).

On land and speculation, the best single source is Rohrbough, *The Land Office Business.* On early speculation in two states, see Stephen Aron, *How the West Was Lost: The Transformation of Kentucky, from Daniel Boone to Henry Clay* (Baltimore: Johns Hopkins University Press, 1996); and, regarding New York, Alan Taylor, *William Cooper's Town: Power and Persuasion on the Frontier of the Early American Republic* (New York: Knopf, 1995).

9. Again the standard account is Rohrbough, *The Land Office Business.* See also Markus Claudius Cachia-Riedl, "Albert Gallatin and the Politics of the New Nation," (Ph.D. diss., University of California, Berkeley, 1998), 246.

10. Cachia-Riedl, "Albert Gallatin and the Politics of the New Nation," 268–269. Mary K. Bonsteel Tachau, *The Federal Courts in the Early Republic: Kentucky, 1789–1816* (Princeton, NJ: Princeton University Press, 1978), shows how overmatched the federal judiciary was in settling competing land claims, some of them dating back to the colonial period.

11. Cachia-Riedl, "Albert Gallatin and the Politics of the New Nation," 247–248 and ch. 7; *Selected Writings of Albert Gallatin,* ed. E. James Ferguson (Indianapolis: Bobbs-Merrill, 1967), 222–224. In 1820, the price was further reduced to $1.25 per acre, the minimum purchase to 80 acres, and the option of paying by credit discontinued. On the settlement of Ohio, see Andrew R. L. Cayton, *The Frontier Republic: Ideology and Politics in the Ohio Country, 1780–1825* (Kent, OH: Kent State University Press, 1986).

12. Cachia-Riedl, "Albert Gallatin and the Politics of the New Nation," 268–269. Gallatin's own possession of lands posed no ethical problems. As always, he was scrupulously honest, and he engaged in no further dealings while he held office.

13. In addition to the Louisiana Purchase of 1804, Gallatin was secretary when Ohio became a state in 1803, when Michigan Territory was divided from Indiana Territory in 1805, and when Illinois Territory was split off from Indiana Territory in 1809. Statehood followed for these areas over the next two decades.

14. Rozann Rothmann, "Political Method in the Federal System: Albert Gallatin's Contribution," *Publius* 1 (1972), 123–141.

15. For an overview of internal improvements from 1788 to 1850, see John Lauritz Larson, *Internal Improvement: National Public Works and the Promise of Popular Government in the Early United States* (Chapel Hill: University of North Carolina Press, 2000).

16. Jefferson is quoted in *Selected Writings of Albert Gallatin,* ed. Ferguson, 228. In the twelve pages immediately following, the same source goes on to include expressions of Gallatin's views on the subject.

17. Gallatin, *Report on Roads and Canals,* April 6, 1808, excerpted in *Selected Writings of Albert Gallatin,* ed. Ferguson, 228–240. Senator Thomas Worthington, a friend of Gallatin's, was instrumental in the resolution asking Gallatin to prepare the report. See Leonard D. White, *The Jeffersonians: A Study in Administrative History, 1801–1829* (New York: Macmillan, 1951), 476. A particularly good analysis of Gallatin's plan is Michael Lacey, "Federalism and National Planning: The Nineteenth-Century Legacy," in Robert Fishman, ed., *The American Planning Tradition: Culture and Legacy* (Washington, DC: Woodrow Wilson Center Press, 2000).

18. Gallatin, *Report on Roads and Canals,* in *Selected Writings of Albert Gallatin,* ed. Ferguson, 235, 237–238.

19. Ibid., 233–235ff. See also Henry Adams, *The Life of Albert Gallatin* (Philadelphia: Lippincott, 1879), 350–352, which emphasizes Gallatin's vision about development through internal improvements.

20. Gallatin, *Report on Roads and Canals,* 229–234.

21. In addition, Gallatin's cost estimates were too low. The federally funded turnpike from Maine to Georgia would have cost far more than his original estimate. Not until the twentieth century did such a road come into existence, as U.S. Highway 1. And the estimated cost of the canals to Lake Ontario and thence to Lake Erie, $3.2 million, may be compared to that of the Erie Canal, built during the 1820s for about $7 million. On the legislation of 1816, see White, *The Jeffersonians: A Study in Administrative History, 1801–1829,* 480–481.

22. Carter Goodrich, "The Gallatin Plan after One Hundred and Fifty Years," *Proceedings of the American Philosophical Society* 102 (Oct. 20, 1958), 435–441.

23. Gallatin to Jefferson, July 27, 1808, in *The Writings of Albert Gallatin,* ed. Henry Adams (Philadelphia: Lippincott, 1879), vol. 1, 395. See also White, *The Jeffersonians: A Study in Administrative History, 1801–1829,* 484–486.

24. On the internal slave market, see Michael Tadman, *Speculators and Slaves: Masters, Traders, and Slaves in the Old South* (Madison: University of Wisconsin Press, 1989); Ira Berlin, *Generations of Captivity: A History of African-American Slaves* (Cambridge, MA: Harvard University Press, 2003); Stephen Deyle, *Carry Me Back: The Domestic Slave Trade in American Life* (New York: Oxford University Press, 2005); and Adam Rothman, *Slave Country: American Expansion and the Origins of the Deep South* (Cambridge, MA: Harvard University Press, 2005), which focuses on Alabama, Mississippi, and Louisiana.

25. The fullest source is William Waller Henning, *The Statutes at Large: Being a Collection of All the Laws of Virginia, from the First Session of the Legislature in the Year 1619* (New York: R. & W. & G. Bartow, 1823). A convenient and

mostly reliable digest, "Virginia Slave Law Summary and Record," is available at www.slaveryinamerica.org/geography/slave_laws_VA.htm (accessed 10/24/11).

26. On Madison's thinking, see Drew McCoy, *The Last of the Fathers: James Madison and the Republican Legacy* (New York: Cambridge University Press, 1989), which concentrates on Madison's post-presidential years, 1817–1836. McCoy's book shows in vivid detail how Madison felt more and more trapped by the issue of slavery; how he fought the nullifiers of the 1820s and 1830s, even though he himself had given them ammunition for their arguments in his Virginia Resolution of 1798.

Of the many books on Jefferson, Joseph J. Ellis, *American Sphinx: The Character of Thomas Jefferson* (New York: Knopf, 1997), captures his ideas on slavery toward the end of his life about as well as any other and more succinctly than most. Ellis's (and many other scholars') conviction that Jefferson did not father the six children of Sally Hemings was substantially overturned by DNA evidence. See Daniel P. Jordan, ed., "Report of the Research Committee on Thomas Jefferson and Sally Hemings," Thomas Jefferson Foundation, 2000, available at www.monticello.org/sites/default/files/inline-pdfs/jefferson-hemings _report.pdf (accessed 10/26/11).

Jefferson did free two brothers of Sally Hemings. Of his six children with her, two died in infancy. He permitted two of the surviving four to leave the plantation as adults, and provided for the freedom of the other two in his will. After his death, his daughter allowed Sally Hemings to live as a freed woman in Charlottesville. The remaining 130 slaves at Monticello were sold at auction in January 1827, six months after Jefferson died. Of the many books that touch on Jefferson and slavery, the most thorough and imaginative is Annette Gordon Reade, *The Hemingses of Monticello: An American Family* (New York: Norton, 2008).

27. Gallatin to William Henry Harrison, Sept. 27, 1809, *The Correspondence of John [Jean] Badollet and Albert Gallatin, 1804–1836*, ed. Gayle Thornbrough (Indianapolis: Indiana Historical Society Publications, no. 22, 1963), 113. Here the context was Badollet's feuds with Harrison, then governor of Indiana Territory, over attempts by settlers to introduce slavery. Harrison, a proponent of slavery, had written to Gallatin complaining of attacks from Badollet. On the pervasive political importance of the slavery issue, see Matthew Mason, *Slavery and Politics in the Early American Republic* (Chapel Hill: University of North Carolina Press, 2006).

28. Gallatin, *Report on Manufactures,* April 19, 1810. The quotation appears on p. 262.

29. Ibid., 262.

30. Compared to the immense legal literature on corporate law, the history of the corporate form in the United States is thin. Three good places to start are Robert E. Wright, "Rise of the Corporate Nation," in Irwin and Sylla, eds., *Founding Choices,* 217–258; Andrew M. Schocket, *Founding Corporate Power in Early National Philadelphia* (Dekalb: Northern Illinois University Press, 2007); and Ronald E. Seavoy, *The Origins of the American Business Corporation, 1784–1855* (Westport, CT: Greenwood Press, 1982).

31. Lawrence A. Peskin, "How the Republicans Learned to Love Manufactur-

ing: The First Parties and the 'New Economy,'" *Journal of the Early Republic* 22 (2002), 235–262, makes the interesting argument that by about 1809 Republicans were more enthusiastic than Federalists about manufacturing. Oddly, he omits any mention of Gallatin's 1810 *Report on Manufactures,* perhaps because his emphasis is on private-sector and state initiatives, rather than on potential federal assistance. Andrew Shankman, in "'A New Thing on Earth': Alexander Hamilton, Pro-Manufacturing Republicans, and the Democratization of American Political Economy," *Journal of the Early Republic* 23 (2003), 342, makes one brief reference to Gallatin's *Report* but—curiously—gives no details about its contents. Shankman's contention is that Republicans, particularly in the Middle Atlantic states, wanted protective tariffs so as to facilitate their bottom-up democratization of the manufacturing sector, in contrast to what he represents as Hamilton's top-down design. This is not an implausible argument, but how Gallatin's proposals fit into it is not explored.

32. Theodore J. Crackel, *Mr. Jefferson's Army: Political and Social Reform of the Military Establishment* (New York: New York University Press, 1987), describes Jefferson's policies aimed at making the army less Federalist in its orientation and more meritocratic. Robert McDonald, ed., *Thomas Jefferson's Military Academy: Founding West Point* (Charlottesville: University of Virginia Press, 2004), is a book of essays explaining Jefferson's purpose in establishing a military school in 1802 in what he hoped would remain a country forever at peace. Hamilton had suggested the establishment of a military academy three years earlier, in 1799. During its earliest years, West Point was not very well organized, but it was reformed and expanded during the War of 1812 and modernized beginning with the superintendency of Sylvanus Thayer in 1817. For the first generation of its existence, West Point was as much an engineering school as a military academy.

33. Hamilton to James Duane, Sept. 3, 1780, *Hamilton Papers,* vol. 2, 406.

34. On Gallatin as an administrator, see Jay C. Heinlein, "Albert Gallatin: A Pioneer in Public Administration," *William and Mary Quarterly* 7 (1950), 64–94; and White, *The Jeffersonians: A Study in Administrative History, 1801–1829,* chs. 10, 11, and 23. The quotation is from Jefferson to Gallatin, Sept. 18, 1801, in *Writings of Gallatin,* ed. Adams, vol. 1, 303. Almost all of Jefferson's biographers note his frequent absences from Washington, D.C. His predecessor, John Adams, had an even worse record of residence in the national capital. As Jefferson's letter to Gallatin put it, "General Washington set the example of those two [summer] months; Mr. Adams extended them to eight months" (ibid). This was an exaggeration, but not by much.

35. Richard Mannix, "Albert Gallatin in Washington, 1801–1813," *Records of the Columbia Historical Society* (Washington, DC: 1971–1972), Book 48, 74, 79.

22. EMBARGO AND FRUSTRATION

1. Among the many books on Monticello, two very different kinds of volumes give a good sense of what life there was like. The first is William L.

Beiswanger, Peter J. Hatch, Lucia Standon, and Susan R. Stein, *Thomas Jefferson's Monticello* (Chapel Hill: University of North Carolina Press, 2001), a coffee-table-sized, photograph-laden book containing essays by Monticello's scholarly staff. The second is Annette Gordon Reade, *The Hemingses of Monticello: An American Family* (New York: Norton, 2008), a sweeping study that analyzes the lives of the most important enslaved family at Monticello, including Jefferson's relationship with Sally Hemings, their children, and other members of the Hemings family.

2. Markus Claudius Cachia-Riedl, "Albert Gallatin and the Politics of the New Nation" (Ph.D. diss., University of California, Berkeley, 1998), 359–360; Anthony Steel, "Anthony Merry and the Anglo-American Dispute about Impressment, 1803–6," *Cambridge Historical Journal* 9 (1949), 331. The impressment issue unfortunately came to a boil at the time of the completion of the Monroe-Pinkney Treaty, which, like the Jay Treaty of 1795, had sought to clarify and preserve British-American trade issues. Because of impressment, however, the Monroe-Pinkney treaty foundered.

3. Donald R. Hickey, "The Monroe-Pinkney Treaty of 1806: A Reappraisal," *William and Mary Quarterly* 44 (1987), 65–88.

4. Madison then suggested that British seamen who had served on ships for under two years and had not yet been naturalized as U.S. citizens be discharged from American ships. Gallatin believed that this plan, too, was unlikely to work. Soon all diplomatic maneuvers over impressment were overtaken by events. Cachia-Riedl, "Albert Gallatin and the Politics of the New Nation," 357–358. Madison thought Gallatin's figure of 9,000 "cannot be as great as he estimates." Madison to Jefferson, April 17, 1807, *Republic of Letters: The Correspondence between Jefferson and Madison, 1776–1826*, ed. James Morton Smith (New York: Norton, 1995), vol. 3, 1467–1468. Gallatin derived his numbers from the federal hospital tax that was deducted from seamen's wages. He calculated that 67,000 sailors were employed in the American merchant marine, including 24,000 in the foreign trade, of whom 9,000 of the latter were British. Ibid., vol. 1, 446n23.

At this time, by no means were all sailors "able seamen." Many were "landsmen" who had recently come aboard either as young men beginning a new career or as impressed civilians—or even as convicts given the choice between imprisonment or naval service. When they learned enough about how to sail the ships (not a simple matter) and, in the case of armed vessels, how to fire the guns, they were "rated able." This process could take anywhere from several months to more than a year. Some inept sailors were never rated able.

5. Jefferson is quoted in *Republic of Letters*, ed. Smith, vol. 3, 1449. For analysis of the *Chesapeake* incident, see Spencer C. Tucker and Frank T. Reuter, *Injured Honor: The Chesapeake-Leopard Affair* (Annapolis, MD: U.S. Naval Institute Press, 2006); and Robert E. Cray, "Remembering the *Chesapeake*: The Politics of Maritime Death and Impressment," *Journal of the Early Republic* 25 (2005), 445–474. A noteworthy aftermath of the affair was the court-martial and suspension of the captain of the *Chesapeake*, James Barron, who was later re-

stored to service. Barron in 1820 fought a duel with Commodore Stephen Decatur, the hero of the First Barbary War and a member of the court-martial. In the duel, Decatur was killed and Barron wounded.

6. The exchanges of letters between Jefferson and Madison on the Chesapeake incident and its aftermath are summarized in *Republic of Letters,* ed. Smith, vol. 3, 1445–1453. The full text of the letters then follows.

7. Gallatin to Hannah Nicholson Gallatin, July 10, 1807, quoted in Richard Mannix, "Albert Gallatin in Washington, 1801–1813," *Records of the Columbia Historical Society* (Washington, DC: 1971–1972), Book 48, 73. Jefferson to William Cabell, March 13, 1808, quoted in Burton Spivak, *Jefferson's English Crisis: Commerce, Embargo, and the Republican Revolution* (Charlottesville: University Press of Virginia, 1979), 105.

8. Gallatin to Jefferson, Oct. 21, 1807, printed in Henry Adams, ed., *The Writings of Albert Gallatin* (Philadelphia: Lippincott, 1879), vol. 1, 359; Gallatin to Jefferson, Dec. 18, 1807, ibid., 368.

9. James Madison's enthusiasm for economic coercion was of long standing and continued when he became president. See, for example, Donald R. Hickey, "Trade Restrictions during the War of 1812," *Journal of American History* 68 (1981), 517–538. Garry Wills, *James Madison* (New York: Times Books, 2002), 52–55, credits the secretary of state with the idea of the embargo; but Wills seems to miss the distinction between an embargo and economic coercion—a distinction that is forcefully argued in Spivak, *Jefferson's English Crisis.*

10. Ralph Ketcham, *James Madison: A Biography* (New York: Macmillan, 1971), 456–466.

11. Gallatin to Jefferson, Dec. 18, 1807, quoted in Richard Mannix, "Gallatin, Jefferson, and the Embargo of 1808," *Diplomatic History* 3 (1979), 153.

12. Gallatin to Jefferson, July 29, August 6, and August 9, 1808, quoted ibid., 167. For evidence of decreased economic activity in Massachusetts and of significant smuggling through Maine, see J. van Fenstermaker and John E. Filer, "The U.S. Embargo Act of 1807: Its Impact on New England Money, Banking, and Economic Activity," *Economic Inquiry* 28 (1990), 163–184.

13. Many letters between Jefferson and Gallatin about the Embargo appear in Henry Adams, *The Life of Albert Gallatin* (Philadelphia: Lippincott, 1879), 372–453. Mannix, in "Gallatin, Jefferson, and the Embargo of 1808," presents copious evidence of the burdens on Gallatin. See also Leonard D. White, *The Jeffersonians: A Study in Administrative History, 1801–1829* (New York: Macmillan, 1951); ch. 11, "The Collectors," well delineates the duties and problems of these important officers, not only during the embargo but for the entire period from 1801 to 1829. On the reluctance of juries to convict violators (though lake traffic is not discussed), see Douglas Lamar Jones, "'The Caprice of Juries': The Enforcement of the Jeffersonian Embargo in Massachusetts," *American Journal of Legal History* 24 (1980), 307–330.

14. Gallatin to Jefferson, July 29, 1808, *Writings of Albert Gallatin,* ed. Adams, vol. 1, 397. One of the best accounts of smuggling into Canada before, during, and after the war is Joshua M. Smith, *Borderland Smuggling: Patriots, Loyal-*

ist, and Illicit Trade in the Northeast, 1783–1820 (Gainesville: University Press of Florida, 2006). Because Gallatin was not heavily involved, I have omitted from this narrative the story of Jefferson's extensive efforts to deal with Spain over Florida, through either purchase or acquisition. Florida was obtained through purchase under the Adams-Onis Treaty of 1819, which also covered large tracts of Mexican territory in the West; there, until the War with Mexico of 1844–1846, the United States tended to compromise with Mexico over the division of territory. Florida became a state in 1845.

15. Adams, *Life of Gallatin,* 365–374; the quoted letters to Hannah Gallatin and from Dallas are on pp. 372–374; see also Gallatin to Dallas, July 30, 1808, and Jefferson to Gallatin, Aug. 11, 1808, quoted in Cachia-Riedl, "Albert Gallatin and the Politics of the New Nation," 409, 410.

16. Among many interpretations of the embargo, see Spivak, *Jefferson's English Crisis,* by far the best single book on the subject; Mannix, "Gallatin, Jefferson, and the Embargo of 1808"; and Forrest McDonald, *The Presidency of Thomas Jefferson* (Lawrence: University Press of Kansas, 1976).

17. Spivak, *Jefferson's English Crisis,* contains a vivid portrayal of Jefferson's increasingly unrealistic views during this period and his evident shift to an anticommercial way of thinking. On the issue of autarky, the fact that enslaved persons—many of them highly skilled craftsmen—did most of the work seemed to loom less important in Jefferson's mind than the self-sufficiency that could be achieved. On the economic results of the embargo, see Douglas A. Irwin, "The Welfare Cost of Autarky: Evidence from the Jeffersonian Trade Embargo, 1807–1809," *Review of International Economics* 13 (2005), 631–645.

In the strict technical sense, the embargo did not bring autarky, since foreign ships could still trade in U.S. ports. But the ban on exports in U.S. ships, which cut total exports by 80 percent, plus the inevitable decline in imports (which eventually had to be paid for using either foreign currency earned through exports, borrowed money, or specie, of which the United States was notably short), was a big step toward autarky.

18. Mannix, "Gallatin, Jefferson, and the Embargo of 1808," 155, 156, 158, 161, 163–170. The letters to Monroe are quoted on p. 167. After Madison won the election of 1808, Jefferson made his withdrawal from authority explicit, even though his term still had four months to run. And two days before he left office, he wrote to his French immigrant friend Pierre-Samuel du Pont, "Never did a prisoner, released from his chains, feel such relief as I shall on shaking off the shackles of power."

19. Many historians have speculated about Jefferson's peculiar behavior. See, for example, Dumas Malone, *Jefferson the President, Second Term* (Boston: Little, Brown, 1974), 621–626, one of the most sympathetic treatments; and Robert M. Johnstone Jr., *Jefferson and the Presidency: Leadership in the Young Republic* (Ithaca, NY: Cornell University Press, 1978), 286–287. Henry Adams, in *Life of Gallatin,* 376–377, is especially rough on Jefferson's conduct: "So cowed was he as to do what no President had ever done before, or has ever done since [Adams was writing in the late 1870s], and what no President has a constitutional right

to do: he abdicated the duties of his office, and no entreaty could induce him to resume them."

20. Gallatin wrote this letter not only on his own behalf, but also on that of Madison, who was not well at the time. Its first sentence reads: "Both Mr. Madison and myself concur in the opinion that, considering the temper of the Legislature, or rather of its members, it would be eligible to point out to them some precise and distinct course." Madison and Gallatin to Jefferson, Nov. 15, 1808, *Republic of Letters,* ed. Smith, vol. 3, 1557–1558.

21. For the numbers cited, see Alexander Balinky, "Gallatin's Theory of War Finance," *William and Mary Quarterly* 16 (1959), 74n6. Randolph's comment is quoted in Adams, *Life of Gallatin,* 391.

22. This poll was taken at a conference of political scientists and historians at the University of Louisville. See php.louisville.edu/news.php?news=533 (accessed 9/23/10). The full list of presidential mistakes was as follows:

1. James Buchanan's inactivity preceding the Civil War (1857–1861);
2. Andrew Johnson's Reconstruction policy favoring southern whites over emancipated slaves (1865–1869);
3. Lyndon Johnson's escalation of the Vietnam War (1964–1967);
4. Woodrow Wilson's refusal to compromise with the Senate on the Treaty of Versailles and the League of Nations (1919–1920);
5. Richard Nixon's Watergate cover-up (1972–1974);
6. James Madison's failure to avoid the War of 1812;
7. Jefferson's embargo (1807–1809);
8. John F. Kennedy's allowing the Bay of Pigs invasion of Cuba (1961);
9. Ronald Reagan's involvement in the Iran-Contra arms-for-hostages bargain (1985–1986);
10. Bill Clinton's sexual relationship with Monica Lewinsky (1995–1996).

A good historical parallel for Jefferson's odd behavior during his last year and a half in office is hard to find. Almost all presidents grow tired of the heavy responsibilities of their office, but few if any have abdicated them to the extent Jefferson did for so long a time. In its effects, perhaps the closest analogy is Woodrow Wilson's incapacity following a serious stroke he suffered in 1919, seventeen months before the expiration of his second term of office. The question of who was running the government during those seventeen months remains, even now, a matter of controversy.

23. One of the strongest indictments of Jefferson's behavior is Leonard W. Levy, *Jefferson and Civil Liberties: The Darker Side* (Cambridge, MA: Harvard University Press, 1963), 93–141. For an econometric argument that the embargo succeeded in hurting the British more than the Americans, see Jeffrey Frankel, "The 1807–1809 Embargo against Great Britain," *Journal of Economic History* 42 (1982), 291–308. Frankel makes the dubious assertion that the embargo was "well-enforced" and goes on to argue that it failed not primarily for economic reasons but for political ones: partisan divisions between the Federalists and Republicans (308).

23. DISPIRITING DIPLOMACY

1. On the issue of Gallatin's being a "foreigner," see Henry Adams, *The Life of Albert Gallatin* (Philadelphia: Lippincott, 1879), 388–389. On the likely vote, Irving Brant, *James Madison: The President, 1809–1812* (Indianapolis: Bobbs-Merrill, 1956), 24–25.

2. Quoted in Adams, *Life of Gallatin,* 391.

3. Gallatin to Jefferson, Nov. 8, 1809, *The Writings of Albert Gallatin,* ed. Henry Adams (Philadelphia: Lippincott, 1879), vol. 1, 465–466.

4. The original Junto had been founded by Benjamin Franklin in 1727 as a small group of men who met on Friday evenings for discussions and proposals for civic improvement. The organization that opposed Gallatin differed from its predecessor of the same name. Some of William Duane's many attacks on Gallatin grew out of the dynamics of Pennsylvania state politics, as opposed to national issues. Duane is quoted in J. C. A. Stagg, *Mr. Madison's War: Politics, Diplomacy, and Warfare in the Early American Republic, 1783–1830* (Princeton, NJ: Princeton University Press, 1983), 61. His role as a party leader is stressed in Jeffrey L. Pasley, *"The Tyranny of Printers": Newspaper Politics in the Early American Republic* (Charlottesville: University Press of Virginia, 2001).

5. On the legislative controversies following the embargo, see Reginald C. Stuart, "James Madison and the Militants: Republican Disunity and Replacing the Embargo," *Diplomatic History* 6, 145–168. The first version of the original bill, Macon's Bill No. 1, was drafted mostly by Gallatin, who, like Madison, had little enthusiasm for it. It would have permitted American merchant ships to travel to any port in any country, and would have prohibited British and French warships as well as merchant ships from entering American ports. Macon's Bill No. 2, however, took a different tack.

6. Adams, *Life of Gallatin,* 416.

24. THE FATE OF THE BANK

1. Jefferson to Gallatin, Dec. 13, 1803, quoted in Henry Adams, *The Life of Albert Gallatin* (Philadelphia: Lippincott, 1879), 321.

2. Ibid. Gallatin's list is quoted in Bray Hammond, *Banks and Politics in America, from the Revolution to the Civil War* (Princeton, NJ: Princeton University Press, 1957), 206–207. Gallatin then had to expend much energy in persuading the bank itself, which was reluctant to extend its operations to such a distant city as New Orleans.

3. Hammond, *Banks and Politics in America,* 209ff.

4. Richard Sylla, John B. Legler, and John J. Wallis, "Banks and State Public Finance in the New Republic: The United States, 1790–1860," *Journal of Economic History* 47 (1987), 391–403. As the nineteenth century progressed, states' income from bank taxation and shareholding became even more important, peaking in about 1840. For the years 1836–1840, 82 percent of Massachusetts's income derived from these sources, 35 percent of Connecticut's, 57 percent of

Delaware's, 39 percent of North Carolina's, 41 percent of South Carolina's, and 61 percent of Georgia's (ibid., 401). Howard Bodenhorn, *State Banking in Early America: A New Economic History* (New York: Oxford University Press, 2002), is a sophisticated theoretical analysis of the role of state banks before the Civil War. Some accounts give the number of state banks in 1811 as 90.

5. Ibid. See also Hammond, *Banks and Politics in America*, chs. 5–8.

6. The importance of the bank to Gallatin is underscored in the middle chapters of Raymond Walters Jr., *Albert Gallatin: Jeffersonian Financier and Diplomat* (New York: Macmillan, 1957), esp. 237–241.

7. Quoted in Hammond, *Banks and Politics in America*, 213. The Second Bank of the United States, chartered in 1816, provided that one-fifth of the twenty-five directors be appointed by the president of the United States.

8. This is the thesis of Hammond, *Banks and Politics in America*, ch. 8.

9. Even Madison's most sympathetic biographer, Irving Brant, in *James Madison: The President, 1809–1812* (Indianapolis: Bobbs-Merrill, 1956), 265–270, acknowledges that, had the president offered even a little active support, recharter would have passed.

10. Hammond, *Banks and Politics in America*, chs. 5–9; Adams, *Life of Gallatin*, 473–475.

11. Lisa R. Morales, "The Financial History of the War of 1812" (Ph.D. diss., University of North Texas, 2009), 195. The haggling over the value of currencies did not begin with the failure of recharter in 1811, but did increase markedly thereafter. The same thing happened on a larger scale in the 1830s, after an explosion in the number of banks, and especially after Andrew Jackson's veto in 1832 of the recharter of the Second Bank of the United States. The currency guidebooks of that era show wildly divergent values for bills of any size—issued not only by banks, but also by mining companies, railroads, and other private firms. For an overview of the problem, see Matthew Carey, *Reflections on the Consequences of the Refusal of the Banks to Receive in Deposit Southern and Western Bank Notes* (Philadelphia: Published by the Author, 1815). Examples of published guides include *Sylvester's Bank-Note and Exchange Manual* (New York: S. J. Sylvester, 1832); and *Thompson's Bank Note and Commercial Reporter* (New York: American Banker, 1842–1858), which was published weekly.

12. Gallatin to Madison, March [n.d.], 1811, *Writings of Albert Gallatin*, ed. Henry Adams (Philadelphia: Lippincott, 1879), vol. 1, 495–496. Madison biographer Irving Brant has speculated that Madison himself initiated these maneuvers as a way to get rid of secretary of state Robert Smith. The wording of Gallatin's letter, however, points in the other direction. See Brant, *James Madison: The President, 1809–1812*, 282, 292–293.

25. FINANCING THE WAYWARD WAR

1. Lawrence A. Peskin, "Conspiratorial Anglophobia and the War of 1812," *Journal of American History* 98 (2011), 647–669.

2. Standard accounts of the War of 1812 include Roger H. Brown, *The Re-*

public in Peril: 1812 (New York: Columbia University Press, 1964); and J. C. A. Stagg, *Mr. Madison's War: Politics, Diplomacy, and Warfare in the Early Republic* (Princeton, NJ: Princeton University Press, 1983). Like much of the historical literature on the early national period, some accounts of the War of 1812 tend toward partisanship. Among many good books on the war that take strong viewpoints are Donald R. Hickey, *The War of 1812: A Forgotten Conflict* (Urbana: University of Illinois Press, 1989), a pro-Federalist argument that the war was unnecessary and filled with bungling by the Madison administration; by contrast, Richard Buel Jr., *America on the Brink: How the Political Struggle over the War of 1812 Almost Destroyed the Young Republic* (New York: Palgrave Macmillan, 2004), blames the causes of the war mostly on Federalists' policies and criticizes their conduct during the war, focusing particularly on Massachusetts. In a short biography entitled *James Madison* (New York: Times Books, 2002), which is mostly about the presidential years, Garry Wills devotes a third of his entire text to the War of 1812 and finds Madison a bumbling wartime president, despite his personal courage. In Ralph Ketcham, *James Madison: A Biography* (New York: Macmillan, 1971), the author allocates about 75 of 671 pages to the war and judges Madison's performance mostly poor but with many extenuating circumstances.

A history from the British and to some extent Canadian perspective is Jon Latimer, *1812: War with America* (Cambridge, MA: Harvard University Press, 2007). See also Alan Taylor, *The Civil War of 1812: American Citizens, British Subjects, Irish Rebels, and Indian Allies* (New York: Knopf, 2010), which pays close attention to the U.S.-Canadian borderlands and is as important in explaining the evolution of Canada as it is in illuminating the American aspects of the war.

3. The role of the war hawks has been a contentious historiographic issue for more than a century. For a quantitative study of voting in the House, see Ronald L. Hatzenbuehler, "The War Hawks and the Question of Congressional Leadership in 1812," *Pacific Historical Review* 45 (1976), 1–22. Jefferson's comment is quoted in Robert Allen Rutland, *The Presidency of James Madison* (Lawrence: University Press of Kansas, 1990), 110. On the importance of Canada as both a potential acquisition and a negotiating pawn in the war, see Stagg, *Mr. Madison's War*, 6–45.

4. Wills, *James Madison*, 82.

5. Edward S. Balinky, "Gallatin's Theory of War Finance," *William and Mary Quarterly* 16 (1959), 74–76.

6. Ibid., 76–82.

7. Gallatin remained nominal secretary until February 1814. Of the six immigrants, only George Campbell had come as a child (his parents had brought him from Scotland to North Carolina when he was three). He interrupted his service as U.S. senator from Tennessee in 1814 to take the treasury post, which he held from February to October, when he was relieved by Dallas. Campbell was a lawyer who had served on the Committee on Ways and Means in the House of Representatives and on the Finance Committee of the Senate. See Weymouth Tyree Jordan, *George Washington Campbell of Tennessee, Western Statesman*

(Tallahassee: Florida State University Press, 1955). On Dallas, see Raymond Walters Jr., *Alexander James Dallas: Lawyer—Politician—Financier, 1759–1817* (Philadelphia: University of Pennsylvania Press, 1943); and George Mifflin, *Life and Writings of Alexander James Dallas* (Philadelphia: J. B. Lippincott, 1871).

8. Gallatin to Madison, March 5, 1813, in *Writings of Albert Gallatin,* ed. Henry Adams (Philadelphia: Lippincott, 1879), vol. 1, 532. As Adams wrote, this action by Gallatin, Parish, Astor, and Girard "saved the United States government for the time from bankruptcy, and perhaps from evils far more fatal; so, at least, the Federalists thought, and they long vented their wrath against these foreigners, as they called them, for an act which was certainly a somewhat bitter satire upon American patriotism"; see Henry Adams, *The Life of Albert Gallatin* (Philadelphia: Lippincott, 1879), 477. See also Lisa R. Morales, "The Financial History of the War of 1812" (Ph.D. diss., University of North Texas, 2009), 158–162.

On Girard, see George Wilson, *Stephen Girard: The Life and Times of America's First Tycoon* (Cambridge, MA: Da Capo Press, 1996); David S. Miller, "The 'Tiara': A Perspective on Merchant Stephen Girard," *Pennsylvania Magazine of History and Biography* 112 (1988), 189–208; Donald R. Adams Jr., *Finance and Enterprise in Early America: A Study of Stephen Girard's Bank, 1812–1831* (Philadelphia: University of Pennsylvania Press, 1978); and John Bach McMaster, *The Life and Times of Stephen Girard: Mariner and Merchant,* 2 vols. (Philadelphia: Lippincott, 1918), an outdated but thorough source. When he died in 1831, Girard left his fortune to philanthropic enterprises, and nearly two centuries later Girard College in Philadelphia is still operating as a large preparatory school for disadvantaged youth. On Astor, the best single source is John D. Haeger, *John Jacob Astor: Business and Finance in the Early Republic* (Detroit: Wayne State University Press, 1991). On Parish, see Philip G. Walters and Raymond Walters Jr., "The American Career of David Parish," *Journal of Economic History* 4 (1944), 149–166; and J. Mackay Hitsman, "David Parish and the War of 1812," *Military Affairs* 26 (1962–63), 171–177. Parish's grandfather had emigrated from Britain to Hamburg.

9. Bray Hammond, *Banks and Politics in America from the Revolution to the Civil War* (Princeton, NJ: Princeton University Press, 1957), 228–229. On the issue of Treasury notes, see Donald H. Kagin, "Monetary Aspects of the Treasury Notes of the War of 1812," *Journal of Economic History* 44 (1984), 69–88. The poor organization of this otherwise informative article reflects, in itself, the confusion that attended the financing of the war. On March 17, 1817, Congress forbade further issue of Treasury notes, a Second Bank of the United States having been established and having begun to issue currency as the first bank had done.

10. For debt figures, see entries for the years 1791–1849 at www.treasurydirect .gov/govt/reports/pd/histdebt/histdebt.htm (accessed 8/25/10). These numbers are in current dollars. Adjusted for inflation (the rate of which is not reliably available for these years), the 1816 figure would be lower, but still well over $110 million and perhaps as high as $120 million.

11. Donald R. Hickey, "American Trade Restrictions during the War of 1812," *Journal of American History* 68 (1981), 517–538.

12. The British action was partly in reprisal for the Americans' earlier burning

of the small town of York (later Toronto), Upper Canada's capital city, whose population was then only 625 as compared with Washington's 8,000. See Robin F. A. Fabel, "The Laws of War in the 1812 Conflict," *Journal of American Studies* 14 (August 1980), 211.

13. Maine did not become a state until 1820. Massachusetts, Connecticut, and Rhode Island sent regular delegations to Hartford; New Hampshire and Vermont were both divided on the issue, but delegations did appear from each state. See James M. Banner Jr., *To the Hartford Convention: The Federalists and the Origins of Party Politics in Massachusetts* (New York: Random House, 1970). The convention explicitly repudiated the idea of secession, but the fact that such a profound issue had been widely discussed suggests how desperate New England had become in its opposition to the war and to prewar Republican policies.

26. WINNING THE PEACE

1. Raymond Walters Jr., *Albert Gallatin: Jeffersonian Financier and Diplomat* (New York: Macmillan, 1957), 258–267.

2. Gallatin to James Witter Nicholson, May 5, 1813, printed in Henry Adams, *The Life of Albert Gallatin* (Philadelphia: Lippincott, 1879), 482.

3. Walters, *Gallatin*, 268–271.

4. Ibid.

5. Ibid., 272–273. Ghent is now in the Flemish sector of Belgium, but was then a possession of the Austrian Habsburgs. In 1815 it became part of the Netherlands for fifteen years, until the Belgian Revolution of 1830.

6. Quoted in Nicholas Dungan, *Gallatin: America's Swiss Founding Father* (New York: New York University Press, 2010), 111.

7. On Indian confederations generally, see Gregory Evans Dowd, *A Spirited Resistance: The North American Indian Struggle for Unity, 1734–1815* (Baltimore: Johns Hopkins University Press, 1992); on Tecumseh before and during the War of 1812, R. David Edmunds, *Tecumseh and the Quest for Indian Leadership* (Boston: Little, Brown, 1984; 2nd ed. Harlow, U.K.: Longman, 2006).

8. Gallatin to Matthew Lyon, May 7, 1816, in *The Writings of Albert Gallatin*, ed. Henry Adams (Philadelphia: Lippincott, 1879), vol. 1, 700. A few prominent historians have recently reinterpreted the War of 1812 in a far more favorable light than did almost all standard accounts written in preceding generations. In particular, Gordon S. Wood, *Empire of Liberty: A History of the Early Republic, 1789–1815* (New York: Oxford University Press, 2009), 662–699, presents the war as something close to an unalloyed triumph of republican (small "r") ideology.

9. That seems to be the nature of any war that can be possibly be represented as a victory. It has been rare in the extreme for an American politician to disparage a war that has not been an unambiguous defeat. Even the leaders of the Confederacy in the 1860s and the advocates of the Vietnam War of the 1960s and 1970s seldom expressed postwar remorse. On this aspect of the War of 1812, see

David Waldstreicher, *In the Midst of Perpetual Fetes: The Making of American Nationalism, 1776–1820* (Chapel Hill: University of North Carolina Press, 1997); the spirited account by Walter R. Borneman, *1812: The War That Forged a Nation* (New York: Harper, 2004); and A. J. Langguth, *Union 1812: The Americans Who Fought the Second War of Independence* (New York: Simon and Schuster, 2006), a popular account emphasizing heroic individuals.

10. Adams, *Life of Albert Gallatin,* 546.

27. HIS LONG AND USEFUL LIFE

1. Gallatin to Jean Badollet, July 29, 1824, quoted in Nicholas Dungan, *Gallatin: America's Swiss Founding Father* (New York: New York University Press, 2010), 134. In 1816 and early 1817, Gallatin had once again hoped to be offered the post of secretary of state. James Monroe had just been elected president, but Monroe chose John Quincy Adams for the State Department, and Gallatin remained in Paris.

2. Gallatin to Badollet, July 29, 1824, in *The Correspondence of John [Jean] Badollet and Albert Gallatin, 1804–1836,* ed. Gayle Thornbrough (Indianapolis: Indiana Historical Society Publications, 1963), 264.

3. Albert Gallatin to James Gallatin, Jan. 13, 1827, in Henry Adams, *The Life of Albert Gallatin* (Philadelphia: Lippincott, 1879), 621–623. This is a long and unusually personal father-to-son letter that covers many other topics as well.

4. Gallatin to Badollet, March 26, 1829, *The Correspondence of John [Jean] Badollet and Albert Gallatin,* ed. Thornbrough, 284–285.

5. In 1822, Gallatin had been offered the presidency of the Second Bank but had declined it on the advice of John Jacob Astor, who, even at this early date, saw where the contentious politics of the bank might eventually lead. See Astor to Gallatin, Oct. 18, 1822, quoted in Dungan, *Gallatin: America's Swiss Founding Father,* 133.

6. The full text of Jackson's long veto message, dated July 10, 1832, is available online at millercenter.org/scripps/archive/speeches/detail/3636 (accessed 10/23/11).

7. Gallatin resigned as president of the Council of the university after less than a year because his colleagues, who wanted to take the institution in a religious direction, gained the upper hand. See Gallatin to Jean Badollet, Feb. 7, 1833, in Thornbrough, ed., *The Correspondence of John [Jean] Badollet and Albert Gallatin,* 312–313.

8. Adams, *Life of Gallatin,* 641; *Register of Debates in Congress,* 22nd Congress, 1st Session (Washington: Gales and Seaton, 1832), vol. 8, 267. Clay went on to say about Gallatin, "The authority of his name has been invoked, and the labors of his pen . . . to overthrow the American system and to substitute the foreign." Here Clay clouded the issue. Free trade was certainly not foreign practice at this time overseas. Even Britain, which later advocated free trade, did not repeal its highly protectionist Corn Laws until 1846.

9. Gallatin's attitude toward Native Americans evolved over the years. In 1805, editing Jefferson's Second Inaugural Address, he advised the president to tone down his comments on the Indians' virtues. "They have but few—I think very few," Gallatin wrote. Their problems arose mainly from "licentiousness . . . and the consequent want of the social institutions which establish and secure *property* and *marriage*." Gallatin to Jefferson, Feb. 12, 1805, *The Writings of Albert Gallatin*, ed. Henry Adams (Philadelphia: Lippincott, 1879), vol. 1, 227. Jefferson's own attitude toward Indians, on the whole, was not particularly generous, despite the comments in the draft of his Second Inaugural.

Gallatin never romanticized Indians, but he gradually became less harsh in judging them. Like many intellectuals, he was part cultural critic, part cautious admirer. Late in life he became fascinated with Indian language and culture. His very important role in ethnology is analyzed in Robert E. Bieder, *Science Encounters the Indian, 1820–1880: The Early Years of American Ethnology* (Norman: University of Oklahoma Press, 1986), 16–55, esp. 20–30. See also Robert E. Bieder, "The Representation of Indian Bodies in Nineteenth-Century American Anthropology," in Devon A. Mihesuah, ed., *Repatriation Reader: Who Owns Indian Remains?* (Lincoln: University of Nebraska Press, 2000), 19–36.

10. See Frederick Merk, *Albert Gallatin and the Oregon Problem* (Cambridge, MA: Harvard University Press, 1950).

11. Raymond Walters Jr., *Albert Gallatin: Jeffersonian Financier and Diplomat* (New York: Macmillan, 1957), 376–379.

12. Gallatin to Baring, April 20, 1842, quoted in Dungan, *Gallatin*, 165. Baring, now Lord Ashburton, was in the United States to negotiate what became the Webster-Ashburton Treaty, clarifying parts of the border between Canada and the United States and issues of rights on the Great Lakes.

13. *Daily National Intelligencer* (Washington, DC), Oct. 6, 1849.

14. *The Hinds County Gazette* (Raymond, Miss.), Sept. 12, 1849; *North American and United States Gazette* (Philadelphia), Aug. 15, 1849.

28. IMMIGRANT EXCEPTIONALISM?

1. Emerson, "Address," *Transactions of the Middlesex Agricultural Society, for the Year 1858* (Concord, MA: Benjamin Tolman, 1858), 45–52. See also *The Collected Works of Ralph Waldo Emerson*, ed. Ronald A. Bosco and Douglas Emory Wilson (Cambridge, MA: Harvard University Press, 2007), vol. 7, ch. 6.

2. This paragraph draws on Thomas K. McCraw, "American Capitalism," *Creating Modern Capitalism*, ed. McCraw (Cambridge, MA: Harvard University Press, 1997), 303–305. Meanwhile, Native Americans living in what became the United States suffered near-genocide. They fought as hard as they could, but lost to superior numbers and technology. See Richard White, *"It's Your Misfortune and None of My Own": A New History of the American West* (Norman: University of Oklahoma Press, 1991).

3. Joseph Schumpeter, the Harvard professor and Austrian immigrant who

popularized the word "entrepreneur," wrote about it at length in his seminal book, *The Theory of Economic Development,* trans. Redvers Opie (Cambridge, MA: Harvard University Press, 1934; first published in German in 1911). Schumpeter described the entrepreneur as one "whose characteristic task" is "breaking up old, and creating new, tradition"; a person who has "the will to conquer: the impulse to fight, to prove oneself superior to others, to succeed for the sake, not of the fruits of success, but of success itself" (pp. 91–94). Appropriately, this is as much a psychological as an economic definition, and many other writers have offered variations on Schumpeter's theme.

4. Robert F. Jones, *"The King of the Alley": William Duer—Politician, Entrepreneur, and Speculator, 1768–1799* (New York: American Philosophical Society, 1992). Duer's son, William Alexander Duer, served on New York's highest court and then as president of Columbia University.

5. Nourse was known for his integrity and ability to work well with people of all political persuasions. He became something of a socialite in New York, then again when the national capital moved to Philadelphia, and ultimately from his fine house in Georgetown after the ultimate relocation of the capital to Washington, D.C. See Oscar P. Fitzgerald, Curator, *In Search of Joseph Nourse, 1754–1841: America's First Civil Servant* (Washington, DC: Dumbarton House, 1994–1995). This fifty-five-page document has sections by four authors, the most relevant to the early years of the Treasury being Mark Walston, "Establishing a National Currency," 29–39. Today, Dumbarton House, Nourse's residence in Georgetown, is a museum and the headquarters of the National Society of the Colonial Dames of America. See also Richard D. White Jr., "A Tale of Two Bureaucrats: Joseph Nourse, Oliver Wolcott, Jr., and the Forerunners of American Public Administration," *Administration and Society* 40 (2008), 384–402.

6. Astor and Parish were also interested in land, as well as in liquid capital. Both became large landowners—Parish in the St. Lawrence Valley, and Astor in New York real estate, as well as in fur-trading lands in the West.

7. For the contents of the following paragraphs, I am indebted to the insights of Harold James, "Comment on Thomas K. McCraw, 'Immigrant Entrepreneurs in U.S. Financial History,'" *Capitalism and Society* 5 (2010), Issue 1, Article 6, 1–2; available at ideas.repec.org/a/bpj/capsoc/v5y2010i1n6.html (accessed 10/5/10).

8. Necker resigned in 1790 and escaped to his sanctuary on the banks of Lake Geneva. In addition to other reasons for his fame, Necker was the father of the woman known as Madame de Staël (1766–1817), who became a political force in France, an eventual opponent of Napoleon, and one of the most widely read writers of her time.

In earlier years, a blow to Necker's reputation began when he published the *Compte rendu au roi* (1781)—a widely read report on the specific sources and uses of the French government's income. This report portrayed the government's finances in a better light than they actually stood. Necker compounded the problem in still another publication, which purported to demonstrate that assistance to the Americans had not caused any significant increase in France's national debt. His most influential economic work was the huge *Traité de l'administration des finances de la France* (1784), a book from which Hamilton learned a great deal.

9. For a broad survey, see Marc Flandreau, ed., *Money Doctors: The Experience of Financial Advising, 1850–2000* (New York: Routledge, 2003). The IMF's "neoliberal" policies of free trade, light governmental interference with business, and floating exchange rates have been especially unpopular in some African and Latin American countries. There, opponents of the IMF frequently point out that nearly all of the developed countries, including the United States, grew to prosperity under the umbrella of high protective tariffs. This is an ongoing debate unlikely to be soon resolved.

10. It is conceivable that had Law and Necker succeeded, they might have stayed in France; but even so, they were not transatlantic immigrants like the ones mentioned in this chapter.

In almost any revolution during any period, rebel leaders will seek and use help from any quarter where they can find it. The decisive Battle of Yorktown, for example, could not have been won without French help under the command of the Comte de Rochambeau of France. George Washington, with an American force of 11,000 soldiers, was assisted by almost 9,000 French troops. In addition, a huge French fleet of twenty-nine ships and 3,200 sailors blocked any seaborne retreat by the British. This joint operation, which was led on the French side by the Comte de Rochambeau, Admiral de Grasse, and the Marquis de Lafayette, was only the most conspicuous episode of foreign assistance. French troops assisted in many other operations as well.

So did military leaders from other countries: Captain John Paul Jones, a Scot who served in the Russian navy after his exploits in the American Revolution; the dashing Casimir Pulaski of Poland, who led U.S. cavalrymen in many battles; General Friedrich Wilhelm von Steuben of Prussia, who helped to train the Continental Army; and the engineering officer Tadeusz Kosciuszko, who served for seven years during the war and designed some of the best American fortifications. Many American towns and counties today are named for Lafayette, Kosciuszko, Pulaski, and von Steuben. Most of these foreign officers returned to Europe, but Pulaski was killed during the siege of Savannah, and von Steuben settled permanently in upstate New York.

29. COMPARISONS AND CONTINGENCIES

1. The Jefferson-Hamilton comparison has been lively from their own time to the present day. For a useful survey of shifting national opinions, see Stephen Knott, "Opposed in Death as in Life," in Robert W. T. Martin and Douglas Ambrose, eds., *The Many Faces of Alexander Hamilton: The Life and Legacy of America's Most Elusive Founding Father* (New York: New York University Press, 2006), 25–53. This same volume contains two other essays bearing on the Hamilton-Jefferson comparison: Robert M. S. McDonald, "The Hamiltonian In-

vention of Thomas Jefferson," ibid., 54–76, which tends to blame Hamilton for the rupture between the two statesmen; and James H. Read, "Alexander Hamilton's View of Thomas Jefferson's Ideology and Character," ibid., 77–106, which takes a position more favorable to Hamilton. For a thorough historical survey of the ups and downs of Hamilton's reputation over the past 200 years, see Stephen F. Knott, *Alexander Hamilton and the Persistence of Myth* (Lawrence: University Press of Kansas, 2002). A similar and likewise thorough book on Jefferson is Merrill Peterson, *The Jefferson Image in the American Mind* (New York: Oxford University Press, 1960). Each of these books is slanted toward the person being studied, at the expense of the other—though less so than most of the biographies. Since the appearance of Peterson's book in 1960, Jefferson's image has been damaged by the revelations about his relationship with Sally Hemings. On balance, however, historians have still tended to favor Jefferson over Hamilton and certainly the Republicans over the Federalists. For an attempt to right this balance, see, for example, Doron Ben-Atar and Barbara B. Oberg, eds., *Federalists Reconsidered* (Charlottesville: University Press of Virginia, 1998).

2. Jefferson fares least well as secretary of state because he lacked the consistent support of President Washington.

3. For a critical analysis of Gallatin as secretary of the treasury, see Alexander Balinky, *Albert Gallatin: Fiscal Theories and Policies* (New Brunswick, NJ: Rutgers University Press, 1958). Balinky's viewpoint is influenced by Keynesianism, and he presents an interesting contrast between Gallatin's actual policies and those he believes would have been more appropriate at the time. He sees no compelling reason to have striven to extinguish the national debt, which is sound economic thinking. But in taking this position he underestimates the power of that goal not merely as a financial aspiration but also as a moral one—an integral part of the heart and soul of Republican ideology.

4. There are some exceptions to the Hamilton-versus-Jefferson oversimplifications. Two classic examples are Alexis de Tocqueville, *Democracy in America,* trans. and ed. Harvey C. Mansfield and Debra Winthrop, 2 vols. (Chicago: University of Chicago Press, 2000; first published 1835–1840); and Herbert Croly, *The Promise of American Life,* ed. Arthur M. Schlesinger Jr. (Cambridge, MA: Harvard University Press, 1965; orig. pub. 1909). The historian George E. Mowry described Theodore Roosevelt's "New Nationalism" program of 1910–1912 as "combining Hamiltonian means with Jeffersonian ends," and went on to say that Franklin D. Roosevelt's New Deal took the New Nationalism a step further. See Mowry, *Theodore Roosevelt and the Progressive Movement* (Madison: University of Wisconsin Press, 1947).

5. Lincoln to Albert G. Hodges, April 4, 1864, epigraph to David Herbert Donald, *Lincoln* (New York: Simon and Schuster, 1995).

6. In 1786, the State of New York blocked federal access to customs duties, much as Rhode Island had done in 1781.

7. In this case the rifts included an ideological split within the Republican Party over how broadly to construe the Constitution.

8. Had the national capital remained in New York, it would have put Wall

Street, the nation's financial center, in the same place as its national government. For a country as large as the United States became, with a political system so permeable to the influence of money, that probably would not have been a good thing.

30. CAPITALISM AND CREDIT

1. James Grant, *Money of the Mind: Borrowing and Lending in America from the Civil War to Michael Milken* (New York: Farrar, Straus and Giroux, 1992).

2. Karl Marx and Friedrich Engels, *The Manifesto of the Communist Party*, in *The Portable Karl Marx*, ed. Eugene Kamenka (New York: Penguin, 1983), 209.

3. Historians and others have argued over whether the slave-plantation system was or was not capitalist. For a variety of reasons that need not be rehearsed here, I do not believe that it was. During the antebellum period, many writers on both sides of the slavery question argued explicitly that it was not like conventional market economies. One vivid example is George Fitzhugh, a proslavery intellectual who published *Sociology for the South; or, The Failure of Free Society* (Richmond, VA: C. H. Wynne, 1854). For a concise and sophisticated modern analysis, see Gavin Wright, *Slavery and Economic Development* (Baton Rouge: Louisiana State University Press, 2006).

4. Hamilton, *Report on a Plan for the Further Support of Public Credit*, Jan. 16, 1795, in *The Papers of Alexander Hamilton*, ed. Harold Syrett et al. (New York: Columbia University Press, 1961–1978), vol. 18, 124–125.

5. Ibid., 126.

6. Ibid., 127–128.

7. Ibid.

31. THE POLITICAL ECONOMY OF HAMILTON AND GALLATIN

1. Thomas K. McCraw, "American Capitalism," in McCraw, ed., *Creating Modern Capitalism* (Cambridge, MA: Harvard University Press, 1997), 315–316. In using this extended hothouse metaphor, I am not unmindful of the heavy human price paid for American economic growth, which was itself part of the pro-business hothouse. There is no denying the brutality of industrialization, although that price was lower in America than in almost all other industrialized countries—with the obvious exception of slavery, which in my view was not "industrial." It retarded long-term economic growth in the South because of the opportunity cost of investing so much capital in the ownership of human beings. The fact that slavery was profitable does not mean that alternative uses of the same capital would not have been more profitable. And the incalculable cruelty and human cost of slavery obviously dwarf these purely economic judgments.

American economic growth had many other downsides. In centers of industrial development, practically no regulations at all existed for environmental protection, and by the late nineteenth century cities such as Pittsburgh and Chicago grew so dirty from the burning of coal that even at midday sunlight could hardly pierce their smoky air. Industrialization also pressed extremely hard on workers. Throughout most of American history until the 1930s, the government often hindered union organizing, and sometimes it directly assisted corporations in their battles against striking employees. In all kinds of disputes, courts tended to side with employers. The law seemed to encourage businesses to treat their workers however they wished, exempting companies from damages from most deaths and injuries suffered on the job. The justification for this policy lay primarily in the doctrine of freedom of contract, which is, of course, a vital prerequisite to capitalist development. In the early years of industrialization, the principle was used to justify the "freedom" of workers, including children, to contract for dangerous jobs and toil seventy-two-hour weeks.

For arguments that the movement to what became American-style capitalism was, on the whole, a regrettable development, see—among many works—Charles G. Sellers, *The Market Revolution: Jacksonian America, 1815–1846* (New York: Oxford University Press, 1992); John Lauritz Larson, *The Market Revolution in America: Liberty, Ambition, and the Eclipse of the Common Good* (New York: Cambridge University Press, 2009); and Richard White, *Railroaded: The Transcontinentals and the Making of Modern America* (New York: Norton, 2011).

2. This framework is foreshadowed in McCraw, "American Capitalism," 317–318. The war experience and its relation to American ideology and government economic intervention is a complex subject difficult to generalize about. See Mark R. Wilson, *The Business of Civil War: Military Mobilization and the State, 1861–1865* (Baltimore: Johns Hopkins University Press, 2006); Robert D. Cuff, *The War Industries Board: Business-Government Relations during World War I* (Baltimore: Johns Hopkins University Press, 1973); Paul A. C. Koistenen, *The Military-Industrial Complex: A Historical Perspective* (New York: Praeger, 1981); and for the period covered by this book, Koistenen, *Beating Plowshares into Swords: The Political Economy of American Warfare, 1606–1865* (Lawrence: University Press of Kansas, 1996).

3. It could be argued that this preference for category two is true of other democratic capitalist countries. But it applies to very few, if any, over such a long and continuous period as the late eighteenth century to the present time. Even Britain belongs in category three for most of the 1940s and parts of the 1950s.

4. As a perceptive historian once wrote about early nineteenth-century American government, "King Laissez Faire" was "not only dead; the hallowed report of his reign had all been a mistake." See Robert A. Lively, "The American System: A Review Article," *Business History Review* 29 (1955), 82. For an argument that the financial system undergirded American economic growth, see Robert E. Wright, *The Wealth of Nations Rediscovered: Expansion of American Financial Markets, 1780–1850* (New York: Cambridge University Press, 2002).

5. Hamilton is quoted in Gerald Stourzh, *Alexander Hamilton and the Idea of Republican Government* (Stanford: Stanford University Press, 1970), 195.

6. Just after Gallatin's time in public office, the greatest of all internal improvements of the early nineteenth century, the Erie Canal, was built entirely with New York State funds. In the two centuries since, a large proportion of public support for economic development has come from state and local funds, as well as federal. On the early years, see Ronald E. Shaw, *Erie Water West: A History of the Erie Canal, 1792–1854* (Lexington: University of Kentucky Press, 1966); and Carter Goodrich, "Internal Improvements Reconsidered," *Journal of Economic History* 30 (1970), 289–311. Soon after the success of the Erie Canal, Pennsylvania, Ohio, Indiana, and Illinois were sponsoring their own elaborate canal projects. Often states depleted their treasuries in futile attempts to duplicate New York's success. After several embarrassing debacles, some states enacted new constitutions forbidding further bond issues of this kind. Many required that budgets be balanced annually, a provision that still survives in many state constitutions. See Harry N. Scheiber, *Ohio Canal Era: A Case Study of Government and the Economy, 1820–1861* (Athens: Ohio University Press, 1969); Carter Goodrich, *Government Promotion of American Canals and Railroads, 1800–1890* (New York: Columbia University Press, 1960); and John Lauritz Larson, *Internal Improvement: National Public Works and the Promise of Popular Government in the Early United States* (Chapel Hill: University of North Carolina Press, 2000).

7. Jefferson to John Holmes, April 22, 1820. This phrase is usually misquoted as "wolf by the ears." See www.monticello.org/site/jefferson/wolf-ears (accessed 11/14/11) for a discussion of the correct quotation. In other writings, Jefferson sometimes did use the plural.

8. Protectionism is discussed later in this chapter. On the earlier period, see also Douglas A. Irwin, "The Aftermath of Hamilton's 'Report on Manufactures,'" in Irwin and Richard Sylla, eds., *Founding Choices: American Economic Policy in the 1790s* (Chicago: University of Chicago Press, 2011), 800–821. Irwin notes that even during the 1790s, before the Jeffersonians took power, protectionists in the United States switched their support from the Federalists to the Jeffersonians because they saw that Hamilton's fiscal program depended so much on import duties, which would have shrunk under high protective tariffs.

9. Gallatin to Jean Badollet, Feb. 7, 1833, *The Correspondence of John [Jean] Badollet and Albert Gallatin*, ed. Gayle Thornbrough (Indianapolis: Indiana Historical Society Publications, 1963), 313. Gallatin added that avoidance of civil war would be "a difficult task, but in my humble opinion not impossible to perform."

10. Madison was one of the leading nationalists of the 1780s, but less so compared to Hamilton in the 1790s and less so compared to Gallatin in the 1800s.

11. See Robert V. Remini, *Henry Clay, Statesman for the Union* (New York: Norton, 1991), ch. 13, which is titled "The American System." On the policies of the United States and other countries during the nineteenth century, see George B. Curtiss, *The Industrial Development of Nations and a History of the Tariff Policies of the United States, and of Great Britain, Germany, France, Russia and Other European Countries* (Binghamton, NY: Curtiss, 1912), vols. 2 and 3.

12. Jackson vetoed both the recharter of the Second Bank and the Maysville Road Bill, an important and highly symbolic internal-improvements project. Other leaders of the fledgling Democratic Party agreed with him. The bank went out of existence in 1836, ushering in a period of "wildcat banking" that would have dismayed Hamilton and did appall Gallatin, who was still alive at the time. As for protective tariffs, which were a keystone of the American System, no other public issue with the exception of slavery proved to be more divisive: the post–Civil War Republican Party was in favor of high tariffs, the Democrats were less so, and southern Democrats were adamantly opposed. Debates over tariff policy constituted a hardy perennial not only of American politics, but also of academic economics in the years when that discipline began to be taught. In the 1880s, the University of Pennsylvania required that its new economics professor not support free trade. Cornell met the problem by appointing two lecturers, one on each side of the controversy. The free traders usually won the academic debates, and they still do so today. But for more than a century, from the 1820s to the 1930s, political forces advocating the protection of infant, adolescent, or ailing industries triumphed in Congress. So, contrary to many popular beliefs, the American economy grew to maturity behind tariff walls averaging close to 30 percent of the value of all imports, and more than that on dutiable imports.

Whether such a high degree of protection was necessary for healthy growth is not at all clear. Most economists believe that the size and integration of the American economy—the world's largest internal free-trade market—spurred domestic competition and lessened the harmful effect that protection from foreign competition would otherwise have had. But there can be no question that the United States protected its home market, just as Germany did during the key period of its leap into modern economic growth (1879–1914), and as Japan did during and after its own "miracle growth" era (1951–1973). The wisdom and efficacy of these policies remain open to question, but their systematic implementation is a settled, though understudied, historical fact. In America throughout the nineteenth century, the law was on the side of producers, who were protected—not that of consumers, who paid higher prices as a result. The immediate impact of tariffs unquestionably damaged consumer interests. But the long-term dynamic effect may have promoted a staged development of some industries from infancy to adolescence to healthy adulthood. These points are summarized for the United States by McCraw, "American Capitalism," in McCraw, ed., *Creating Modern Capitalism,* ch. 9; for Germany by Jeffrey Fear, "German Capitalism," ibid., ch. 5; and for Japan by Jeffrey Bernstein, "Japanese Capitalism," ibid., ch. 12.

In the large but still inadequate literature on this subject, see J. J. Pincus, "Tariffs," in Glenn Porter, ed., *Encyclopedia of American Economic History* (New York: Scribner's, 1980), especially the table on p. 440; Frank W. Taussig, *The Tariff History of the United States,* 8th ed. (New York: Putnam's Sons, 1930); Sidney Ratner, *The Tariff in American History* (New York: Van Nostrand, 1972); G. R. Hawke, "The United States Tariff and Industrial Protection in the Late Nineteenth Century," *Economic History Review* 28 (1975), 84–99; Bennett D. Baack and John Ray, "Tariff Policy and Comparative Advantage in the Iron and Steel

Industry: 1870–1929," *Explorations in Economic History* 11 (1974), 3–23; Keith Head, "Infant Industry Protection in the Steel Rail Industry," *Journal of International Economics* 37 (1994), 141–165. Lance Davis et al., *American Economic History: The Development of a National Economy* (Homewood, IL: Irwin, 1969), Table 16–2, shows that American manufacturing benefited far more than any other segment of the economy from tariff protection.

Acknowledgments

Writing a book on this remarkably rich subject was a tremendous pleasure. It's a delight to thank those who helped me do it.

Susan McCraw, with whom I've been madly in love since she was seventeen years old and I was eighteen, helped the most, by far. She's done that with all my work, while excelling in her many other roles: as the mother of our three wonderful children, as a tax lawyer who knows more about some aspects of finance than I do, as a nationally recognized fabric artist, and as the spiritual core of our now extended family. With infinite patience and generosity, she helped me to conceive the book, write it, and—with her acute editorial eye—rewrite it and decide how to organize ten of its thirty-one chapters.

I could not have worked effectively without the extremely able research assistance of Felice Whittum. With unvarying promptness, and in response to what must sometimes have seemed bizarre requests, she provided me with a mountain of research materials, most of which appear in the endnotes. She checked almost all of those notes and caught several mistakes. She is a model of efficiency.

Susan Wallace Boehmer, the very creative editor-in-chief at Harvard University Press, helped me to plan the book. She read early drafts on Hamilton and Gallatin, and wrote a long memorandum that helped me to rethink proportions, pacing, and organization. In many back-and-forth emails, she answered my queries and gave unfailing support to the project. So did Michael Aronson of the Press, with whom I've had the pleasure of working for many years, on this book and others as well. I also benefited to an unusual degree from the very perceptive suggestions of two anonymous referees who read the completed manuscript for the Press.

My good friends Jim Baughman, Glenn Porter, Richard Tedlow, Jack High, and Walter Friedman—all former Harvard Business School colleagues and, like me, editors of the *Business History Review*, the preeminent journal in its field—turned their superior intelligence, knowledge of finance, and editorial acumen to the task of helping decide what to include in the book and what to leave out. Jim Baughman was especially helpful in the earliest stage of the project, and convinced me to change part of its direction. He, Glenn Porter, and Jack High read parts of the manuscript as it evolved, and Richard Tedlow and Walter Friedman read all of it. Each made numerous suggestions on how to improve it, in ways big and small.

Three friends from other universities helped me enormously: Thomas S. Hines of UCLA bent the twig as I was conceiving the book. William Childs of Ohio State and Lewis Gould of the University of Texas read the entire manuscript and provided invaluable criticism and commentary.

For additional help in understanding the political economy of the early Republic, I am deeply indebted to three other scholars: Richard Sylla of NYU, the world's leading expert on Hamilton's economic program, who read an early draft of the Hamilton chapters and pointed out several errors; Burton Spivak of the New York Bar, a brilliant interpreter of Thomas Jefferson's thinking and the chief authority on the Embargo of 1807–1809; and Gautham Rao, a young scholar wholly conversant with the copious historical literature on the period from 1760 to 1830. Professor Rao knows almost as much about the customs service—the chief source of federal revenues during the Hamilton and Gallatin years—as they themselves did. Both he and Burton Spivak read the full manuscript, discussed it with me by telephone and email, and made innumerable helpful suggestions.

I had the great advantage of trying out many of the book's arguments in publications such as the *American Scholar,* the *New York Times,* and the online journal *Capitalism and Society.* I also benefited mightily from discussing Hamilton's economic program with about thirty students and colleagues in Harvard's Business History Seminar and—over the course of a decade—with my classes of about 160 students per year in the Harvard Business School's popular elective, "The Coming of Managerial Capitalism."

The Harvard Business School generously supported the research for this book. I especially appreciate the efforts of Professor Geoffrey Jones, as a Director of Research, to secure the resources necessary to complete the project.

In no aspect of the book's evolution did I benefit more than from editorial help. In addition to the many persons named above, I received priceless advice from three absolutely splendid editors: Jeff Strabone, Cynthia Baughman, and Maria Ascher. All three involved themselves in both the substance of the story as well as its form, and the result was a vastly improved book.

To everyone named here, I extend the strongest and sincerest thanks that I am able to give. For errors and infelicities that remain, the fault is mine alone, and I take full responsibility.

Credits

1. Statue of Alexander Hamilton by James Earle Fraser. Kim Baker/Getty Images.
2. Alexander Hamilton drawn from life by an unknown artist, January 11, 1773. Courtesy of the Prints and Photographs Division, Library of Congress.
3. George Washington at Princeton, by Charles Willson Peale, 1779. Pennsylvania Academy of Fine Arts, Philadelphia. Gift of Maria McKean Allen and Phebe Warren Downes through the bequest of their mother, Elizabeth Wharton McKean.
4. Alexander Hamilton at Yorktown, by Alonzo Chappel, c. 1857. Museum of the City of New York.
5. Elizabeth Hamilton, by Ralph Earl, 1787. Museum of the City of New York.
6. Gouverneur Morris and Robert Morris, by Charles Willson Peale, 1783. Pennsylvania Academy of Fine Arts, bequest of Richard Ashhurst.
7. Bank of the United States, Wm. Birch & Son, c. 1800. Courtesy of the Prints and Photographs Division, Library of Congress.
8. Alexander Hamilton, by John Trumbull, 1792. Courtesy of the Prints and Photographs Division, Library of Congress.
9. Bust of Alexander Hamilton, by Giuseppe Ceracchi, c. 1793. Collection of the New-York Historical Society.
10. Alexander Hamilton, by John Trumbull, 1804. National Portrait Gallery, Smithsonian Institution. Gift of Henry Cabot Lodge.
11. The Grange, n.d. Drawing by OH. F. Langmann. Courtesy of the Prints and Photographs Division, Library of Congress.
12. Philip Hamilton, n.d. Reproduced in Allan McLane Hamilton, *Intimate Life*

444

of Alexander Hamilton (New York: Charles Scribner's Sons, 1911), opposite p. 210.

13. Alexander Hamilton, by Ezra Ames, c. 1810. Courtesy of the Union College Permanent Collection, Schenectady, NY.

14. Statue of Albert Gallatin, by James Earle Fraser, dedicated in 1947. Kim Baker/Getty Images.

15. Albert Gallatin, 1803. Engraving by American Bank Note Co., after a painting by Gilbert Stuart. Collection of the New-York Historical Society.

16. Thomas Jefferson, 1805, by Gilbert Stuart. National Portrait Gallery, Smithsonian Institution, and Thomas Jefferson Foundation, Inc., at Monticello. Gift of the Regents of the Smithsonian Institution, the Thomas Jefferson Foundation, and the Enid and Crosby Kemper Foundation.

17. James Madison, 1804, by Gilbert Stuart. Colonial Williamsburg Foundation, gift of Mrs. George S. Robbins.

18. Albert Gallatin, 1805, by Rembrandt Peale. Courtesy of Independence National Historical Park, Philadelphia.

19. Monticello, n.d. Special Collections, Fine Arts Library, Harvard University, Cambridge, MA.

20. Montpelier, n.d. Lithographer unknown. Yale University Art Gallery, Mabel Brady Garvan Collection.

21. Friendship Hill, n.d. Photograph by Thomas Markwardt. Courtesy of the U.S. National Park Service.

22. Burned Capitol, c. 1814, by George Muger. Courtesy of the Prints and Photographs Division, Library of Congress.

23. Albert Gallatin, 1815. Sketch by Pieter Van Huffel, print created in 1915. Courtesy of the Prints and Photographs Division, Library of Congress.

24. Albert Gallatin, 1841, by William H. Powell. Collection of the New-York Historical Society.

Index

Constitutional Convention, 80–81;
and Hamilton's bank bill, 116; and
Hamilton's *Report on the Subject of
Manufactures*, 129, 130; and Hamilton's reputation, 167, 170; health
problems of, 228; and impressment,
422n4; indecisiveness of, 181; inheritance of, 103; and Jay Treaty, 148,
149, 150, 346; and Jefferson, 141,
228, 233, 284, 341; and land, 369n8;
and land development, 253; and
landed estates in Virginia, 352; leaves
House of Representatives, 215; letter
from Gallatin of March 5, 1813, 302;
letter from Jefferson of September 21,
1795, 148, 149; letter to Jefferson of
March 6, 1796, 205; letter to Jefferson
of March 9, 1794, 208; letter to Jefferson of October 20, 1797, 162; loan
from Solomon, 67; and Macon's Bill
No. 1, 426n5; and Macon's Bill No. 2,
288; and military, 237, 263–264, 265;
and Monroe-Pinkney Treaty, 273; and
Montpelier, 269, 285; and Morris, 69;
and *National Gazette*, 153; and national honor, 237; as nationalist, 363;
and navy, 208; and neutrality, 221;
and New Orleans, 240; newspaper
contributions of, 154; notes on Philadelphia Convention of 1787, 381n13;
and original holders vs. purchasers of
government securities, 102; and peace
negotiations for War of 1812, 306;
and political base in Virginia, 75; on
political parties, 139; and political
theory, 342; political victories of, 346;
portrait by Gilbert Stuart, 1804, 244;
and John Randolph, 416n37; as Republican leader in Congress, 284; and
Republican Party, 139, 205; and Second Bank of the United States, 361; as
secretary of state, 228; and secretary
of treasury, 382n20; and slavery, 258,
259, 260, 269, 361, 420n26; and
Robert Smith, 285–286, 297, 427n12;
and strong federal government, 260;
and Tariff Act of 1789, 102; and
three-fifths clause, 79; and trade, 346;
and Treaty of Ghent, 343; and Virginia, 363; Virginia constituents of,

102, 141; and Virginia Plan, 80; and
Virginia Resolution, 219–220, 304,
362; and war between France and
Great Britain, 146, 147; war experi-
ence of, 265; and War of 1812, 298,
299, 344, 387n9; and Washington,
139, 150, 154, 284; and Washington,
D.C. as national capital, 221; world-
view of, 4
Madison River, 243
Maier, Pauline, 371n3, 372n5
Main, Gloria, 377n12
Maine, 254, 255, 318, 430n13
Maitland, F. W., 348
Malone, Dumas, 424n19
Mandler, Peter, 399n29
Manifest Destiny, 322
Mann, Bruce H., 383n21, 385n12
Manning, William, 103–104, 388n10
Mannix, Richard, 411n15, 412n1,
421n35, 423n7, 424n16
Mansfield, Jared, 252
Manufactures/manufacturing, 64, 122;
and banks, 5; and Brown family, 127;
credit-based, 353; encouragement of,
128–129, 363; and Federalists,
420n31; and France, 339; and Galla-
tin, 213, 255, 261–263, 360, 361;
Hamilton on, 122, 123, 124, 125,
127–128, 136, 360–361; imported
from Great Britain, 48; and North,
49; in Pennsylvania, New York, and
New England, 74; and protective tar-
iffs, 362; and Republicans, 420n31;
United States as leading producer of,
364–365
Marie Antoinette, 339
Market economy, 35, 350. *See also* Capitalism; Credit; Trade
Markets, foreign, 88, 125
Market value of national and state debt,
99
Marshall, John, 73, 118, 188, 392n18
Martin, Robert W. T., 434n1
Martis, Kenneth C., 411n21
Marx, Karl, *The Communist Manifesto*,
351–352, 436n2
Maryland, 57, 106, 198, 224, 225, 259,
380n5
Mason, Matthew, 420n27